THE WRITER'S I

PERSONAL VIEWPOINTS FOR READING AND WRITING

SHEENA GILLESPIE
LINDA STANLEY

Queensborough Community College
City University of New York

Scott, Foresman/Little, Brown College Division

Scott, Foresman and Company

Glenview, Illinois
Boston
London

Library of Congress Cataloging-in-Publication Data
Gillespie, Sheena.
  The writer's I.

  Includes index.
  1. College readers. 2. English language—Rhetoric.
I. Stanley, Linda.   . II. Title.
PE1417.G52   1987   808'.0427   87-23467
ISBN 0-673-39722-X

1   2   3   4   5   6   7   8   9   10—MPC—93   92   91   90   89   88   87

Printed in the United States of America

Acknowledgments

Ved Mehta, reprinted from *Sound-Shadows of the New World* by Ved Mehta by
permission of W. W. Norton & Company, Inc. Copyright 1985 by Ved Mehta.
Mary Ann Lynch, "December 22, 1972, New York City" by Mary Ann Lynch.
From *Ariadne's Thread*, edited by Lyn Lifshin. Copyright 1982 by Lyn Lifshin.
Reprinted by permission of Harper & Row, Publishers, Inc.
Toi Derricotte, "The Black Notebooks" by Toi Derricotte. From *Ariadne's Thread*,
edited by Lyn Lifshin. Copyright 1982 by Lyn Lifshin. Reprinted by permission
of Harper & Row, Publishers, Inc.
John Coleman, from *Blue Collar Journal: A College President's Sabbatical* by John R.
Coleman (J. B. Lippincott Company). Copyright 1974 by John R. Coleman.
Reprinted by permission of the author.
Wright Morris, pages 3–8 from *Will's Boy: A Memoir* by Wright Morris.
Copyright 1981 by Wright Morris. Reprinted by permission of Harper & Row,
Publishers, Inc.
Zora Neale Hurston, "I Get Born," pp. 27–32 from *Dust Tracks on the Road: An
Autobiography*, Second Edition by Zora Neale Hurston (J. B. Lippincott
Company). Copyright 1942 by Zora Neale Hurston; copyright renewed 1970
by John C. Hurston. Reprinted by permission of Harper & Row, Publishers, Inc.
Richard Rodriguez, "Hunger of Memory." From *Hunger of Memory* by Richard
Rodriguez. Copyright 1981 by Richard Rodriguez. Reprinted by permission of
David R. Godine, Boston.
William Carlos Williams, "Danse Russe." From William Carlos Williams,
Collected Earlier Poems. Copyright 1938 by New Directions Publishing Corporation.
Reprinted by permission of New Directions Publishing Corporation.

(continued on page 329)

To Patrick Fenton, who is always willing to share his craft with our students, both in our classrooms and in our textbooks.

PREFACE

OVERVIEW

By writing in the first person, students, we believe, will better develop a sense of their own possibilities—both in what they have to say and in how they can best say it. It is our firm conviction that when students can sense the person behind the pen both when they read and when they write, they will become better readers and better writers.

In *The Writer's I*, we have included thirty-eight essays written in the first person, arranged them according to theme, added stories, poems and journal entries that further elucidate these themes, and used all selections to suggest aspects of the methods by which a writer goes about writing. For the eight chapters, we selected as our themes writings about the self, people, places, events and experiences, goals, emotions, choices, and philosophies. We have collected in each chapter essays that are written in the first person, most using the singular "I" but some using the plural "we." Our general orientation and organization will be recognizable to those who have used *Someone Like Me: Images for Writing* in its five editions since 1972.

We have divided the book into two parts, the first including essays of an autobiographical or otherwise personal purpose, the second including essays of an expository or persuasive intent. In the rhetorical sections in the first four chapters (Part One), we suggest a process of writing useful for the personal or autobiographical essay; in the second part of the book, Chapters 5–8, we concentrate on the more formal methods of generating ideas as well as on audience evaluation and revision for style—all aspects of writing useful for the writer with an expository or persuasive purpose. Our rhetoric is inductive, and uses writing to induce writing rather than to prescribe or merely to exemplify it.

READINGS

We have grouped our essays, journal entries, stories, and poems according to the eight themes of self, people, places, events and experiences, goals, emotions, choices, and philosophies because we feel these topics represent basic responses to life. We see the self as continually forging paths between particular and personal perceptions and experiences and the perceptions and experiences of the larger society. This need to build a relationship between the self and society has provided a catalyst for many of our best professional writers, and we believe it provides an important impetus for our student writers as well.

In Part One, the writers muse on personal responses to particular people, places, events, experiences through journal entry, memoir, autobiography, personal essay, short story, and poem. In Part Two, the writers convey their personal responses to the larger issues of the society such as the importance of work, the importance of play, the success credo, marriage, alienation, loneliness, affirmative action, materialism, the need for simplicity, language, death, and the need for metaphysical meaning. While this is not a "writing across the curriculum" anthology as generally conceived, we have included the writings of such eminent writer/scientists as Lewis Thomas, Loren Eiseley, and Richard Selzer; extensive social criticism (all essays in Part Two can be construed as such), and several works of journalism. One third of the selections are by women, one fifth by minority writers. Fully one half of the selections are fresh and, to our knowledge, have never been anthologized before.

Students will invariably descry some readings as "boring," and we have made every effort to choose works that strike chords in the student reader. Not all readings, however, are immediately accessible; one third we would consider "challenging" reading for some students. We teach our students that reading, as well as writing, is a difficult process but one they can learn. We help students to learn to read an essay through the rhetorical section after Thoreau's essay "Simplicity" —undoubtedly, for students, the most difficult essay in the book.

FIRST PERSON

We subscribe to James Britton's tripartite classification of the purposes of written discourse in his *Development of Writing Abilities (London, MacMillan Education, Ltd., 1975)* as expressive, transactional, and poetic; all three are represented in the selections in our book. Expressive writing he defines as "utterance at its most relaxed and intimate, as free as possible from outside demands, whether those of a task or of an audience" (82). Expressive writing is represented by the several journal selections in Chapter 1 and by Anne Morrow Lindbergh's journal entries in Chapter 8. To the extent that personal and autobiographical essays are freer than expository writings from outside demands, the other selections in Part One may be said to be expressive as well. Writing that aims to express the writer is generally written in the first person.

"Transactional" writing corresponds to what we in the profession generally call expository writing. As Britton describes it, transactional writing uses "language to get things done: to inform people . . . to advise or persuade or instruct people" (88). The essays in Part Two may be said to have a transactional purpose. Poetic use of language creates a text as an object of contemplation, not as a means to achieve an effect upon the reader or a release for a writer; the poems and stories typify poetic writing. Poetic writing may or may not be written in the first person (about half the stories and poems here are), but transactional writing often is not. In fact, in the twentieth century, dominated as it is by science and technology, people have developed a distrust of writers who use the first person in any but the most personal writing. "Objectivity" has become the aim.

We recognize that an equally strong tide is pulling society back to personal expression. The written communication of business and industry is now seen to be inflated, jargon-filled prose, created by as well as creating methods of conducting business in which the personality of the writer is submerged in an impersonal corporate atmosphere. At the same time, the renewed emphasis on critical thinking is undermining belief in objectivity. And the most memorable thinkers and stylists have retained their belief in and use of the personal essay.

William Zinsser, author of *On Writing Well* (New York, Harper & Row, 1980), says Americans must once again be willing to reveal themselves and to cease hiding behind impersonal expression. Writing in the first person *is* dignified, he maintains, and furthermore warms up one's style. A writer, he says, "is obviously at his most natural and relaxed when he writes in the first person" (22). Even when "I" is not permitted, as in the most technical or academic writing, he adds, "It's still possible to convey a sense of I-ness. . . . Good writers are always visible just behind their words" (24).

STRUCTURE

As we have said, we have divided the book into two parts. The first focuses on personal or expressive writing, including journals and personal and autobiographical essays, and the second moves to the expository or transactional essay. Because of our desire to present learning about writing as an inductive process, we have included rhetorical sections *after* the first and second essay in each chapter so that we can draw in our discussion on the style and structure of the essayist for our presentation. In Part One, the discussions focus on a writing process for expressive writing that includes using the journal, memory, and the imagination as means of generating ideas; planning for and organizing the effective personal essay; developing the paragraph; describing a place; narrating an event; and revising the rough draft. An extensive introduction to personal writing and to its process precedes Part One.

In Part Two we present the classical questions as a more formal way of generating ideas for the expository essay, discuss patterns of arrangement, suggest how to both respond to an essay as a reader and how to respond to readers as a writer, and finally, suggest how to revise for coherence and style. An introduction to expository writing precedes Part Two.

Before each selection, we include a headnote giving background on the writer and asking questions that can serve as prereading and prewriting aids. After each selection we ask questions on meaning and questions on method.

At the end of each chapter we list possible topics for students' own writing.

An Instructor's Manual offers additional writing topics, discussions of each selection, and suggestions for how to teach the course in twelve or fifteen weeks.

ACKNOWLEDGMENTS

We wish to thank those teachers of composition who generously offered suggestions, particularly those reviewers who had used the fifth edition of *Someone Like Me: Images for Writing*, the forerunner to this book: John Dick of the University of Texas at El Paso, Mary Gulbranson of the North Dakota School of Science, C. Jeriel Howard of Northeastern Illinois University, Sylvia Kostecki of Massasoit Community College, Peter Markman of Fullerton College, Mary McGann of Rhode Island College, Harvey S. Weiner of LaGuardia Community College, and Frances Winter of Massachusetts Bay Community College.

We also are grateful to Joe Opiela, our editor, who helped us shape this project, if not quite as a phoenix from the ashes, then at least as a rebirth; to Billie Ingram, our production editor, for a beautiful product; and to Nan Upin, Joe's editorial assistant, who was always cheerful as well as helpful. Our especial thanks to Margaret Cavanaugh, Sylvia Katcher, Evelyn Pomann, and Marge Caronna for their generous assistance in the preparation of yet another manuscript.

CONTENTS

CHAPTER 3

Places: *Writing the Essay—Describing a Place, Developing the Paragraph*   *89*

CHAPTER 4

Events and Experiences: *Writing and Rewriting the Essay—Narrating an Event, Revising the Essay*   *123*

PART TWO
THE WRITER'S I AND THE PUBLIC WORLD   171

CHAPTER 5

Goals: *Generating Ideas—Generalizing about Observations, Observing To Support Generalizations*   175

CHAPTER 6

Emotions: *Generating Ideas, Planning the Essay— Asking Questions, Arranging the Answers*   215

PART ONE:

THE WRITER's I AND THE PRIVATE WORLD

The essays in this book are written in the first-person pronoun, the writers having announced that "I am the writer of this essay, and what you see and what you feel and what you learn will be experienced through my sight, my emotions, and my understanding." Once on stage, these writers have not buried themselves in a group of "we's," nor hidden behind another "one," nor has any become supporting player to a "he" or "she" or "they." Each writer is the main actor, interpreting the drama and enjoying the applause and taking any hisses. All communications with the audience are person to person.

Many good writers do not, of course, use the pronoun "I"—they refer to themselves as "one" or "we" or "they." You may have been told by teachers, in fact, never to write in the first person, and there are situations in which you would not want to do so: a newspaper article, a report, a research paper, a textbook, for example. In these instances, objectivity is the goal. However, the essay form provides ample opportunity for you to declare yourself—your experiences, your thoughts, and your feelings—directly to your reader, and the essays of professional writers who have taken this opportunity we have collected here.

Why communicate so directly with your reader? One answer is "personality." By writing naturally in the first person, you will be communicating who you are. You will be writing as a person with particular experiences, particular thoughts, and particular emotions, even with particular quirks and dreams. You will distinguish yourself from other writers; your writing will be uniquely expressive, uniquely alive. Even your words and sentences will not sound like those of other writers: they will sound like *you*. Two distinct personalities emerge, for example, from these introductions to "I Discover My Father" by Sherwood Anderson and "Sister Flowers" by Maya Angelou, both from Chapter 2:

> *You hear it said that fathers want their sons to be what they feel they cannot themselves be, but I tell you it also works the other way. A boy wants something very special from his father. I know that as a small boy I wanted my father to be a certain thing he was not. I wanted him to be a proud, silent, dignified father. When I was with other boys and he passed along the street, I wanted to feel a flow of pride. "There he is. That is my father."*

> *For nearly a year, I sopped around the house, the Store, the school and the church, like an old biscuit, dirty and inedible. Then I met, or rather got to know, the lady who threw me my first life line.*

Another characteristic that makes the personal essay so effective is honesty. The writer asks, "What did I really feel? What did I really see? What really happened?" By pursuit of honesty, we mean you attempt to get through to the truth of the experience or feeling. Not that writers lie, but often they do not tell the truth because capturing the truth is difficult. Truth is like a drop of mercury: just as you think you have cornered it, it slides away. You will need to concentrate, even meditate perhaps, in order to understand the truth of an experience, and even then you will want to find the right words to express what you have discovered. The poets and short story writers in these chapters have been particularly good at discovering truth and revealing it in words, but as a personal essayist you can reveal truth also. Loren Eiseley, in "Sparrow Hawks" (Chapter 7), has found the words and the details to express the intense impact of the cry of the sparrow hawk:

> *I was young then and had seen little of the world, but when I heard that cry my heart turned over. It was not the cry of the hawk I had captured; for, by shifting my position against the sun, I was now seeing further up. Straight out of the sun's eye, where she must have been soaring restlessly above us for untold hours, hurtled his mate. And from far up, ringing from peak to peak of the summits over us, came a cry of such unutterable and ecstatic joy that it sounds down across the years and tingles among the cups on my quiet breakfast table.*

In pursuing honesty and revealing personality, does the personal essayist stand naked before the audience? Not if he or she does not want to, certainly, and how many of us do want to reveal ourselves completely? The writer has the power to select both what is said and how it is said. Our personalities are complex, composed as they are of many often-conflicting desires, attitudes, and expressions; so too, we play many roles in life—parent, child, sibling, friend, lover, employee, student. In writing personal essays, you can choose to reveal any one of these personality traits and write from the perspective of any one of these roles. You can adopt a role and a tone of voice that reveal what you want to reveal—no more, no less. For example, in the following paragraph from Zora Neale Hurston's essay in Chapter 1, "I Get Born," the author is clearly playing the role of the daughter of a father who wished she had been born a boy, but rather than adopting the tone of voice of a sullen, resentful child, the author chooses to be humorous.

> The saying goes like this. My mother's time had come and my father was not there. Being a carpenter, successful enough to have other helpers on some jobs, he was away often on building business, as well as preaching. It seems that my father was away from home for months this time. I have never been told why. But I did hear that he threatened to cut his throat when he got the news. It seems that one daughter was all that he figured he could stand. My sister, Sarah, was his favorite child, but that one girl was enough. Plenty more sons, but no more girl babies to wear out shoes and bring in nothing. I don't think he ever got over the trick he felt that I played on him by getting born a girl, and while he was off from home at that. A little of my sugar used to sweeten his coffee right now. That is a Negro way of saying his patience was short with me. Let me change a few words with him—and I am of the word-changing kind—and he was ready to change ends. Still and all, I looked more like him than any child in the house. Of course, by the time I got born, it was too late to make any suggestions, so the old man had to put up with me. He was nice about it in a way. He didn't tie me in a sack and drop me in the lake, as he probably felt like doing.

On the other hand, personal writing does narrow the distance between writer and reader; the relationship can be quite intimate. You should assume your reader is both interested and sympathetic, perhaps selecting a friend as your intended audience, so that you can write honestly and reveal your personality. If your reader is chosen for you, then assume that the reader will play the role of friend or at least of sympathetic acquaintance. What relationship do you think that Anderson, Angelou, Eiseley, and Hurston, in the passages quoted above, have established with their readers?

Writing with a personal voice is more vivid writing. The writer is speaking of events experienced, emotions felt, ideas developed. This immediacy—this lack of distance between writer and subject as well as between writer and reader—encourages a search for the precise word, the most telling detail. Just as Loren Eiseley discovered how to describe the cry of the hawk, so Saul Bellow evokes so many sensory details of his day on the kibbutz in Israel that his reader can feel and smell the soil in the citrus groves and see the fruit:

> *We walk in the citrus groves after breakfast, taking Mississippi with us (John is seldom without her); the soil is kept loose and soft among the trees, the leaves are glossy, the ground itself is fragrant. Many of the trees are still unharvested and bending, tangerines and lemons as dense as stars. "Oh that I were an orange tree/That busie plant!" wrote George Herbert. To put forth such leaves, to be hung with oranges, to be a blessing—one feels the temptation of this on such a morning and I even feel a fibrous woodiness entering my arms as I consider it. You want to take root and stay forever in the most temperate and blue of temperate places. John mourns his son, he always mourns his son, but he is also smiling in the sunlight.*

The writings in Part 1 are journal entries, personal essays, autobiographical essays, stories, and poems. The writers write about themselves, about other people, about places, about experiences. All these writings reveal the personalities of the writers as well as their attempts at honesty about facets of their lives.

These first four chapters also explain, in discussions placed after the first and second essay in each chapter, how to go about writing a personal or autobiographical essay of your own. Chapter 1 indicates that keeping a journal might give you ideas about which to write an essay, or that you might locate factual records or search your memories or, more important, your imagination. Chapter 2 suggests ways to plan your essay once you have generated some ideas for it: how to create an effective subject and then organize it.

Chapters 3 and 4 help you begin writing the paper by discussing methods of describing a place and narrating an event, as well as of developing paragraphs. Chapter 4 concludes with some suggestions for revising your essay once you have completed a rough draft.

CHAPTER ONE

The Self:
Generating Ideas
Keeping a Journal
Writing Autobiography

Walt Whitman described the self as a "miracle of miracles, beyond statement, most spiritual and vaguest of earth's dreams, yet hardest basic fact, and only entrance to all facts." The self, as Whitman indicates, is indeed paradoxical, and if it is to remain dynamic, it must constantly evolve. To insure self-growth, we must evaluate all that happens to us, however seemingly insignificant. What you will discover in reading the selections in this chapter is that regardless of whether the writers choose to keep a journal or write an autobiographical essay, a poem, or a short story, what they have in common is an interest in and knowledge about themselves.

Ved Mehta, a blind student from India, for example, records in his journal his impressions of America and their effects on him. Mary Ann Lynch recounts what was for her a harrowing experience in a New York City bus terminal, while Toi Derricotte describes her emotional responses to being part of the only black family in an upper-middle-class New Jersey suburb. John Coleman's journal is a personal record of the blue-collar work he did for eight weeks while on sabbatical from his college presidency. Henry David Thoreau's journal, written over a century ago, records his initial reactions to moving to a small cabin in the woods near Walden Pond in Concord, Massachusetts. All these writers use the journal to chart the growth of the paradoxical self, often in confrontation with a paradoxical society. A discussion of keeping a journal follows Ved Mehta's entries, beginning on page 10.

In their autobiographical essays, both Wright Morris and Zora Neale Hurston write about their own births, while Richard Rodriguez writes about choosing to learn English, although it meant sacrificing the emotional security he associated with Spanish, the language of his family. All three writers found these early experiences crucial to their development as individual selves and record them with passion, pain, and humor. A discussion of how to write an autobiographical essay begins on page 27, after Wright Morris's essay.

The short story "Father and I" also reflects the complexity of the self through a ten-year-old boy's realization that his father could not protect him from the "anguish that was to come, the unknown," and the poem "Danse Russe" portrays the self's sometimes conflicting needs for solitude and companionship.

VED MEHTA

FROM *Sound-Shadows of the New World*

Ved Mehta (b. 1934) was born in India and became blind at the age of four. He left his country in 1949 to study at the Arkansas School for the Blind and continued his education at Pomona College, Oxford, and Harvard. He has written several autobiographical volumes including The Ledge Between the Streams *(1981), and in 1982 he was awarded a MacArthur Prize Fellowship. In these journal entries published in the most recent volume of his autobiography,* Sound-Shadows of the New World, *Mehta talks about his initial reaction to Arkansas and to keeping a journal. How do his thoughts about keeping a journal differ from those you may have?*

Soon after I arrived at the school, I started keeping a journal, and I continued it intermittently during my stay in Arkansas. I always typed my entries, though this meant that, as with my letters, I had no way of reading what I'd written. But, unlike my letters, the entries tended to be short, and I was able to compose them in my head before I typed them. Then again, sometimes I was too tired to care what I typed, but it didn't seem to matter, since I never imagined that anyone would ever read them. Typing the journal was for me like talking to my pillow, which could neither remember nor repeat one syllable.

My Arkansas journal remained silent for some thirty years. Then, while I was going through some old papers in preparation for writing this narrative, I happened upon it. Even though the events recounted in it were ancient personal history, as it were, I was loath to break the seal of silence, for it would mean confronting what I dimly remembered as my embarrassing adolescent self, and exposing it to the adult eyes of someone else—those of the person who would read it to me. After a struggle, I sat down with my reader and gave myself over to my unvarnished, lonely voice speaking in the middle of Arkansas.

September 16, 1949
Daddyjee wrote and told me that I should write something every day. He said that it should be material with universal appeal. I can write such material. But I don't quite understand what he expects me to do with it. Anyway, I've made a resolution to type out my reactions to the happenings of the day whenever I can. I would like to write about my impressions of America and myself—to put my memories in a neat order and explain the new country and my character. I think I will find this task very enjoyable and pleasant. I won't have too much time to devote to it, though. No doubt I'll make many mistakes in grammar and typing.

September 18
On Sundays, there is no supper here. When we leave the noon meal, we pick up a bag of sandwiches. I ate mine at tea time and was very hungry all evening. So I drank a lot of water. Sometimes I wake up in the night and I'm so hungry that I could eat my bed.

September 24
There was a social hour in the gym this evening. We new students were introduced, and were required to mix with the faculty. We were judged by how good mixers we were, I think. Daddyjee is a much better mixer than I am.

Most students talked about the summer. They all seemed to have sat around on porches and listened to the radio. The blind here, outside of school, seem to be little better off than I was at home, when I was idle all day long and longed for something to do.

September 28
Choir is getting really interesting. Today we learned the words to "Skip to Maloo," "Oh Promise Me," and "Be Still My Heart." What is "Maloo"? Must somehow find out discreetly.

September 30
Lois cleared her throat in English class today. I thought of Mamajee's cough. Then I heard Mamajee clicking the knitting needles as she hummed to herself.

I heard the scraping sound of Daddyjee's pumps on the bare floor as he worked his feet into them. There were raindrops on the tin roof of our Simla cottage and the hiss and rattle as the coals finally caught fire in the fireplace.

October 8
Today I went with McNabb to Stifft's Station, to take my jacket to Bumpus Cleaners. We had to cross the very busy West Markham Street in front of the school to get to it. Stifft's Station was a wondrous little place—it had only three or four shops, but you could get anything there. There was also a telephone that worked automatically when you put a nickel into it. Most surprisingly, there was no sentry at the intersection, as at home. There was just a traffic light which turned different colors, and the drivers obeyed it by themselves. What self-discipline Americans have!

October 10
After study hall, we went to the student dining room to fold Christmas seals. The tables were covered with stacks of long envelopes and sheets of what felt like stamps. McNabb explained to me that the seals said "Be Thankful You Can See," and were supposed to raise money for the Rehabilitation Center for the Blind in Little Rock.

   In order to make us work faster, Mr. Woolly organized us into teams and ran contests among tables. But no matter how fast we worked, there were always more stacks of seals. We worked for four hours. At the end of the evening we were given a free Coke.

October 12
This was the third evening of folding seals. But Mr. Woolly told us that he was cancelling school tomorrow so that we could spend the whole day folding more seals. He said there was to be no school the day after, either, and we would spend that morning folding seals, too. I wish we could get on with our studies.

October 14
After folding seals, we went to the circus at Robinson Auditorium with a group called the Shriners. Most of us totally blind boys sat with partially sighted fellows so that they could tell us what was going on. There were clowns throwing buckets of confetti, acrobats flying through the air, bears, elephants, and horses running and jumping. I wish I could say that I enjoyed it, but it was mostly a lot of noise.

October 15
This evening we had a "Backward Dance." Girls asked boys for dates. No girl asked me. Everyone walked up the steps to the gym backward, went in back-

ward, danced backward. No girl asked me to dance, although now I know a little foxtrot and waltz.

October 16
This being Sunday, we had a special lunch of Southern fried chicken and a lot of corn bread. But Joe complained that the peas were hard. Mr. Hartman overheard him, and told Joe off. He said that the students who fussed most about the food were usually those who had come from poor families and had far worse food at home than we had at school.

October 21
I got my report card for the first six-week period today. It's not very good, but I set it down here so that I can later compare it with better report cards: English—A; Civics—C+; Junior Business Training—B; General Science—C+; Industrial Arts—Incomplete; Physical Education—B; Piano—B+; Orchestral Instruction (Violin)—Incomplete; Public School Music (Choir)—A−. I was also graded on my character, and because I can't remember the character part to copy it, I'm stapling it to this entry:

Characteristics	School Life		
	Good	Average	Poor
Co-operation		✓	
Courtesy		✓	
Attitude		✓	
Personal Appearance		✓	
Dining Room Etiquette		✓	
Housekeeping			

Characteristics	Dormitory Life		
	Good	Average	Poor
Co-operation		✓	
Courtesy	✓		
Attitude		✓	
Personal Appearance		✓	
Dining Room Etiquette			
Housekeeping		✓	

PROBING FOR MEANING

1. Mehta's father told him he should write every day in his journal about "material with universal appeal." To what extent do his entries indeed have universal appeal and to what extent are they essentially a personal record of a particular experience?

2. Mehta describes his entries as "unvarnished." To what extent does he in fact appear to represent truthfully the thoughts of a fifteen-year-old blind student?

3. In his introduction, Mehta indicates he now believes his entries to be "embarrassing" and "adolescent." Why might he think so? Why do you think he has published them anyway?

PROBING FOR METHOD

1. How would you characterize the content of Mehta's journal entries? To what extent does he use the journal merely to record the day's events? At what points does he also analyze his reactions to America and to himself?

2. What is Mehta's attitude toward himself and his school experiences? How consistent is this attitude—or tone—throughout his entries?

Keeping a Journal

How did Ved Mehta go about keeping a journal?
In his introduction to these entries, kept thirty years earlier when he was fifteen, Mehta gives us many details about how he kept his journal. He tells us he wrote intermittently, that he typed his entries though he had no way of reading what he had written because of his blindness, that his entries were short, that he composed them in his head beforehand, and that he never "imagined that anyone would ever read them." He explains, "Typing the journal was for me like talking to my pillow, which could neither remember nor repeat one syllable."

In his first entry, he explains why he kept a journal. He wanted "to put my memories in a neat order and explain the new country and my character." He adds that the journal is an assignment given him by his father and that he didn't "quite understand what he expects me to do with it."

In writing his entries, Mehta primarily related the happenings of his day and often his reactions to them. Occasionally, he found that occurrences in the present suggest memories of his past in India. As he reflects in his introduction, he wrote in an "unvarnished, lonely voice" that exposed his "embarrassing adolescent self."

Keeping a journal.
In keeping a journal, you can write about any subject you wish, using any form for doing so. You can record the events of your day, like Mehta, analyzing them as you go along; concentrate on a dramatic episode, like

Lynch; focus on a theme, as Derricotte seems to do; write in response to a particular period of your life or activity in which you are participating, as Coleman, Thoreau, and also Mehta do; or record memories and explore thoughts, as Thoreau does. You can respond to school and instructors, to reading you are doing, to friends and lovers, to your developing sense of self, to observations and thoughts and feelings.

You can adopt one style of writing or experiment with several. You can write in whole sentences or fragments and whole paragraphs or fragments; you can use standard punctuation, create your own, or use none at all. The journal-keepers here provide an impressive array of possibilities.

One method of writing down thoughts that you might find useful in keeping a journal is freewriting. Freewriting is writing in which you proceed as fast as possible from thought to thought, not pausing to construct sentences or punctuate them, or even worry about logical progression, but simply recording whatever comes into your mind. Freewriting attempts to capture the speech of thought. By forcing yourself to keep writing, you also force your mind to loosen up and let the memories, thoughts, and emotions flow. Freewriting encourages free association; it is a magnet for thoughts and emotions. Lynch and Derricotte demonstrate the uses of freewriting in their journal entries.

Why do people keep journals? Mehta kept his first in response to his father's request; subsequently, he found a reason of his own in recording his experiences and explaining both himself and his new country. The other writers here write for similar reasons—to record experiences, memories, and thoughts and, in some cases, to analyze them as well.

Another reason for keeping a journal is to use the material for other writing—in Chapter 7 see "Simplicity," Thoreau's essay from *Walden*, which is based on the journal entries here, and in Chapter 8, see Anne Morrow Lindbergh's journal entries and essay "Channelled Whelk" from *Gift of the Sea*. Still another reason is to publish the journal itself. Mehta claims not to have intended to publish his journal, but the other writers here probably did write with possible publication in mind.

Whether writing for themselves or for publication, most journal writers aim for an honest voice, what Mehta calls an "unvarnished" voice, one that attempts to capture in words and details the most private thoughts and feelings. Even when they write with a reader in mind, they still search for specific language and details to capture the essence of their experience. Regardless of their purpose in keeping journals, they attempt to make the record as accurate as possible.

Procedures for keeping a journal.

A. Purchase a notebook that you will enjoy writing in.
B. Find a quiet place in which to write.

C. Write daily ("journal" is based on the French word *jour*, meaning "day") or as often during the week as you can.

D. Begin simply by writing. Try filling a page. If the thoughts do not come easily, try freewriting. Write for ten minutes whatever comes into your head without concern for style or grammar; this shotgun approach should dislodge your thoughts and feelings, memories and dreams, events and experiences.

E. Write some entries for your eyes alone; write others for an audience. Experiment with how your content and style change, depending on whether you are writing for a reader or not. Like Mehta, write with an "unvarnished" voice that expresses how you think and feel as honestly as you can.

F. If, after a week of writing in your journal, you are not yet comfortable with the process, experiment with changing the place in which you are writing, the time of day when you write, what you are writing about, or how you are writing. Perhaps the library is quieter than your room, morning a fresher time to think than evening, memories more interesting than your daily occurrences, less structured writing more conducive than "correct" writing.

G. Keep experimenting until you find a combination of place, time, content, and style that works best for you. Make the journal your own; work on making it belong to you; as much as possible banish the sense that someone is looking over your shoulder as you write. The writing that results may resemble none of the entries here as you develop your own sense of what you want to say and how you want to say it.

H. Reread your journal at some point and write an entry responding to what you have written. In the aggregate, what does your journal tell you about yourself, your responses to school or to a particular class, to reading you have done, to writing itself? Would material in these entries provide the basis of other writing: an essay for class, an article for the school newspaper, a letter home? You may see a purpose for keeping a journal, as Mehta did, beyond simply fulfilling an assignment.

MARY ANN LYNCH

December 22, 1972, New York City

Mary Ann Lynch is a photographer as well as the editor and publisher of Combinations, A Journal of Photography. *She is currently the director of communications for a New York State agency. As you read her journal entry, notice the stylistic changes that occur as her emotional tension builds.*

December 22, 1972. New York City
A nightmarish trip to Port Authority, our flight canceled, all planes grounded. At the bus terminal, down so many stairs, my knees want to buckle. I am afraid I will drop Margot onto these concrete steps. Jack parks us near the snack shop, by a wall; there are no seats available. He constructs a fortress of luggage around us, then leaves us with a caveat to stay put no matter what. If he does manage to get tickets for the last stretch of this interminable holiday journey home, we may have to leave very quickly. Keep everything packed up and stay put. His is gone. People all around and every person desperate, except Margot, peaceful on my lap. I hold her tightly as if I were clinging to her instead of my being the mother lion.

A few yards away from us, in the center of the room, a wild-eyed, drunken ragged limping man is playing to the crowd, cajoling, confronting people for money and cigarettes. He has seen Margot, she is looking in his direction, and he is stumbling over to where we are. He reels before my eyes, speaks broken English, sings in Spanish, a lullaby, in a voice that once perhaps was beautiful but which now quakes and is off key, drunken. He is inside the barricade, he has shoved one foot in between two suitcases, he wants to hold the baby. *Do you mind*, reaching down for her, *do you mind*, touching her, *do you mind*, we are both touching her, where can I go I mind I mind no you cannot hold her.

He is holding her, the dirty ragged filthy foul vile drunken bum animal he is holding her my sweet baby and my god i am standing here alone watching him with her. His cigarette what if she thinks it is food she will get burned he is holding her i must have said something because he has put his cigarette on the floor she will not get burned by it but oh god he is holding my only baby my sweet margot my and i have her back.

He had thought of *leche leche* when she had started to cry, the baby don't want cigarettes, baby want *leche* he had said not wanting her to cry and somewhere in between the cigarette and the *leche* i got her back and he was gone, into the coffee shop, to get *leche* for the baby, *leche* for the baby.

now jack is here we have no time he says we have to hurry i managed to get us tickets but the bus is leaving he says. he doesn't hear what i hear through the thick glass next to us, doesn't hear the cries for *leche leche,* doesn't feel the cigarette ash hot against flesh he cant see it burn deeply. we are running we will have no *leche* from this place this night.

PROBING FOR MEANING

1. What do you think Lynch might have felt the significance was of her experience in the busy terminal?

2. Why does she describe herself as "clinging" to her daughter instead of being "the mother lion"?

3. Lynch reveals her feelings about the vagrant with complete honesty. Do you

think she overreacted? Would you have edited this entry or do you admire her for conveying her fear and loathing?

PROBING FOR METHOD

1. What effect does Lynch's use of freewriting have on the meaning of her entry?
2. What is the difference between the style of the first paragraph of her entry as opposed to the last? What does the last entry reveal about her emotional state?
3. How would you describe the tone of Lynch's entry? Is it consistent with the essay's meaning? Why or why not?

Toi Derricotte

FROM *The Black Notebooks*

TOI DERRICOTTE (b. 1941) is from Detroit, Michigan. She has taught for several years and has received numerous fellowships and awards for creative writing. Her published poetry includes The Empress of the Death House *(1978) and* Natural Birth *(1983). Of the journal entries published below from her work in progress,* The Black Notebooks, *Derricotte states: "I write about our family's experiences as one of the first black families in Upper Montclair, of my problems being unrecognized because of my light complexion, and my love and rage toward my neighbors."*

July 1977

Yesterday I put my car in the shop. The neighborhood shop. When I went to pick it up I held a conversation with the man who worked on it. I told him I had been afraid to leave the car there at night with the keys in it. "Don't worry," he said. "You don't have to worry about stealing in Upper Montclair as long as the niggers don't move in." I couldn't believe it. I hoped I had heard him wrong. "What did you say?" I asked. He repeated the same thing without hesitation.

In the past my anger would have swelled quickly. I would have blurted out something, hotly demanded he take my car down off the rack immediately though he had not finished working on it, and taken off in a blaze. I love that reaction. The only feeling of power one can possibly have in a situation in which there is such a sudden feeling of powerlessness is to "do" something, handle the situation. When you "do" something, everything is clear. But for some reason yesterday, I, who have been more concerned lately with understanding my feelings than in reacting, repressed my anger. Instead of reacting, I leaned back in myself, dizzy with pain, fear, sadness, and confused.

I go home and sit with myself for an hour, trying to grasp the feeling— the odor of self-hatred, the biting stench of shame.

December 1977

About a month ago we had the guy next door over for dinner. He's about twenty-six. The son of a banker. He lived in a camper truck for a year and came home recently with his dog to "get himself together."

After dinner we got into a conversation about the Hartford Tennis Club, where he is the swimming instructor. I asked him, hesitantly, but unwilling not to get this firsthand information, if blacks were allowed to join. (Everybody on our block belongs to Hartford, were told about "the club" and asked to join as soon as they moved in. We were never told about it or asked to join.) Unemotionally, he said, "No. The man who owns the club won't let blacks in." I said, "You mean the people on this block who have had us over to dinner and who I have invited to my home for dinner, the people I have lived next door to for three years, these same people are ones I can't swim in a pool with?" "That's the rule," he said, as if he were stating a fact with mathematical veracity and as if I would have no feelings. He told us about one girl, the daughter of the president of a bank, who worked on the desk at the Hartford Club. When they told her black people couldn't join, she quit her job. I looked at him. He is the swimming instructor at the club.

My husband and I are in marriage counseling with a white therapist. The therapist sees us separately. When I came in upset about that conversation, he said he didn't believe people were like this anymore. He said I would have to try to join the club to tell whether in fact this was true.

Four days ago, the woman down the street called me, asking if my son could baby-sit for her. I like this woman, I don't know why. She is Dutch and has that ruddy coloring, red hair, out of a Rubens painting. Easy to talk to. She and her husband are members of the club and I couldn't resist telling her the story of the guy next door to get her reaction. She said, "Oh, Toi, two years ago, John and I wanted to have you and Bruce be our guests at a dinner party at the club. I was just picking up the phone to call and ask you when Holly called [a woman who lives across the street] and said, 'Do you think that's a good idea? You better check with the Fullers [old members of the club] first before you call Bruce and Toi.' I called Steve and he called a meeting of the executive committee. We met together for four hours. Several of us said we would turn in our resignations unless you could come. But the majority of people felt that it wouldn't be a good idea because you would see all the good things about the club and want to join. And since you couldn't join, it would just hurt you and be frustrating. John and I wanted to quit. I feel very ashamed of myself, but the next summer, when I was stuck in the house with the kids with nothing to do, we joined again."

May 1978
I had a dinner party last week. Saturday night, the first dinner party in over a year. The house was dim & green with plants & flowers, light & orange like a fresh fruit tart, openings of color in darkness, shining, the glass in the dark heart of the house opening out.

    & i made sangria with white wine adding strawberries & apples & oranges & limes & lemon slices & fresh squeezed juice in an ice clear pitcher with cubes like glass lighting the taste with sound & color.

    & the table was abundant.

    & they came. one man was a brilliant conversationalist & his wife was happy to offer to help in the kitchen & one woman was quiet & seemed rigid as a fortress & black & stark as night, a wall falling quickly, her brow, that swarthy drop without her, that steep incline away . . . & her husband was a doctor & introduced himself as "dr." & i said "charmed. contessa toinette."

    & we were black & white together, we were middle class & we had "been to europe" & the doctors were black & the businessmen were white & the doctors were white & the businessmen were black & the bankers were there too.

    & the black people sat on this side of the room & the white people sat on that & they ate cherried chocolates with dainty fingers & told stories.

    & soon i found that one couple belonged to the Hartford Club & my heart closed like my eyes narrowing on that corner of the room on that conversation like a beam of light & they said "it isn't our fault. it's the man who owns it." & i was angry & i said it is your fault for you belong & no one made you & suddenly i wanted to belong i wanted them to let me in or die & wanted to go to court to battle to let crosses burn on my lawn let anything happen they will i will go to hell i will break your goddamned club apart don't give me shit anymore.

    bruce said it is illegal & if we wanted to we could get in no matter what the man at the top did & everyone is blaming it on that one ugly man & behind him they hide their own ugliness & behind his big fat ass they hide their puny hopes & don't want to be seen so god will pass over their lives & not touch, hide their little house & little dishwasher, hide like the egyptians hid their children from the face of god, hide their soaked brown evil smelling odor dripping ass. and they were saying don't blame me please throwing up their hands begging not to be seen, but i see them, my eye like a cat seeing into x-ray the bird's blood-brain: i will not pass, like god i will not pass over their evil.

    the next day bruce & i talk about it. he still doesn't want to pay 200 dollars to belong. he says it's not worth it to fight about, he doesn't want to fight to belong to something stupid, would rather save his energy to fight for something important.

important.

what is important to me?

no large goal like integrating a university. just living here on this cruddy street, taking the street in my heart like an arrow.

PROBING FOR MEANING

1. Why does Derricotte experience "the odor of self-hatred, the biting stench of shame" after her encounter with the car mechanic?

2. What is your response to her December 1977 entry? Would you have acted differently from either of her neighbors?

3. Is there a logical and emotional connection among the three entries? Why or why not?

PROBING FOR METHOD

1. Derricotte experiments with different techniques. How would you characterize her style in the July 1977 and December 1977 entries?

2. In her May 1978 entry, Derricotte uses freewriting. What is the effect of her cataloging?

3. How do the first paragraph and the last eight lines of the May 1978 entry differ stylistically from the rest of the entry? How does this difference affect the meaning of the entry?

John Coleman

FROM *Blue Collar Journal: A College President's Sabbatical*

John Coleman (b. 1921) was born in Canada. He received his Ph.D. from the University of Chicago and has written several books on labor and economics. While president of Haverford College, Coleman took a sabbatical leave in the spring of 1973 and worked at several blue-collar jobs, including ditch-digging. As you read this excerpt from Blue Collar Journal: A College President's Sabbatical *(1974), jot down your ideas about why Coleman thought it important to try such radically different things during his sabbatical.*

Tuesday, March 27

One of the waitresses I find hard to take asked me at one point today, "Are you the boy who cuts the lemons?"

"I'm the man who does," I replied.

"Well, there are none cut." There wasn't a hint that she heard my point.

Dana, who has cooked here for twelve years or so, heard that exchange.

"It's no use, Jack," he said when she was gone. "If she doesn't know now, she never will." There was a trace of a smile on his face, but it was a sad look all the same.

In that moment, I learned the full thrust of those billboard ads of a few years ago that said "BOY. Drop out of school and that's what they'll call you the rest of your life." I had read those ads before with a certain feeling of pride; education matters, they said, and that gave a lift to my field. Today I saw them saying something else. They were untrue in part; it turns out that you'll get called "boy" if you do work that others don't respect even if you have a Ph.D. It isn't education that counts, but the job in which you land. And the ads spoke too of a sad resignation about the world. They assumed that some people just won't learn respect for others, so you should adapt yourself to them. Don't try to change them. Get the right job and they won't call *you* boy any more. They'll save it for the next man.

It isn't just people like this one waitress who learn slowly, if at all. Haverford College has prided itself on being a caring, considerate community in the Quaker tradition for many long years. Yet when I came there I soon learned that the cleaning women in the dormitories were called "wombats" by all the students. No one seemed to know where the name came from or what connection, if any, it had with the dictionary definition. *The American College Dictionary* says a wombat is "any of three species of burrowing marsupials of Australia . . . somewhat resembling ground hogs." The name was just one of Haverford's unexamined ways of doing things.

It didn't take much persuasion to get the name dropped. Today there are few students who remember it at all. But I imagine the cleaning women remember it well.

Certainly I won't forget being called a boy today.

Wednesday, March 28
A day off once again.

I went into a restaurant downtown, the first time since I started work as a sandwich man. My curiosity won out. I ordered a club sandwich just to see how well it held together. It was noon, and I knew the man or woman in the kitchen must be having a rough time at that hour, but I ordered it just the same.

The sandwich looked fine, and its ingredients were fresh. I sent my compliments to the sandwich man, but I think the waitress thought I was nuts.

The place where I really wanted to eat was the Oyster House. I wanted to sit down at one of the tables and have someone—one of the many waitresses I like—bring me the menu. I wanted to order that stuffed fillet of sole, after some oysters at the bar. And I wanted the salad on the side, complete with cherry tomato and cucumber slice, and blue cheese dressing on top. I know some of the inside secrets of the place. I know, for example, that yesterday a customer got a thumbtack in his corn chowder (he was very nice about it). But I know too that the sanitation is generally good and that the people who work here care. I just wanted to see the whole meal come together as a production, fashioned by people whom I knew.

I'll eat there someday as a customer. And nothing that happens will escape my eye.

Sunday, April 1
It was hard, steady work all day long.

The rhythm of each day and even of each week is familiar enough that it should be getting boring by now. It doesn't seem that way yet. There is enough variety in the flow of orders and of people too that I seldom feel I have been through all this before. Cleaning up the aluminum trays, where my supplies are kept, at the end of each day is dull; I'd happily skip that if I could. But even in that there is a small element of suspense: the question each time is how far I can get with closing up for the night before the last waitress comes in with an order that requires getting the supplies out again.

I wonder how many loaves of bread and heads of lettuce I'd go through if I stuck at this job until retirement age.

Tuesday, April 3
The last day once again.

Joey's parting words to me were that I had been "more than just satisfactory." He said that, if I ever came back to Boston to work, I should try the Oyster House first. That's worth as much as getting an honorary degree any day.

Tonight I dropped my uniform in the dirty linen basket and punched the clock for the last time. The happy news is that Lonnie will be back from the hospital tomorrow and ready to take up his place once again. I looked at the salad bar as I walked out at 10:00. It had been mine for a while, but it was now Lonnie's once more.

Wednesday, April 4. Haverford, Pennsylvania
I drove back to Haverford today. There is a meeting of the Federal Reserve Bank's directors tomorrow morning. That meeting should end by noon. Then I can take off the director's disguise and put on the workman's again.

The time left is so short that I don't want to spend much of it looking for a job. I had enough of that in those three days of walking Boston's streets. So for the past week I have been buying whatever out-of-town papers I could get at a newsstand off Washington Street and studying want ads again. The area around Washington, D.C., looks most promising this time. Unless our directors' meeting is unusually long, I should be there by midafternoon. So I can start the next job hunt before dark.

Tonight I'm in my own home on the campus. There are lights and noises in the dormitories across the cricket field. A few recent issues of the students' newspaper are lying on the coffee table downstairs. The telephone is at my side. It's tempting to get back into Haverford affairs once again. A lot must be happening here.

Maybe one short visit to a dorm. Maybe just one issue of the *News*. Maybe just a couple of calls to colleagues to see how things are doing while I'm away.

But I don't feel ready to come back. Not yet. I went downstairs and turned out all the lights. The president isn't at home.

PROBING FOR MEANING

1. To what extent do you agree or disagree with Coleman's March 27 entry, particularly his statement that "it isn't education that counts, but the job in which you land."

2. What points about boredom is he making in his April 1 entry?

3. Coleman juxtaposes two ways of life in the April 3 and April 4 entries. Is his reaction to Joey's parting compliment plausible? Why or why not?

PROBING FOR METHOD

1. Coleman uses dialogue in his journal entries. To what extent does this technique affect their impact?

2. Define Coleman's purpose in writing these journal entries. Is he seeking to influence his readers in any way? Explain your answer.

HENRY DAVID THOREAU

FROM *The Journals*

Henry David Thoreau (1817–1862) was an American essayist and poet who was part of the American romantic literary movement. In 1845 he built a cabin at Walden Pond in Massachusetts, where he lived for the next two years, and in Walden *(1854), he describes his daily experiences. A nonconformist, Thoreau was imprisoned for failing to pay his taxes and recorded the episode in his essay "Civil Disobedience." He is recognized today not only for his prose style but also for his individualism, which challenged the status quo not only of his society but of ours today as well. He was also a major influence on Gandhi and Martin Luther King, Jr. As you read his journal entries, notice how much attention he pays to detail and try to sharpen your own powers of observation by writing in your journal a descriptive paragraph on your room or a place that is important to you.*

Volume I

(1845)

July 5. Saturday. Walden.—Yesterday I came here to live. My house makes me think of some mountain houses I have seen, which seemed to have a fresher auroral atmosphere about them, as I fancy of the halls of Olympus. I lodged at the house of a saw-miller last summer, on the Caatskill Mountains, high up as Pine Orchard, in the blueberry and raspberry region, where the quiet and cleanliness and coolness seemed to be all one,—which had their ambrosial character. He was the miller of the Kaaterskill Falls. They were a clean and wholesome family, inside and out, like their house. The latter was not plastered, only lathed, and the inner doors were not hung. The house seemed high-placed, airy, and perfumed, fit to entertain a travelling god. It was so high, indeed, that all the music, the broken strains, the waifs and accompaniments of tunes, that swept over the ridge of the Caatskills, passed through its aisles. Could not man be man in such an abode? And would he ever find out this grovelling life? It was the very light and atmosphere in which the works of Grecian art were composed, and in which they rest. They have appropriated to themselves a loftier hall than mortals ever occupy, at least on a level with the mountain-brows of the world. There was wanting a little of the glare of the lower vales, and in its place a pure twilight as became the precincts of heaven. Yet so equable and calm was the season there that you could not tell whether it was morning or noon or evening. Always there was the sound of the morning cricket.

July 6. I wish to meet the facts of life—the vital facts, which are the phenomena or actuality the gods meant to show us—face to face, and so I came down here. Life! who knows what it is, what it does? If I am not quite right here, I am less wrong than before; and now let us see what they will have. The preacher, instead of vexing the ears of drowsy farmers on their day of rest, at the end of the week,—for Sunday always seemed to me like a fit conclusion of an ill-spent week and not the fresh and brave beginning of a new one,—with this one other draggletail and postponed affair of a sermon, from thirdly to fifteenthly, should teach them with a thundering voice pause and simplicity. "Stop! Avast! Why so fast?" In all studies we go not forward but rather backward with redoubled pauses. We always study *antiques* with silence and reflection. Even time has a depth, and below its surface the waves do not lapse and roar. I wonder men can be so frivolous almost as to attend to the gross form of negro slavery, there are so many keen and subtle masters who subject us both. Self-emancipation in the West Indies of a man's thinking and imagining provinces, which should be more than his island territory,—one emancipated heart and intellect! It would knock off the fetters from a million slaves. . . .

Aug. 23. Saturday. I set out this afternoon to go a-fishing for pickerel to eke out my scanty fare of vegetables. From Walden I went through the woods to Fair Haven, but by the way the rain came on again, and my fates compelled me to stand a half-hour under a pine, piling boughs over my head, and wearing my pocket handkerchief for an umbrella; and when at length I had made one cast over the pickerel-weed, the thunder gan romblen in the heven with that grisly steven that Chaucer tells of. (The gods must be proud, with such forked flashes and such artillery to rout a poor unarmed fisherman.) I made haste to the nearest hut for a shelter. This stood a half a mile off the road, and so much the nearer to the pond. There dwelt a shiftless Irishman, John Field, and his wife, and many children, from the broad-faced boy that ran by his father's side to escape the rain to the wrinkled and sibyl-like, crone-like infant, not knowing whether to take the part of age or infancy, that sat upon its father's knee as in the palaces of nobles, and looked out from its home in the midst of wet and hunger inquisitively upon the stranger, with the privilege of infancy; the young creature not knowing but it might be the last of a line of kings instead of John Field's poor starveling brat, or, I should rather say, still knowing that it was the last of a noble line and the hope and cynosure of the world. An honest, hard-working, but shiftless man plainly was John Field; and his wife, she too was brave to cook so many succeeding dinners in the recesses of that lofty stove; with round, greasy face and bare breast, still thinking to improve her condition one day; with the never absent mop in hand, and yet no effects of it visible anywhere. The chickens, like members of the family, stalked about the room, too much humanized to roast well. They stood and looked in my eye or pecked at my shoe. He told me his story, how hard he worked bogging for a neighbor, at ten dollars an acre and the use of the land with manure for one year, and the little broad-faced son worked cheerfully at his father's side the while, not knowing, alas! how poor a bargain he had made. Living, John Field, alas! without arithmetic; failing to live.

PROBING FOR MEANING

1. What particular house is Thoreau reminded of as he comes to Walden?
2. How are your thoughts about Sundays similar to or different from Thoreau's?
3. What is your impression of John Field? Do you think Thoreau's last comment concerning him is too harsh? Why or why not?
4. What impression did you form of Thoreau from his three journal entries?

PROBING FOR METHOD

1. To what senses does Thoreau appeal in the descriptive passages of his journal?
2. What is Thoreau's purpose in coming to Walden?
3. How would you characterize Thoreau's audience? Is he writing for the average reader? Explain your answer.

WRIGHT MORRIS

FROM *Will's Boy*

Wright Morris (b. 1910) was born in Nebraska. He has published many novels and short stories, including The Field of Vision *(1956), and for his most recent novel* Plains Song *(1981), he won the American Book Award. In the following excerpt from his memoir* Will's Boy, *he raises many interesting ideas about childhood memories. As you read his essay, think about the similarities and differences between your childhood and his.*

I was born on the sixth of January, 1910, in the Platte Valley of Nebraska, just south of the 41st parallel, just west of the 98th meridian, just to the north, or south, or a bit to the east of where it sometimes rained, but more than likely it didn't, less than a mile from what had once been the Lone Tree station of the Pony Express on the Overland Trail.

My father had come west from Ohio to begin a new life with the Union Pacific Railroad in Chapman, Nebraska. My mother had been born on the bluffs south of the Platte in a house with the cupola facing the view to the west. They met in the barber shop of Eddie Cahow, who had come up from Texas on the Chisholm Trail, but found that he preferred barbering to a life in the saddle. The open range had been closed by strips of barbed wire, and the plow, for both better and worse, had replaced the six-shooter and the man on horseback, a change predicted when the town called Lone Tree at its founding was changed to Central City before I was born. Early settlers felt, and with reason, that a Lone Tree might encourage maverick, wandering males, but discourage most marriageable females. My childhood impressions were not of the big sky, and the endless vistas, but of the blaze of light where the trees ended, the sheltered grove from where I peered at the wagons of the gypsies camped at its edge.

Six days after my birth my mother died. Having stated this bald fact, I ponder its meaning. In the wings of my mind I hear voices, I am attentive to the presence of invisible relations, I see the ghosts of people without faces. Almost twenty years will pass before I set knowing eyes on my mother's people. Her father, a farmer and preacher of the Seventh-Day Adventist gospel, shortly after her death would gather up his family and move to a new Adventist settlement near Boise, Idaho. My life begins, and will have its ending, in this abiding chronicle of real losses and imaginary gains.

My father, William Henry Morris, born on a farm near Zanesville, Ohio, was one of fourteen children, all of whom grew to maturity. In the early 1890s, with his older brother, Harry, he came west to the treeless plains of Nebraska. To my knowledge no one ever referred to my father as Bill. Both friends and relations called him Will. The housekeeper, Anna, brought up from Aurora to take care of a house, a widower, and a motherless child, pronounced this word as in whippoorwilllll, the sound tailing off like the bird's song, greatly enhancing my impression of the man who often took his meals with his hat on. He was a busy father; the bicycle he rode to and from his work often lay on its side, the front wheel still spinning.

On weekends in Chapman the farmers parked their buggies at the hitch bar in front of Cahow's barber shop. This provided free bleacher seat views, for those in the buggies, of the man being clipped or shaved in the chair. If the chair was pumped up, and the occupant erect rather than horizontal, he was able to exchange glances with those peering over the half curtain. In this manner, according to Eddie Cahow, my father first set eyes on my mother, leaping from the chair, the cloth dangling from his collar, to help her down from the buggy. That is the story, and who am I to change it? She was the youngest, and most favored, of the four Osborn girls. Her name was Grace. Her sisters, Winona, Violet and Marion. Grace Osborn and Will Morris were soon married, and used his recently acquired railroad pass to spend their honeymoon in San Francisco, from where he wired the bank to send him another fifty dollars. A son, Fayette Mitchell, born in 1904, lived for only a few days. Six years will pass before I am born, and a few days later Grace Osborn Morris is dead, having given her life that I might live.

On her death a debate arose as to who should raise me, my father or my mother's married sister, Violet. More than sixty years later my Aunt Winona wrote me:

> When your mother died my sister Violet wanted to take you, but your father would not consent to it. He said, "He is all I have left of Grace." O dear boy, you were the center of so much suffering, so many losses you will never realize, know or feel . . .

This decision would be crucial to the child who played no part in it. Much of my life would be spent in an effort to recover the losses I never knew, realized or felt, the past that shaped yet continued to elude me. Had Grace Osborn lived, my compass would have been set on a different course, and my sails full of more than the winds of fiction. Am I to register that as a child's loss, or a man's gain?

*The small creatures of this world, and not a few of the large ones, are only at their ease under something. The cat crawls under the culvert, the infant under the table, screened off by the cloth that hangs like a curtain . . . in the Platte Valley of Nebraska, street culverts, piano boxes, the seats of wagons and buggies, railroad trestles, low bridges, the dark caves under front porches were all favored places of concealment. With Br'er Fox I shared the instinct to lie low. Seated in dust as fine as talcum, my lap and hands overlaid with a pattern of shadows, I peered out at the world through the holes between the slats.**

In a room of lampglow, where the shadows waver on a low ceiling, I lie full of longing at the side of a woman whose bosom heaves, but she is faceless. Would this be my father's second wife, in a marriage soon ended? Not knowing the nature of the longing I felt, would it persist and reappear as a poignant yearning for what it is in the past that eludes me?

I have another memory of lampglow and shadow. A figure looms above me, swaying like smoke, and against the flickering lamplight I see her fingers unbraid her hair. I hear the lisp of the comb, and the rasp of the brush. This will prove to be Anna, a friend of my mother's sisters, who has been hired to take care of me. Heavily, her arms resting on the bed, she kneels to pray. Her hushed whispering voice fills me with awe. To test the height of the wick's flame she stretches one of her gray hairs across the top of the chimney. Did I see it glow, like the filament of a light bulb, or is that something I have imagined, a luminous fiber in my mind, rather than the lamp? My child's soul is enlarged by this nightly ceremony of light and shadow, and the voice of prayer. It is appropriate to this emotion that the details are vague. Later, gripping her hand in the church pew, I feel the throb of her voice before I hear it, and share her passion with fear and trembling.

*One reason I see it all so clearly is that I have so often put it into writing. Perhaps it is the writing I remember, the vibrant image I have made of the memory impression. A memory for just such details is thought to be characteristic of the writer, but the fiction is already at work in what he remembers. No deception is intended, but he wants to see clearly what is invariably, intrinsically vague. So he imagines. Image-making is indivisibly a part of remembering.**

In this same house, in my sleepers with the "feet," I hurry to stand on

*Earthly Delights, Unearthly Adornments, 1978.

the hot-air floor radiator while I am dressed. In the kitchen my eyes are below the level of the table where raw sugar cookies are being rolled for baking. I reach and clutch some of the dough: I love its sweet, raw taste.

In the large room at the front, where I lie with pneumonia, the panels of colored glass in the window make a bright pattern on the bedclothes. With my warm breath, and the sleeve of my elbow, I rub a hole in the frosted window and peer out. The world is white. I am able to see the white birches in the yard against the black, twisted buggy lanes in the road. Gifts are placed on the bed. The flames of candles glitter on the Christmas tree tinsel. A huge bearlike man, with a booming voice, comes in with the winter trapped in his coat. He is Dr. Brown. I am puzzled why the fur of his coat is on the inside. For reasons that are not clear he comes to see me only when I am sick.

*If I attempt to distinguish between fiction and memory, and press my nose to memory's glass to see more clearly, the remembered image grows more illusive, like the details in a Pointillist painting. I recognize it, more than I see it. This recognition is a fabric of emotion as immaterial as music. In this defect of memory do we have the emergence of imagination? . . . Precisely where memory is frail and emotion is strong, imagination takes fire. . . .**

PROBING FOR MEANING

1. What picture of life in Nebraska does Morris provide in the first two paragraphs of the essay?

2. How does his mother's death six days after his birth affect the course of his life?

3. What is your response to his father's decision to raise him himself? What portrait of his father emerges in the essay?

4. Express in your own words the meaning of the paragraph beginning "This decision would be crucial. . . . " What does the last sentence mean?

5. What is the significance of his memories of "lampglow and shadow" and their relationship to Anna?

6. What contrast about his childhood experiences does Morris make in the second and third paragraphs from the end?

7. Morris, Hurston, and Rodriguez all focus on childhood memories. To what extent is Morris's emphasis on memory similar to or different? How did reading about their concepts of the importance of memory affect your views on the topic?

PROBING FOR METHOD

1. Morris included in his memoir physical descriptions of Nebraska and facts about his mother's death and her family, as well as details about his father. How does he integrate all of these and still provide a portrait of himself?

*Earthly Delights, Unearthly Adornments, 1978.

2. What is the effect of the italicized passages in his essay? How would their *exclusion* affect the meaning of what he is trying to convey?

3. What is Morris's purpose in recalling these childhood memories? Is he writing only for other writers or for a more general audience? Explain your answer.

Writing Autobiography

How did Wright Morris write his autobiography?
In the selection we have reprinted here, which begins Morris's book, the writer indicates he has relied on several sources: facts, memories, earlier writing, and imagination. He begins with the facts of his life—his birth, his birthplace, his parents' lives before his birth. He also calls on early memories of sense impressions and emotional responses—the memories in "lampglow and shadow" of lying "full of longing" beside a woman who may have been his father's second wife and of observing Anna's evening prayers, memories of the sweet, raw taste of cookie dough and of glittering frost and candle flames one Christmas when he was sick.

He makes much use of earlier writing he has done, perhaps in journals ("One reason I see it all so clearly is that I have so often put it into writing"), and particularly in earlier books he has published. He indicates his most vital source is his imagination: "Precisely where memory is frail and emotion is strong, imagination takes fire." In so doing, he casts doubt on the accuracy of his memories: "A memory for just such details is thought to be characteristic of the writer, but the fiction is already at work in what he remembers. No deception is intended, but he wants to see clearly what is invariably, intrinsically vague."

Writing autobiography.
Morris indicates that the aim of autobiographical writing is not so much to recount the facts of our lives as to supply the details and interpretations that ignite the facts so they glow with life. In writing autobiography as in keeping a journal, we want to reward ourselves and our readers not merely with the facts but also with the truth.

Facts themselves can be gleaned from many sources: from family records, family members, photograph albums, our own and others' diaries. Memory may also supply facts, as Richard Rodriguez's memory seems to have done in his autobiography *Hunger of Memory*, although he suggests that memory played a larger role in his recalling his emotional reactions to the facts: "Memory teaches me what I know of these matters; the boy reminds the adult."

Capturing memories is more difficult for most writers than is locating facts in records and through conversations. Most writers record their experiences in writing—in journals, particularly—but what of the earliest memories, those of experiences of earliest childhood? Meditation can aid the memory: by relaxing and letting the mind wander freely about a subject, the writer can often recover memories that elude more concentrated efforts.

The imagination fuses fact and memory, often unconsciously, as Morris suggests, but often consciously, artfully. Autobiography is above all writing intended for a reader, and where facts are few and memory frail, imagination must find ways of dramatizing the truth. Details of place, persons, conversations, sights, sounds, and smells may be added to present a complete landscape and the activities and significances within it. Zora Neale Hurston's essay appears to fuse fact, memory, and imagination in her vivid and humorous account of her birth.

Procedures for writing autobiography.

A. In writing an autobiographical essay about yourself, select an aspect of your life that you want to convey to a reader. For example, write about a phase you went through, an experience that formulated your personality or outlook in some way, an aspect of your character that interests you.

B. Call upon the facts of your subject. What facts do you remember? What can you learn by talking to friends and family members? Peruse family records, albums, and diaries for what they may tell you about dates, feelings, the clothing you wore, the people you were with, the room you were in, the weather, and so on.

C. Where facts cannot be obtained, what memories can you call on? Meditate in a quiet place or use your journal to explore your memories of your subject. Freewriting may be a way of capturing a particularly vivid memory or of dislodging a stubbornly resistant one.

D. You might next consider how to fuse your facts and memories imaginatively with what seems to you to be the truth of your subject, of its meaning for you. Morris fused what he had been told and what he remembered with imaginative images of "lampglow and shadow" and with excerpts from others of his writings. Rodriguez has focused very specifically on his struggle to retain his family language, despite years of schooling in English. Hurston has created meaning through her analysis and dramatization of her father's reaction to her birth.

E. In creating unity, you will also want to choose to remain a consistent distance from your subject. The writers of the essays in this chapter achieve varying distances from their subjects. Morris is intensely private and subjective, Rodriguez is also very intense but less private in his awareness of the public ramifications of his subject, and Hurston is humorous, achieving the greatest distance from her subject of the three.

F. Also, choose a consistent attitude or tone toward your subject. Morris and Rodriguez are both extremely serious in tone, Morris achieving a profundity, Rodriguez desiring to be moralistic. Other tones adopted by writers of autobiography are nostalgia, whimsy, and humor, as Hurston's essay exemplifies.

G. Most of the essays in this book are autobiographical, as the writers consider people they have known, places they have been, events and experiences they have gone through, emotions they have had, choices they have made, and philosophies they have worked out. The writing discussions in each chapter will supply further suggestions for successful autobiographical writing.

ZORA NEAL HURSTON

I Get Born

Zora Neal Hurston (1901–1961) was a black American novelist, journalist, and critic who sought in her many writings to communicate the beauty, complexity, and wisdom of black experience and tradition. Her novels include Their Eyes Were Watching God *(1937). In this excerpt from* I Love Myself When I Am Laughing *(edited in 1979), notice how she uses humor not only to reveal information about herself but also to engage her reader. What did you find most involving about "I Get Born"?*

This is all hear-say. Maybe some of the details of my birth as told me might be a little inaccurate, but it is pretty well established that I really did get born.

The saying goes like this. My mother's time had come and my father was not there. Being a carpenter, successful enough to have other helpers on some jobs, he was away often on building business, as well as preaching. It seems that my father was away from home for months this time. I have never been told why. But I did hear that he threatened to cut his throat when he got the news. It seems that one daughter was all that he figured he could stand. My sister, Sarah, was his favorite child, but that one girl was enough. Plenty more sons, but no more girl babies to wear out shoes and bring in nothing. I don't think he ever got over the trick he felt that I played on him by getting born a girl, and while he was off from home at that. A little of my sugar used to sweeten his coffee right now. That is a Negro way of saying his patience was short with me. Let me change a few words with him—and I am of the word-changing kind—and he was ready to change ends. Still and all, I looked more like him than any child in the house. Of course, by the time I got born, it was too late to make any suggestions, so the old man had to put up with me. He was nice about it in a way. He didn't tie me in a sack and drop me in the lake, as he probably felt like doing.

People were digging sweet potatoes, and then it was hog-killing time. Not at our house, but it was going on in general over the country like, being January and a bit cool. Most people were either butchering for themselves, or off helping other folks do their butchering, which was almost just as good. It is a gay time. A big pot of hasslits cooking with plenty of seasoning, lean slabs of fresh-killed pork frying for the helpers to refresh themselves after the work is done. Over and above being neighborly and giving aid, there is the food, the drinks and the fun of getting together.

So there was no grown folks close around when Mama's water broke. She sent one of the smaller children to fetch Aunt Judy, the mid-wife, but she was gone to Woodbridge, a mile and a half away, to eat at a hog-killing. The child was told to go over there and tell Aunt Judy to come. But nature, being indifferent to human arrangements, was impatient. My mother had to make it alone. She was too weak after I rushed out to do anything for herself, so she just was lying there, sick in the body, and worried in mind, wondering what would become of her, as well as me. She was so weak, she couldn't even reach down to where I was. She had one consolation. She knew I wasn't dead, because I was crying strong.

Help came from where she never would have thought to look for it. A white man of many acres and things, who knew the family well, had butchered the day before. Knowing that Papa was not at home, and that consequently there would be no fresh meat in our house, he decided to drive the five miles and bring a half of a shoat, sweet potatoes, and other garden stuff along. He was there a few minutes after I was born. Seeing the front door standing open, he came on in, and hollered, "Hello, there! Call your dogs!" That is the regular way to call in the country because nearly everybody who has anything to watch has biting dogs.

Nobody answered, but he claimed later that he heard me spreading my lungs all over Orange County, so he shoved the door open and bolted on into the house.

He followed the noise and then he saw how things were, and, being the kind of a man he was, he took out his Barlow Knife and cut the navel cord, then he did the best he could about other things. When the mid-wife, locally known as a granny, arrived about an hour later, there was a fire in the stove and plenty of hot water on. I had been sponged off in some sort of a way, and Mama was holding me in her arms.

As soon as the old woman got there, the white man unloaded what he had brought, and drove off cussing about some blankety-blank people never being where you could put your hands on them when they were needed.

He got no thanks from Aunt Judy. She grumbled for years about it. She complained that the cord had not been cut just right, and the bellyband had not been put on tight enough. She was mighty scared I was going to have a weak back, and that I would have trouble holding my water until I reached puberty. I did.

The next day or so a Mrs. Neale, a friend of Mama's, came in and re-minded her that she had promised to let her name the baby in case it was a girl. She had picked up a name somewhere which she thought was very pretty. Perhaps she had read it somewhere, or somebody back in those woods was smoking Turkish cigarettes. So I became Zora Neale Hurston.

There is nothing to make you like other human beings so much as doing things for them. Therefore, the man who grannied me was back next day to see how I was coming along. Maybe it was a pride in his own handiwork, and his resourcefulness in a pinch, that made him want to see it through. He remarked that I was a God-damned fine baby, fat and plenty of lung-power. As time went on, he came infrequently, but somehow kept a pinch of interest in my welfare. It seemed that I was spying noble, growing like a gourd vine, and yelling bass like a gator. He was the kind of man that had no use for puny things, so I was all to the good with him. He thought my mother was justified in keeping me.

But nine months rolled around, and I just would not get on with the walking business. I was strong, crawling well, but showed no inclination to use my feet. I might remark in passing, that I still don't like to walk. Then I was over a year old, but still I would not walk. They made allowances for my weight, but yet, that was no real reason for my not trying.

They tell me that an old sow-hog taught me how to walk. That is, she didn't instruct me in detail, but she convinced me that I really ought to try.

It was like this. My mother was going to have collard greens for dinner, so she took the dishpan and went down to the spring to wash the greens. She left me sitting on the floor, and gave me a hunk of cornbread to keep me quiet. Everything was going along all right, until the sow with her litter of pigs in convoy came abreast of the door. She must have smelled the cornbread I was messing with and scattering crumbs about the floor. So, she came right on in, and began to nuzzle around.

My mother heard my screams and came running. Her heart must have stood still when she saw the sow in there, because hogs have been known to eat human flesh.

But I was not taking this thing sitting down. I had been placed by a chair, and when my mother got inside the door, I had pulled myself up by that chair and was getting around it right smart.

As for the sow, poor misunderstood lady, she had no interest in me except my bread. I lost that in scrambling to my feet and she was eating it. She had much less intention of eating Mama's baby, than Mama had of eating hers.

With no more suggestions from the sow or anybody else, it seems that I just took to walking and kept the thing a-going. The strangest thing about it was that once I found the use of my feet, they took to wandering. I always wanted to go. I would wander off in the woods all alone, following some in-side urge to go places. This alarmed my mother a great deal. She used to say that she believed a woman who was an enemy of hers had sprinkled "travel dust" around the doorstep the day I was born. That was the only explanation she could find. I don't know why it never occurred to her to connect my tendency with my father, who didn't have a thing on his mind but this town and the next one. That should have given her a sort of hint. Some children are just bound to take after their fathers in spite of women's prayers.

PROBING FOR MEANING

1. What is Hurston's father's reaction to the birth of his daughter?

2. Hurston explains in the third and fourth paragraphs the unusual circumstances surrounding her birth. What else does she add to the essay's meaning in paragraph three?

3. How do you respond to the intervention of the white man? What is your reaction to Aunt Judy's complaints about him?

4. Why does Hurston include the episode of her learning to walk? What do we find out about her from this inclusion?

5. What is the significance of the last line of the essay? How does it contribute to the essay's meaning?

PROBING FOR METHOD

1. How effective is Hurston's use of humor?

2. How would you classify her choice of words—formal, informal, colloquial? Is it consistent with her subject matter? Why or why not?

3. Read over the first and last paragraphs of the essay. How does the allusion to her father in both contribute to the essay's coherence?

4. Although Hurston's essay is autobiographical, how does she use hyperbole to make it more effective?

RICHARD RODRIGUEZ

FROM *Hunger of Memory*

Richard Rodriguez (b. 1944) is a Mexican-American writer who grew up in Sacramento, California. As a child, Rodriguez struggled in parochial school with the task of learning his "public" language—English. He subsequently studied at Stanford and Columbia and did graduate work at the Warburg Institute

in London and the University of California at Berkeley. In 1981 he wrote
Hunger of Memory: The Education of Richard Rodriguez, *in which he*
describes the complexities and contradictions—personal and political—of growing
up bilingual in America. In the following essay, Rodriguez recalls his struggle
to learn English. How does his reaction to the English language compare
with yours?

I remember to start with that day in Sacramento—a California now nearly thirty years past—when I first entered a classroom, able to understand some fifty stray English words.

The third of four children, I had been preceded to a neighborhood Roman Catholic school by an older brother and sister. But neither of them had revealed very much about their classroom experiences. Each afternoon they returned, as they left in the morning, always together, speaking in Spanish as they climbed the five steps of the porch. And their mysterious books, wrapped in shopping-bag paper, remained on the table next to the door, closed firmly behind them.

An accident of geography sent me to a school where all my classmates were white, many the children of doctors and lawyers and business executives. All my classmates certainly must have been uneasy on that first day of school— as most children are uneasy—to find themselves apart from their families in the first institution of their lives. But I was astonished.

The nun said, in a friendly but oddly impersonal voice, "Boys and girls, this is Richard Rodriguez." (I heard her sound out: *Rich-heard Road-ree-guess*). It was the first time I had heard anyone name me in English. "Richard," the nun repeated more slowly, writing my name down in her black leather book. Quickly I turned to see my mother's face dissolve in a watery blur behind the pebbled glass door.

Many years later there is something called bilingual education—a scheme proposed in the late 1960s by Hispanic-American social activists, later endorsed by a congressional vote. It is a program that seeks to permit non-English-speaking children, many from lower-class homes, to use their family language as the language of school. (Such is the goal its supporters announce.) I hear them and am forced to say no: it is not possible for a child—any child—ever to use his family's language in school. Not to understand this is to misunderstand the public uses of schooling and to trivialize the nature of intimate life—a family's "language."

Memory teaches me what I know of these matters; the boy reminds the adult. I was a bilingual child, a certain kind—socially disadvantaged—the son of working-class parents, both Mexican immigrants.

In the early years of my boyhood, my parents coped very well in America. My father had steady work. My mother managed at home. They were nobody's victims. Optimism and ambition led them to a house (our home) many blocks from the Mexican south side of town. We lived among *gringos* and only a block from the biggest, whitest houses. It never occurred to my parents that they couldn't live wherever they chose. Nor was the Sacramento of the fifties bent on teaching them a contrary lesson. My mother and father were more annoyed than intimidated by those two or three neighbors who tried initially to make us unwelcome. ("Keep your brats away from my sidewalk!") But despite all they achieved, perhaps because they had so much to achieve, any deep feeling of ease, the confidence of "belonging" in public was withheld from them both. They regarded the people at work, the faces in crowds, as very distant from us. They were the others, *los gringos*. That term was interchangeable in their speech with another, even more telling, *los americanos*.

I grew up in a house where the only regular guests were my relations. For one day, enormous families of relatives would visit and there would be so many people that the noise and the bodies would spill out to the backyard and front porch. Then, for weeks, no one came by. (It was usually a salesman who rang the doorbell.) Our house stood apart. A gaudy yellow in a row of white bungalows. We were the people with the noisy dog. The people who raised pigeons and chickens. We were the foreigners on the block. A few neighbors smiled and waved. We waved back. But no one in the family knew the names of the old couple who lived next door; until I was seven years old, I did not know the names of the kids who lived across the street.

In public, my father and mother spoke a hesitant, accented, not always grammatical English. And they would have to strain—their bodies tense—to catch the sense of what was rapidly said by *los gringos*. At home they spoke Spanish. The language of their Mexican past sounded in counterpoint to the English of public society. The words would come quickly, with ease. Conveyed through those sounds was the pleasing, soothing, consoling reminder of being at home.

During those years when I was first conscious of hearing, my mother and father addressed me only in Spanish; in Spanish I learned to reply. By contrast, English *(inglés)*, rarely heard in the house, was the language I came to associate with *gringos*. I learned my first words of English overhearing my parents speak to strangers. At five years of age, I knew just enough English for my mother to trust me on errands to stores one block away. No more.

I was a listening child, careful to hear the very different sounds of Spanish and English. Wide-eyed with hearing, I'd listen to sounds more than words. First, there were English *(gringos)* sounds. So many words were still unknown that when the butcher or the lady at the drugstore said something to me, exotic polysyllabic sounds would bloom in the midst of their sentences. Often, the speech of people in public seemed to me very loud, booming with confidence. The man behind the counter would literally ask, "What can I do for you?" But by being so firm and so clear, the sound of his voice said that he was a *gringo*; he belonged in public society.

I would also hear then the high nasal notes of middle-class American speech. The air stirred with sound. Sometimes, even now, when I have been traveling abroad for several weeks, I will hear what I heard as a boy. In hotel lobbies or airports, in Turkey or Brazil, some Americans will pass, and suddenly I will hear it again—the high sound of American voices. For a few seconds I will hear it with pleasure, for it is now the sound of *my* society—a reminder of home. But inevitably—already on the flight headed for home, the sound fades with repetition. I will be unable to hear it anymore.

When I was a boy, things were different. The accent of *los gringos* was never pleasing nor was it hard to hear. Crowds at Safeway or at bus stops would be noisy with sound. And I would be forced to edge away from the chirping chatter above me.

I was unable to hear my own sounds, but I knew very well that I spoke English poorly. My words could not stretch far enough to form complete thoughts. And the words I did speak I didn't know well enough to make into distinct sounds. (Listeners would usually lower their heads, better to hear what I was trying to say.) But it was one thing for *me* to speak English with difficulty. It was more troubling for me to hear my parents speak in public: their high-whining vowels and guttural consonants; their sentences that got stuck with "eh" and "ah" sounds; the confused syntax; the hesitant rhythm of sounds so different from the way *gringos* spoke. I'd notice, moreover, that my parents' voices were softer than those of *gringos* we'd meet.

I am tempted now to say that none of this mattered. In adulthood I am embarrassed by childhood fears. And, in a way, it didn't matter very much that my parents could not speak English with ease. Their linguistic difficulties had no serious consequences. My mother and father made themselves understood at the county hospital clinic and at government offices. And yet, in another way, it mattered very much—it was unsettling to hear my parents struggle with English. Hearing them, I'd grow nervous, my clutching trust in their protection and power weakened.

There were many times like the night at a brightly lit gasoline station (a blaring white memory) when I stood uneasily, hearing my father. He was talking to a teenaged attendant. I do not recall what they were saying, but I cannot forget the sounds my father made as he spoke. At one point his words slid together to form one word—sounds as confused as the threads of blue and green oil in the puddle next to my shoes. His voice rushed through what he had left to say. And, toward the end, reached falsetto notes, appealing to his listener's understanding. I looked away to the lights of passing automobiles. I tried not to hear anymore. But I heard only too well the calm, easy tone in the attendant's reply. Shortly afterward, walking toward home with my father, I shivered when he put his hand on my shoulder. The very first chance that I got, I evaded his grasp and ran on ahead into the dark, skipping with feigned boyish exuberance.

But then there was Spanish. *Español*: my family's language. *Español*: the language that seemed to me a private language. I'd hear strangers on the radio and in the Mexican Catholic church across town speaking in Spanish, but I couldn't really believe that Spanish was a public language, like English. Spanish speakers, rather, seemed related to me, for I sensed that we shared— through our language—the experience of feeling apart from *los gringos*. It was thus a ghetto Spanish that I heard and I spoke. Like those whose lives are bound by a barrio, I was reminded by Spanish of my separateness from *los otros, los gringos* in power. But more intensely than for most barrio children— because I did not live in a barrio—Spanish seemed to me the language of home. (Most days it was only at home that I'd hear it.) It became the language of joyful return.

A family member would say something to me and I would feel myself specially recognized. My parents would say something to me and I would feel embraced by the sounds of their words. Those sounds said: *I am speaking with ease in Spanish. I am addressing you in words I never use with* los gringos. *I recognize you as someone special, close, like no one outside. You belong with us. In the family.*

(Ricardo)

At the age of five, six, well past the time when most other children no longer easily notice the difference between sounds uttered at home and words spoken in public, I had a different experience. I lived in a world magically compounded of sounds. I remained a child longer than most; I lingered too long, poised at the end of language—often frightened by the sounds of *los gringos*, delighted by the sounds of Spanish at home. I shared with my family a language that was startlingly different from that used in the great city around us.

For me there were none of the gradations between public and private society so normal to a maturing child. Outside the house was public society; inside the house was private. Just opening or closing the screen door behind me was an important experience. I'd rarely leave home all alone or without reluctance. Walking down the sidewalk, under the canopy of tall trees, I'd warily notice the —suddenly—silent neighborhood kids who stood warily watching me. Nervously, I'd arrive at the grocery store to hear there the sounds of the *gringo*— foreign to me—reminding me that in this world so big, I was a foreigner. But then I'd return. Walking back toward our house, climbing the steps from the sidewalk, when the front door was open in summer, I'd hear voices beyond the screen door talking in Spanish. For a second or two, I'd stay, linger there, listening. Smiling, I'd hear my mother call out, saying in Spanish (words): "Is that you, Richard?" All the while her sounds would assure me: *Your are home now; come closer; inside. With us.*

Sí, I'd reply.

Once more inside the house I would resume (assume) my place in the family. The sounds would dim, grow harder to hear. Once more at home, I would grow less aware of that fact. It required, however, no more than the blurt of the doorbell to alert me to listen to sounds all over again. The house would turn instantly still while my mother went to the door. I'd hear her hard

English sounds. I'd wait to hear her voice return to soft-sounding Spanish, which assured me, as surely as did the clicking tongue of the lock on the door, that the stranger was gone.

Plainly, it is not healthy to hear such sounds so often. It is not healthy to distinguish public words from private sounds so easily. I remained cloistered by sounds, timid and shy in public, too dependent on voices at home. And yet it needs to be emphasized: I was an extremely happy child at home. I remember many nights when my father would come back from work, and I'd hear him call out to my mother in Spanish, sounding relieved. In Spanish, he'd sound light and free notes he never could manage in English. Some nights I'd jump up just at hearing his voice. With *mis hermanos* I would come running into the room where he was with my mother. Our laughing (so deep was the pleasure!) became screaming. Like others who know the pain of public alienation, we transformed the knowledge of our public separateness and made it consoling—the reminder of intimacy. Excited, we joined our voices in a celebration of sounds. *We are speaking now the way we never speak out in public. We are alone—together,* voices sounded, surrounded to tell me. Some nights, no one seemed willing to loosen the hold sounds had on us. At dinner, we invented new words. (Ours sounded Spanish, but made sense only to us.) We pieced together new words by taking, say, an English verb and giving it Spanish endings. My mother's instructions at bedtime would be lacquered with mock-urgent tones. Or a word like *sí* would become, in several notes, able to convey added measures of feeling. Tongues explored the edges of words, especially the fat vowels. And we happily sounded that military drum roll, the twirling roar of the Spanish *r*. Family language: my family's sounds. The voices of my parents and sisters and brother. Their voices insisting: *You belong here. We are family members. Related. Special to one another. Listen!* Voices singing and sighing, rising, straining, then surging, teeming with pleasure that burst syllables into fragments of laughter. At times it seemed there was steady quiet only when, from another room, the rustling whispers of my parents faded and I moved closer to sleep.

PROBING FOR MEANING

1. Rodriguez says that he was "a listening child." What does he mean?

2. How did Rodriguez feel about the sounds of English when he was a boy? How have his feelings changed now that he is grown?

3. What effect did his parents' halting English have upon Rodriguez when he was growing up?

4. Why did Spanish seem like "a private language" to him? What positive and negative effects did his early feelings about Spanish have upon him?

5. Do you get a sense from this short excerpt why Rodriguez is opposed to bilingual education? Explain your answer.

PROBING FOR METHOD

1. Rodriguez begins the essay by recalling how, on his first day in public school, he watched his mother's face "dissolve in a watery blur behind the pebbled glass door." In what sense is the image of the door symbolic?

2. Where else in the essay is the image of a door important? What other images does Rodriguez use to evoke his thoughts and feelings?

3. What effect does the repeated use of the Spanish word *"gringos"* have on the reader?

4. What other Spanish words does Rodriguez introduce into the essay, and to what effect?

WILLIAM CARLOS WILLIAMS

Danse Russe

William Carlos Williams (1883–1963) was born in Rutherford, New Jersey. He was a physican by vocation and a poet and short story writer by avocation. He wrote in simple language and tried to capture the immediacy of life's experiences. His publications include The Collected Later Poems of William Carlos Williams *(1963). As you read "Danse Russe," published in 1916, compare your ideas about loneliness with those of this dancing celebrant of life.*

If I when my wife is sleeping
and the baby and Kathleen
are sleeping
and the sun is a flame-white disc
in silken mists
above shining trees,—
if I in my north room
dance naked, grotesquely
before my mirror
waving my shirt round my head
and singing softly to myself:
"I am lonely, lonely.
I was born to be lonely,
I am best so!"

If I admire my arms, my face
my shoulders, flanks, buttocks
against the yellow drawn shades,—

Who shall say I am not
the happy genius of my household?

PROBING FOR MEANING

1. What connotations does the poet give the word "lonely"? Keep in mind that he purposely dances when no one is awake, is "best" lonely, and is "the happy genius of his household."
2. What details enhance his description of his "Danse Russe" (Russian dance)?
3. What is his motivation for dancing?

PROBING FOR METHOD

1. What effect does the place of the sun as well as his description of it have on his dance, particularly since his is a "north" room and the drawn shade is "yellow"?
2. Characterize the tone of the poem. How does it contribute to the poem's overall effect?

PÄR LAGERKVIST

Father and I

Pär Lagerkvist (1891–1974) was a Swedish poet, novelist, and playwright whose humanism and agonized honesty led him to actively oppose the Nazi regime of the 1930s and all forms of tyranny and totalitarianism. His determination to probe deeply and honestly into the human heart and mind brought him acclaim for his novel The Hangman *(1935), a poignant and revealing portrait of the destructive nature of violence. As a testament to his genius, he won the Nobel Prize for Literature in 1951. His best-known works internationally are* The Dwarf *(1945),* Barabbas *(1950) and* The Sibyl *(1956). As you read "Father and I," written from the point of view of the son, compare the narrator's experience of his father with your own, or with other father-child relationships you have observed or read about.*

When I was getting on toward ten, I remember, Father took me by the hand one Sunday afternoon, as we were to go out into the woods and listen to the birds singing. Waving good-bye to Mother, who had to stay at home and get the evening meal, we set off briskly in the warm sunshine. We didn't make any great to-do about this going to listen to the birds, as though it were something extra special or wonderful; we were sound, sensible people, Father and I, brought up with nature and used to it. There was nothing to make a fuss about. It was just that it was Sunday afternoon and Father was free. We walked along the railway line, where people were not allowed to go as a rule, but Father worked on the railway and so he had a right to. By doing this we could get straight into the woods, too, without going a round-about way.

Soon the bird song began and all the rest. There was a twittering of finches and willow warblers, thrushes and sparrows in the bushes, the hum that goes on all around you as soon as you enter a wood. The ground was white with wood anemones, the birches had just come out into leaf, and the spruces had fresh shoots; there were scents on all sides, and underfoot the mossy earth lay steaming in the sun. There was noise and movement everywhere; bumblebees came out of their holes, midges swarmed wherever it was marshy, and birds darted out of the bushes to catch them and back again as quickly.

All at once a train came rushing along and we had to go down on to the embankment. Father hailed the engine driver with two fingers to his Sunday hat and the driver saluted and extended his hand. It all happened quickly; then on we went, taking big strides so as to tread on the sleepers and not in the gravel, which was heavy going and rough on the shoes. The sleepers sweated tar in the heat, everything smelled, grease and meadowsweet, tar, and heather by turns. The rails glinted in the sun. On either side of the line were telegraph poles, which sang as you passed them. Yes, it was a lovely day. The sky was quite clear, not a cloud to be seen, and there couldn't be any, either, on a day like this, from what Father said.

After a while we came to a field of oats to the right of the line, where a crofter we knew had a clearing. The oats had come up close and even. Father scanned them with an expert eye and I could see he was satisfied. I knew very little about such things, having been born in a town. Then we came to the bridge over a stream, which most of the time had no water to speak of but which now was in full spate. We held hands so as not to fall down between the sleepers. After that it is not long before you come to the platelayer's cottage lying embedded in greenery, apple trees and gooseberry bushes. We called in to see them and were offered milk, and saw their pig and hens and fruit trees in blossom; then we went on. We wanted to get to the river, for it was more beautiful there than anywhere else; there was something special about it, as farther upstream it flowed past where Father had lived as a child. We usually liked to come as far as this before we turned back, and today, too, we got there after a good walk. It was near the next station, but we didn't go so far. Father just looked to see that the semaphore was right—he thought of everything.

We stopped by the river, which murmured in the hot sun, broad and friendly. The shady trees hung along the banks and were reflected in the back-water. It was all fresh and light here; a soft breeze was blowing off the small lakes higher up. We climbed down the slope and walked a little way along the bank, Father pointing out the spots for fishing. He had sat here on the stones as a boy, waiting for perch all day long; often there wasn't even a bite, but it was a blissful life. Now he didn't have time. We hung about on the bank for a good while, making a noise, pushing out bits of bark for the current to take, throwing pebbles out into the water to see who could throw farthest; we were both gay and cheerful by nature, Father and I. At last we felt tired and that we had had enough, and we set off for home.

It was beginning to get dark. The woods were changed—it wasn't dark there yet, but almost. We quickened our steps. Mother would be getting anx-ious and waiting with supper. She was always afraid something was going to happen. But it hadn't; it had been a lovely day, nothing had happened that shouldn't. We were content with everything.

The twilight deepened. The trees were so funny. They stood listening to every step we took, as if they didn't know who we were. Under one of them was a glow-worm. It lay down there in the dark staring at us. I squeezed Fa-ther's hand, but he didn't see the strange glow, just walked on. Now it was quite dark. We came to the bridge over the stream. It roared down there in the depths, horribly, as though it wanted to swallow us up; the abyss yawned below us. We trod carefully on the sleepers, holding each other tightly by the hand so as not to fall in. I thought Father would carry me across, but he didn't say anything; he probably wanted me to be like him and think nothing of it.

We went on. Father was so calm as he walked there in the darkness, with even strides, not speaking, thinking to himself. I couldn't understand how he could be so calm when it was so murky. I looked all around me in fear. Noth-ing but darkness everywhere. I hardly dared take a deep breath, for then you got so much darkness inside you, and that was dangerous. I thought it meant you would soon die. I remember quite well that's what I thought then. The embankment sloped steeply down, as though into chasms black as night. The telegraph poles rose, ghostly, to the sky. Inside them was a hollow rumble, as though someone were talking deep down in the earth and the white porcelain caps sat huddled fearfully together listening to it. It was all horrible. Nothing was right, nothing real; it was all so weird.

Hugging close to Father, I whispered, "Father, why is it so horrible when it's dark?"

"No, my boy, it's not horrible," he said, taking me by the hand.

"Yes, Father, it is."

"No, my child, you mustn't think that. Not when we know there is a God."

I felt so lonely, forsaken. It was so strange that only I was afraid, not Father, that we didn't think the same. And strange that what he said didn't me and stop me from being afraid. Not even what he said about God helped me. I thought he too was horrible. It was horrible that he was everywhere here in the darkness, down under the trees, in the telegraph poles which rumbled— that must be he—everywhere. And yet you could never see him.

We walked in silence, each with his own thoughts. My heart contracted, as though the darkness had got in and was beginning to squeeze it.

Then, as we were rounding a bend, we suddenly heard a mighty roar behind us! We were awakened out of our thoughts in alarm. Father pulled me down on to the embankment, down into the abyss, held me there. Then the train tore past, a black train. All the lights in the carriages were out, and it was going at frantic speed. What sort of train was it? There wasn't one due now! We gazed at it in terror. The fire blazed in the huge engine as they shovelled in coal; sparks whirled out into the night. It was terrible. The driver stood there in the light of the fire, pale, motionless, his features as though turned to stone. Father didn't recognize him, didn't know who he was. The man just stared straight ahead, as though intent on rushing into the darkness, far into the darkness that had no end.

Beside myself with dread, I stood there panting, gazing after the furious vision. It was swallowed up by the night. Father took me up on to the line; we hurried home. He said, "Strange, what train was that? And I didn't recognize the driver." Then we walked on in silence.

But my whole body was shaking. It was for me, for my sake. I sensed what it meant: it was the anguish that was to come, the unknown, all that Father knew nothing about, that he wouldn't be able to protect me against. That was how this world, this life, would be for me; not like Father's, where everything was secure and certain. It wasn't a real world, a real life. It just hurtled, blazing, into the darkness that had no end.

PROBING FOR MEANING

1. What characteristics of his father and of himself does the boy reveal in the first paragraph? What similar comments does he make later in the story?

2. How does the second paragraph contradict what he says of himself in the first? Are there other contradictions elsewhere? What significance do these contradictions have?

3. What do we learn about the boy's mother from the story? Is the boy's insight about his mother important? Why or why not?

4. What does the second train incident in the latter section of the story suggest to the boy about his relationship with his father and about life itself? What emotions or images does the black train evoke? To what extent do you empathize with the boy?

PROBING FOR METHOD

1. The author uses time settings to convey different moods of the narrator. How is the mood different at night from in the day? Give examples.

2. Lagerkvist is writing as an adult but uses a child as narrator. What does the reader learn that is strictly from the child's point of view? Ho do his insights differ from those filtered through the adult narrator?

3. Comment on the effectiveness of Lagerkvist's use of dialogue. How does it add to your impressions of the boy and the father?

WRITING TOPICS
Generating Ideas on the Self

Freewrite, brainstorm or write a journal entry in response to one or more of the following:

The unexamined life is not worth living.

Plato

I celebrate myself, and sing myself.

Walt Whitman

I'm nobody! Who are you?
  Are you—nobody too?
Then there's a pair of us
  Don't tell! They'd advertise—you know

How dreary—to be—somebody!
  How public—like a frog—
To tell one's name—the live long June
  To an admiring bog.

Emily Dickinson

I am lonely, lonely
I was born to be lonely,
I am best so

William Carlos Williams

I need more willpower. It's not impossible to write even under my conditions. The trouble is I'm lazy.

Mario Puzo

Writing comes out of life, life must *come first.*
Anne Morrow Lindberg

That favorite subject, myself.

James Boswell

I only regret that everyone wants to deprive me of the journal, which is the only steadfast friend I have, the only one which makes my life bearable; because my happiness with human beings is precarious, my confiding moods rare, and the least sign of non-interest is enough to silence me. In the journal I am at ease.

Playing so many roles, dutiful daughter, devoted sister, mistress, protector, my father's new found illusion, Henry's needed, all-purpose friend, I had to find one place of truth, one dialogue without falsity. This is the role of the diary.

Anaïs Nin

I put a piece of paper and a pencil under my pillow, and when I could not sleep I wrote in the dark.

Henry David Thoreau

I'm pore, I'm black, I may be ugly and can't cook, a voice say to everything, listening. But I'm here. Amen, say shug. Amen. Amen.

Alice Walker

Topics for Essays on the Self

1. Lynch's journal entry is concerned with an unpleasant memory of a trip she had taken. Write an essay about a trip you have taken that evokes a similar emotion *or* describe a frightening encounter you have had. What insights about yourself did you gain?
2. Both Coleman and Derricotte write about experiences of discrimination. Write a personal essay about a similar experience you have had, making sure that you include what you learned about yourself as a result.
3. Develop an approach to freewriting similar to that of Derricotte. Then freewrite about one or two of the statements from "Generating Ideas" and develop an essay about yourself based on your freewriting.
4. Both Morris and Hurston write about their earliest memories. Freewrite about one of your earliest memories that had a significant impact upon you and then expand on it for a fully developed essay.
5. Analyze the *kinds* of topics the journal-keepers in chapter 1 discuss. Notice, for example, that Mehta records daily observations while Coleman's entries are more analytical. Experiment with keeping a journal on six successive days imitating either of their styles. What did you learn about yourself as a result? Write an essay analyzing this experiment.
6. Rodriguez writes about growing up as a Mexican-American in California: Zora Neale Hurston describes black life in a small town in Florida. Write an essay describing how your cultural background has affected your concept of yourself.
7. Wright Morris emphasizes the relationship between memory and writing. Students often complain that nothing has happened to them that is interesting

enough to write about. Conduct an experiment to test whether or not this is true of you. Each day for a week write a journal entry that focuses on a different memory. Then, write an essay developing these memories.

8. Go through a family photograph album and select a picture or pictures that evoke a powerful memory and write about it. You might then show the picture you selected to another family member and compare and contrast his or her memories with yours. Consider whether or not you should modify your essay in any way as a result of what you have learned.

9. Both Rodriguez and Lagerkvist write about an experience children have—realizing that parents are fallible and cannot protect them. If you have a similar memory, develop it into an essay, explaining the effect upon you.

CHAPTER TWO

People:

Planning the Essay
Creating an Effective Subject
Organizing an Essay

In his poem "People," Yevgeny Yevtushenko seeks to convey the uniqueness of each individual:

> *Nothing in them is not particular,*
> *and planet is dissimilar from planet.*

Pardoxically, however, although people are dissimilar, they also have many qualities in common. In this chapter, you will encounter people who have had experiences, felt emotions, and developed thoughts that are common to all human beings. In reading about them, you will no doubt recognize yourself.

We are unique, but we are also influenced by those who share our daily lives, and five of the essayists in this chapter write about a person who influenced them. In "Discovery of a Father," for example, Sherwood Anderson announces that as a child, he did not get that special thing a boy wants from his father. Maya Angelou in "Sister Flowers" portrays the woman who threw her her "first life line," and in "Quintana" John Gregory Dunne explains his relationship with his daughter and describes his thoughts on being the parent of an adopted child. In his essay Alfred Kazin explains why Cousin Sophie was his family's "constant charge and preoccupation," and Joyce Maynard recognizes the importance of the continuity of her own family through her last encounter with her grandmother.

In his poem "People," Yevtushenko explains why "no people are uninteresting," and in the short story "Phineas," John Knowles dramatizes the complex friendship of his protagonists Gene and Finny.

Discussions on planning your essay on a person are included as well. "Creating an Effective Subject" begins on page 51, and "Organizing an Essay" begins on page 59.

SHERWOOD ANDERSON

Discovery of a Father

Sherwood Anderson (1876–1941) was an American novelist and short story writer whose collection of short stories **Winesburg, Ohio** *(1919), reflecting life in a small midwestern town, brought him instant recognition. Anderson was convinced that the growth of urban centers would result in the disintegration of the personal life. His interest in the individual and his connection to his community is reflected in his autobiographical essay "Discovery of a Father." As you read about Anderson's expectations of his father, compare them with your idea of what a father should be.*

You hear it said that fathers want their sons to be what they feel they cannot themselves be, but I tell you it also works the other way. A boy wants something very special from his father. I know that as a small boy I wanted my father to be a certain thing he was not. I wanted him to be a proud, silent, dignified father. When I was with other boys and he passed along the street, I wanted to feel a flow of pride. "There he is. That is my father."

But he wasn't such a one. He couldn't be. It seemed to me then that he was always showing off. Let's say someone in our town had got up a show. They were always doing it. The druggist would be in it, the shoe-store clerk, the horse doctor, and a lot of women and girls. My father would manage to get the chief comedy part. It was, let's say, a Civil War play and he was a comic Irish soldier. He had to do the most absurd things. They thought he was funny, but I didn't.

I thought he was terrible. I didn't see how mother could stand it. She even laughed with the others. Maybe I would have laughed if it hadn't been my father.

Or there was a parade, the Fourth of July or Decoration Day. He'd be in that, too, right at the front of it, as Grand Marshal or something, on a white horse hired from a livery stable.

He couldn't ride for shucks. He fell off the horse and everyone hooted with laughter, but he didn't care. He even seemed to like it. I remember once when he had done something ridiculous, and right out on Main Street, too. I was with some other boys and they were laughing and shouting at him and he was shouting back and having as good a time as they were. I ran down an alley back of some stores and there in the Presbyterian Church sheds I had a good long cry.

Or I would be in bed at night and father would come home a little lit up and bring some men with him. He was a man who was never alone. Before he went broke, running a harness shop, there were always a lot of men loafing in the shop. He went broke, of course, because he gave too much credit. He couldn't refuse it and I thought he was a fool. I had got to hating him.

There'd be men I didn't think would want to be fooling around with him. There might even be the superintendent of our schools and a quiet man who ran the hardware store. Once I remember there was a white-haired man who was a cashier of the bank. It was a wonder to me they'd want to be seen with such a windbag. That's what I thought he was. I know now what it was that attracted them. It was because life in our town, as in all small towns, was at times pretty dull and he livened it up. He made them laugh. He could tell stories. He'd even get them to singing.

If they didn't come to our house they'd go off, say at night, to where there was a grassy place by a creek. They'd cook food there and drink beer and sit about listening to his stories.

He was always telling stories about himself. He'd say this or that wonderful thing had happened to him. It might be something that made him look like a fool. He didn't care.

If an Irishman came to our house, right away father would say he was Irish. He'd tell what county in Ireland he was born in. He'd tell things that happened there when he was a boy. He'd make it seem so real that, if I hadn't known he was born in southern Ohio, I'd have believed him myself.

If it was a Scotchman the same thing happened. He'd get a burr into his speech. Or he was a German or a Swede. He'd be anything the other man was. I think they all knew he was lying, but they seemed to like him just the same. As a boy that was what I couldn't understand.

And there was mother. How could she stand it? I wanted to ask but never did. She was not the kind you asked such questions.

I'd be upstairs in my bed, in my room above the porch, and father would be telling some of his tales. A lot of father's stories were about the Civil War. To hear him tell it he'd been in about every battle. He'd known Grant, Sherman, Sheridan and I don't know how many others. He'd been particularly intimate with General Grant so that when Grant went East to take charge of all the armies, he took father along.

"I was an orderly at headquarters and Sim Grant said to me, 'Irve,' he said, 'I'm going to take you along with me.' "

It seems he and Grant used to slip off sometimes and have a quiet drink together. That's what my father said. He'd tell about the day Lee surrendered and how, when the great moment came, they couldn't find Grant.

"You know," my father said, "about General Grant's book, his memoirs. You've read of how he said he had a headache and how, when he got word that Lee was ready to call it quits, he was suddenly and miraculously cured.

"Huh," said father. "He was in the woods with me.

"I was in there with my back against a tree. I was pretty well corned. I had got hold of a bottle of pretty good stuff.

"They were looking for Grant. He had got off his horse and come into the woods. He found me. He was covered with mud.

"I had the bottle in my hand. What'd I care? The war was over. I knew we had them licked."

My father said that he was the one who told Grant about Lee. An orderly riding by had told him, because the orderly knew how thick he was with Grant. Grant was embarrassed.

"But, Irve, look at me. I'm all covered with mud," he said to father.

And then, my father said, he and Grant decided to have a drink together. They took a couple of shots and then, because he didn't want Grant to show up potted before the immaculate Lee, he smashed the bottle against the tree.

"Sim Grant's dead now and I wouldn't want it to get out on him," my father said.

That's just one of the kind of things he'd tell. Of course the men knew he was lying, but they seemed to like it just the same.

When we got broke, down and out, do you think he ever brought anything home? Not he. If there wasn't anything to eat in the house, he'd go off visiting around at farmhouses. They all wanted him. Sometimes he'd stay away for weeks, mother working to keep us fed, and then home he'd come bringing, let's say, a ham. He'd got it from some farmer friend. He'd slap it on the table in the kitchen. "You bet I'm going to see that my kids have something to eat," he'd say, and mother would just stand smiling at him. She'd never say a word about all the weeks and months he'd been away, not leaving us a cent for food. Once I heard her speaking to a woman in our street. Maybe the woman had dared to sympathize with her. "Oh," she said, "it's all right. He isn't ever dull like most of the men in this street. Life is never dull when my man is about."

But often I was filled with bitterness, and sometimes I wished he wasn't my father. I'd even invent another man as my father. To protect my mother I'd make up stories of a secret marriage that for some strange reason never got known. As though some man, say the president of a railroad company or maybe a Congressman, had married my mother, thinking his wife was dead and then it turned out she wasn't.

So they had to hush it up but I got born just the same. I wasn't really the son of my father. Somewhere in the world there was a very dignified, quite wonderful man who was really my father. I even made myself half believe these fancies.

And then there came a certain night. He'd been off somewhere for two or three weeks. He found me alone in the house, reading by the kitchen table.

It had been raining and he was very wet. He sat and looked at me for a long time, not saying a word. I was startled, for there was on his face the saddest look I had ever seen. He sat for a time, his clothes dripping. Then he got up.

"Come on with me," he said.

I got up and went with him out of the house. I was filled with wonder but I wasn't afraid. We went along a dirt road that led down into a valley, about a mile out of town, where there was a pond. We walked in silence. The man who was always talking had stopped his talking.

I didn't know what was up and had the queer feeling that I was with a stranger. I don't know whether my father intended it so. I don't think he did.

The pond was quite large. It was still raining hard and there were flashes of lightning followed by thunder. We were on a grassy bank at the pond's edge when my father spoke, and in the darkness and rain his voice sounded strange.

"Take off your clothes," he said. Still filled with wonder, I began to undress. There was a flash of lightning and I saw that he was already naked.

Naked, we went into the pond. Taking my hand he pulled me in. It may be that I was too frightened, too full of a feeling of strangeness, to speak. Before that night my father had never seemed to pay any attention to me.

"And what is he up to now?" I kept asking myself. I did not swim very well, but he put my hand on his shoulder and struck out into the darkness.

He was a man with big shoulders, a powerful swimmer. In the darkness I could feel the movement of his muscles. We swam to the far edge of the pond and then back to where we had left our clothes. The rain continued and the wind blew. Sometimes my father swam on his back and when he did he took my hand in his large powerful one and moved it over so that it rested always on his shoulder. Sometimes there would be a flash of lightning and I could see his face quite clearly.

It was as it was earlier, in the kitchen, a face filled with sadness. There would be the momentary glimpse of his face and then again the darkness, the wind and the rain. In me there was a feeling I had never known before.

It was a feeling of closeness. It was something strange. It was as though there were only we two in the world. It was as though I had been jerked suddenly out of myself, out of my world of the schoolboy, out of a world in which I was ashamed of my father.

He had become blood of my blood; he the strong swimmer and I the boy clinging to him in the darkness. We swam in silence and in silence we dressed in our wet clothes, and went home.

There was a lamp lighted in the kitchen and when we came in, the water dripping from us, there was my mother. She smiled at us. I remember that she called us "boys."

"What have you boys been up to," she asked, but my father did not answer. As he had begun the evening's experience with me in silence, so he ended it. He turned and looked at me. Then he went, I thought, with a new and strange dignity out of the room.

I climbed the stairs to my own room, undressed in the darkness and got into bed. I couldn't sleep and did not want to sleep. For the first time I knew that I was the son of my father. He was a story teller as I was to be. It may be that I even laughed a little softly there in the darkness. If I did, I laughed knowing that I would never again be wanting another father.

PROBING FOR MEANING

1. In the first part of the essay, what impression of his father does Anderson create? What examples of his father's behavior are given to achieve this impression?

2. What differences does the boy discover about his father in the swimming scene?

3. Explain the phrase "a face filled with sadness," which is used at least twice in the second part of the essay.

4. Anderson gains recognition about himself and his father as a result of this encounter. What does he find out?

5. What kind of man was Anderson's father? Why was he a clown? Why didn't he support his family? Would a father like Anderson's have embarrassed and angered you if you had been in Anderson's place?

6. How important are the roles that society has given us to play?

7. Why do you think Anderson wrote this essay?

PROBING FOR METHOD

1. Why does Anderson focus on the swimming scene in writing about his father?

2. What effect does he create by using dialogue and anecdotes?

3. How would you classify Anderson's level of language? What does that suggest about the audience he was trying to reach? Explain your answer.

Creating an Effective Subject

How did Anderson create an effective subject?

At some point in his thinking and writing about his father, Anderson decided that his purpose should be to convey his childhood feelings about him. He therefore decided to eliminate all information about his father except that which was necessary to explain their evolving relationship. He also made a decision to focus on the swimming scene because this one event served best to indicate what he had learned about his father. He both eliminated and added material to fulfill his purpose.

He decided to show us his father in action so that we would understand both his early hatred and his subsequent admiration of the man. He chose to write an autobiographical personal essay filled with conversation and anecdote. His informality and simple vocabulary indicate that his desired audience was the common reader—the majority of Americans, regardless of the level of their education.

Creating an effective subject.
In choosing a subject, several considerations must be kept in mind: the purpose of your writing, the audience to whom you are writing, your knowledge of your subject, and the proposed length of the piece. Once you have taken these aspects into account, you can begin to formulate an effective subject.

In writing for English classes, your purpose is usually to write an informative essay, and your audience is usually your instructor and your classmates. However, your instructor may also ask you to write an autobiographical essay, a business letter, an evaluative report, a scientific research essay, an editorial, or an informative magazine article. Likewise, you may be asked to write for various audiences during the semester: your peers, an employer, your coworkers, or the readers common to a particular publication, such as your college newspaper or a magazine. If your purpose and your audience vary, your choice or presentation of a subject will also vary. What is suitable to one purpose and one audience is not suitable to another.

For example, as you read the other essays in this chapter, compare them for audience and purpose. You will notice that they were written for different audiences and with different purposes. The simple vocabulary level, the use of dialogue, and the relatively uncomplicated ideas indicate that Maya Angelou's informal autobiographical essay, like Sherwood Anderson's, is written for the average person. In their likewise autobiographical essays, Kazin writes about Cousin Sophie and Maynard writes about her visit to her grandmother with a sophisticated vocabulary and with complex ideas, indicating they wrote for a more educated audience than did Anderson and Angelou. In drawing a portrait of Quintana, John Gregory Dunne writes not only to express his own feelings about his adopted daughter, but also to tell his reader about the "moment" adoptive parents must face. His vocabulary and references, or allusions, to figures from history, sports, and films indicate that he too writes for an educated reader.

A third consideration in choosing an effective subject is your knowledge of it. You write most easily about what you know best, as did all the writers in this chapter. Unless you are given an assignment to research your subject, choose one with which you are familiar, about which you have knowledge sufficient for your purpose. A good way to tell how much you know about a subject is to freewrite about it; if you cannot produce much freewriting on a subject, then you might consider another subject.

A final consideration is length. Most assignments in English classes call for much shorter essays than those written by the professional writers in this chapter—usually in the 500- to 1000-word range. You will therefore want to focus more narrowly than they in order not to sacrifice the concreteness of detail that is the mark of any successful essay. It is much more effective to devote full attention to one specific aspect of your subject than to try to tell everything about it in a short space. If you have many pages of freewriting or many entries in your journal, you might consider narrowing your subject to just one aspect of it.

Once you have taken into account purpose, audience, your knowledge of the subject, and the length called for, you should be able to shape an effective subject.

Procedures to follow in creating an effective subject.

A. Define your purpose in writing. Is it to express your feelings, give information, persuade? How would each purpose affect your presentation of your material?

B. Consider your audience. What is your reader most likely to be interested in and know about? If you are writing an informal essay to your classmates, then consider how the material might best be presented in an essay written for this audience. If you are given the assignment of writing instead for your instructor, consider how your presentation of the material will differ.

C. Determine how much writing will be necessary to develop your purpose specifically, even dramatically. If you find you have too much material for the length of your paper, reexamine your material for an aspect or aspects that you can develop specifically in the allotted space.

D. In order to be as specific as possible, explore your subject further through freewriting or, if further knowledge is required, conduct some research.

E. Phrase a sentence to clarify for yourself exactly what you intend to write about. Be as specific as possible. For example, Anderson's thesis sentence might have been, "While for many of my childhood years I was ashamed of my clownish father, I one night came to realize his serious side, which made me proud to be his son." While Anderson did not include this sentence in his essay, you may wish to include your thesis sentence in your introductory paragraph.

MAYA ANGELOU

Sister Flowers

Maya Angelou (b. 1928) is a black American author, poet, playwright, stage and screen performer, and singer born in St. Louis, Missouri. After a tragic childhood ("from a broken family, raped at eight, unwed mother at sixteen"), Angelou first joined a dance company and then went on to star in an off-Broadway play. She has written three books of poetry, produced a series on Africa for PBS-TV, and served as a coordinator for the Southern Christian Leadership Conference. Angelou has been awarded three honorary doctorates. She is best known for the four books that comprise her autobiography, including I Know Why the Caged Bird Sings *(1970),* The Heart of a Woman *(1981), and* All God's Children Need Traveling Shoes *(1986). As you read about Sister Flowers's influence on Maya Angelou, think about someone who made an impact on your life as you were growing up.*

For nearly a year, I sopped around the house, the Store, the school and the church, like an old biscuit, dirty and inedible. Then I met, or rather got to know, the lady who threw me my first life line.

Mrs. Bertha Flowers was the aristocrat of Black Stamps. She had the grace of control to appear warm in the coldest weather, and on the Arkansas summer days it seemed she had a private breeze which swirled around, cooling her. She was thin without the taut look of wiry people, and her printed voile dresses and flowered hats were as right for her as denim overalls for a farmer. She was our side's answer to the richest white woman in town.

Her skin was a rich black that would have peeled like a plum if snagged, but then no one would have thought of getting close enough to Mrs. Flowers to ruffle her dress, let alone snag her skin. She didn't encourage familiarity. She wore gloves too.

I don't think I ever saw Mrs. Flowers laugh, but she smiled often. A slow widening of her thin black lips to show even, small white teeth, then the slow effortless closing. When she chose to smile on me, I always wanted to thank her. The action was so graceful and inclusively benign.

She was one of the few gentlewomen I have ever known, and has remained throughout my life the measure of what a human being can be.

Momma had a strange relationship with her. Most often when she passed on the road in front of the Store, she spoke to Momma in that soft yet carrying voice, "Good day, Mrs. Henderson." Momma responded with "How you, Sister Flowers?"

Mrs. Flowers didn't belong to our church, nor was she Momma's familiar. Why on earth did she insist on calling her Sister Flowers? Shame made me want to hide my face. Mrs. Flowers deserved better than to be called Sister. Then, Momma left out the verb. Why not ask, "How *are* you, *Mrs.* Flowers?" With the unbalanced passion of the young, I hated her for showing her ignorance to Mrs. Flowers. It didn't occur to me for many years that they were as alike as sisters, separated only by formal education.

Although I was upset, neither of the women was in the least shaken by what I thought an unceremonious greeting. Mrs. Flowers would continue her easy gait up the hill to her little bungalow, and Momma kept on shelling peas or doing whatever had brought her to the front porch.

Occasionally, though, Mrs. Flowers would drift off the road and down to the Store and Momma would say to me, "Sister, you go on and play." As she left I would hear the beginning of an intimate conversation. Momma persistently using the wrong verb, or none at all.

"Brother and Sister Wilcox is sho'ly the meanest—" "Is," Momma? "Is"? Oh, please, not "is," Momma, for two or more. But they talked, and from the side of the building where I waited for the ground to open up and swallow me, I heard the soft-voiced Mrs. Flowers and the textured voice of my grandmother merging and melting. They were interrupted from time to time by giggles that must have come from Mrs. Flowers (Momma never giggled in her life). Then she was gone.

She appealed to me because she was like people I had never met personally. Like women in English novels who walked the moors (whatever they were) with their loyal dogs racing at a respectful distance. Like the women who sat in front of roaring fireplaces, drinking tea incessantly from silver trays full of scones and crumpets. Women who walked over the "heath" and read morocco-bound books and had two last names divided by a hyphen. It would be safe to say that she made me proud to be Negro, just by being herself.

She acted just as refined as whitefolks in the movies and books and she was more beautiful, for none of them could have come near that warm color without looking gray by comparison.

I was fortunate that I never saw her in the company of po-whitefolks. For since they tend to think of their whiteness as an evenizer, I'm certain that I would have had to hear her spoken to commonly as Bertha, and my image of her would have been shattered like the unmendable Humpty-Dumpty.

One summer afternoon, sweet-milk fresh in my memory, she stopped at the Store to buy provisions. Another Negro woman of her health and age would have been expected to carry the paper sacks home in one hand, but Momma said, "Sister Flowers, I'll send Bailey up to your house with these things."

She smiled that slow dragging smile, "Thank you, Mrs. Henderson. I'd prefer Marguerite, though." My name was beautiful when she said it. "I've been meaning to talk to her, anyway." They gave each other age-group looks.

Momma said, "Well, that's all right then. Sister, go and change your dress. You going to Sister Flowers's."

The chifforobe was a maze. What on earth did one put on to go to Mrs. Flowers' house? I knew I shouldn't put on a Sunday dress. It might be sacrilegious. Certainly not a house dress, since I was already wearing a fresh one. I chose a school dress, naturally. It was formal without suggesting that going to Mrs. Flowers' house was equivalent to attending church.

I trusted myself back into the Store.

"Now, don't you look nice." I had chosen the right thing, for once. . . .

There was a little path beside the rocky road, and Mrs. Flowers walked in front swinging her arms and picking her way over the stones.

She said, without turning her head, to me, "I hear you're doing very good school work, Marguerite, but that it's all written. The teachers report that they have trouble getting you to talk in class." We passed the triangular farm on our left and the path widened to allow us to walk together. I hung back in the separate unasked and unanswerable questions.

"Come and walk along with me, Marguerite." I couldn't have refused even if I wanted to. She pronounced my name so nicely. Or more correctly, she spoke each word with such clarity that I was certain a foreigner who didn't understand English could have understood her.

"Now no one is going to make you talk—possibly no one can. But bear in mind, language is man's way of communicating with his fellow man and it is language alone which separates him from the lower animals." That was a totally new idea to me, and I would need time to think about it.

"Your grandmother says you read a lot. Every chance you get. That's good, but not good enough. Words mean more than what is set down on paper. It takes the human voice to infuse them with the shades of deeper meaning."

I memorized the part about the human voice infusing words. It seemed so valid and poetic.

She said she was going to give me some books and that I not only must read them, I must read them aloud. She suggested that I try to make a sentence sound in as many different ways as possible.

"I'll accept no excuse if you return a book to me that has been badly handled." My imagination boggled at the punishment I would deserve if in fact I did abuse a book of Mrs. Flowers's. Death would be too kind and brief.

The odors in the house surprised me. Somehow I had never connected Mrs. Flowers with food or eating or any other common experience of common people. There must have been an outhouse, too, but my mind never recorded it.

The sweet scent of vanilla had met us as she opened the door.

"I made tea cookies this morning. You see, I had planned to invite you for cookies and lemonade so we could have this little chat. The lemonade is in the icebox."

It followed that Mrs. Flowers would have ice on an ordinary day, when most families in our town bought ice late on Saturdays only a few times during the summer to be used in the wooden ice-cream freezers.

She took the bags from me and disappeared through the kitchen door. I looked around the room that I had never in my wildest fantasies imagined I would see. Browned photographs leered or threatened from the walls and the white, freshly done curtains pushed against themselves and against the wind. I wanted to gobble up the room entire and take it to Bailey, who would help me analyze and enjoy it.

"Have a seat, Marguerite. Over there by the table." She carried a platter covered with a tea towel. Although she warned that she hadn't tried her hand at baking sweets for some time, I was certain that like everything else about her the cookies would be perfect.

They were flat round wafers, slightly browned on the edges and butter-yellow in the center. With the cold lemonade they were sufficient for child-hood's lifelong diet. Remembering my manners, I took nice little lady-like bites off the edges. She said she had made them expressly for me and that she had a few in the kitchen that I could take home to my brother. So I jammed one whole cake in my mouth and the rough crumbs scratched the insides of my jaws, and if I hadn't had to swallow, it would have been a dream come true.

As I ate she began the first of what we later called "my lessons in living." She said that I must always be intolerant of ignorance but understanding of illiteracy. That some people, unable to go to school, were more educated and even more intelligent than college professors. She encouraged me to listen care-fully to what country people called mother wit. That in those homely sayings was couched the collective wisdom of generations.

When I finished the cookies she brushed off the table and brought a thick, small book from the bookcase. I had read *A Tale of Two Cities* and found it up to my standards as a romantic novel. She opened the first page and I heard po-etry for the first time in my life.

"It was the best of times and the worst of times . . ." Her voice slid and curved down through and over the words. She was nearly singing. I wanted to look at the pages. Were they the same that I had read? Or were there notes, music, lined on the pages, as in a hymn book? Her sounds began cascading gently. I knew from listening to a thousand preachers that she was nearing the end of her reading, and I hadn't really heard, heard to understand, a single word.

"How do you like that?"

It occurred to me that she expected a response. The sweet vanilla flavor was still on my tongue and her reading was a wonder in my ears. I had to speak.

I said, "Yes, ma'am." It was the least I could do, but it was the most also.

"There's one more thing. Take this book of poems and memorize one for me. Next time you pay me a visit, I want you to recite."

I have tried often to search behind the sophistication of years for the enchantment I so easily found in those gifts. The essence escapes but its aura remains. To be allowed, no, invited, into the private lives of strangers, and to share their joys and fears, was a chance to exchange the Southern bitter wormwood for a cup of mead with Beowulf or a hot cup of tea and milk with Oliver Twist. When I said aloud, "It is a far, far better thing that I do, than I have ever done . . ." tears of love filled my eyes at my selflessness.

On that first day, I ran down the hill and into the road (few cars ever came along it) and had the good sense to stop running before I reached the Store.

I was liked, and what a difference it made. I was respected not as Mrs. Henderson's grandchild or Bailey's sister but for just being Marguerite Johnson.

Childhood's logic never asks to be proved (all conclusions are absolute). I didn't question why Mrs. Flowers had singled me out for attention, nor did it occur to me that Momma might have asked her to give me a little talking to. All I cared about was that she had made tea cookies for *me* and read to *me* from her favorite book. It was enough to prove that she liked me.

PROBING FOR MEANING

1. What is Marguerite like before Sister Flowers takes an interest in her? Why is the attention of Sister Flowers important to her?

2. Marguerite calls Sister Flowers "one of the few gentlewomen" she has ever known. What does she mean? What is it that makes Sister Flowers a gentlewoman in her eyes?

3. What sort of lessons does Sister Flowers give Marguerite? Why does she encourage Marguerite to be "intolerant of ignorance but understanding of illiteracy"? Why does she insist that Marguerite read aloud?

4. After she has grown up, what does Marguerite realize about her relationship with Sister Flowers?

5. Marguerite says that Sister Flowers made her "proud to be Negro." How does Sister Flowers do that? Is this the most important thing she does for Marguerite?

PROBING FOR METHOD

1. Why does Angelou choose to write about Sister Flowers? Which sentence best explains the significance of her subject for her?

2. In what ways does Angelou contrast Momma with Sister Flowers? In what ways does she contrast herself as a child with each woman? How do these contrasts help us to understand Marguerite better?

3. Angelou chooses to focus on the first time Marguerite goes to Sister Flowers's house. What do we learn about Marguerite through this experience? What, for example, do we learn about her when Angelou writes that the odors in the house surprised her?

4. Angelou begins the essay by comparing herself to "an old biscuit, dirty and inedible." What does this image tell us about her? How does the image of the tea cookies help us to understand the kind of effect Sister Flowers will have on her?

Organizing an Essay

What framework is evident in Angelou's essay?
Maya Angelou introduces her essay with a one-sentence description of her life before meeting Sister Flowers and then introduces her subject in the final sentence of the first paragraph: "Then I met, or rather got to know, the lady who threw me my first life line." In her next four paragraphs, she describes Sister Flowers's appearance and demeanor as a gentlewoman.

She devotes paragraphs 6–10 to Momma's relationship with Sister Flowers and 11–13 to the reasons why Sister Flowers appealed to her, and then in paragraph 14, beginning "One summer afternoon . . .," she begins narrating her visit to Sister Flowers's home. She proceeds chronologically from Sister Flowers's invitation to her subsequent preparation for the visit, her walk with Sister Flowers to her home, her eating the cookies Sister Flowers had prepared, and finally the first of her "lessons in living." She concludes her essay with her jubilant reaction to the interest this gentlewoman had taken in her.

Like Anderson's, Angelou's essay is divided into two major sections, the first giving background, the second focusing on one event that best dramatizes her thesis, the visit to Sister Flowers's house. Her outline might look like this:

I. Introduction (Paragraph 1)
II. My admiration for Sister Flowers from afar (Paragraphs 1–13)
   A. Sister Flowers, the aristocrat (Paragraphs 2–5)
      1. Her grace
      2. Her clothing
      3. Her reserve
   B. Momma's relationship with Sister Flowers (6–10)
      1. Momma called her by the familiar name "Sister"
      2. Momma used the wrong verb
      3. Only as an adult does Angelou realize they were alike as sisters, separated only by formal education
   C. Sister Flowers's appeal to Angelou (11–13)
      1. She reminds her of heroines in novels
      2. She acted as refined as whitefolks
III. One summer afternoon's visit to Sister Flowers's home (14 to third paragraph from end)
   A. The invitation
   B. The preparation
   C. The discussion about talking as well as reading
   D. The odors in the house
   E. The cookies

F. The first "lesson in living"
G. The reading from *A Tale of Two Cities*
H. The gift of the book of poems
I. The exit running down the hill
IV. Conclusion: Reaction to being liked (last two paragraphs)

Organizing the paper.

Good writing results from much effort. One important step in writing the essay, which is time-consuming but necessary, is developing the outline. The outline helps you focus sharply on a subject by eliminating wandering from the subject, repeating earlier points, or neglecting major aspects of the subject. The outline also helps the writer focus on the order in which he presents his points.

There are at least two ways of approaching the organization of an essay through outlining. The traditional method is to list all aspects of a topic, arrange them in appropriate sequence, and proceed to write. Many writers find that a second method works better since they do not know what they want to say until they actually begin writing. These writers prefer to make their outlines after they have engaged in freewriting or have written a first draft. With all their ideas down on paper, they then sort them into a logical sequence. After changing, rearranging, eliminating, and/or adding, they proceed to the final draft.

These are various patterns of organization, and we will be exploring some of these in subsequent chapters: Chapter 3 (descriptive arrangement), Chapter 4 (narrative arrangement), and Chapter 6 (arranging material generated by asking various questions about the subject).

These patterns apply largely to the middle, or body, of the essay. The introduction has a dual function: to interest the reader in the essay and to give him or her some idea of its purpose (the thesis statement is usually located in this paragraph). The introduction should present the subject in such a way as to make the audience aware that the writer is interested in the reader's reactions to his subject matter.

The conclusion to a short essay should do more than simply summarize the paper; only in long essays, where the reader might forget earlier points, is the summary conclusion effective. The conclusion instead should present to the reader aspects of the subject about which he or she might think further. It should also leave an impact on the reader's mind. Most important, it should have a note of finality that assures the reader that the essay has been concluded.

Procedures to follow in organizing your paper.

A. Write your thesis sentence at the top of the page, making sure it is phrased as clearly as possible.

B. Make an outline under the first method: (1) List all of the ideas that occur to you in thinking about your topic. (2) Once you have made an extensive list, rearrange the items into headings and subheadings. Your headings will form the major points that will later constitute the body of your paper. (3) Group all the other items under the major headings, eliminating those that, on second thought, obviously do not fit in. Your subheadings should develop your headings, just as your headings develop your paper topic. (4) Check to see that each division is distinct from the others to avoid overlapping. (5) Determine if any major points have been omitted. (6) Arrange your points in a logical order.

C. If you prefer the second method of outlining, begin with freewriting or a first draft of your topic. Next, make an outline based on what you have written. Scrutinize your outline carefully. Does each heading belong? Are any repeated? Are the points arranged in a logical order? What other points can you now think of to include? Once you have answered these questions and made the necessary adjustments, you are ready to begin what may be your final draft.

JOHN GREGORY DUNNE

Quintana

John Gregory Dunne (b. 1932) was educated at Princeton University, served in the Army, and was a staff writer for Time Magazine *for several years. He has written several screenplays with his wife, novelist and essayist Joan Didion, including* Play It as It Lays *(1972) and* True Confessions *(1982). His publications include* The Studio *(1969) and* Quintana and Her Friends *(1978). In this essay about his daughter, Dunne shares his views on adoption. As you read "Quintana," make some notes on your ideas about this vital issue.*

Quintana will be eleven this week. She approaches adolescence with what I can only describe as panache, but then watching her journey from infancy has always been like watching Sandy Koufax pitch or Bill Russell play basketball. There is the same casual arrogance, the implicit sense that no one has ever done it any better. And yet it is difficult for a father to watch a daughter grow up. With each birthday she becomes more like us, an adult, and what we cling to is the memory of the child. I remember the first time I saw her in the nursery at Saint John's Hospital. It was after visiting hours and my wife and I stood staring through the soundproof glass partition at the infants in their cribs, wondering which was ours. Then a nurse in a surgical mask appeared from a back room carrying a fierce, black-haired baby with a bow in her hair. She was just seventeen hours old and her face was still wrinkled and red and the identification beads on her wrist had not our name but only the letters "NI." "NI" stood for "No Information," the hospital's code for an infant to be placed for adoption. Quintana is adopted.

It has never been an effort to say those three words, even when they occasion the well-meaning but insensitive compliment, "You couldn't love her more if she were your own." At moments like that, my wife and I say nothing and smile through gritted teeth. And yet we are not unaware that sometime in the not too distant future we face a moment that only those of us who are adoptive parents will ever have to face—our daughter's decision to search or not to search for her natural parents.

I remember that when I was growing up, a staple of radio drama was the show built around adoption. Usually the dilemma involved a child who had just learned by accident that it was adopted. This information could only come accidentally, because in those days it was considered a radical departure from the norm to inform your son or daughter that he or she was not your own flesh and blood. If such information had to be revealed, it was often followed by the specious addendum that the natural parents had died when the child was an infant. An automobile accident was viewed as the most expeditious and efficient way to get rid of both parents at once. One of my contemporaries, then a young actress, was not told that she was adopted until she was twenty-two and the beneficiary of a small inheritance from her natural father's will. Her adoptive mother could not bring herself to tell her daughter the reason behind the bequest and entrusted the task to an agent from the William Morris office.

Today we are more enlightened, aware of the psychological evidence that such barbaric secrecy can only inflict hurt. When Quintana was born, she was offered to us privately by the gynecologist who delivered her. In California, such private adoptions are not only legal but in the mid-sixties, before legalized abortion and before the sexual revolution made it acceptable for an unwed mother to keep her child, were quite common. The night we went to see Quintana for the first time at Saint John's, there was a tacit agreement between us that "No Information" was only a bracelet. It was quite easy to congratulate ourselves for agreeing to be so open when the only information we had about her mother was her age, where she was from and a certified record of her good health. What we did not realize was that through one bureaucratic slipup we would learn her mother's name and that through another she would learn ours, and Quintana's.

From the day we brought Quintana home from the hospital, we tried never to equivocate. When she was little, we always had Spanish-speaking help and one of the first words she learned, long before she understood its import, was *adoptada*. As she grew older, she never tired of asking us how we happened to adopt her. We told her that we went to the hospital and were given our choice of any baby in the nursery. "No, not that baby," we had said, "not that baby, not that baby . . ." All this with full gestures of inspection, until finally: "That baby!" Her face would always light up and she would say: "Quintana." When she asked a question about her adoption, we answered, never volunteering more than she requested, convinced that as she grew her questions would become more searching and complicated. In terms I hoped she would understand, I tried to explain that adoption offered to a parent the possibility of escaping the prison of the genes, that no matter how perfect the natural child, the parent could not help acknowledging in black moments that some of his or her bad blood was bubbling around in the offspring; with an *adoptada*, we were innocent of any knowledge of bad blood.

In time Quintana began to intuit that our simple parable of free choice in the hospital nursery was somewhat more complex than we had indicated. She now knew that being adopted meant being born of another mother, and that person she began referring to as "my other mommy." How old, she asked, was my other mommy when I was born? Eighteen, we answered, and on her stubby little fingers she added on her own age, and with each birthday her other mommy became twenty-three, then twenty-five and twenty-eight. There was no obsessive interest, just occasional queries, some more difficult to answer than others. Why had her other mother given her up? We said that we did not know—which was true—and could only assume that it was because she was little more than a child herself, alone and without the resources to bring up a baby. The answer seemed to satisfy, at least until we became close friends with a young woman, unmarried, with a small child of her own. The contradiction was, of course, apparent to Quintana, and yet she seemed to understand, in the way that children do, that there had been a millennium's worth of social change in the years since her birth, that the pressures on a young unmarried mother were far more in 1966 than they were in 1973. (She did, after all, invariably refer to the man in the White House as President Nixon Vietnam Watergate, almost as if he had a three-tiered name like John Quincy Adams.) We were sure that she viewed her status with equanimity, but how much so we did not realize until her eighth birthday party. There were twenty little girls at the party, and as little girls do, they were discussing things gynecological, specifically the orifice in their mothers' bodies from which they had emerged at birth. "I didn't," Quintana said matter-of-factly. She was sitting in a large wicker fan chair and her pronouncement impelled the other children to silence. "I was adopted." We had often wondered how she would handle this moment with her peers, and we froze, but she pulled it off with such élan and aplomb that in moments the other children were bemoaning their own misfortune in not being adopted, one even claiming, "Well, I was almost adopted."

Because my wife and I both work at home, Quintana has never had any confusion about how we make our living. Our mindless staring at our respective typewriters means food on the table in a way the mysterious phrase "going to the office" never can. From the time she could walk, we have taken her to meetings whenever we were without help, and she has been a quick study on the nuances of our life. "She's remarkably well adjusted," my brother once said about her. "Considering that every time I see her she's in a different city." I think she could pick an agent out of a police lineup, and out of the blue one night at dinner she offered that all young movie directors were short and had frizzy hair and wore Ditto pants and wire glasses and shirts with three buttons opened. (As far as I know, she had never laid eyes on Bogdanovich, Spielberg or Scorsese.) Not long ago an actress received an award for a picture we had written for her. The actress's acceptance speech at the televised award ceremony drove Quintana into an absolute fury. "She never," Quintana reported, "thanked *us*." Since she not only identifies with our work but at times even considers herself an equal partner, I of course discussed this piece with her before I began working on it. I told her what it was about and said I would drop it if she would be embarrassed or if she thought the subject too private. She gave it some thought and finally said she wanted me to write it.

I must, however, try to explain and perhaps even try to justify my own motives. The week after *Roots* was televised, each child in Quintana's fifth-grade class was asked to trace a family tree. On my side Quintana went back to her great-grandfather Burns, who arrived from Ireland shortly after the Civil War, a ten-year-old refugee from the potato famine, and on her mother's side to her great-great-great-great-grandmother Cornwall, who came west in a wagon train in 1846. As it happens, I have little interest in family beyond my immediate living relatives. (I can never remember the given names of my paternal grandparents and have never known my paternal grandmother's maiden name. This lack of interest mystifies my wife.) Yet I wanted Quintana to understand that if she wished, there were blood choices other than Dominick Burns and Nancy Hardin Cornwall. Over the past few years, there has been a growing body of literature about adoptees seeking their own roots. I am in general sympathetic to this quest, although not always to the dogged absolutism of the more militant seekers. But I would be remiss if I did not say that I am more than a little sensitive to the way the literature presents adoptive parents. We are usually shown as frozen in the postures of radio drama, untouched by the changes in attitudes of the last several generations. In point of fact we accept that our children might seek out their roots, even encourage it; we accept it as an adventure like life itself—perhaps painful, one hopes enriching. I know not one adoptive parent who does not feel this way. Yet in the literature there is the implicit assumption that we are threatened by the possibility of search, that we would consider it an act of disloyalty on the part of our children. The patronizing nature of this assumption is never noted in the literature. It is as if we were Hudson and Mrs. Bridges, below-stairs surrogates taking care of the wee one, and I don't like it one damn bit.

Often these days I find myself thinking of Quintana's natural mother. Both my wife and I admit more than a passing interest in the woman who produced this extraordinary child. (As far as we know, she never named the father, and even more interesting, Quintana has never asked about him.) When Quintana was small, and before the legalities of adoption were complete, we imagined her mother everywhere, a wraithlike presence staring through the chain-link fence at the blond infant sunbathing in the crib. Occasionally today we see a photograph of a young woman in a magazine—the mother as we imagine her to look—and we pass it to each other without comment. Once we even checked the name of a model in *Vogue* through her modeling agency; she turned out to be a Finn. I often wonder if she thinks of Quintana, or of us. (Remember, we know each other's names.) There is the possibility that having endured the twin traumas of birth and the giving up of a child, she blocked out the names the caseworker gave her, but I don't really believe it. I consider it more likely that she has followed the fairly well-documented passage of Quintana through childhood into adolescence. Writers are at least semipublic figures, and in the interest of commerce or selling a book or a movie, or even out of simple vanity, we allow interviews and photo layouts and look into television cameras; we even write about ourselves, and our children. I recall wondering how this sentient young woman of our imagination had reacted to four pages in *People*. It is possible, even likely, that she will read this piece. I know that it is an almost intolerable invasion of her privacy. I think it probable, however, that in the dark reaches of night she has considered the possibility of a further incursion, of opening a door one day and seeing a young woman who says, "Hello, Mother, I am your daughter."

Perhaps this is romantic fantasy. We know none of the circumstances of the woman's life, or even if she is still alive. We once suggested to our lawyer that we make a discreet inquiry and he quite firmly said that this was a quest that belonged only to Quintana, if she wished to make it, and not to us. What is not fantasy is that for the past year, Quintana has known the name of her natural mother. It was at dinner and she said that she would like to meet her one day, but that it would be hard, not knowing her name. There finally was the moment: we had never equivocated; did we begin now? We took a deep breath and told Quintana, then age ten, her mother's name. We also said that if she decided to search her out, we would help her in any way we could. (I must allow, however, that we would prefer she wait to make this decision until the Sturm and Drang of adolescence is past.) We then considered the possibility that her mother, for whatever good or circumstantial reasons of her own, might prefer not to see her. I am personally troubled by the militant contention that the natural mother has no right of choice in this matter. "I did not ask to be born," an adoptee once was quoted in a news story I read. "She has to see me." If only life were so simple, if only pain did not hurt. Yet we would never try to influence Quintana on this point. How important it is to know her parentage is a question only she can answer; it is her decision to make.

All parents realize, or should realize, that children are not possessions, but are only lent to us, angel boarders, as it were. Adoptive parents realize this earlier and perhaps more poignantly than others. I do not know the end of this story. It is possible that Quintana will find more reality in family commitment and cousins across the continent and heirloom orange spoons and pictures in an album and faded letters from Dominick Burns and diary entries from Nancy Hardin Cornwall than in the uncertainties of blood. It is equally possible that she will venture into the unknown. I once asked her what she would do if she met her natural mother. "I'd put one arm around Mom," she said, "and one arm around my other mommy, and I'd say, 'Hello, Mommies.' "

If that's the way it turns out, that is what she will do.

PROBING FOR MEANING

1. Where does the author first state the main idea of the essay? Cite other instances where he restates it.

2. What portrait emerges of Quintana from the first paragraph of the essay? What other examples does Dunne give to support his point that Quintana has "panache"?

3. What did you learn about adoption from the author's account of his and his wife's experiences?

4. Do you agree with Dunne that parents who adopt a child should be totally honest with him or her? Why or why not?

PROBING FOR METHOD

1. Dunne is writing about his daughter but he also states his ideas about the relationship between adopted children and their parents. What techniques does he use to merge the two subjects successfully?

2. What is Dunne's purpose in writing this essay? Is he merely informing his readers about his views or is he seeking to persuade them? Did he influence your point of view on adoption? Why or why not?

3. For what audience is Dunne writing? Is it limited to people involved in a situation similar to his, or is he addressing a wider audience? Cite evidence for your point of view.

ALFRED KAZIN

Cousin Sophie

Alfred Kazin (b. 1915) is an American literary critic, essayist, and teacher. He has taught in universities throughout the country and lectured in Germany,

*England, France, and Norway. His writings include many volumes of criticism
as well as several autobiographical works including* On Native Grounds
(1942), Starting Out in the Thirties *(1965), and* New York Jew *(1978). One
reviewer wrote of Kazin, "He rarely allows people to emerge through
anecdote . . . instead he explains people." As you read "Cousin Sophie," study
the techniques Kazin uses to "explain" his protagonist to his readers.*

Our cousin Sophie was a difficult case. Because she had always lived with us,
and had often taken care of me as a child when my mother was ill, I could have
thought of her as my other mother, but she always seemed too young, restless,
tormented. Although she was certainly not pretty—her long face usually looked
sad or bitter, and when she was gay, wildly and almost desperately gay—she
radiated, as if it were warmth from her body, a passionate and angry vivid-
ness. All my life I had seen her, with the long black hair which had never been
cut, her embroidered Russian blouses and velvet skirts, against the background
of a tiny rectangle room scented with musk, with patchouli, while above the
bed covered with a tickly India spread there hung, side by side, two pictures.
One (I learned their names only much later) was Sir George Frederic Watts's
Hope—a blindfolded young lady with bare feet sat on a globe earnestly listening for the vibration of the single string on her harp; the other was Pierre-
Auguste Cot's *The Storm*. As the lovers raced before the storm, their heads
were apprehensively yet exultantly turned back; and the cloak that the godlike
lover was tenderly holding over the woman's shoulders, so light and flimsy that
it barely covered her nakedness, seemed woven in its lightness and transpar-
ency of "love" itself, so that the gauze veil which together they held over their
heads, though too flimsy to shield them from the storm, carried some deeper
knowledge of desire that explained the shyness of the woman and the confi-
dent and protective smile of the man. As they ran together, just ahead of the
storm, they seemed to be running not only under the same veil, but with the
same feet.

I had looked at Sophie under those two pictures all my life, just as I had
looked at her blouses, her skirts and her petticoats—there was no closet—or
could smell from her warm and fragrant flesh, as soon as she came near me,
the musk and sandalwood, or could feel her presence again whenever I touched
her velvet skirts on the hangers and the stiff crinkly surface of the India spread
on her bed. She was never easy with anyone, never tender; there was something about her long sweeping hair and the ungraspable scent of her body that
was like the resistance of velvet, which retreats back into itself, in soft and
recessive lines, after you have touched it. As a child I had often watched her,
while she sat doing her hair in front of the mirror, suddenly in despair let the
great mane fall over her face; or else she would sit coldly coiling her hair,
doubling and then binding with long black hairpins each sheaf she caught up
in her hand. Her moods were always extreme. The whole long day for her was
like a sundial, either washed in sunlight or cold-gray in shadow; the moody,

somber Sophie, in whose face one saw the control of her despair, alternated with a Sophie reckless, agonized, violently gay, who as she threw her great hair back, or bent over the mandolin with the little black pick in her hand, or coldly stared at some possible suitor stiffly seated at our dinner table whom my mother had hopefully brought in, impressed herself all through my boyhood with that proud and flashing loneliness that I was to recognize immediately when I first saw *Carmen*.

Sophie was not just the unmarried cousin who had always lived with us; her unmarriedness, her need of a husband, of some attachment, was our constant charge and preoccupation. To this my mother gave as much thought as she did to us, and at the center of our household, whether she was off in her room under the picture of the two lovers fleeing from the storm, or in the kitchen with her friends from "the shop," drinking tea, eating fruit, or playing at the mandolin, one always saw or felt the vividly resentful figure of Sophie— Sophie beating at the strings of that yellow-shining, deep-bosomed, narrow-waisted mandolin, Sophie standing in front of the great mirror in the kitchen combing up her black black hair. As I watched with amazement, she kept one plait of hair suspended in her hand and then unceasingly and rhythmically, with the curved comb glistening in rhinestones, drew it with her long bony fingers through her hair, back and forth, until, when she had sifted and coiled and piled it up again, she would gather out the last straggle-thin threads in her hand as if it were a claw, and with a last sidelong look, manage with one gesture to throw a little ball of hair away and give herself one last approving glance in the mirror. How natural it had always been to stand behind Sophie and to watch her combing her hair; or to steal into her room to smell the musk, the patchouli, the stingingly sweet face powder, the velvet skirts whose creases seemed to mark the pressure of her body, the slips whose straps seemed just to have slipped off her shoulders. In the sepia dusk of the old prints, the lovers still ran rapturously before the storm, *Hope* held up her harp, and the bony gnarled wicker bookstand was filled with romantic English novels like *The Sheik* and Russian novels in stippled blue bindings which Sophie and Sophie alone could have brought into the house. And as if the difference had not already been made sufficiently clear between a mother who always seemed old to me and Sophie forever sultry and vivid, it was brought closer by the fact that my mother was home all day and that Sophie appeared only in the evenings; when she was home, she was often elaborately sick in bed, with a bed jacket, while my mother brought her soft-boiled eggs and toast. The difference in their status was established by the way my mother worked, and waited on her, and told us to be quiet when Sophie was ill; we knew from my mother's constant expression of anxiety over her, from her anguished sulky looks of demanding love, that Sophie lacked something that everyone else in the world possessed.

PROBING FOR MEANING

1. What specific examples does Kazin offer in paragraph 1 to support his asser-

tion that "cousin Sophie was a difficult case"? To what extent do you find them convincing? What other adjectives would you use to describe Sophie?

2. In paragraph 2, Kazin recalls his boyhood impressions of Sophie. Why did she appear to him as proud and lonely?

3. "Sophie was not just the unmarried cousin who had always lived with us; her unmarriedness, her need of a husband, of some attachment, was our constant charge and preoccupation." Why did the family become so involved with Sophie?

4. Explain your reaction to the last sentence of the essay. What effect does it have on your impression of Sophie?

5. Kazin's essay concerns growing up in America in the 1930s. To what extent would a family be likely to respond to Sophie in a similar way today?

PROBING FOR METHOD

1. Kazin repeats important details in his sketch of Sophie. Choose two or three and discuss the effect of the repetition.

2. Why does Kazin describe in such detail the pictures hanging over Sophie's bed? Do they in any way help to explain Sophie to the reader? Why or why not?

JOYCE MAYNARD

My Grandmother

Joyce Maynard (b. 1954) was born in Durham, New Hampshire. At eighteen she was one of the youngest writers ever published in the New York Times. *In her freshman year at Yale, she wrote an autobiography,* Looking Back: A Chronicle of Growing Up Old in the Sixties *(1973). She lives in New Hampshire with her husband and two children and is a frequent contributor to the "Hers" column of the* New York Times, *a column written by and about women. As you read "My Grandmother," formulate your thoughts on whether her essay is relevant only to women or if it has something to say to men as well.*

My mother called last week to tell me that my grandmother is dying. She has refused an operation that would postpone, but not prevent, her death from pancreatic cancer. She can't eat, she has been hemorrhaging, and she has severe jaundice. "I always prided myself on being different," she told my mother. "Now I *am* different. I'm yellow."

My mother, telling me this news, began to cry. So I became the mother for a moment, reminding her, reasonably, that my grandmother is eighty-seven, she's had a full life, she has all her faculties, and no one who knows her could wish that she live long enough to lose them. Lately my mother has been finding notes in my grandmother's drawers at the nursing home, reminding her, "Joyce's husband's name is Steve. Their daughter is Audrey." In the last few years she hasn't had the strength to cook or garden, and she's begun to say she's had enough of living.

My grandmother was born in Russia, in 1892—the oldest daughter in a large and prosperous Jewish family. But the prosperity didn't last. She tells stories of the pogroms and the cossacks who raped her when she was twelve. Soon after that, her family emigrated to Canada, where she met my grandfather.

Their children were the center of their life. The story I loved best, as a child, was of my grandfather opening every box of Cracker Jacks in the general store he ran, in search of the particular tin toy my mother coveted. Though they never had much money, my grandmother saw to it that her daughter had elocution lessons and piano lessons, and assured her that she would go to college.

But while she was at college, my mother met my father, who was blue-eyed and blond-haired and not Jewish. When my father sent love letters to my mother, my grandmother would open and hide them, and when my mother told her parents she was going to marry this man, my grandmother said if that happened, it would kill her.

Not likely, of course. My grandmother is a woman who used to crack Brazil nuts open with her teeth, a woman who once lifted a car off the ground, when there was an accident and it had to be moved. She has been representing her death as imminent ever since I've known her—twenty-five years—and has discussed, at length, the distribution of her possessions and her lamb coat. Every time we said goodbye, after our annual visit to Winnipeg, she'd weep and say she'd never see us again. But in the meantime, while every other relative of her generation, and a good many of the younger ones, has died (nursed usually by her), she has kept making knishes, shopping for bargains, tending the healthiest plants I've ever seen.

After my grandfather died, my grandmother lived, more than ever, through her children. When she came to visit, I would hide my diary. She couldn't understand any desire for privacy. She couldn't bear it if my mother left the house without her.

This possessiveness is what made my mother furious (and then guilt-ridden that she felt that way, when of course she owed so much to her mother). So I harbored the resentment that my mother—the dutiful daughter—would not allow herself. I—who had always performed specially well for my grandmother, danced and sung for her, presented her with kisses and good report cards—stopped writing to her, ceased to visit.

But when I heard that she was dying, I realized I wanted to go to Winnipeg to see her one more time. Mostly to make my mother happy, I told myself (certain patterns being hard to break). But also, I was offering up one more particularly fine accomplishment: my own dark-eyed, dark-skinned, dark-haired daughter, whom my grandmother had never met.

I put on my daughter's best dress for our visit to Winnipeg, the way the best dresses were always put on me, and I filled my pockets with animal crackers, in case Audrey started to cry. I scrubbed her face mercilessly. On the elevator going up to her room, I realized how much I was sweating.

Grandma was lying flat with an IV tube in her arm and her eyes shut, but she opened them when I leaned over to kiss her. "It's Fredelle's daughter, Joyce," I yelled, because she doesn't hear well anymore, but I could see that no explanation was necessary. "You came," she said. "You brought the baby."

Audrey is just one, but she has seen enough of the world to know that people in beds are not meant to be so still and yellow, and she looked frightened. I had never wanted, more, for her to smile.

Then Grandma waved at her—the same kind of slow, finger-flexing wave a baby makes—and Audrey waved back. I spread her toys out on my grandmother's bed and sat her down. There she stayed, most of the afternoon, playing and humming and sipping on her bottle, taking a nap at one point, leaning against my grandmother's leg. When I cranked her Snoopy guitar, Audrey stood up on the bed and danced. Grandma couldn't talk much anymore, though every once in a while she would say how sorry she was that she wasn't having a better day. "I'm not always like this," she said.

Mostly she just watched Audrey. Sometimes Audrey would get off the bed, inspect the get-well cards, totter down the hall. "Where is she?" Grandma kept asking. "Who's looking after her?" I had the feeling, even then, that if I'd said, "Audrey's lighting matches," Grandma would have shot up to rescue her.

We were flying home that night, and I had dreaded telling her, remembering all those other tearful partings. But in the end, I was the one who cried. She had said she was ready to die. But as I leaned over to stroke her forehead, what she said was, "I wish I had your hair" and "I wish I was well."

On the plane flying home, with Audrey in my arms, I thought about mothers and daughters, and the four generations of the family that I know most intimately. Every one of those mothers loves and needs her daughter more than her daughter will love or need her some day, and we are, each of us, the only person on earth who is quite so consumingly interested in our child.

Sometimes I kiss and hug Audrey so much she starts crying—which is, in effect, what my grandmother was doing to my mother, all her life. And what makes my mother grieve right now, I think, is not simply that her mother will die in a day or two, but that, once her mother dies, there will never again be someone to love her in quite such an unreserved, unquestioning way. No one else who believes that, fifty years ago, she could have put Shirley Temple out of a job, no one else who remembers the moment of her birth. She will only be a mother, then, not a daughter anymore.

Audrey and I have stopped over for a night in Toronto, where my mother lives. Tomorrow she will go to a safe-deposit box at the bank and take out the receipt for my grandmother's burial plot. Then she will fly back to Winnipeg, where, for the first time in anybody's memory, there was waist-high snow on April Fool's Day. But tonight she is feeding me, as she always does when I come, and I am eating more than I do anywhere else. I admire the wedding china (once my grandmother's) that my mother has set on the table. She says (the way Grandma used to say to her, of the lamb coat), "Some day it will be yours."

PROBING FOR MEANING

1. What do we learn in the first three paragraphs about Maynard's mother as well as her grandmother? In what ways does Maynard contrast her mother to her grandmother? How are they similar?

2. "My grandmother is a woman who used to crack Brazil nuts open with her teeth." What other details does Maynard cite to give the reader a sense of her grandmother? How do you respond to her?

3. What quality about the grandmother did Maynard's mother resent? Is she justified in this resentment? Do you empathize with her feeling?

4. What new characteristics of the grandmother emerge in the hospital when she meets her great-granddaughter for the first time?

5. In paragraph 16, what point is Maynard making about not only her own family but also families in general? To what extent do you agree with her?

6. What examples does Maynard give in the last two paragraphs to emphasize the continuity of the generations of women in her family? What is your reaction to her point of view?

7. What does Maynard learn about herself through this experience?

PROBING FOR METHOD

1. Anderson uses the swimming scene to portray the change that occurs in his relationship with his father while Maynard uses her grandmother's approaching death to evaluate her relationship with her mother and her grandmother. How does limiting her subject in this way make it easier for her to communicate her thoughts?

2. Read over Maynard's topic sentences. To what extent is she consistent in supporting them? How would you characterize her style? Does she succeed in sustaining your interest? Why or why not?

3. How does Maynard use images of the china and the lamb coat to help us better understand her mother and her grandmother?

YEVGENY YEVTUSHENKO

People

Yevgeny Yevtushenko (b. 1933) is a Russian poet and author who was born in Siberia. Yevtushenko first became prominent in the Soviet Union with the publication of his poem "Babi Yar" (1962) and was criticized by the Soviet regime for his censure of its anti-Semitic actions. He has subsequently toured the United States and Europe, drawing record audiences to his poetry readings. His collections include City Lights *(1961),* Selected Poems *(1963), and* Stolen Apples *(1971). In his later work he has shifted his thematic emphasis from the political to the personal. As you read his poem "People," formulate your responses to his view that all people are interesting.*

No people are uninteresting.
Their fate is like the chronicle of planets.

Nothing in them is not particular,
and planet is dissimilar from planet.

And if a man lived in obscurity
making his friends in that obscurity
obscurity is not uninteresting.

To each his world is private,
and in that world one excellent minute.

And in that world one tragic minute.
These are private.

In any man who dies there dies with him
his first snow and kiss and fight.
It goes with him.

They are left books and bridges
and painted canvas and machinery

Whose fate is to survive.
But what has gone is also not nothing:

by the rule of the game something has gone.
Not people die but worlds die in them.

Whom we knew as faulty, the earth's creatures.
Of whom, essentially, what did we know?

Brother of a brother? Friend of friends?
Lover of lover?

We who knew our fathers
in everything, in nothing.

They perish. They cannot be brought back.
The secret worlds are not regenerated.

And every time again and again
I make my lament against destruction.

PROBING FOR MEANING

1. Explain your response to the first line of the poem.

2. To what extent do you agree with Yevtushenko that "obscurity is not uninteresting"?

3. To what events might the "excellent minute" and "tragic minute" refer?

4. What is the significance of the contrast made between "first snow and kiss and fight" and "books and bridges and painted canvas and machinery"?

5. Explain the line "Not people die but worlds die in them" and characterize your response to it.

6. What is Yevtushenko implying in his concept of knowing "everything" and "nothing" about the people we cherish? Is this contradictory? To what extent is it true of your experience with people?

7. For what reasons does the poet "lament against destruction"?

8. How would you characterize your response to the poem? Is it pessimistic? Depressing? Realistic?

PROBING FOR METHOD

1. How effectively does Yevtushenko support his point of view that "no people are uninteresting." What examples did you find most convincing?

2. The poet departs from a traditional rhyme scheme—to what extent did this affect your response to the poem?

3. Point out examples of repetition in the poem. How does this technique affect the poem's impact?

JOHN KNOWLES

Phineas

John Knowles (b. 1926) is from Fairmont, West Virginia, is a graduate of Yale University, and currently lives in New York City. He was a reporter for the Hartford Courant *for two years and later a free-lance writer. For his first novel,* A Separate Peace *(1960), he received both the Rosenthal Award from the National Institute of Arts and Letters and the William Faulkner Foundation Award. As you read "Phineas," the short story on which the novel was based, compare Gene and Finny's friendship with one that you experienced or know about.*

It was the kind of place I expected all right, an old, rooted Massachusetts town. All of the homes along Main Street, from solid white mansions to neat saltboxes, were settled behind their fences and hedges as though invulnerable to change.

I approached a particular house. The yard was large but the house had been built close to the street. A hedge as high as my shoulder separated it from the sidewalk. I kept calm until I reached the break in the hedge and saw the marker. It was the name, in small, clear letters. I stood beneath an ancient, impregnable elm and got myself ready to knock at Finny's door.

Three months before, I had gone unsuspectingly to another door and first encountered him. The summer session of the Devon School convened that year in June, and when I opened the door of the room assigned me, there was Finny, standing in the middle of the floor and pulling handfuls of clothes carelessly out of a suitcase.

I had seen him at a distance around the school the previous winter and gotten the impression that he was bigger than I was. But when he straightened up, our eyes met dead level. For a second I thought he was going to say, "I'll bet my old man can lick your old man." Then his mouth broke into a grin, and he said, "Where did you get that dizzy shirt?"

It was like one of the shifts which made him so good at sports: exactly what the opponent didn't expect. I had been prepared to introduce myself, or to waive that and exclaim, "Well, I guess we're roommates!" or to begin negotiating an immediate, hostile division of the available floor space. Instead, he cut through everything and began criticizing my clothes—*my* clothes—while he stood there in hacked-off khaki pants and an undershirt. As a matter of fact, I was wearing a lime-green, short-sleeved sports shirt with the bottom squared and worn outside the pants, much admired in the South. "At home," I said. "Where did you think?"

"I don't know, but I can see that home is *way* down yonder." He had an unusual voice, as though he had some baritone instrument in his chest which would amaze you if he didn't keep it under control. You could clearly hear the music in it when he spoke: it was only when he tried to sing, which he often did, that music fled and his voice wailed off key ("Like an Arabian lament," the director of the Glee Club once commented).

Finny made me understand that we should be close friends at once. That first day, standing in our comfortless room amid his clothes, he began to talk and I began to listen. He wanted to establish a firm understanding on all subjects, so he covered the field, beginning with God and moving undeviatingly through to sex. "I'm not too bright about all this," he began, "and I don't understand much about theories, but the way it's always seemed to me . . ." and then he outlined his beliefs. I didn't like them much; they had an eccentric, first-hand originality which cut straight across everything I had been told to believe. God, he felt, was Someone you had to discover for yourself. Nothing important had ever been written or said about Him. Sermons were usually hot air; formal prayers were drill.

Sex was vital, and that was why it was surrounded by even more fantasy than God. He had experienced it three times, and gave detailed, completely matter-of-fact and unboastful accounts of all three, omitting only the girls' names out of gallantry.

"How many times have you slept with a girl?" he asked, fixing his interested eyes on mine.

I was supposed to take up my story at this point. But my ideas would have been as dull as a catechism after his; it seemed as though I had never had an original thought in my life. Besides, this wasn't the way we talked with strangers in the South.

I hadn't asked for all these confidences, and I wasn't going to give mine in return. "I'll tell you about it someday," I answered in what I thought was a cool, rebuffing tone.

"All right," exclaimed Finny with cheerful unconcern. "Will I be interested?"

"You'll be as interested as I was in yours." I liked the screened irony of this reply, lie though it was.

"Good!" He flung his empty suitcase into a corner, where it landed at an angle against the wall and stayed that way for the rest of the summer.

I wasn't going to be opened up like that suitcase, to have him yank out all my thoughts and feelings and scatter them around under foot. So he went on talking and I kept on restively listening through the first weeks of summer.

Finny declared himself especially pleased with this weather, but I found later that all weathers delighted Phineas.

For that was his real name, and it is important for two reasons: first, it was just the kind of special old New England name he would have, and second, no one ever thought to kid him about it. At the Devon School kidding people, or "cutting them down," as it was called, gave place only to athletics as a field of concentration. No one could be allowed to grow above the prevailing level; anyone who threatened to must be instantly and collectively cut down. But Phineas at Devon was like the elms I came to find in his home town, so rooted and realized and proportional that the idea of felling them was unthinkable. Not that he wasn't kidded: his amazing way of dressing, his enjoyment of singing and his inability ever to be on key, the score of fourteen he got on a Latin examination, his habit of emptying his pockets on the floor at night, the icebox he bought which wouldn't hold ice or water, his failure to realize that he was naked when he went calling around the dormitory after a shower, all of these habits were kidded endlessly. But not cut down; they were too exceptional for that. We searched for ways to get at him for a while and then realized that it was impossible, because he never forced himself up.

All of us were at Devon for the summer session, the first in the history of the school. It was because of the war, to hurry us toward graduation before we became eighteen and draftable. We sixteen-year-olds were brought back for the summer and our pace stepped up noticeably. It's odd that such a peaceful summer should have resulted from war.

We became a muted New England adaptation of gilded youth that summer, we boys of sixteen. The masters were more benevolent toward us than at any other time. I think we relieved them of some of their pressure; we reminded them of what peace was like, of lives not bound up with destruction.

Phineas was the essence of this careless peace. Not that he was unconcerned about the war. On the third morning of the session he decided to wear his pink shirt, to memorialize the bombing of the Ploesti oil fields. It was a finely woven broadcloth, carefully cut, and very pink. No one else in the school could have worn it without some risk of having it torn from his back. But Finny put it on with the air of a monarch assuming the regalia. As he was buttoning the collar he at last acknowledged my absorbed stare, letting his eyes slide slowly from the mirror around to me.

"I figured it was a good day to put in on," he said stoutly, "on account of the oil fields." I just kept staring at him in my mystification. "Well, you've got to do *something* to celebrate," he added rebukingly. "You can't just let something like that go by."

"Talk about *my* dizzy shirt!" I broke out indignantly at last.

"Yeah, but yours really is just a dizzy shirt. This is an emblem."

"Is that right!"

"Yeah, that *is* right."

It was right. I watched him break it out during the next weeks for certain specific triumphs—his grade of C on a history quiz, the Battle of Midway, the retirement of Mrs. Carrian, our school dietitian, or "Lucrezia," as we called her. During the regular school terms, Phineas told me, he wore the shirt principally to celebrate the victories of the soccer, hockey, and lacrosse squads. He had elected to play, and therefore inevitably to star, on these three teams the previous year. He excelled at any sport because he had never yet realized that a player had to work for years to master completely one co-ordinated athletic movement, such as swinging a golf club. He thought an athlete naturally was good at everything at once. And he was right, for himself.

But why had he picked these teams, which drew smaller crowds and commanded less prestige than some of the others? It looked a little phony to me, deliberately turning his back on fame so that people would admire him even more. That might be it. So I asked him.

"Football!" he exclaimed in a tone of thrilling scorn. "Who would ever want to play football!" We were walking across the playing fields toward the gym after an hour of compulsory calisthenics. "It's just like those damn push-ups and knee bends today. 'All together now, one-two-three,' that's football. Do you know they draw a map of every player's move, like it was geometry or something?"

Privately I thought that gave football a praiseworthy orderliness. I was going to say so, but Finny had encountered one of his principles, and wanted to enlarge on it.

"In a sport you've got to be loose," he went on. "You have to invent something new all the time. It's no fun if you don't."

This, as it turned out, was his personal athletic code. To be free, to invent, to create without any imposed plan. There was the essence of happiness. Or at least, as we walked back to the gym that late afternoon, so he gave me to believe.

He applied the same individualism, or anarchy, to his studies. We were sitting in our room memorizing the Presidents of the United States one night. "Washington-Adams-Jefferson-Madison-Monroe-Adams-Jackson," said Finny. "I've got those guys cold. Then who was there?"

"Van Buren-Harrison-Tyler-Polk-Taylor-Fillmore."

"What!" Finny cried. "Who ever heard of *them!*"

"Well, they were President of the United States once."

He smiled as though at a wry, touching dream. "I guess *somebody* has to make up lists for schoolboys."

I turned back to the Cleveland-Harrison-Cleveland-McKinley-Roosevelt-Taft period with a divided mind. With Phineas sitting next to me day after day like some guiltless doubting Thomas, I began to wonder not whether history was real, but whether it was important.

I didn't do well in that course; that is, I got a B. At the end of the summer Mr. Patch-Withers told me that I didn't receive an A because of a "veiled flippance" in some of my work. But by that time nothing like grades mattered any more.

I knew Finny was interfering with my studies, and then I began to suspect why. I was smarter than he was. He couldn't stand that. I wasn't deceived by that amazed, happy grin of his when he learned I'd scored the highest grade in Latin, or his candid questions about how I balanced trigonometry equations in three steps while he took twelve. He was trying to take me in; he hated the fact that I could beat him at this. He might be the best natural athlete in the school, the most popular boy, but I was winning where it counted. Of all that there was to know about Phineas, I grasped this hidden enmity best.

And then I realized, with relief, that we were equals. He wasn't so unlike me, so peacefully himself, unconscious of conflict and rivalry, after all. He was as vulnerable and treacherous as everybody else. I began to feel more comfortable with him; I almost even liked him.

Summer moved on in its measureless peace. Finny put up with the compulsory calisthenics in the afternoons, but it was in the hour or two of daylight after supper that he set out to enjoy himself. One evening when five of us were sitting around the Common Room, all bored except Phineas, the idea came to him. His face lit up in inspiration. "I know, let's go jump in the river!" The rest of us looked up warily. "You know," he said, already full of enthusiasm, "out of that tree the seniors use to practice abandoning a troopship." He looked at us in the amused, cajoling way he had, as though we were a good but reluctant team and he was the coach. "Come on, don't just sit there waiting for the end of the world."

So we went out across the empty campus. There was a heightened, theatrical glow around us, as though we were crossing an empty stage with light flooding out from the wings. It gave what we were about to do the aura of a drama.

The tree grew alone and leaned out slightly over the river's edge. We looked up at its extraordinary height, and none of us believed that we would jump from it. None but Phineas. He stripped to his underpants and began scrambling up the wooden rungs nailed on the side of the tree. At last he stepped onto a branch which reached out a little farther over the water. "Is this the one they jump from?" he called down. None of us knew. "If I do it, will everybody do it?" We didn't say anything very clearly. "Well," he cried out, "here's my contribution to the war effort!" and he sprang out, fell through the tips of some lower branches, and smashed into the water.

"Great!" he cried, bobbing instantly to the surface again. "That's the most fun I've had this whole week. Who's next?"

I was. I hated the very existence of that tree. The idea of jumping from it revolted every instinct for self-preservation I had. But I would not lose in this to Phineas. I took off my clothes and began to climb. The branch he had jumped from was more slender than it looked from the ground, and much higher. It was impossible to walk out on it far enough to be well over the river. I would have to spring far out or risk falling into the shallows next to the bank. "Come on," drawled Finny from below, "don't admire the view. When they torpedo the troopship you can't stand around admiring the waves. Jump!"

It took one hatred to overcome another. I hated him at that moment, always trying to show me up, to get revenge for my procession of A's and his D's. Damn him. I jumped.

The tips of branches snapped past me and then I crashed into the water. An instant later I was on the surface getting congratulations.

"I think that was better than Finny's," said Bobby Zane, who was bidding for an ally in the dispute he foresaw.

"Oh, yeah?" Finny grimaced in pretended fury. "Let's see you pass the course before you start handing out grades. The tree's all yours."

Bobby's mouth closed as though forever. He didn't argue or refuse. He became inanimate. But the other two, Chet Douglass and Leper Lepellier, were vocal enough, complaining about school regulations, the danger of stomach cramps, chronic infirmities they had never mentioned before.

"It's you, pal," Finny said to me at last, "just you and me." He and I started back across the campus, preceding the others like two seigneurs.

But this made me feel no closer to Phineas. Neither did the document he drew up, the Charter of the Super Suicide Society of the Summer Session, inscribing his name and mine as charter members. He listed Chet, Bobby, and Leper as "trainees," and posted the paper in the Common Room. A few added their names to the trainee list and came with us in the evenings. The thing was respected: Finny's direct and aspiring pleasure in this game carried the whole dormitory with him.

August arrived with a deepening of all the summertime splendors of New Hampshire. There was a latent freshness in the air, as though spring were returning in the middle of the summer.

But examinations were at hand. I wasn't as ready for them as I should have been. The Suicide Society now met almost every evening, and all members were required to attend and jump. I never got inured to it. But when Phineas did it backwards one evening, so did I, with the sensation that I was throwing my life away. He promoted both of us on the spot to Senior Overseer Charter Members.

I would not let myself be shaken off, even though I began to see that it didn't really matter whether he showed me up at the tree or not. Because it was what you had in your heart that counted. And I had detected that Finny's was a den of lonely, selfish ambition. He was not better than I was, no matter who won all the contests.

A French examination was announced for one Friday late in August. Finny and I studied for it in the library Thursday afternoon; I went over vocabulary lists, and he wrote messages and passed them with great seriousness to me, as *aides-mémoire*. Of course I didn't get any work done. After supper I went to our room to try again. Phineas came in.

"Arise," he began airily, "Senior Overseer Charter Member! Elwin 'Leper' Lepellier has announced his intention to make the leap this very night, to qualify, to save his face at last."

I didn't believe it. Leper Lepellier would go down paralyzed with panic on any sinking troopship before making such a jump. Finny had put him up to it, to finish me for good on the exam. I turned around with elaborate resignation. "If he jumps out of that tree I'm Mahatma Gandhi."

"All right," Finny agreed. He had a way of turning clichés inside out like that. "Come on. We've got to be there. Maybe he *will* do it this time."

"Jee-sus!" I slammed the French book shut.

"What's the matter?"

What a performance! His face was completely questioning and candid. "Studying!" I snarled. "You know, books. Examinations."

"Yeah . . ." He waited for me to go on, as though he didn't see what I was getting at yet.

"Oh, of course, *you* wouldn't know what I'm talking about. Not you." I stood up and slammed the chair against the desk. "Okay, we go. We watch little lily-liver Lepellier not jump from the tree, and I ruin my grade."

He looked at me with an interested expression. "You want to study?"

I sighed heavily. "Never mind, forget it. I know. I joined the club. I'm going."

"Don't go!" He shrugged. "What the hell, it's only a game."

I stopped halfway to the door. "What d'you mean?" I muttered. What he meant was clear enough, but I was groping for what lay behind his words. I might have asked, "Who are you, then?" instead. I was facing a total stranger.

"I didn't know you needed to study," he said simply. "I didn't think you ever did. I thought it just came to you."

It seemed that he had made some kind of parallel between my studies and his sports. He probably thought anything you were good at came without effort. He didn't know yet that he was unique.

I couldn't quite achieve a normal speaking voice. "If I need to study, then so do you."

"Me?" He smiled faintly. "Listen, I could study forever and I'd never break C. But it's different for you, you're good. You really are. If I had a brain like that, I'd—I'd have my head cut open so people could look at it."

He put his hands on the back of a chair and leaned toward me. "I know. We kid around a lot, but you have to be serious sometime, about something. If you're really good at something, I mean if there's nobody, or hardly anybody, who's as good as you are, then you've got to be serious about that. Don't mess around." He frowned. "Why didn't you say you had to study before?"

"Wait a minute," I said.

"It's okay. I'll oversee old Leper. I know he's not going to do it." He was at the door.

"Wait a minute," I said more sharply. "I'm coming."

"No you aren't, pal, you're going to study."

"Never mind my studying."

"You think you've done enough already?"

"Yes." I let this drop curtly, to bar him from telling me what to do about my work. He let it go at that, and went out the door ahead of me, whistling off key.

We followed our gigantic shadows across the campus, and Phineas began talking in wild French, to give me a little extra practice. I said nothing, my mind exploring the new dimensions of isolation around me. Any fear I had ever had of the tree was nothing beside this. It wasn't my neck but my understanding that was menaced. He had never been jealous of me. Now I knew that there never had been and never could have been any rivalry between us. I was not of the same quality as he.

I couldn't stand this. We reached the others loitering around the base of the tree, and Phineas began exuberantly to throw off his clothes, delighted by the challenge, the competitive tension of all of us. "Let's go, you and me," he called. A new idea struck him. "We'll go together, a double jump! Neat, eh?"

None of this mattered now: I would have listlessly agreed to anything. He started up the wooden rungs and I began climbing behind, up to the limb high over the bank. Phineas ventured a little way along it, holding a thin, nearby branch for support. "Come out a little way," he said, "and then we'll jump side by side." The countryside was striking from here, a deep-green sweep of playing fields and bordering shrubbery, with the school stadium white and miniature-looking across the river. From behind us the last long rays of light cut across the campus.

Holding firmly to the trunk, I took a step toward him, and then my knees bent and I jounced the limb. Finny, his balance gone, swung his head around to look at me for an instant with extreme interest, and then he tumbled sideways, broke through the little branches below and hit the bank with a sickening, unnatural thud. It was the first clumsy physical action I had ever seen him make. With unthinking sureness I moved out on the limb and jumped into the river, every trace of my fear of this forgotten.

None of us was allowed near the infirmary during the next days, but I heard all the rumors that came out of it. Eventually a fact emerged: one of his legs had been "shattered." I learned no more, although the subject was discussed endlessly. Everyone talked about Phineas to me. I suppose this was natural. I had been right beside him when it happened: I was his roommate.

I couldn't go on hearing about it much longer. If anyone had been suspicious of me, I might have developed some strength to defend myself. But no one suspected. Phineas must still be too sick, or too noble, to tell them.

I spent as much time as I could alone in our room, trying to empty my mind of every thought, to forget where I was, even who I was. One evening when I was dressing for dinner an idea occurred to me, the first with any energy behind it since Finny fell from the tree. I decided to put on his clothes. We wore the same size, and although he always criticized my clothes, he used to wear them frequently, quickly forgetting what belonged to him and what to me. I never forgot, and that evening I put on his cordovan shoes and his pants, and I looked for and finally found his pink shirt neatly folded, in a drawer. Its high stiff collar against my neck, the rich material against my skin excited a sense of strangeness and distinction; I felt like some nobleman, some Spanish grandee.

But when I looked in the mirror it was no remote aristocrat I had become. I was Phineas, Phineas to the life. I even had his humorous expression on my face, his sharp awareness. I had no idea why this gave me such intense relief, but it seemed, as I stood there in Finny's shirt, that I would never stumble over the twists and pitfalls of my own character again.

I didn't go down to dinner. The sense of transformation stayed with me throughout the evening, and even when I undressed and went to bed. That night I slept easily, and it was only on waking up that this illusion was gone, and I was confronted with myself, and what I had done to Finny.

Sooner or later it had to happen, and that morning it did. "Finny's better!" Dr. Stanpole called to me on the chapel steps. He steered me amiably into the lane leading toward the infirmary. "He could stand a visitor or two now, after these very nasty few days."

"You—you don't think I'll upset him or anything?"

"You? No, why? It'll do him good."

"I suppose he's still pretty sick."

"It was a messy break, but we'll have him walking again."

"*Walking* again!"

"Yes." The doctor didn't look at me, and barely changed his tone of voice. "Sports are finished for him after an accident like that, of course."

"But he must be able to," I burst out, "if his leg's still there, if you aren't going to amputate it—you aren't, are you?—then it must come back the way it was, why shouldn't it? Of course it will."

Dr. Stanpole hesitated, and I think glanced at me for a moment. "Sports are finished. As a friend you ought to help him face that and accept it."

I grabbed my head and the doctor, trying to be kind, put his hand on my shoulder. At his touch I lost all hope of controlling myself. I burst out crying into my hands; I cried for Phineas and for myself and for this doctor who believed in facing things. Most of all I cried because of kindness, which I had not expected.

"Now, that's no good. You've got to be cheerful and hopeful. He needs that from you. He wanted especially to see you. You were the one person he asked for."

That stopped my tears. Of course I was the first person he wanted to see. Phineas would say nothing behind my back; he would accuse me, face to face.

We were walking up the steps of the infirmary. Everything was very swift, and next I was in a corridor, being nudged by Dr. Stanpole toward a door. "He's in there. I'll be with you in a minute."

I pushed back the door, which was slightly ajar, and stood transfixed on the threshold. Phineas lay among pillows and sheets, his left leg, enormous in its white bindings, suspended a little above the bed. A tube led from a glass bottle into his right arm. Some channel began to close inside me and I knew I was about to black out.

"Come on in," he said. "You look worse than I do." The fact that he could make a light remark pulled me back a little, and I went to a chair beside his bed. He seemed to have diminished physically in the few days which had passed, and to have lost his tan. His eyes studied me as though I were the patient. They no longer had their sharp good humor, but had become clouded and visionary. After a while I realized he had been given a drug. "What are *you* looking so sick about?" he went on.

"Finny, I—" there was no controlling what I said; the words were instinctive, like the reactions of someone cornered. "What happened at the tree? That damn tree, I'm going to cut down that tree. Who cares who can jump out of it? How did you fall, how could you fall off like that?"

"I just fell." His eyes looked vaguely into my face. "Something jiggled and I fell over. I remember I turned around and looked at you; it was like I had all the time in the world. I thought I could reach out and get hold of you."

I flinched violently away from him. "To drag me down too!"

He kept looking vaguely over my face. "To get hold of you, so I wouldn't fall."

"Yes, naturally." I was fighting for air in this close room. "I tried, you remember? I reached out but you were gone, down through those little branches."

"I remember looking at your face for a second. Funny expression you had. Very shocked, like you have right now."

"Right now?" Well, of course, I *am* shocked. It's terrible."

"But I don't see why you should look so *personally* shocked. You look like it happened to you or something."

"It's almost like it did! I was right there, right on the limb beside you!"

"Yes, I know. I remember it all."

There was a hard block of silence, and then I said quietly, as though my words might detonate the room, "Do you remember what made you fall?"

His eyes continued their roaming across my face. "I don't know. I must have lost my balance. It must have been that. I did have this feeling that when you were standing there beside me, y—I don't know. I must have been delirious. So I just have to forget it. I just fell, that's all." He turned away to grope for something among the pillows. "I'm sorry about that feeling I had."

I couldn't say anything to this sincere, drugged apology for having suspected the truth. He was never going to accuse me. It was only a feeling he had, and at this moment he must have been formulating a new commandment in his personal decalogue: Never accuse a friend of a crime if you only have a feeling he did it.

It was his best victory. If I had been the one in the hospital bed I would have brought Devon down around his ears with my accusations; I would have hounded him out of the school. And I had thought we were competitors! It was so ludicrous I wanted to cry.

And if Phineas had been sitting here in this pool of guilt, how would he have felt, what would he have done?

He would have told the truth.

I got up so suddenly that the chair overturned. I stared at him in amazement, and he stared back, his mouth gradually breaking into a grin. "Well," he said in his friendly, knowing voice, "what are you going to do, hypnotize me?"

"Finny, I've got something to tell you. You're going to hate it, but there's something I've got to tell you."

But I didn't tell him. Dr. Stanpole came in before I was able to, and then a nurse came in, and I was sent away. I walked down the corridor of elms descending from the infirmary to the dormitories, and at every tree I seemed to leave something I had envied Finny—his popularity, his skill at sports, his background, his ease. It was none of these I had wanted from him. It was the honesty of his every move and his every thought.

But the story wasn't yet complete. I had to wait for a while before ending it, because the day after I saw Finny, the doctor decided that he was not yet well enough for visitors, even old pals like me, after all. The summer session closed. Phineas was taken by ambulance to his home outside Boston, and I went south for a month's vacation. At the end of September I came back to Boston, en route to Devon for the fall term. I found the town where he lived, and I waited a little longer under that tree in front of Finny's house, struggling, maybe for the last time, with the risky emotions I had had for years. Tomorrow, back at Devon, I would be someone else. A week later I was going to turn seventeen and begin the last acceleration which would pitch me into some corner of the war.

The sun was going down much earlier those days, and it began to get chilly. I rehearsed what I was going to say once more, and then turned in through the hedge and knocked at Finny's door.

PROBING FOR MEANING

1. Characterize Finny, using all the details in the story in your characterization: his attitude toward the war, sports, grades, friendship. Why, of all the boys at Devon, has he alone been exempted from being ridiculed or "cut down" by his peers? What is your reaction to Finny? Is he someone you would choose as a friend? Why or why not?

2. The narrator reveals himself indirectly through his reactions to Finny. What kind of person is the narrator? What stages do his attitudes toward Finny go through? What precipitates each stage? To what extent do you agree with his assessment of Finny?

3. How does the narrator feel about Finny at the end? What "risky" emotions

does he struggle with "for the last time" before visiting his sick friend at home? Has the narrator changed through his friendship with Finny? Has Finny changed? Explain.

4. The narrator describes Finny's attitudes toward life as "victorious." What does he mean? Do you believe Finny is as victorious and worthy of envy as the narrator thinks he is? Explain.

5. How would you state the theme of the story in a sentence?

PROBING FOR METHOD

1. The story ends with a knock on Finny's door, and what is going to happen next can only be imagined. Why did the author elect not to tell the reader any more? Write two sentences stating what you imagine the narrator planned to say to Finny.

2. The backdrop of the story is World War II. What effect does the war in Europe have on the action at Devon? What other symbolic subjects and/or situations does the story include?

3. A part of the tone of the selection is developed by the author's skillful use of setting. Exactly what contribution does the setting make to the mood of the story?

WRITING TOPICS
Generating Ideas About a Person

Freewrite, or write a journal entry in response to one of the following:

No people are uninteresting.

> *Yevgeny Yevtushenko*

My neighbor is hell.

> *Jean-Paul Sartre*

Your friend is your need answered.

> *Kahlil Gibran*

A boy wants something very special from his father.

> *Sherwood Anderson*

And what makes my mother grieve right now, I think, is not simply that her mother will die in a day or two, but that, once her mother dies, there will never again be someone to love her in quite such an unreserved, unquestioning way.

> *Joyce Maynard*

He was as vulnerable and treacherous as everybody else. I began to feel more comfortable with him; I almost even liked him.

> *John Knowles*

Good fences make good neighbors.

Robert Frost

All parents realize, or should realize, that children are not possessions, but are only lent to us, angel boarders, as it were.

John Gregory Dunne

Wishing to be friends is quick work, but friendship is a slow-ripening process.

Aristotle

Topics for Essays on a Person

1. Who are the most important people in your life? Is there one person whom you understand as well as Anderson understood his father or Joyce Maynard her mother and grandmother? If you can think of one person you would like to write about, choose one event, action, or conversation through which you can best reveal that person and write an essay in which you portray him or her through this special moment. Did you also learn something about yourself through this encounter?

2. Perhaps an important person in your experience is one you were acquainted with briefly, like Sister Flowers, who influenced you at a special period in your life. This relationship may be easier to describe than one with a person you know well, for if you do not have as many details from which to select, you can be less concerned with limiting the topic. Write an essay in which your emphasis is on creating a dominant mood about the person. Describe this individual, conveying through your choice of words your attitude toward him or her.

3. Perhaps there is a person in your family who, like Kazin's cousin Sophie, was or is "a difficult case." Write a portrait of that person, emphasizing, as does Kazin, the particular characteristics that make him or her difficult.

4. Look over what you have written on the statement you chose for the Generating Ideas section of this chapter. Consider whether this material can be revised into an essay or if any part of it can be expanded into a formal piece of writing. In either case, develop an essay on the topic.

5. John Knowles in "Phineas" focuses on the intensity and ambivalence of an adolescent friendship. Using a close friend as your subject, write an essay about friendship.

6. "Phineas" and "Cousin Sophie" make statements for or against conformity to accepted norms. Choosing one or two of these norms, write an essay in which you discuss the extent to which conformity or nonconformity has a part in the effectiveness of a person's development. Use examples from the selections and your own experience in your response.

7. Self-doubt is a theme of some of the selections in this chapter, including "Phineas" and "Sister Flowers." In an essay, discuss how self-doubt affects the main characters in both selections. What affect can self-doubt have on a person's development?

8. Social class plays a role in several of the selections. Discuss the importance of class distinctions in the main character's lives in the Angelou or Knowles selections. Does social class also play a part in your life? If so, include that in your essay.

9. The understanding of parent by child or child by parent in this universally significant relationship occupies the people in "Father and I" (Chapter 1), "I Discover My Father," "My Grandmother," and "Quintana." Choose one or two of these selections and write an essay discussing what the protagonists learned about their relationships. Include a paragraph comparing their discoveries to your own.

10. Write an essay discussing your point of view on the subject of adoption that includes your thoughts about whether adopted children should be encouraged to seek their natural parents.

11. A common human tendency is to fail to notice special qualities in people we see every day. Write an essay about someone you once thought of as being ordinary but whom you now recognize as having unique qualities that you appreciate, much as Maya Angelou reevaluated her grandmother.

Chapter Three

Places:
Writing the Essay
Describing a Place
Developing the Paragraph

"Although it wasn't wild, it was a fairly large and undisturbed lake and there were places in it which, to a child at least, seemed infinitely remote and primeval." In "Once More to the Lake," E. B. White succeeds in showing us that a place can have a considerable effect on our lives, while Saul Bellow's senses and imagination are captivated by a place—a very different kind of place, a kibbutz, which he describes as "a homeplace for body and soul."

We react to places usually because of our emotional associations with them. Pete Hamill, for example, remembers the hall of his home on "378 Seventh Avenue" as a place where as a child he had dreaded everything from "sudden attacks from the open door leading to the cellar, to rats feasting on the wet garbage, to unnamed things, specters, icy hands, the vengeance of God." Russell Baker's childhood memories are more pleasant as he remembers "summer days drenched with sunlight, fields yellow with butterflies, and barn lofts sweet with hay," while in "In the Fig Tree" Lillian Hellman recalls her thrilling experiences in a special childhood place of refuge.

A candy store is the setting of both a short story and a poem, but the reactions of the protagonists are quite different. For Ferlinghetti, "the pennycandystore beyond the El" was the place where he first sensed the magic and brevity of childhood, whereas Tommy Castelli in "The Prison" finds the store where he works claustrophobic.

A discussion of how to write an effective place description begins on page 94. On page 102, after E. B. White's essay, is a discussion on developing effective paragraphs.

SAUL BELLOW

On a Kibbutz

Saul Bellow (b. 1915) is a Jewish-American writer who was born in Quebec but has spent most of his life in Chicago. He deals in his novels with "intelligent beings in a complex society struggling with absurdity, meaning, ignominy, and their own emotions." Bellow writes: "As human isolation increases, while education and abilities multiply, the most vital questions and answers become the internal ones." Bellow believes strongly in the primacy of the emotions. His novels include Dangling Man *(1944),* The Victim *(1947),* The Adventures of Augie March *(1953),* Seize the Day *(1956),* Henderson the Rain King *(1959),* Herzog *(1964),* Humboldt's Gift *(1975), and* The Dean's December *(1982). In 1976 he received the Nobel Prize for literature. As you read his account of being on a kibbutz (a type of commune) from* To Jerusalem and Back, *think about a place that has had a strong positive or negative influence on you.*

On a kibbutz.

Lucky is Nola's dog. John's dog is Mississippi. But John loves Lucky too, and Nola dotes on Mississippi. And then there are the children—one daughter in the army, and a younger child who still sleeps in the kibbutz dormitory. Lucky is a woolly brown dog, old and nervous. His master was killed in the Golan. When there is a sonic boom over the kibbutz, the dog rushes out, growling. He seems to remember the falling bombs. He is too feeble to bark, too old to run, his teeth are bad, his eyes under the brown fringe are dull, and he is clotted under the tail. Mississippi is a big, long-legged, short-haired, brown-and-white, clever, lively, affectionate, and greedy animal. She is a "child dog"—sits in your lap, puts a paw on your arm when you reach for a tidbit to get it for herself. Since she weighs fifty pounds or more she is not welcome in my lap, but she sits on John and Nola and on the guests—those who permit it. She is winsome but also flatulent. She eats too many sweets but is good company, a wonderful listener and conversationalist; she growls and snuffles when

you speak directly to her. She "sings" along with the record player. The Auer-
bachs are proud of this musical yelping.

In the morning we hear the news in Hebrew and then again on the BBC.
We eat an Israeli breakfast of fried eggs, sliced cheese, cucumbers, olives, green
onions, tomatoes, and little salt fish. Bread is toasted on the coal-oil heater.
The dogs have learned the trick of the door and bang in and out. Between the
rows of small kibbutz dwellings the lawns are ragged but very green. Light and
warmth come from the sea. Under the kibbutz lie the ruins of Herod's Caesarea.
There are Roman fragments everywhere. Marble columns in the grasses. Fallen
capitals make garden seats. You have only to prod the ground to find fragments of pottery, bits of statuary, a pair of dancing satyr legs. John's tightly
packed bookshelves are fringed with such relics. On the crowded desk stands a
framed photograph of the dead son, with a small beard like John's, smiling
with John's own warmth.

We walk in the citrus groves after breakfast, taking Mississippi with us
(John is seldom without her); the soil is kept loose and soft among the trees,
the leaves are glossy, the ground itself is fragrant. Many of the trees are still
unharvested and bending, tangerines and lemons as dense as stars. "Oh that
I were an orange tree/That busie plant!" wrote George Herbert. To put forth
such leaves, to be hung with oranges, to be a blessing—one feels the temptation of this on such a morning and I even feel a fibrous woodiness entering my
arms as I consider it. You want to take root and stay forever in the most temperate and blue of temperate places. John mourns his son, he always mourns
his son, but he is also smiling in the sunlight.

In the exporting of oranges there is competition from the North African
countries and from Spain. "We are very idealistic here, but when we read
about frosts in Spain we're glad as hell," John says.

All this was once dune land. Soil had to be carted in and mixed with the
sand. Many years of digging and tending made these orchards. Relaxing, breathing
freely, you feel what a wonderful place has been created here, a homeplace for
body and soul; then you remember that on the beaches there are armed pa-
trols. It is always possible that terrorists may come in rubber dinghies that
cannot be detected by radar. They entered Tel Aviv itself in March 1975 and
seized a hotel at the seashore. People were murdered. John keeps an Uzi in his
bedroom cupboard. Nola scoffs at this. "We'd both be dead before you could
reach your gun," she says. Cheerful Nola laughs. An expressive woman—she
uses her forearm to wave away John's preparations. "Sometimes he does the
drill and I time him to see how long it takes to jump out of bed, open the
cupboard, get the gun, put in the clip, and turn around. They'd mow us down
before he could get a foot on the floor."

Mississippi is part of the alarm system. "She'd bark," says John.

Just now Mississippi is racing through the orchards, nose to the ground.
The air is sweet, and the sun like a mild alcohol makes you yearn for good
things. You rest under a tree and eat tangerines, only slightly heavyhearted.

From the oranges we go to the banana groves. The green bananas are tied up in plastic tunics. The great banana flower hangs groundward like the sexual organ of a stallion. The long leaves resemble manes. After two years the ground has to be plowed up and lie fallow. Groves are planted elsewhere—more hard labor. "You noticed before," says John, "that some of the orange trees were withered. Their roots get into Roman ruins and they die. Some years ago, while we were plowing, we turned up an entire Roman street."

He takes me to the Herodian Hippodrome. American archeologists have dug out some of the old walls. We look down into the diggings, where labels flutter from every stratum. There are more potsherds than soil in these bluffs—the broken jugs of the slaves who raised the walls two thousand years ago. At the center of the Hippodrome, a long, graceful ellipse, is a fallen monolith weighing many tons. We sit under fig trees on the slope while Mississippi runs through the high smooth grass. The wind is soft and works the grass gracefully. It makes white air courses in the green.

Whenever John ships out he takes the dog for company. He had enough of solitude when he sailed on German ships under forged papers. He does not like to be alone. Now and again he was under suspicion. A German officer who sensed that he was Jewish threatened to turn him in, but one night when the ship was only hours out of Danzig she struck a mine and went down, the officer with her. John himself was pulled from the sea by his mates. Once he waited in a line of nude men whom a German doctor, a woman, was examining for venereal disease. In that lineup he alone was circumcised. He came before the woman and was examined; she looked into his face and she let him live.

John and I go back through the orange groves. There are large weasels living in the bushy growth along the pipeline. We see a pair of them at a distance in the road. They could easily do for Mississippi. She is luckily far off. We sit under a pine on the hilltop and look out to sea where a freighter moves slowly toward Ashkelon. Nearer to shore, a trawler chuffs. The kibbutz does little fishing now. Off the Egyptian coast, John has been shot at, and not long ago several members of the kibbutz were thrown illegally into jail by the Turks, accused of fishing in Turkish waters. Twenty people gave false testimony. They could have had a thousand witnesses. It took three months to get these men released. A lawyer was found who knew the judge. His itemized bill came to ten thousand dollars—five for the judge, five for himself.

Enough of this sweet sun and the transparent blue-green. We turn our backs on it to have a drink before lunch. Kibbutzniks ride by on clumsy old bikes. They wear cloth caps and pedal slowly; their day starts at six. Plain-looking working people from the tile factory and from the barn steer toward the dining hall. The kibbutzniks are a mixed group. There is one lone Ortho-dox Jew, who has no congregation to pray with. There are several older gen-tiles, one a Spaniard, one a Scandinavian, who married Jewish women and settled here. The Spaniard, an anarchist, plans to return to Spain now that Franco has died. One member of the kibbutz is a financial wizard, another was a high-ranking army officer who for obscure reasons fell into disgrace. The dusty tarmac path we follow winds through the settlement. Beside the undistinguished houses stand red poinsettias. Here, too, lie Roman relics. Then we come upon a basketball court, and then the rusty tracks of a children's choo-choo, and then the separate quarters for young women of eighteen, and a museum of antiquities, and a recreation hall. A strong odor of cattle comes from the feeding lot. I tell John that Gurdjiev had Katherine Mansfield resting in the stable at Fontainebleau, claiming that the cows' breath would cure her tuberculosis. John loves to hear such bits of literary history. We go into his house and Mississippi climbs into his lap while we drink Russian vodka. "We could live with those bastards if they limited themselves to making this Stolichnaya."

These words put an end to the peaceful morning. At the north there swells up the Russian menace. With arms from Russia and Europe, the PLO and other Arab militants and the right-wing Christians are now destroying Lebanon. The Syrians have involved themselves; in the eyes of the Syrians, Israel is Syrian land. Suddenly this temperate Mediterranean day and the orange groves and the workers steering their bikes and the children's playground flutter like illustrated paper. What is there to keep them from blowing away?

PROBING FOR MEANING

1. What pleasures does life on the kibbutz offer, according to Bellow?
2. How would you characterize John? What sort of a life has he had? How does he feel about his life on the kibbutz?
3. John calls himself and his fellow kibbutzniks "idealistic." What does he mean?
4. How does what Bellow calls "the Russian menace" affect the quality of life on the kibbutz?
5. Bellow tells us that John mourns his son yet smiles in the sunlight. What is Bellow's attitude toward John? How does his attitude toward John reflect his attitude toward the kibbutz in general?

PROBING FOR METHOD

1. Bellow refers to the Roman ruins twice in the essay. Why are the ruins a significant detail in his description?
2. Why does Bellow tell us about the incident of the Turks' illegally jailing several members of the kibbutz?
3. Why does Bellow begin the essay by describing Lucky and Mississippi? What do the dogs help us to understand about life on the kibbutz?
4. What examples of sensory detail do you find effective?
5. What overall impression does Bellow's description convey?

Describing a Place

How does Bellow describe his place?

Bellow has decided upon a circular spatial pattern for presenting the sensuous details of his day on an Israeli kibbutz. Beginning with breakfast in a kibbutz dwelling, he describes the various tastes of fish, tomatoes, cucumbers, and cheese and, briefly, the appearance of the house both from inside and from without. As he and his host move away from the kibbutz toward the citrus groves, he evokes a third sense, touch, as the warm breeze from the sea and rays of the sun reach him. He also comments that the air is sweet. As he and his host pass through the citrus to the banana groves and beyond them to the Hippodrome, and then continue the cycle until they end up back at John's house, he constantly evokes other sensuous details—the sight of green grass waving white in the wind, the taste of tangerines, the strong odor of cattle.

Throughout this sensuous description of his day, Bellow weaves warnings that this peaceful, almost pagan atmosphere can suddenly be disrupted. He first warns us in the opening paragraph where he contrasts the two dogs: Lucky, who is old and nervous from his experiences of war, and Mississippi, who seems to be a dog of peacetime Israel. Bellow frequently mentions also John's son who was killed in the Golan. These dark details in the bright day prepare us for Bellow's concluding paragraph that cements our sense of the precariousness of the Israeli existence.

Describing a place.

Description involves both content and arrangement. You need to be concerned both with what you want to say about the place and the manner in which you present your subject to the reader.

Description of a place generally involves two aspects: how a place is experienced sensuously—by the senses—and how it is experienced emotionally. A good description may concentrate on either the sensuous or the emotional, or it may combine them. The sensuous description usually evokes primarily visual details, because sight is ordinarily our strongest sense and the one on which we depend the most, although smells, sounds, and even taste and touch may be brought to bear on what the writer wishes the reader to experience. A mood description, which seeks to implant a particular emotion about a place, may use sensuous details, or the writer may employ emotional scenes or encounters in the description of the place.

In this chapter, for example, E. B. White's essay is largely a mood piece infused with sensuous detail. Visual detail is present, as are sound, smell, taste, and touch, and he uses them very skillfully in conveying his emotional reactions to the lake. Bellow uses the senses in describing his place—the kibbutz—even more than does White, as his purpose is to contrast the fruitful lushness of the land with the fear the people constantly experience. Sensuous and emotional details are here played off against each other.

The object of description is to aid your reader in sharing your experience of the place. This sharing is done by supplying details that paint a picture or evoke a mood. The more vividly these details are presented, the more vividly the scene is shared by the reader.

The arrangement of description depends upon one's purpose in writing. If purely sensuous description is the aim, then the writer can choose one of several spatial or visual patterns or orientations for describing the place:

Left to right (for rooms, stages, or landscapes)

Top to bottom (for buildings, people, or objects)

Outer to inner (for buildings, or other places that permit several perspectives; the Grand Canyon, for example)

Main impression to detail (similar to the motion-film technique of "panning"; for places, objects, or people)

Other sense impressions can be described as one moves along visually, or the essay can be divided into sections for the different senses: sight, sounds, smells. It is also possible, of course, to describe a place as though you were blind, and to let the senses other than sight dominate.

In writing a mood piece, any spatial pattern can be used to organize the description. However, main-impression-to-detail (or its reverse) is the most frequent pattern of arrangement. The writer states the main impression (mood) of the place and then proceeds to support that impression with details, or uses details to lead to a conclusion about the emotional atmosphere. The writer of a mood description may also work out two arrangements simultaneously: one for the mood of the piece, the other for the sensuous details.

Several of the writers in this chapter use a climactic arrangement in presenting the details of their places. For example, White begins with relaxed moments shared with his son and gradually builds up to the terror of his final dual experience. On the other hand, Bellow, as we have seen, moves the reader spatially in a circle from kibbutz dwelling to citrus and banana groves to Roman ruins and then back to groves and dwelling, while simultaneously he leads the reader emotionally from the family life of the kibbutz with its relative harmony to the terror facing Israel politically.

Procedures to follow in describing a place.

A. What is the purpose of your description? Is it sensuous or emotional or a combination?

B. Observe what details must be included to convey the main impression. What details could be omitted without distortion or blurring?

C. Determine how best to present your description. The following are two useful patterns of organization that work for both types of description:
   1. Begin with an overall impression and then add contributing details.
   2. Begin with details and conclude with an overall impression for a climactic effect.
D. For purely sensuous description, choose a pattern that works from left to right, inner to outer, top to bottom, or the reverse of any of these. Follow your order carefully so as not to confuse your reader.

E. B. WHITE

Once More to the Lake

E. B. White (1899–1985) was an American humorist, poet, storyteller, and essayist who began his career as a journalist with the New Yorker *in 1926. He also wrote a monthly column for* Harper's *in which he expressed his views on contemporary life in witty and succinct prose. He is perhaps best known for* Charlotte's Web, *a book written for children. In "Once More to the Lake" (1941), White recalls a special summer when he took his son back to the Maine lake where he had spent many vacations as a child. As you read White's essay, think of a place that holds special memories for you.*

One summer, along about 1904, my father rented a camp on a lake in Maine and took us all there for the month of August. We all got ringworm from some kittens and had to rub Pond's Extract on our arms and legs night and morning, and my father rolled over in a canoe with all his clothes on; but outside of that the vacation was a success and from then on none of us ever thought there was any place in the world like that lake in Maine. We returned summer after summer—always on August 1st for one month. I have since become a salt-water man, but sometimes in summer there are days when the restlessness of the tides and the fearful cold of the sea water and the incessant wind which blows across the afternoon and into the evening make me wish for the placid-ity of a lake in the woods. A few weeks ago this feeling got so strong I bought myself a couple of bass hooks and a spinner and returned to the lake where we used to go, for a week's fishing and to revisit old haunts.

I took along my son, who had never had any fresh water up his nose and who had seen lily pads only from train windows. On the journey to the lake I began to wonder what it would be like. I wondered how time would have marred this unique, this holy spot—the coves and streams, the hills that the sun set behind, the camps and the paths behind the camps. I was sure the tarred road would have found it out and I wondered in what other ways it would be desolated. It is strange how much you can remember about places like that once you allow your mind to return into the grooves which lead back. You remember one thing, and that suddenly reminds you of another thing. I guess I remembered clearest of all the early mornings, when the lake was cool and motionless, remembered how the bedroom smelled of the lumber it was made of and of the wet woods whose scent entered through the screen. The partitions in the camp were thin and did not extend clear to the top of the rooms, and as I was always the first up I would dress softly so as not to wake the others, and sneak out into the sweet outdoors and start out in the canoe, keeping close along the shore in the long shadows of the pines. I remembered being very careful never to rub my paddle against the gunwale for fear of disturbing the stillness of the cathedral.

The lake had never been what you would call a wild lake. There were cottages sprinkled around the shores, and it was in farming country although the shores of the lake were quite heavily wooded. Some of the cottages were owned by nearby farmers, and you would live at the shore and eat your meals at the farmhouse. That's what our family did. But although it wasn't wild, it was a fairly large and undisturbed lake and there were places in it which, to a child at least, seemed infinitely remote and primeval.

I was right about the tar: it led to within half a mile of the shore. But when I got back there, with my boy, and we settled into a camp near a farmhouse and into the kind of summertime I had known, I could tell that it was going to be pretty much the same as it had been before—I knew it, lying in bed the first morning, smelling the bedroom, and hearing the boy sneak quietly out and go off along the shore in a boat. I began to sustain the illusion that he was I, and therefore, by simple transposition, that I was my father. This sensation persisted, kept cropping up all the time we were there. It was not an entirely new feeling, but in this setting it grew much stronger. I seemed to be living a dual existence. I would be in the middle of some simple act, I would be picking up a bait box or laying down a table fork, or I would be saying something, and suddenly it would be not I but my father who was saying the words or making the gesture. It gave me a creepy sensation.

We went fishing the first morning. I felt the same damp moss covering the worms in the bait can, and saw the dragonfly alight on the tip of my rod as it hovered a few inches from the surface of the water. It was the arrival of this fly that convinced me beyond any doubt that everything was as it always had been, that the years were a mirage and there had been no years. The small waves were the same, chucking the rowboat under the chin as we fished at anchor, and the boat was the same boat, the same color green and the ribs broken in the same places, and under the floor-boards the same freshwater leavings and debris—the dead helgramite,* the wisps of moss, the rusty discarded fishhook, the dried blood from yesterday's catch. We stared silently at the tips of our rods, at the dragonflies that came and went. I lowered the tip of mine into the water, tentatively, pensively dislodging the fly, which darted two feet away, posed, darted two feet back, and came to rest again a little farther up the rod. There had been no years between the ducking of this dragonfly and the other one—the one that was part of memory. I looked at the boy, who was silently watching his fly, and it was my hands that held his rod, my eyes watching. I felt dizzy and didn't know which rod I was at the end of.

We caught two bass, hauling them in briskly as though they were mackerel, pulling them over the side of the boat in a businesslike manner without any landing net, and stunning them with a blow on the back of the head. When we got back for a swim before lunch, the lake was exactly where we had left it, the same number of inches from the dock, and there was only the merest suggestion of a breeze. This seemed an utterly enchanted sea, this lake you could leave to its own devices for a few hours and come back to, and find that it had not stirred, this constant and trustworthy body of water. In the shallows, the dark, water-soaked sticks and twigs, smooth and old, were undulating in clusters on the bottom against the clean ribbed sand, and the track of the mussel was plain. A school of minnows swam by, each minnow with its small individual shadow, doubling the attendance, so clear and sharp in the sunlight. Some of the other campers were in swimming, along the shore, one of them with a cake of soap, and the water felt thin and clear and insubstantial. Over the years there had been this person with the cake of soap, this cultist, and here he was. There had been no years.

Up to the farmhouse to dinner through the teeming, dusty field, the road under our sneakers was only a two-track road. The middle track was missing, the one with the marks of the hooves and the splotches of dried, flaky manure. There had always been three tracks to choose from in choosing which track to walk in; now the choice was narrowed down to two. For a moment I missed terribly the middle alternative. But the way led past the tennis court, and something about the way it lay there in the sun reassured me; the tape had loosened along the backline, the alleys were green with plantains and other weeds, and the net (installed in June and removed in September) sagged in the dry noon, and the whole place steamed with midday heat and hunger and emptiness. There was a choice of pie for dessert, and one was blueberry and one was apple, and the waitresses were the same country girls, there having been no passage of time, only the illusion of it as in a dropped curtain—the waitresses were still fifteen; their hair had been washed, that was the only difference— they had been to the movies and seen the pretty girls with the clean hair.

---

*The nymph of the May-fly, used as bait.

Summertime, oh summertime, pattern of life indelible, the fade-proof lake, the woods unshatterable, the pasture with the sweet fern and the juniper forever and ever, summer without end; this was the background, and the life along the shore was the design, the cottages with their innocent and tranquil design, their tiny docks with the flagpole and the American flag floating against the white clouds in the blue sky, the little paths over the roots of the trees leading from camp to camp and the paths leading back to the outhouses and the can of lime for sprinkling, and at the souvenir counters at the store the miniature birch-bark canoes and the post cards that showed things looking a little better than they looked. This was the American family at play, escaping the city heat, wondering whether the newcomers in the camp at the head of the cove were "common" or "nice," wondering whether it was true that the people who drove up for Sunday dinner at the farmhouse were turned away because there wasn't enough chicken.

It seemed to me, as I kept remembering all this, that those times and those summers had been infinitely precious and worth saving. There had been jollity and peace and goodness. The arriving (at the beginning of August) had been so big a business in itself, at the railway station the farm wagon drawn up, the first smell of the pine-laden air, the first glimpse of the smiling farmer, and the great importance of the trunks and your father's enormous authority in such matters, and the feel of the wagon under you for the long ten-mile haul, and at the top of the last long hill catching the first view of the lake after eleven months of not seeing this cherished body of water. The shouts and cries of the other campers when they saw you, and the trunks to be unpacked, to give up their rich burden. (Arriving was less exciting nowadays, when you sneaked up in your car and parked it under a tree near the camp and took out the bags and in five minutes it was all over, no fuss, no loud wonderful fuss about trunks).

Peace and goodness and jollity. The only thing that was wrong now, really, was the sound of the place, an unfamiliar nervous sound of the outboard motors. This was the note that jarred, the one thing that would sometimes break the illusion and set the years moving. In those other summertimes all motors were inboard; and when they were at a little distance, the noise they made was a sedative, an ingredient of summer sleep. They were one-cylinder and two-cylinder engines, and some were make-and-break and some were jump-spark,* but they all made a sleepy sound across the lake. The one-lungers throbbed and fluttered and the twin-cylinder ones purred and purred, and that was a quiet sound too. But now the campers all had outboards. In the daytime, in the hot mornings, these motors made a petulant, irritable sound; at night, in the still evening when the afterglow lit the water, they whined about one's ears like mosquitoes. My boy loved our rented outboard, and his great desire was to achieve singlehanded mastery over it, and authority, and he soon learned the trick of choking it a little (but not too much), and the adjustment of

*Methods of ignition timing.

the needle valve. Watching him I would remember the things you could do with the old one-cylinder engine with the heavy flywheel, how you could have it eating out of your hand if you got really close to it spiritually. Motor boats in those days didn't have clutches, and you would make a landing by shutting off the motor at the proper time and coasting in with a dead rudder. But there was a way of reversing them, if you learned the trick, by cutting the switch and putting it on again exactly on the final dying revolution of the flywheel, so that it would kick back against compression and begin reversing. Approaching a dock in a strong following breeze, it was difficult to slow up sufficiently by the ordinary coasting method, and if a boy felt he had complete mastery over his motor, he was tempted to keep it running beyond its time and then reverse it a few feet from the dock. It took a cool nerve, because if you threw the switch a twentieth of a second too soon you would catch the flywheel when it still had speed enough to go up past center, and the boat would leap ahead, charging bull-fashion at the dock.

We had a good week at the camp. The bass were biting well and the sun shone endlessly, day after day. We would be tired at night and lie down in the accumulated heat of the little bedrooms after the long hot day and the breeze would stir almost imperceptibly outside and the smell of the swamp drift in through the rusty screens. Sleep would come easily and in the morning the red squirrel would be on the roof, tapping out his gay routine. I kept remembering everything, lying in bed in the morning—the small steamboat that had a long rounded stern like the lip of a Ubangi, and how quietly she ran on the moonlight sails; when the older boys played their mandolins and the girls sang and we ate doughnuts dipped in sugar, and how sweet the music was on the water in the shining light, and what it had felt like to think about girls then. After breakfast we would go up to the store and the things were in the same place—the minnows in a bottle, the plugs and spinners disarranged and pawed over by the youngsters from the boys' camp, the fig newtons and the Beeman's gum. Outside, the road was tarred and cars stood in front of the store. Inside, all was just as it had always been, except there was more Coca-Cola and not so much Moxie and root beer and birch beer and sarsaparilla. We would walk out with a bottle of pop apiece and sometimes the pop would backfire up our noses and hurt. We explored the streams, quietly, where the turtles slid off the sunny logs and dug their way into the soft bottom; and we lay on the town wharf and fed worms to the tame bass. Everywhere we went I had trouble making out which was I, the one walking at my side, the one walking in my pants.

One afternoon while we were there at that lake a thunderstorm came up. It was like the revival of an old melodrama that I had seen long ago with childish awe. The second-act climax of the drama of the electrical disturbance over a lake in America had not changed in any important respect. This was the big scene, still the big scene. The whole thing was so familiar, the first feeling of oppression and heat and a general air around camp of not wanting to go very far away. In midafternoon (it was all the same) a curious darkening of the sky, and a lull in everything that had made life tick; and then the way the boats suddenly swung the other way at their moorings with the coming of a breeze out of the new quarter, and the premonitory rumble. Then the kettle drum, then the snare, then the bass drum and cymbals, then crackling light against the dark, and the gods grinning and licking their chops in the hills. Afterward the calm, the rain steadily rustling in the calm lake, the return of light and hope and spirits, and the campers running out in joy and relief to go swimming in the rain, their bright cries perpetuating the deathless joke about how they were getting simply drenched, and the children screaming with delight at the new sensation of bathing in the rain, and the joke about getting drenched linking the generations in a strong indestructible chain. And the comedian who waded in carrying an umbrella.

When the others went swimming my son said he was going in too. He pulled his dripping trunks from the line where they had hung all through the shower, and wrung them out. Languidly, and with no thought of going in, I watched him, his hard little body, skinny and bare, saw him wince slightly as he pulled up around his vitals the small, soggy, icy garment. As he buckled the swollen belt suddenly my groin felt the chill of death.

PROBING FOR MEANING

1. White describes the Maine lake as a "holy spot." What details from the essay defend this description?

2. What particular features distinguish this lake from others?

3. What does the author mean by "I seemed to be living a dual existence"? What importance does this statement have for the essay?

4. "Arriving was less exciting nowadays." What other differences does the author discover between his childhood and adult visits to the lake?

5. What does the last sentence mean? What connection does it have with the rest of the essay?

PROBING FOR METHOD

1. White writes of canoeing in the "long shadow of the pines" and taking care not to disturb "the stillness of the cathedral." What other metaphors and similes does he use?

2. To what extent did White limit his topic? What might his broader topic have been? What sentence might be his thesis sentence?

3. What was White's purpose in writing his essay? How would you categorize the audience he is writing for?

4. Where in the essay does White foreshadow the last sentence? Does he prepare us for it in any way?

Developing the Paragraph

How does White structure his paragraphs?
Each paragraph of his essay develops one major aspect of his thesis so that the essay proceeds in an orderly way from main contention to elaboration of the thesis and supporting examples to a conclusion that hints at the wider implications of the thesis. An outline of the piece might look like this:

I. Introduction (paragraphs 1 to 3)
   A. Background (paragraph 1)
      1. Childhood trips to the lake
      2. Decision to return
   B. Current trip to the lake (paragraph 2)
   C. General description of the lake (paragraph 3)
II. "Dual existence" experiences (paragraphs 4 to 11)
   A. Introduction (paragraph 4) including thesis statement
   B. Fishing (paragraphs 5 and 6)
   C. Dinner at the farmhouse (paragraph 7)
   D. The American family at play (paragraph 8)
   E. The arriving (paragraph 9)
   F. Unfamiliar sound (paragraph 10)
   G. Conclusion (paragraph 11)
      1. Sleeping
      2. Waking
      3. Visiting the store
      4. Exploring
III. Conclusion (paragraphs 12 and 13)
   A. The thunderstorm (paragraph 12)
   B. Final realization of meaning of experience at lake (paragraph 13)

In each paragraph, White employs a technique used by many good writers, which is to express the main idea concretely in one sentence somewhere in the paragraph, usually in the beginning or concluding sentence. Notice, for example, that the topic sentence comes at the end of paragraph 1, is the second sentence of paragraph 2 and the first sentence of paragraph 3, and in the fourth paragraph comes in the middle of the paragraph. This sentence, "I began to sustain the illusion that he was I, and therefore, by simple transposition, that I was my father," and a following one, "I seemed to be leading a dual existence," also state the thesis of the entire essay.

Paragraphs 5 and 11 contain both introductory and concluding topic sentences. Which sentences in the remaining paragraphs summarize the topics of those units?

White has developed the main idea of each paragraph in various ways throughout the essay—through the use of description, narration, example, cause and effect, and comparison and contrast. The sentences in paragraph 1, for example, relate why he has come once more to the lake.

In his second and third paragraphs, he lists his memories as well as describes what the lake shore once looked like. In paragraph 4, he compares the present experience with the past; in paragraph 5, he compares a present fishing trip with a childhood one, using description, narration, and cause and effect. Paragraphs 6 through 11 cite other examples of this "dual experience" at the lake, also using description, comparison and contrast, and cause and effect. Paragraph 12 both describes and narrates the thunderstorm, and his final paragraph narrates his son's preparations for swimming and their effect on him.

Developing the paragraph.
The basic structure of the paragraph is similar to that of the essay as a whole. Like the essay, the paragraph is limited to one topic that can be expanded within a limited space. Also, just as the essay outline follows a certain method of development, so the sentences in the paragraph must develop the topic logically. The first paragraph of the essay usually introduces the thesis, and correspondingly, the first sentence of the paragraph often is an introduction or topic sentence. Finally, in a long paragraph, the last sentence may act as a conclusion.

A simplified method of forming good paragraphs with effective topic sentences involves the use of the essay outline. Each of the major headings when stated in sentence form can serve as the topic sentence of a paragraph. The development of each paragraph requires the development of the point in the topic sentence.

A method of paragraph development that writers frequently use is to give examples that illustrate the topic sentence. Paragraphs may also be expanded by adapting those methods that apply to the essay as a whole: spatial order, chronological order, contrast and comparison, cause and effect, definition, process analysis, and so forth.

Paragraphs, regardless of the method of their development, follow variations on one of two possible patterns: Ideas are either coordinate (of equal value) or subordinate (unequal). The introduction to White's essay, for example, contains three sentences of equal value (the first, third, and fifth) and two that are subordinate in some way to the others (second and fourth). Outlined, the paragraph looks like this:

Sentence 1: One summer, along about 1904, my father rented a camp on a lake in Maine and took us all there for the month of August.

Sentence 2: We all got ringworm from some kittens . . . , and my father rolled over in a canoe . . . ; but outside of that the vacation was a success. . . .

Sentence 3: We returned summer after summer. . . .

   Sentence 4: I have since become a salt-water man, but sometimes in summer there are days. . . .

Sentence 5: A few weeks ago this feeling got so strong I . . . returned to the lake where we used to go, . . .

His second paragraph also follows a coordinate/subordinate pattern:

Sentence 1: I took along my son. . . .

Sentence 2: On the journey to the lake I began to wonder what it would be like.

   Sentence 3: I wondered how time would have marred this unique, this holy spot. . . .

      Sentence 4: I was sure the tarred road would have found it out. . . .

         Sentence 5: It is strange how much you can remember about places like that once you allow your mind to return. . . .

            Sentence 6: You remember one thing, . . .

Sentence 7: I guess I remembered clearest of all the early mornings, . . .

Sentence 8: The partitions in the camp were thin. . . .

Sentence 9: I remembered being very careful never to rub my paddle against the gunwale for fear of disturbing the stillness of the cathedral.

Procedures to follow in developing paragraphs.

Method 1: Write each major heading in your outline in sentence form. Use each sentence as the topic sentence of a paragraph in your paper. Once you have formulated the topic sentence for each paragraph, use the sub-headings in your outline to develop the rest of the paragraph.

   Method 2: If you prefer to outline your essay after writing the first draft, then once you have determined the major points of your draft, make sure each one forms a separate paragraph.

A. Develop each paragraph logically; that is, arrange the sentences in an effective pattern.

   1. If the paragraph describes a place, follow the spatial pattern described in Chapter 3.

   2. If it narrates an event, develop a chronological arrangement (Chapter 4).

   3. For the more complex methods of paragraph development, see Chapter 6 for organization by cause and effect and by contrast and comparison. Paragraphs developed by these methods will also follow a coordinate or subordinate pattern. If you wish to explain your causes or comparisons to your reader, arrange your details in a subordinate pattern. If you wish simply to list them, follow a coordinate pattern. Most paragraphs both list ideas and explain them.

B. No rules have been formulated for the length of paragraphs, but some guidelines are useful:

1. A heading from your outline that can be explained in a sentence or two is not usually worth a separate paragraph. Unless you want a short paragraph for emphasis, you should, if possible, join it to either the preceding or the following heading or simply delete it.
2. Some headings may need to be divided into two paragraphs if the subject requires more than five or six well-developed sentences. In this case, each subheading should be written in sentence form and serve as a topic sentence for each paragraph.
3. Short paragraphs create dramatic emphasis if used at the right point in an essay and if used sparingly.
4. Longer paragraphs can be used to develop major points but should at most be half a page in length so as not to engulf the reader.

C. Use your thesis sentence in developing your introduction. Your introduction should fulfill two purposes: it should state the topic and it should engage the reader (see Chapter 2, p. 60).

D. The conclusion should not simply summarize the essay; it should stress a particular aspect of the topic for the reader to think about on his or her own. Its tone of finality should clearly indicate that the essay is concluded (see Chapter 2, p. 60).

PETE HAMILL

Home—378 Seventh Avenue

Pete Hamill (b. 1935) was born in Brooklyn, New York, and attended Pratt Institute. He has had many careers, first as a sheetmetal-worker in the Brooklyn Navy Yard, then as a reporter with the Saturday Evening Post. *During the Vietnam War, he was a correspondent in South Vietnam and received many awards for his outstanding reporting. Hamill's writings include* Irrational Ravings *(1971),* The Gift *(1973), and numerous screenplays. He is currently a free-lance writer who contributes to* Esquire, New York Times Magazine, *and other periodicals. As you read his description of 378 Seventh Avenue, pay particular attention to his eye for detail and his succinct prose style.*

The house was at 378 Seventh Avenue. There was a small butcher shop to the left and Teddy's Sandwich Shop to the right, and when I went in, I saw that the mailbox was still broken and the hall smelled of backed-up sewers and wet garbage. There were, of course, no locks on the doors, and I stood for a while in the yellow light of the thirty-watt bulb, and shifted the sea bag to the other shoulder. Two baby carriages were parked beside the stairs, and in the blackness at the back of the hall, I caught a glimpse of battered garbage cans. A small shudder went through me; the back of that hall had always been a fearful place when I was small, a place where I always felt vulnerable: to sudden attacks from the open door leading to the cellar, to rats feasting on the wet garbage, to unnamed things, specters, icy hands, the vengeance of God. Once, I'd had to go to the cellar late at night. To the right, inside the cellar door, there was a light switch, covered with a ceramic knob. I reached for the knob and it was gone, and there was a raw wire there instead and the shock knocked me over backwards, into the garbage cans, my heart spinning and racing away, and then rushing back again. I thought of that night trip, the strangeness later when I realized for the first time what it must feel like to die, and I started up the stairs.

It was a hall as familiar as anything I've ever known before or since. First floor right, Mae McAvoy; on the left, Poppa Clark; second floor right, Anne Sharkey and Mae Irwin; left, Carrie Woods. Carrie was a tiny sparrow of a woman who kept dogs and drank whiskey, and the dogs started a ferocious attack on the locked door, trying to get at me—alarmed, I suppose, by a smell they had not sensed for many weeks. All the apartments had the feeling of tossing bodies within, and I remembered fragments of other nights: the scream when a husband punched out a wife, and how he left and never came back; the glasses breaking at some forgotten party and the blood in the hall later; how they all hated one of the women because she was a wine drinker and therefore a snob; the great large silent man in one of those apartments, who played each Christmas with a vast Lionel electric train set, while forcing his only daughter to play at an untuned upright piano, who rooted for the Giants in that neighborhood of Dodger fans, and who had a strange tortured set of eyes. At each landing there were sealed metal doors where the dumbwaiter once had been, a pit that dropped away, like some bottomless well, to a boarded-over access door in the cellar, and which I thought, when I was eight, was the way to Hell itself, or at the very least, to the secret cave where Shazam granted Billy Batson the magic powers. There were two more baby carriages at the top of the second floor, the floor where my father had so often stopped on his way home, emptied of songs, dry and hoarse, unable to make that one final flight of stairs to bed. Billy Batson. Billy Hamill. Shazam.

There were traces of dinner smells in the hall, as if you could chew the air itself. It was almost three.

The door to our apartment was not locked. I dropped the sea bag, pushed the door open easily, and stepped into the dark kitchen, groping for the light cord in the center of the room. I bumped into a chair, then the table, and then found the light cord. A transformer hummed for a few seconds and then the round fluorescent ceiling light blinked on. The room was as I had remembered it: a white-topped gas range against the far wall where the old coal stove had once stood, a tall white cabinet to the left, and then the sink, high, one side shallow and the other deep, next to the window that never opened. A Servel refrigerator with a broken handle was next to the bathroom door. A closet loomed behind me next to the front door, with a curtain covering the disorder within, and there was a table in the center of the room, linoleum on the floor, and a clothesline running the length of the room because there was no back-yard, and in winter the clothes froze on the line on the roof. There was a picture of Franklin Roosevelt on one wall, a map of Ireland from the *Daily News* on another, and beside it I saw some of the drawings I had sent from boot camp. Some of them were cartoons, drawings of soldiers and pilots I had cop-ied from Milton Caniff; the others were something new, drawings of sailors' faces, done in ink washes, the first drawings I had made that didn't look like comic-strip figures. Roaches scurried across the table, panicked by the harsh-ness of the sudden blue-tinged light. I could hear movement at the other end of the railroad flat, the smell of heavy breathing and milk, and then my mother was coming through the rooms.

"Oh Peter," she said. "You're home."

And she hugged me.

PROBING FOR MEANING

1. Describe your impression of 378 Seventh Avenue from the first paragraph of Hamill's essay, in which he describes the hallway of his home.

2. What kind of people live at 378 Seventh Avenue? Does Hamill convey his atti-tude toward them in any way? Explain.

3. In the fourth paragraph Hamill describes his kitchen. Which details tell you something about his family?

4. Why are the last two lines so important to the essay? How does Hamill intend them to affect the reader?

PROBING FOR METHOD

1. Hamill includes specific details in the first paragraph of his essay as well as conveys a dominant impression. What details does he highlight? What techniques does he use to combine details and dominant impression successfully?

2. What does Hamill accomplish by referring to so many of his neighbors in para-graph 2?

3. Hamill's description of his home is relatively short, yet he succeeds in describ-ing the place, his own memories of it, and the people who live there. What makes his description so effective? To what senses does he appeal? What use does he make of spatial description?

4. Compare your reaction to the two lines of paragraph 3 with your reaction to the last two lines of the essay. What does Hamill achieve in contrasting these four lines?

RUSSELL BAKER

Morrisonville

Russell Baker (b. 1925) is a regular columnist for the New York Times. *He began his career in journalism with the* Baltimore Sun, *and in 1954 he joined the Washington bureau of the* Times. *His books include* An American in Washington *(1961),* All Things Considered *(1965),* Poor Russell's Almanac *(1972), and his Pulitzer-Prize-winning autobiography* Growing Up *(1982). As you read this selection about "Morrisonville" from* Growing Up, *think about Baker's comment that it was "a delightful place to spend a childhood."*

Morrisonville was a poor place to prepare for a struggle with the twentieth century, but a delightful place to spend a childhood. It was summer days drenched with sunlight, fields yellow with buttercups, and barn lofts sweet with hay. Clusters of purple grapes dangled from backyard arbors, lavender wisteria blossoms perfumed the air from the great vine enclosing the end of my grandmother's porch, and wild roses covered the fences.

On a broiling afternoon when the men were away at work and all the women napped, I moved through majestic depths of silences, silences so immense I could hear the corn growing. Under these silences there was an orchestra of natural music playing notes no city child would ever hear. A certain cackle from the henhouse meant we had gained an egg. The creak of a porch swing told of a momentary breeze blowing across my grandmother's yard. Moving past Liz Virts's barn as quietly as an Indian, I could hear the swish of a horse's tail and knew the horseflies were out in strength. As I tiptoed along a mossy bank to surprise a frog, a faint splash told me the quarry had spotted me and slipped into the stream. Wandering among the sleeping houses, I learned that tin roofs crackle under the power of the sun, and when I tired and came back to my grandmother's house, I padded into her dark cool living room, lay flat on the floor, and listened to the hypnotic beat of her pendulum clock on the wall ticking the meaningless hours away.

I was enjoying the luxuries of a rustic nineteenth-century boyhood, but for the women Morrisonville life had few rewards. Both my mother and grandmother kept house very much as women did before the Civil War. It was astonishing that they had any energy left, after a day's work, to nourish their mutual disdain. Their lives were hard, endless, dirty labor. They had no electricity, gas, plumbing, or central heating. No refrigerator, no radio, no telephone, no automatic laundry, no vacuum cleaner. Lacking indoor toilets, they had to empty, scour, and fumigate each morning the noisome slop jars which sat in bedrooms during the night.

For baths, laundry, and dishwashing, they hauled buckets of water from a spring at the foot of a hill. To heat it, they chopped kindling to fire their wood stoves. They boiled laundry in tubs, scrubbed it on washboards until knuckles were raw, and wrung it out by hand. Ironing was a business of lifting heavy metal weights heated on the stove top.

They scrubbed floors on hands and knees, thrashed rugs with carpet beaters, killed and plucked their own chickens, baked bread and pastries, grew and canned their own vegetables, patched the family's clothing on treadle-operated sewing machines, deloused the chicken coops, preserved fruits, picked potato bugs and tomato worms to protect their garden crop, darned stockings, made jelly and relishes, rose before the men to start the stove for breakfast and pack lunch pails, polished the chimneys of kerosene lamps, and even found time to tend the geraniums, hollyhocks, nasturtiums, dahlias, and peonies that grew around every house. By the end of the summer day a Morrisonville woman had toiled like a serf.

At sundown the men drifted back from the fields exhausted and steaming. They scrubbed themselves in enamel basins and, when supper was eaten, climbed up onto Ida Rebecca's porch to watch the night arrive. Presently the women joined them, and the twilight music of Morrisonville began:

The swing creaking, rocking chairs whispering on the porch planks, voices murmuring approval of the sagacity of Uncle Irvey as he quietly observed for probably the ten-thousandth time in his life, "A man works from sun to sun, but woman's work is never done."

Ida Rebecca, presiding over the nightfall from the cane rocker, announcing, upon hearing of some woman "up there along the mountain" who had dropped dead hauling milk to the creamery, that "man is born to toil, and woman is born to suffer."

The timelessness of it: Nothing new had been said on that porch for a hundred years. If one of the children threw a rock close to someone's window, Uncle Harry removed his farmer's straw hat, swabbed the liner with his blue bandanna, and spoke the wisdom of the ages to everyone's complete satisfaction by declaring, "Satan finds work for idle hands to do."

If I interrupted the conversation with a question, four or five adults competed to be the first to say, "Children are meant to be seen and not heard."

If one of my aunts mentioned the gossip about some woman "over there around Bollington" or "out there towards Hillsboro," she was certain to be silenced by a scowl from Ida Rebecca or Uncle Irvey and a reminder that "little pitchers have big ears."

I was listening to a conversation that had been going on for generations. Someone had a sick cow.

The corn was "burning up" for lack of rain.

If the sheriff had arrested a local boy for shooting somebody's bull: "That boy never brought a thing but trouble to his mother, poor old soul."

Old Mr. Cooper from out there around Wheatland had got his arm caught in the threshing machine and it had to be taken off, "poor old soul."

Ancient Aunt Zell, who lived "down there around Lucketts," had to be buried on a day "so hot the flowers all wilted before they could get her in the ground, poor old soul."

When the lamps were lit inside, someone was certain to say to the children, "Early to bed and early to rise makes a man healthy, wealthy, and wise."

Uncle Harry usually led the departures, for he lived outside Morrisonville proper and had to walk a half mile to get home. Only a year younger than Uncle Irvey, Harry was Ida Rebecca's quiet son. A dour man in sweat-stained work shirts, baggy trousers held up by yellow galluses, he worked in the fields, did some carpentry, turned up on a building job occasionally. He was gray, solemn, and frosty. A lonely man. His wife had died in childbirth twenty years earlier.

I knew he was slightly scandalous. Lately he had taken an interest in a younger woman who had borne an illegitimate child and been abandoned by her lover. Everybody knew Uncle Harry had "gone to housekeeping" with her and was devoted to her child, but he did not bring either mother or daughter to sit on Ida Rebecca's porch. Morrisonville's social code was rigid about such things.

Another person who did not join our evening assemblies was Annie Grigsby, Ida Rebecca's next-door neighbor. Annie had been born in slavery, and this made her a notable citizen. Her log house was pointed out to travelers as one of the Morrisonville sights not to be ignored. "Annie was born in slavery," the visitor was always advised.

"Born in slavery." That phrase was uttered as though it were an incredible accomplishment on Annie's part. Elsewhere, people boasted of neighbors who had tamed lightning, invented the wind-up Victrola, and gone aloft in flying machines, but we in Morrisonville didn't have to hang our heads. We had Annie. "Born in slavery." My mother told me about Abraham Lincoln, a great man who freed the slaves, and living so close to Annie, who had been freed by Lincoln himself, made me feel in touch with the historic past.

Annie was not much older than Ida Rebecca, who was born in 1861. She was a short, gray-haired, rotund woman of weary carriage and a dignity appropriate to her remarkable birth. Now and then she unbent enough to invite Doris or my cousin Kenneth or me into her dark kitchen for a piece of butter bread, Morrisonville's universal treat. One afternoon I wandered into her backyard to find her hacking the meat out of a huge, freshly killed terrapin.

"What's that, Annie?"

"It's a tarpon."

"What's a tarpon?"

"Tarpon's big turtle, child."

"Why're you cutting it up like that?"

"To make soup. You come back over here when I get it done, and I'll give you some."

White Morrisonville's hog-meat diet hadn't prepared me for terrapin soup. I hurried back across the road giggling to my mother that colored people ate turtles.

"Colored people are just like everybody else," she said.

Despite the respect accorded Annie, no one else in Morrisonville held my mother's radical view. Nor did Annie. Only when there was death or sickness did Annie presume the social freedom of white households. Then she came to help in the sickroom or sit in a rocker on Ida Rebecca's porch comforting a sobbing child in her lap. In time of crisis her presence was expected, for she was a citizen of stature. An historical monument. A symbol of our nation's roots. "Born in slavery."

PROBING FOR MEANING

1. What details does Baker offer to support his point that Morrisonville was "a delightful place to spend a childhood"? Why did it not prepare him "for a struggle with the twentieth century"?

2. Describe a typical day in the life of a woman in Morrisonville at that time. Why do you think Baker includes this in his essay?

3. "The timelessness of it: Nothing new had been said on that porch for a hundred years." What is your reaction to the porch conversations? Are your family's conversations different from those Baker overheard? Explain the reasons for any similarities or differences.

4. What do we learn about Morrisonville's social code through Baker's inclusion of Uncle Harry and Annie Grigsby? Are today's social codes more flexible?

5. What do you think about Annie's exclusion from the porch conversations but her presence being expected in times of crisis because she was a "citizen of stature"?

6. What is the overall impression that Baker offers of Morrisonville life? Would you have liked to grow up there? Why or why not?

PROBING FOR METHOD

1. To what senses does Baker appeal in the first two paragraphs of the essay?

2. What effect does he achieve by contrasting his own days to those of his mother and grandmother? Does the inclusion of this contrast affect the unity of his essay? Explain.

3. What mood does he create by describing evening hours on the porch? What do these descriptions contribute to your dominant impression of the essay?

LILLIAN HELLMAN

In the Fig Tree

Lillian Hellman (1900—1984) was an American playwright, journalist, and essayist who was born in New Orleans but spent many years in New York City and New England. Her autobiographical essays include An Unfinished Woman *(1969),* Pentimento *(1973), and* Scoundrel Time *(1976). As you read "In the Fig Tree," taken from* An Unfinished Woman, *write down two or three of your associations with a childhood place.*

There was a heavy fig tree on the lawn where the house turned the corner into the side street, and to the front and sides of the fig tree were three live oaks that hid the fig from my aunts' boardinghouse. I suppose I was eight or nine before I discovered the pleasures of the fig tree, and although I have lived in many houses since then, including a few I made for myself, I still think of it as my first and most beloved home.

I learned early, in our strange life of living half in New York and half in New Orleans, that I made my New Orleans teachers uncomfortable because I was too far ahead of my schoolmates, and my New York teachers irritable because I was too far behind. But in New Orleans, I found a solution: I skipped school at least once a week and often twice, knowing that nobody cared or would report my absence. On those days I would set out for school done up in polished strapped shoes and a prim hat against what was known as "the climate," carrying my books and a little basket filled with delicious stuff my Aunt Jenny and Carrie, the cook, had made for my school lunch. I would round the corner of the side street, move on toward St. Charles Avenue, and sit on a bench as if I were waiting for a streetcar until the boarders and the neighbors had gone to work or settled down for the post-breakfast rest that all Southern ladies thought necessary. Then I would run back to the fig tree, dodging in and out of bushes to make sure the house had no dangers for me. The fig tree was heavy, solid, comfortable, and I had, through time, convinced myself that it wanted me, missed me when I was absent, and approved all the rigging I had done for the happy days I spent in its arms: I had made a sling to hold the school books, a pulley rope for my lunch basket, a hole for the bottle of afternoon cream-soda pop, a fishing pole and a smelly little bag of elderly bait, a pillow embroidered with a picture of Henry Clay on a horse that I had stolen from Mrs. Stillman, one of my aunts' boarders, and a proper nail to hold my dress and shoes to keep them neat for the return to the house.

It was in that tree that I learned to read, filled with the passions that can only come to the bookish, grasping, very young, bewildered by almost all of what I read, sweating in the attempt to understand a world of adults I fled from in real life but desperately wanted to join in books. (I did not connect the grown men and women in literature with the grown men and women I saw around me. They were, to me, another species.)

It was in the fig tree that I learned that anything alive in water was of enormous excitement to me. True, the water was gutter water and the fishing could hardly be called that: sometimes the things that swam in New Orleans gutters were not pretty, but I didn't know what was pretty and I liked them all. After lunch—the men boarders returned for a large lunch and a siesta—the street would be safe again, with only the noise from Carrie and her helpers in the kitchen, and they could be counted on never to move past the back porch, or the chicken coop. Then I would come down from my tree to sit on the side street gutter with my pole and bait. Often I would catch a crab that had wandered in from the Gulf, more often I would catch my favorite, the crayfish, and sometimes I would, in that safe hour, have at least six of them for my basket. Then, about 2:30, when house and street would stir again, I would go back to my tree for another few hours of reading or dozing or having what I called the ill hour. It is too long ago for me to know why I thought the hour "ill," but certainly I did not mean sick. I think I meant an intimation of sadness, a first recognition that there was so much to understand that one might never find one's way and the first signs, perhaps, that for a nature like mine, the way would not be easy. I cannot be sure that I felt all that then, although I can be sure that it was in the fig tree, a few years later, that I was first puzzled by the conflict which would haunt me, harm me, and benefit me the rest of my life: simply, the stubborn, relentless, driving desire to be alone as it came into conflict with the desire not to be alone when I wanted not to be. I already guessed that other people wouldn't allow that, although, as an only child, I pretended for the rest of my life that they would and must allow it to me.

PROBING FOR MEANING

1. Why does Hellman think of the fig tree as her "most beloved home"?
2. What does she learn about herself from her experiences in the fig tree?
3. What exactly is Hellman trying to convey by using the phrase "ill hour" in reference to the fig tree?
4. Explain in your own words the meaning of the last two sentences of the essay.

PROBING FOR METHOD

1. Hellman recalls many experiences and emotions associated with the fig tree. Why does she not describe the tree in any detail? Would including a description of the tree affect the meaning of the essay? How?

2. How would you characterize the mood of the essay? Is it suggested by Hellman's use of the phrase "ill hour"? Why or why not?

3. Hellman personifies the tree. To what extent does this technique help the reader to understand better what the fig tree means to the writer?

LAWRENCE FERLINGHETTI

The pennycandystore beyond the El

Lawrence Ferlinghetti (b. 1919) is a poet, playwright, and editor. He is co-owner of City Lights Books in San Francisco and founder and editor of City Lights Publishing House. Ferlinghetti was an important figure in the beat poetry movement of the 1950s, which was primarily concerned with rebelling against society and taking strong stands on political issues. Ferlinghetti writes in common everyday language rather than in formal poetic structures. In his poem published below from A Coney Island of the Mind *(1958), he laments the brevity of childhood and innocence. To what extent do you agree with his point of view?*

> The pennycandystore beyond the El
> is where I first
>   fell in love
>   with unreality
> Jellybeans glowed in the semi-gloom
> of that september afternoon
>
> A cat upon the counter moved among
>   the licorice sticks
>   and tootsie rolls
>   and Oh Boy Gum
>
> Outside the leaves were falling as they died
>
> A wind had blown away the sun

A girl ran in
Her hair was rainy
Her breasts were breathless in the little room

Outside the leaves were falling
                and they cried
                        Too soon! too soon!

PROBING FOR MEANING

1. Approximately how old is the speaker of the poem?
2. Why does he think of the candy store as having always been "unreal" to him?
3. What do the dying leaves, the vanishing sun, and the girl have in common?
4. Why do the leaves cry "Too soon! too soon!"?

PROBING FOR METHOD

1. What spatial details describing the penny candy store are included in the poem?
2. What mood does the poem convey? How does the structure of the lines contribute to the mood?
3. What is the effect of writing "pennycandystore" as one word?
4. This short poem does much to help you experience what is being described. Which scene seems the most vivid to you? Why?

BERNARD MALAMUD

The Prison

Bernard Malamud (1914–1986) was a Jewish-American fiction writer who was born in Brooklyn, New York, the setting for many of his works. In The Assistant *(1957), he presents the struggle of Morris Bober, a good man who fails to attain success in society's terms. For his collection of short stories,* The Magic Barrel *(1958), he received the National Book Award. His other novels include* A New Life *(1961) and* The Fixer *(1967), for which he received both the Pulitzer Prize and the National Book Award. As you read "The Prison," think about how you may have responded in Tommy's situation and if you would have chosen as he did.*

Though he tried not to think of it, at twenty-nine Tommy Castelli's life was a screaming bore. It wasn't just Rosa or the store they tended for profits counted in pennies, or the unendurably slow hours and endless drivel that went with selling candy, cigarettes, and soda water; it was this sick-in-the-stomach feeling of being trapped in old mistakes, even some he had made before Rosa changed Tony into Tommy. He had been as Tony a kid of many dreams and schemes, especially getting out of this tenement-crowded, kid-squawking neighborhood, with its lousy poverty, but everything had fouled up against him before he could. When he was sixteen he quit the vocational school where they were making him into a shoemaker, and began to hang out with the gray-hatted, thick-soled-shoe boys, who had the spare time and the mazuma and showed it in fat wonderful rolls down in the cellar clubs to all who would look, and everybody did, popeyed. They were the ones who had bought the silver caffe espresso urn and later the television, and they arranged the pizza parties and had the girls down; but it was getting in with them and their cars, leading to the holdup of a liquor store, that had started all the present trouble. Lucky for him the coal-and-ice man who was their landlord knew the leader in the district, and they arranged something so nobody bothered him after that. Then before he knew what was going on—he had been frightened sick by the whole mess—there was his father cooking up a deal with Rosa Agnello's old man that Tony would marry her and the father-in-law would, out of his savings, open a candy store for him to make an honest living. He wouldn't spit on a candy store, and Rosa was too plain and lank a chick for his personal taste, so he beat it off to Texas and bummed around in too much space, and when he came back everybody said it was for Rosa and the candy store, and it was all arranged again and he, without saying no, was in it.

That was how he had landed on Prince Street in the Village, working from eight in the morning to almost midnight every day, except for an hour off each afternoon when he went upstairs to sleep, and on Tuesdays, when the store was closed and he slept some more and went at night alone to the movies. He was too tired always for schemes now, but once he tried to make a little cash on the side by secretly taking in punchboards some syndicate was distributing in the neighborhood, on which he collected a nice cut and in this way saved fifty-five bucks that Rosa didn't know about; but then the syndicate was written up by a newspaper, and the punchboards all disappeared. Another time, when Rosa was at her mother's house, he took a chance and let them put in a slot machine that could guarantee a nice piece of change if he kept it long enough. He knew of course he couldn't hide it from her, so when she came and screamed when she saw it, he was ready and patient, for once not yelling back when she yelled, and he explained it was not the same as gambling because anybody who played it got a roll of mints every time he put in a nickel. Also the machine would supply them a few extra dollars cash they could use to buy television so he could see the fights without going to a bar; but Rosa wouldn't let up screaming, and later her father came in shouting that he was a criminal and chopped the machine apart with a plumber's hammer. The next day the cops raided for slot machines and gave out summonses wherever they found them, and though Tommy's place was practically the only candy store in the neighborhood that didn't have one, he felt bad about the machine for a long time.

Mornings had been his best time of day because Rosa stayed upstairs cleaning, and since few people came into the store till noon, he could sit around alone, a toothpick in his teeth, looking over the *News* and *Mirror* on the fountain counter, or maybe gab with one of the old cellar-club guys who had happened to come by for a pack of butts, about a horse that was running that day or how the numbers were paying lately; or just sit there, drinking coffee and thinking how far away he could get on the fifty-five he had stashed away in the cellar. Generally the mornings were this way, but after the slot machine, usually the whole day stank and he along with it. Time rotted in him, and all he could think of the whole morning, was going to sleep in the afternoon, and he would wake up with the sour remembrance of the long night in the store ahead of him, while everybody else was doing as he damn pleased. He cursed the candy store and Rosa, and cursed, from its beginning, his unhappy life.

It was on one of these bad mornings that a ten-year-old girl from around the block came in and asked for two rolls of colored tissue paper, one red and one yellow. He wanted to tell her to go to hell and stop bothering, but instead went with bad grace to the rear, where Rosa, whose bright idea it was to keep the stuff, had put it. He went from force of habit, for the girl had been coming in every Monday since the summer for the same thing, because her rock-faced mother, who looked as if she arranged her own widowhood, took care of some small kids after school and gave them the paper to cut out dolls and such things. The girl, whose name he didn't know, resembled her mother, except her features were not quite so sharp and she had very light skin with dark eyes; but she was a plain kid and would be more so at twenty. He had noticed, when he went to get the paper, that she always hung back as if afraid to go where it was dark, though he kept the comics there and most of the other kids had to be slapped away from them; and that when he brought her the tissue paper her skin seemed to grow whiter and her eyes shone. She always handed him two hot dimes and went out without glancing back.

It happened that Rosa, who trusted nobody, had just hung a mirror on the back wall, and as Tommy opened the drawer to get the girl her paper this Monday morning that he felt so bad, he looked up and saw in the glass something that made it seem as if he were dreaming. The girl had disappeared, but he saw a white hand reach into the candy case for a chocolate bar and for another, then she came forth from behind the counter and stood there, innocently waiting for him. He felt at first like grabbing her by the neck and socking till she threw up, but he had been caught, as he sometimes was, by his thought of how his Uncle Dom, years ago before he went away, used to take with him Tony alone of all the kids, when he went crabbing to Sheepshead Bay. Once they went at night and threw the baited wire traps into the water and after a while pulled them up and they had this green lobster in one, and just then this fat-faced cop came along and said they had to throw it back unless it was nine inches. Dom said it was nine inches, but the cop said not to be a wise guy so Dom measured it and it was ten, and they laughed about that lobster all night. Then he remembered how he had felt after Dom was gone, and tears filled his eyes. He found himself thinking about the way his life had turned out, and then about this girl, moved that she was so young and a thief. He felt he ought to do something for her, warn her to cut it out before she got trapped and fouled up her life before it got started. His urge to do this was strong, but when he went forward she looked up frightened because he had taken so long. The fear in her eyes bothered him and he didn't say anything. She thrust out the dimes, grabbed at the tissue rolls and ran out of the store.

He had to sit down. He kept trying to make the desire to speak to her go away, but it came back stronger than ever. He asked himself what difference does it make if she swipes candy—so she swipes it; and the role of reformer was strange and distasteful to him, yet he could not convince himself that what he felt he must do was unimportant. But he worried he would not know what to say to her. Always he had trouble speaking right, stumbled over words, especially in new situations. He was afraid he would sound like a jerk and she would not take him seriously. He had to tell her in a sure way so that even if it scared her, she would understand he had done it to set her straight. He mentioned her to no one but often thought about her, always looking around whenever he went outside to raise the awning or wash the window, to see if any of the girls playing in the street was her, but they never were. The following Monday, an hour after opening the store he had smoked a full pack of butts. He thought he had found what he wanted to say but was afraid for some reason she wouldn't come in, or if she did, this time she would be afraid to take the candy. He wasn't sure he wanted that to happen until he had said what he had to say. But at about eleven, while he was reading the *News*, she appeared, asking for the tissue paper, her eyes shining so he had to look away. He knew she meant to steal. Going to the rear he slowly opened the drawer, keeping his head lowered as he sneaked a look into the glass and saw her slide behind the counter. His heart beat hard and his feet felt nailed to the floor. He tried to remember what he had intended to do, but his mind was like a dark, empty room so he let her, in the end, slip away and stood tongue-tied, the dimes burning his palm.

Afterwards, he told himself that he hadn't spoken to her because it was while she still had the candy on her, and she would have been scared worse than he wanted. When he went upstairs, instead of sleeping, he sat at the kitchen window, looking out into the back yard. He blamed himself for being too soft, too chicken, but then he thought, no there was a better way to do it. He would do it indirectly, slip her a hint he knew, and he was pretty sure that would stop her. Sometime after, he would explain to her why it was good she had stopped. So next time he cleaned out this candy platter she helped herself from, thinking she might get wise he was on to her, but she seemed not to, only hesitated with her hand before she took two candy bars from the next plate and dropped them into the black patent leather purse she always had with her. The time after that he cleaned out the whole top shelf, and still she was not suspicious, and reached down to the next and took something different. One Monday he put some loose change, nickels and dimes, on the candy plate, but she left them there, only taking the candy, which bothered him a little. Rosa asked him what he was mooning about so much and why was he eating chocolate lately. He didn't answer her, and she began to look suspiciously at the women who came in, not excluding the little girls; and he would have been glad to rap her in the teeth, but it didn't matter as long as she didn't know what he had on his mind. At the same time he figured he would have to do something sure soon, or it would get harder for the girl to stop her stealing. He had to be strong about it. Then he thought of a plan that satisfied him. He would leave two bars on the plate and put in the wrapper of one a note she could read when she was alone. He tried out on paper many messages to her, and the one that seemed best he cleanly printed on a strip of cardboard and slipped it under the wrapper of one chocolate bar. It said, "Don't do this any more or you will suffer your whole life." He puzzled whether to sign it A Friend or Your Friend and finally chose Your Friend.

This was Friday, and he could not hold his impatience for Monday. But on Monday she did not appear. He waited for a long time, until Rosa came down, then he had to go up and the girl still hadn't come. He was greatly disappointed because she had never failed to come before. He lay on the bed, his shoes on, staring at the ceiling. He felt hurt, the sucker she had played him for and was now finished with because she probably had another on her hook. The more he thought about it the worse he felt. He worked up a splitting headache that kept him from sleeping, then he suddenly slept and woke without it. But he had awaked depressed, saddened. He thought about Dom getting out of jail and going away God knows where. He wondered whether he would ever meet up with him somewhere, if he took the fifty-five bucks and left. Then he remembered Dom was a pretty old guy now, and he might not know him if they did meet. He thought about life. You never really got what you wanted. No matter how hard you tried you made mistakes and couldn't get past them. You could never see the sky outside or the ocean because you were in a prison, except nobody called it a prison, and if you did they didn't know what you were talking about, or they said they didn't. A pall settled on him. He lay motionless, without thought or sympathy for himself or anybody.

But when he finally went downstairs, ironically amused that Rosa had allowed him so long a time without bitching, there were people in the store and he could hear her screeching. Shoving his way through the crowd he saw in one sickening look that she had caught the girl with the candy bars and was shaking her so hard the kid's head bounced back and forth like a balloon on a stick. With a curse he tore her away from the girl, whose sickly face showed the depth of her fright.

"Whatsamatter," he shouted at Rosa, "you want her blood?"

"She's a thief," cried Rosa.

"Shut your face."

To stop her yowling her slapped her across her mouth, but it was a harder crack than he had intended. Rosa fell back with a gasp. She did not cry but looked around dazedly at everybody, and tried to smile, and everybody there could see her teeth were flecked with blood.

"Go home," Tommy ordered the girl, but then there was a movement near the door and her mother came into the store.

"What happened?" she said.

"She stole my candy," Rosa cried.

"I let her take it," said Tommy.

Rosa stared at him as if she had been hit again, then with mouth distorted began to sob.

"One was for you, Mother," said the girl.

Her mother socked her hard across the face. "You little thief, this time you'll get your hands burned good."

She pawed at the girl, grabbed her arm and yanked it. The girl, like a grotesque dancer, half ran, half fell forward, but at the door she managed to turn her white face and thrust out at him her red tongue.

PROBING FOR MEANING

1. Malamud portrays two different stages in the life of the central character. What were the characteristics of Tony's life as opposed to Tommy's? Why does Tommy keep remembering his Uncle Dom? What was his role in Tony's life?

2. Why did Tommy return from Texas? What does this point out about him?

3. What is your reaction to Rosa? To what extent is she to blame for Tommy's conception of life as a prison?

4. What function does the little girl have in the story? Why is Tommy so upset about her? Why doesn't he confront her? Is Tommy naive in thinking that he could influence her? Why does she react to him as she does at the end?

5. What is Malamud's attitude toward Tommy? Compare Malamud's attitude to your own.

PROBING FOR METHOD

1. From whose point of view is the story told—the author's or Tony's? What effect does this narrative point of view achieve?

2. Describe the introduction to the story. How does the opening set the tone for the entire story?

3. What details does Malamud include to create a claustrophobic atmosphere for the reader as well as for Tommy?

WRITING TOPICS
Generating Ideas on a Place

Freewrite, perhaps in your journal entry in response to one of the following statements.

> *Home is the place where, when you have to go there, They have to take you in.*
>
> Robert Frost

> *Straight wilderness would wipe me out faster than cancer from cigarette smoke.*
>
> Al Young

> *This world is more wonderful than convenient.*
>
> Henry David Thoreau

> *Summertime, oh summertime, pattern of life indelible, the fade-proof lake, the woods unshatterable, the pasture with the sweet fern and the juniper forever and ever, summer without end.*
>
> E. B. White

> *Most places, you can usually be free some of the time if you wake up before other people.*
>
> William Stafford

> *The pennycandystore beyond the el is where I first fell in love with unreality.*
>
> Lawrence Ferlinghetti

> *All the world's a stage.*
>
> William Shakespeare

Topics for Essays on a Place

1. Has any place affected you as intensely as the lake did White, the fig tree did Hellman, or the penny candy store did Ferlinghetti? Describe this place, conveying your response to it through your use of sensuous detail.

2. Write a visual description of a place that you know well. Choose a

specific spatial order as does Hamill to help your reader see it as you do or once did. Select only those sensuous details that create a dominant impression.

3. We all have places of our own that may seem unappealing to other people but that we like very much. Your room, for example, may be messy and chaotic but a refuge nevertheless. Write an essay about a place that is paradoxical in this way, including what is both appealing and unappealing at the same time.

4. In "Once More to the Lake," "On a Kibbutz," and "In the Fig Tree," place evokes an important insight for the author or a character. Write about a place that had a similar effect on you or discuss the interaction between person and place in any two of these selections that made the insight possible.

5. Look over what you have written on the statement you chose for Generating Ideas. Consider whether this material can be revised into an essay or whether any one of the thoughts you expressed can now be expanded into a formal piece of writing. In either case, develop an essay on the topic.

6. Hamill, Malamud, and Ferlinghetti write about places in the city. Write an essay comparing the attitude of one writer toward the city with your own.

7. Places often affect people's behavior. Discuss the influence of the lake, the kibbutz, and 378 Seventh Avenue on the characters in one or two of the selections. How might these or similar places affect people in general? How do you think they would affect you?

8. Discuss the responses to nature of White, Baker, and Bellow. Account as much as possible for the differences in their attitudes. How is their response similar to or different from yours?

9. People's behavior also affects the atmosphere of a place. To what extent has the candy store in "The Prison" been shaped by personal or cultural behavior or attitudes?

10. Ferlinghetti's poem describes place at a moment when a major truth comes into focus for the young narrator. Recall some major awakening in your life—love, death, religion, hatred—and then describe briefly but exactly the place where the awakening occurred so that your mood is also evident.

CHAPTER FOUR

Events and Experiences:

Writing and Rewriting the Essay
Narrating an Event
Revising the Essay

"I was introduced to mortality, not by the old and failing, but by beautiful young men who lay wrecked after sudden explosions of violence," writes Brent Staples in a poignant essay about the murder of his 22-year-old brother. Staples's purpose in writing this intensely personal experience is not only to reveal the complexity of his relationship with his brother, but also to inform his readers of the terrifying reality of ghetto life in America. An essential role of a survivor of any horrifying experience is to testify, to write about the experience because of its value for others; you will share another survivor's experience in Hana Wehle's account of her ambivalence as she returns from the concentration camps to her native city of Prague.

As do Staples and Wehle, the other writers in this chapter recall experiences and narrate events, some pleasant, some unpleasant. In "A Style of My Own," Patrick Fenton, for example, recalls the excitement of becoming a writer, whereas Richard Selzer recounts a horrifying experience in a windowless room, and Alice Walker learns from a traumatic event in her childhood.

In "Trying to Talk with a Man," poet Adrienne Rich explores the complexity of the man-woman relationship, while in a short story Kate Chopin's protagonist "celebrates" the freedom she feels from her husband's death.

A discussion of how to narrate an event begins on page 129, and an analysis of Patrick Fenton's first draft indicates how to revise a piece of writing (pages 136 to 149).

RICHARD SELZER

An Absence of Windows

Richard Selzer (b. 1928) has recently retired as Professor of Surgery at the Yale School of Medicine, and he has written extensively about his experiences as a physician. In 1975 he won the National Magazine Award from Columbia University School of Journalism for his essays published in Esquire. *His books include* Rituals of Surgery *(1974), a volume of short stories, and* Mortal Lessons *(1977) and* Letters to a Young Doctor, *(1982), collections of essays on the life of a physician. As you read Selzer's essay, think about how you might respond to working in "windowless rooms."*

Not long ago, operating rooms had windows. It was a boon and a blessing in spite of the occasional fly that managed to strain through the screens and threaten our very sterility. For the adventurous insect drawn to such a ravishing spectacle, a quick swat and, Presto! The door to the next world sprang open. But for us who battled on, there was the benediction of the sky, the applause and reproach of thunder. A Divine consultation crackled in on the lightning! And at night, in Emergency, there was the pomp, the longevity of the stars to deflate a surgeon's ego. It did no patient a disservice to have Heaven looking over his doctor's shoulder. I very much fear that, having bricked up our windows, we have lost more than the breeze; we have severed a celestial connection.

Part of my surgical training was spent in a rural hospital in eastern Connecticut. The building was situated on the slope of a modest hill. Behind it, cows grazed in a pasture. The operating theater occupied the fourth, the ultimate floor, wherefrom huge windows looked down upon the scene. To glance up from our work and see the lovely cattle about theirs, calmed the frenzy of the most temperamental of prima donnas. Intuition tells me that our patients had fewer wound infections and made speedier recoveries than those operated upon in the airless sealed boxes where now we strive. Certainly the surgeons were of a gentler stripe.

I have spent too much time in these windowless rooms. Some part of me would avoid them if I could. Still, even here, in these bloody closets, sparks fly up from the dry husks of the human body. Most go unnoticed, burn out in an instant. But now and then, they coalesce into a fire which is an inflammation of the mind of him who watches.

Not in large cities is it likely to happen, but in towns the size of ours, that an undertaker will come to preside over the funeral of a close friend; a policeman will capture a burglar only to find that the miscreant is the uncle of his brother's wife. Say that a fire breaks out. The fire truck rushes to the scene; it proves to be the very house where one of the firemen was born, and the luckless man is now called on to complete, axe and hose, the destruction of his natal place. Hardly a civic landmark, you say, but for him who gulped first air within those walls, it is a hard destiny. So it is with a hospital, which is itself a community. Its citizens—orderlies, maids, nurses, x-ray technicians, doctors, a hundred others.

A man whom I knew has died. He was the hospital mailman. It was I that presided over his death. A week ago I performed an exploratory operation upon him for acute surgical abdomen. That is the name given to an illness that is unknown, and for which there is no time to make a diagnosis with tests of the blood and urine, x-rays. I saw him writhing in pain, rolling from side to side, his knees drawn up, his breaths coming in short little draughts. The belly I lay the flat of my hand upon was hot to the touch. The slightest pressure of my fingers caused him to cry out—a great primitive howl of vowel and diphthong. This kind of pain owns no consonants. Only later, when the pain settles in, long and solid, only then does it grow a spine to sharpen the glottals and dentals a man can grip with his teeth, his throat. Fiercely then, to hide it from his wife, his children, for the pain shames him.

In the emergency room, fluid is given into the mailman's veins. Bags of blood are sent for, and poured in. Oxygen is piped into his nostrils, and a plastic tube is let down into his stomach. This, for suction. A dark tarry yield slides into a jar on the wall. In another moment, a second tube has sprouted from his penis, carrying away his urine. Such is the costume of acute surgical abdomen. In an hour, I know that nothing has helped him. At his wrist, a mouse skitters, stops, then darts away. His slaty lips insist upon still more oxygen. His blood pressure, they say, is falling. I place the earpieces of my stethoscope, this ever-asking Y, in my ears. Always, I am comforted a bit by this ungainly little hose. It is my oldest, my dearest friend. More, it is my lucky charm. I place the disc upon the tense mounding blue-tinted belly, gently, so as not to shock the viscera into commotion (those vowels!), and I listen for a long time. I hear nothing. The bowel sleeps. It plays possum in the presence of the catastrophe that engulfs it. We must go to the operating room. There must be an exploration. I tell this to the mailman. Narcotized, he nods and takes my fingers in his own, pressing. Thus has he given me all of his trust.

A woman speaks to me.

"Do your best for him, Doctor. Please."

My best? An anger rises toward her for the charge she has given. Still, I cover her hand with mine.

"Yes," I say, "my best."

An underground tunnel separates the buildings of our hospital. I accompany the stretcher that carries the mailman through that tunnel, cursing for the thousandth time the demonic architect that placed the emergency room in one building, and the operating room in the other.

Each tiny ridge in the cement floor is a rut from which rise and echo still more vowels of pain, new sounds that I have never heard before. Pain invents its own language. With this tongue, we others are not conversant. Never mind, we shall know it in our time.

We lift the mailman from the stretcher to the operating table. The anesthetist is ready with still another tube.

"Go to sleep, Pete," I say into his ear, my lips so close it is almost a kiss. "When you wake up, it will all be over, all behind you."

I should not have spoken his name aloud! No good will come of it. The syllable has peeled from me something, a skin that I need. In a minute, the chest of the mailman is studded with electrodes. From his mouth a snorkel leads to tanks of gas. Each of these tanks is painted a different color. One is bright green. That is for oxygen. They group behind the anesthetist, hissing. I have never come to this place without seeing that dreadful headless choir of gas tanks.

Now red paint tracks across the bulging flanks of the mailman. It is a harbinger of the blood to come.

"May we go ahead?" I ask the anesthetist.

"Yes," he says. And I pull the scalpel across the framed skin, skirting the navel. There are arteries and veins to be clamped, cut, tied, and cauterized, fat and fascia to divide. The details of work engage a man, hold his terror at bay. Beneath us now, the peritoneum. A slit, and we are in. Hot fluid spouts through the small opening I have made. It is gray, with flecks of black. Pancreatitis! We all speak the word at once. We have seen it many times before. It is an old enemy. I open the peritoneum its full length. My fingers swim into the purse of the belly, against the tide of the issuing fluid. The pancreas is swollen, necrotic; a dead fish that has gotten tossed in, and now lies spoiling across the upper abdomen. I withdraw my hand.

"Feel," I invite the others. They do, and murmur against the disease. But they do not say anything that I have not heard many times. Unlike the mailman, who was rendered eloquent in its presence, we others are reduced to the commonplace at the touch of such stuff.

We suction away the fluid that has escaped from the sick pancreas. It is rich in enzymes. If these enzymes remain free in the abdomen, they will digest the tissues there, the other organs. It is the pancreas alone that can contain them safely. This mailman and his pancreas—careful neighbors for fifty-two years until the night the one turned rampant and set fire to the house of the other. The digestion of tissues has already begun. Soap has formed here and there, from the compounding of the liberated calcium and the fat. It would be good to place a tube (still another tube) into the common bile duct, to siphon away the bile that is a stimulant to the pancreas. At least that. We try, but we cannot even see the approach to that duct, so swollen is the pancreas about it. And so we mop and suck and scour the floors and walls of this ruined place. Even as we do, the gutters run with new streams of the fluid. We lay in rubber drains and lead them to the outside. It is all that is left to us to do.

"Zero chromic on a Lukens," I say, and the nurse hands me the suture for closure.

I must not say too much at the operating table. There are new medical students here. I must take care what sparks I let fly toward such inflammable matter.

The mailman awakens in the recovery room. I speak his magic name once more.

"Pete." Again, "Pete," I call.

He sees me, gropes for my hand.

"What happens now?" he asks me.

"In a day or two, the pain will let up," I say. "You will get better."

"Was there any . . .?"

"No," I say, knowing. "There was no cancer. You are clean as a whistle."

"Thank God," he whispers, and then, "Thank *you*, Doctor."

It took him a week to die in fever and pallor and pain.

It is the morning of the autopsy. It has been scheduled for eleven o'clock. Together, the students and I return from our coffee. I walk slowly. I do not want to arrive until the postmortem examination is well under way. It is twenty minutes past eleven when we enter the morgue. I pick the mailman out at once from the others. Damn! They have not even started. Anger swells in me, at being forced to face the *whole* patient again.

It isn't fair! Dismantled, he would at least be at some remove . . . a tube of flesh. But look! There is an aftertaste of life in him. In his fallen mouth a single canine tooth, perfectly embedded, gleams, a badge of better days.

The pathologist is a young resident who was once a student of mine. A tall lanky fellow with a bushy red beard. He wears the green pajamas of his trade. He pulls on rubber gloves, and turns to greet me.

"I've been waiting for you," he smiles. "Now we can start."

He steps to the table and picks up the large knife with which he will lay open the body from neck to pubis. All at once, he pauses, and, reaching with his left hand, he closes the lids of the mailman's eyes. When he removes his hand, one lid comes unstuck and slowly rises. Once more, he reaches up to press it down. This time it stays. The gesture stuns me. My heart is pounding, my head trembling. I think that the students are watching me. Perhaps my own heart has become visible, beating beneath this white laboratory coat.

The pathologist raises his knife.

"Wait," I say. "Do you always do that? Close the eyes?"

He is embarrassed. He smiles faintly. His face is beautiful, soft.

"No," he says, and shakes his head. "But just then, I remembered that he brought the mail each morning . . . how his blue eyes used to twinkle."

Now he lifts the knife, and, like a vandal looting a gallery, carves open the body.

To work in windowless rooms is to live in a jungle where you cannot see the sky. Because there is no sky to see, there is no grand vision of God. Instead, there are the numberless fragmented spirits that lurk behind leaves, beneath streams. The one is no better than the other, no worse. Still, a man is entitled to the temple of his preference. Mine lies out on a prairie, wondering up at Heaven. Or in a many windowed operating room where, just outside the panes of glass, cows graze, and the stars shine down upon my carpentry.

PROBING FOR MEANING

1. Why does Selzer feel that windows in an operating room are "a boon and a blessing"?

2. What was wrong with the mailman? What does Selzer mean when he writes that "pain invents its own language"?

3. Why does Selzer regret having spoken the mailman's name? How does the fact that he knows the mailman personally affect him?

4. What is it that embarrasses the pathologist?

5. At the end of the essay, Selzer writes that windowless rooms are really no better or worse than rooms with windows. What prompts him to write this? Why, despite this, would he prefer to avoid windowless rooms?

PROBING FOR METHOD

1. How does the introductory description of the operating room in the rural hospital in Connecticut help to illustrate the essay's thematic focus?

2. At times, Selzer states directly what he is feeling, as when he becomes angry at finding that the autopsy has not started. What does his narrative help us to understand about his feelings about himself and his profession?

3. Selzer compares the mailman's pancreas to a dead fish. What does this comparison capture about the man's condition? What other analogies does he draw? What effect do they have on the reader?

4. Selzer does not stop to define all the medical terms that he uses. To what

extent does this make his narrative more difficult to understand? What effect does it have on our understanding of the theme of the essay?

5. During the operation, Selzer warns himself against saying too much in front of the new medical students. "I must take care," he says, "what sparks I let fly toward such inflammable matter." Where else do images of sparks and inflammation appear in the essay? What might these images evoke?

Narrating an Event

How does Selzer narrate the events of "An Absence of Windows"?
Selzer begins by comparing and contrasting operating rooms of the past, which had windows, with those of the present, which are windowless, dramatizing as he does so why he prefers those with windows. In his fourth paragraph, which is still an introductory paragraph, he focuses on the hospital as a community in which everyone knows everyone else. In his fifth paragraph, he introduces his subject with the thesis statement. "A man whom I knew has died."

Selzer thus employs a flashback technique for narrating this event. After informing us of the man's death, he returns to the day a week earlier when he had first noticed that the man, the hospital mailman, was in pain. He then proceeds chronologically through the events leading to the man's death: his examination of him in the emergency room, the operation, their conversation in the recovery room, his death, and the autopsy. He concludes the essay by returning to his preference for rooms with windows, thus building a frame around the essay.

Why did Selzer inform us of the man's death at the beginning? His purpose was not to build suspense, which a straight chronological order would have done, but to diffuse the suspense and instead concentrate on how he felt about failing to save someone he knew, about having to perform an autopsy on his body. His emphasis was not on what happened but on his reactions to what happened.

Selzer enriched his narrative in several ways. He uses vivid imagery to enable the reader to picture the man's body, both before and after death: "My fingers swim into the purse of the belly." "The pancreas is swollen, necrotic; a dead fish that has gotten tossed in, and now lies spoiling across the abdomen." He describes the man's belly as a house, a "ruined place," the man and his pancreas as "careful neighbors for fifty-two years until the night the one turned rampant and set fire to the house of the other." He describes the man's death as "a fire which is an inflammation of the mind of him who watches," cautioning himself to "take care what sparks I let fly toward such inflammable matter" as new medical students.

He also uses the present verb tense: "A man whom I knew has

died" through to the end of the narrative: "Now he lifts the knife, and, like a vandal looting a gallery, carves open the body." The present tense creates a sense of immediacy, a sense that the reader is living through the experience the narrator is relating.

Selzer has answered vividly the questions any narrator must answer: the who, where, when, how, why, and what happened of the event. We know the patient is the hospital mailman and that he had blue eyes that twinkled when he brought the mail each morning, and we know that the pathologist, "a tall lanky fellow with a bushy red beard" and dressed in "the green pajamas of his trade," has a beautiful, soft face. We do not need to know more about either man, but we do need to know these things about both men.

As a physician, Selzer concentrates primarily on answering the "how" question, supplying, as we have seen, great detail about how doctors both examine patients and operate on them. Perhaps unlike most physicians he also attempts to explain "why" in his discussion of preferring windowed rooms (the "where") that allow Heaven to look over his shoulder as he performs his "carpentry."

Narrating an event.
A good narration includes a meaningful event, thoughtful organization, a clear point of view, and telling details that evoke interest and contribute to meaning.

Many events seem to happen at random, either because they are unexpected or because the participants do not invest them with meaning. In narrating an event, however, you, as narrator, should decide beforehand what meaning you wish to convey to the reader. This meaning will give unity to your essay if you select your organization, point of view, and details with this theme in mind. This meaning does not have to be earth-shattering, just as the event you write about need not be cataclysmic; it must, however, matter to you.

How you organize the essay often helps to convey the meaning of an event. In the essays in this chapter, Richard Selzer and Brent Staples use flashback techniques that allow them to announce that the event has significance from the outset, and Hana Wehle's flashbacks immeasurably enrich her narrative of her train ride home from the concentration camp. Whereas Selzer's and Staples's pattern is fairly simple in that they begin at the end of the event, flash back to the beginning, and proceed chronologically to the end again, Wehle's is much more complex, as her mind darts back and forth across her life in no discernible pattern. On the other hand, Alice Walker uses a straight chronological approach, perhaps because the events she recounts are dramatic enough by themselves to suggest meaning, as Wehle's train ride, Selzer's hospital routine, and Staples's occupation are not.

All of the narrators are involved in the action, as indeed are most narrators of personal experience. However, the degree of their involvement differs. Wehle and Walker are the foci of their narratives, whereas Selzer shares the stage with the ailing mailman and Staples is concerned with his brother's life as well as his own.

Telling details flesh out the framework provided by meaning, organization, and point of view. Without them, the narrative is a spindly skeleton indeed. Telling a good story is an ancient art, and people still love to hear one. They love the suspense and appreciate the meaning, but above all they remember the details. Having finished Selzer's essay, one remembers the vivid descriptions of the patient's cavernous stomach; once finished with "A Brother's Murder," one remembers the "line of stitches [that] lay between the thumb and index finger," just as one is most impressed with Wehle's grandmother's dumplings and the "glob of whitish scar tissue" on Walker's blind eye. Through details, the narrative springs to life.

Procedures to follow in narrating an event.

A. Choose an event that you have witnessed or an experience you have had that you wish to convey to a reader. Impart the meaning of the event to the reader as you narrate the experience.
B. Organize your essay to establish a narrative pattern—either straight chronology or a flashback arrangement.
C. Decide on your point of view as narrator. Will you be an actor in the event or a spectator on the sidelines—or somewhere in between?
D. Select telling details that will grasp the imagination of the reader. Answer the journalist's questions—who, where, when, how, what happened, and why—as fully as is necessary for your reader to participate in your narrative.

PATRICK FENTON

A Style of My Own

Patrick Fenton (b. 1941) is a free-lance writer who was born in Brooklyn's Irish tenements on St. Patrick's Day. His writing has appeared in the New York Times, New York Magazine, Newsday, *and the* New York Daily News. *He has appeared on radio and television programs and has often spoken on col-*

lege campuses. He wrote this essay specifically for this book and his first draft appears immediately following, along with his comments about writing and revising the essay.

During the '50s, a grammar school education at Holy Name parochial school in the Park Slope section of Brooklyn was as good as any you might receive at an exclusive private school today, probably better. I spent the most impressive part of my youth there learning to read and learning the mechanics of writing the composition. But there was one important thing the nuns of Holy Name failed to teach me about writing: how to be sloppy, how to cross out sentences over and over again in the search for the right words—how to indulge in creative scribbling. I still remember the nuns in their black and white habits walking between the rows of desks, nodding in approval as they looked down at neat sentences all lined up properly—like soldiers in formation. Guilt would run through me whenever I drifted away from this style and filled a page with cross-outs, write-ins, and notes to myself. For a long time I felt that even if you did manage to write something good from this creative scribbling, how could you ever tell someone you had to write a paragraph ten times before you felt it was finished?

It was common in the neighborhood to leave school at an early age and go off to work in the factories of Bay Ridge. At sixteen, I dropped out of high school and went to work down in Quaker Maid, a gray, prison-like factory on the Brooklyn waterfront. I spent my teenage years working in factories like this, running up and down the hard slats of wooden floors as I tried to keep up with the race of conveyor belts around me. Formal education was over for me, but the part of me that wanted to be a writer was beginning to stir as I looked around me at people who had spent their whole lives working in the bleakness of Brooklyn's waterfront factories.

I spent all my free time reading, reading on the Hamilton Avenue bus as it bounced down Prospect Avenue towards Industry City, reading up on the hot tar roofs of the tenements that surrounded 17th Street like walls, reading down on the long bays of the beaches of Coney Island. I read things like Harold Robbins' *A Stone For Danny Fisher* (called junk by most literary critics of the '50s, but to me it had a sort of Brooklyn pathos to it), *The Amboy Dukes,* and occasionally something truly great, like Alfred Kazin's, *A Walker In The City.* I remember buying this book kind of by accident, because I liked the line drawings inside it of elevated train stations and wash flying like flags of poverty in tenement yards, the very props that made up the stage of my own life.

Slowly my reading built up to more sophisticated levels. I started to read collections of *The New Yorker* stories and articles, which were filled with brilliant work by Eudora Welty, V. S. Pritchett, J. D. Salinger, Saul Bellow, and Roger Angell. When I discovered an author that I really liked, I would go to the library and take out all his or her books.

My head was full of words that would help me explain some of the swells of emotion that I felt in the factories, but when I tried to get it down on paper I just couldn't make the connection of mind to page. In the beginning I thought it should come more easily to me. I was afraid to take chances, afraid to move away from the comfortable clichés that were set in my mind by the nuns of Holy Name. There were two significant incidents in my life that changed this. One happened by accident. One day I was up in the great books section of the New York Public Library on 5th Avenue and I saw something that amazed me. I looked at the actual, rough drafts of the poet Walt Whitman's *Leaves of Grass*, and I saw that it was filled with the same false starts, the same cross-outs, and the same write-ins that covered my own writing.

The other incident was getting my first by-line in a Brooklyn weekly newspaper, the *Park Slope News*, a local paper whose editors were known to have worked with several Brooklyn writers who went on to the daily newspapers. It was here that I learned to think an article out. I learned to write under a deadline, which forces you to get it all down on paper so you can see what you have, or what you don't have. Most beginning writers make the mistake of mulling over the opening paragraph of a story too long. They lose the chance to have three or four paragraphs down on paper, which presents choices. They lose the choice of moving up one of the new paragraphs to the opening, which often results in a more dramatic beginning.

With the encouragement of a young editor on the *Park Slope News*, Marian Leifsen, who saw a spark of talent in the rubble of an overwritten piece I sent her about the Irish tenements of Brooklyn, I was invited to submit more stories to the paper. With her help, I spent the next three years learning how to write a sentence with a goal other than just winning the approval of a nun. I wrote about what I knew best, my world, which was made up of swing shifts in factories, sounds of garbage bags crashing in tenement yards, junk men screaming in hallways on Saturday mornings, and Sunday afternoons where life was celebrated over pitchers of beer at christenings and weddings in brightly lit American Legion halls.

The night that the politician George Wallace was shot, I received a phone call from Marian Leifsen asking me to come to the paper's office, which was in Bay Ridge, and do a piece on my reaction to it. They were closing out the week's issue, so I would have to write it on deadline. If I had known what that was like, I probably would not have shown up.

I usually did my first drafts in long hand on long, yellow legal pads (I still use them to work out tough paragraphs), but I knew they would want me to write it right from the typewriter. "Don't worry," Marian assured me. "I'll give you a hand if you get stuck." The most nerve-wracking part was, every five minutes the owner of the paper would stick his head out of the office and yell, "for Christ's sake, hasn't he got it yet?" The finished essay, "A Gut Reaction To The Wallace Shooting," turned out to be among some of the more lasting pieces that I did for the *Park Slope News*. More than that, it taught me that sometimes you have to force it out; you have to reach inside of yourself and take chances.

There was always a feeling of awe whenever something I wrote for the paper drew letters—letters that acknowledged my very existence as a writer. I experienced other times when just writing a simple sentence became so difficult it left me drained. At these times, I felt that I had no right to call myself a writer. By studying the lives of other writers, however, I learned that even professionals go through this sort of writer's block. The important thing was not to give up, to keep the words coming, like a prize fighter trying to bust out of the ropes with a flurry of punches—hoping some of them will land on target. Jack Kerouac, the Beat Generation writer who wrote *On The Road*, had a strong influence on me with the way he was able to get a great amount of New England, small town gloominess into the long, rolling sentences he used in *Dr. Sax*. I learned a lot about using the short sentence by reading the Nick Adams stories of Ernest Hemingway. I thought over the importance of what George Orwell had to say in his essay, "Why I Write." He warned that if a writer "escapes from his early influences altogether, he will have killed his impulse to write." For me, that was the single, most important lesson I ever learned about writing: write about what you know best. Write about who you are.

I read all the Orwell essays, studying his crisp style, his ability to take the most common theme, man's everyday existence, and to build on it until he turned it into something with the brilliance of *Down and Out in Paris and London*. I read the tabloids, the *New York Post* and the *Daily News*, where Jimmy Breslin and Pete Hamill wrote about the city in prose that caught the very soul of it. I studied the *New York Times* for its great foreign dispatch stories that made you feel you were in Istanbul or Paris.

I was fortunate to be learning to write in a time when good writing was everywhere. The *Village Voice*, a New York weekly, was filled with the writing of some of the freshest writers in the country. There was much to be learned from the work of Jean Shepherd, Joe Flaherty, Norman Mailer, Jack Newfield, and Jack Deacy. It was encouraging to know that Jack Deacy and Joe Flaherty had also started on the *Park Slope News*.

The *Park Slope News* was a great place to spend time finding a style, a place to come out of. I interviewed local celebrities, covered beauty contests in Bay Ridge, wrote about politicians, food, bar fights. I wrote about growing up on 17th Street in Park Slope when it was the hub of one of the greatest Irish working-class sections of Brooklyn, a time of pie hawkers, rag men and ice men selling kerosene to warm the tenements.

One night, after covering a story down at the Brooklyn Navy Yard, where the writer Pete Hamill's movie, *Badge 373*, was being filmed, his brother Denis invited me back to their house for a beer. Denis told me that Charlie Monaghan, a local editor, had read one of my stories, "My Night in Ryan's Bar," and that he wanted to speak to me about it. He pushed me to call Monaghan, which eventually I did, and it led to an interview with Byron Dobell, who was the editor of *New York* magazine.

After a long talk in his office, Byron looked over my clips from the paper, stared at me for a second, and said—"you're a writer." After three years of writing, reading, grinding out stories for the *Park Slope News*, my writing had started to shape into that mysterious thing called "a style of your own." I went home and wrote "Confessions Of A Working Stiff," a long personal story that really should have been a book. It took me just three nights to write it. The story just flowed out.

After "Confessions" came out in *New York* magazine in 1973, it led to a career in free-lance writing for me. There are still nights that I find myself struggling with a sentence, unable to get what I want from a word, a phrase, but I get over it by looking at a letter I received from the writer, Alfred Kazin. It hangs in a frame above my work area. In it, he has revised the first part of it by bolding crossing out some words in the fourth sentence with blue pen. It is marked with some of the same cross-outs and write-ins that I once felt so guilty about when I first started to write.

PROBING FOR MEANING

1. What did Fenton "learn" about writing from the nuns? Is his experience familiar to you? Why or why not?

2. Although he dropped out of school at sixteen, why was Fenton still interested in reading? To what extent do you share his love of books?

3. Why, despite all he was learning about words, did Fenton have trouble writing about his experiences?

4. What two incidents helped him get rid of his "writer's block"?

5. Some of the writers Fenton talks about, like Saul Bellow, Alfred Kazin, Pete Hamill, and George Orwell, are included in this anthology. Read the selections of those writers with whom you are unfamiliar.

6. "Write about what you know best. Write about who you are." Why is this good advice?

7. Describe your overall response to Fenton's struggle to become a writer. Are there any aspects of his experience with which you identify? Why or why not?

PROBING FOR METHOD

1. How effectively does Fenton's introductory paragraph prepare the reader for what will follow in the essay?

2. What was Fenton's purpose in writing this essay? Is he mainly recalling his own experiences as a writer or does he also want to influence his readers? Explain your answer.

3. Fenton wrote this essay for a particular audience—college students like yourself. To what extent is he successful in reaching that audience?

4. How would you characterize the tone of the essay? Is his tone consistent with his purpose and audience? Why or why not?

5. Although Fenton is writing an essay about his experiences in becoming a writer, how does the inclusion of specific details about people and places make his essay more effective?

Rough Draft

A Style of My Own

~~Early Influences~~

by

Patrick Fenton

Manual

Writing came hard to me. At sixteen, I dropped out of ~~Manalel~~
Training High School in South Brooklyn and went to work down in
Industry City, a factorey town that ran along the Brooklyn waterfront. My head was always full of the words that would help me
explain some of the swells of emotions that were going on inside
of me at this time, but when I tryed to get them down on paper I
couldn't make the connection of mind to page. In the beginning I
was afraid to take chances, afraid to move away from the comfort-

cliches   strict
able ~~cliques~~ that were set in my mind by ~~aiged~~ nuns in the ~~AA444A~~
classrooms of Holy Name Parochial school.

OPEN WITH THIS?
                                                    Parochial
                                                    School
During the '50s, a grammer school education at Holy Name was
in the Park Slope Section of Brooklyn
                                                         n
as good as any~~thing~~ you might ~~learn~~ at a exclusive private school
                              receive
today, probably better. But there was one thing the nuns failed to
teach me about writing; how to be sloppy, how to cross out sentences
over and over again in the search for the right words––how to indulge in creative scribbling. I still remember them walking be-
                    in their black and white habits

tween the desks, nodding as they looked down at neat sentences *in approval*

properly lined up, like soldiers in formation.

NEW
PAR Guilt would run through me whenever I drifted away from this style

and filled a page with crooss-outs, write-ins, and notes to my-

self. For a long time I felt that even if you did manage to write

something good from this creative scribbling, how could you ever

tell someone you had to write one paragraph ten times before you

were finished?

~~With the help of Mariann Leifsen~~

This guilt stayed with me even after I managed to ~~sell~~ *get* a story

published in ~~to~~ the Park Slope News, a local newspaper in our area that was know

to have worked with several Brookly writers who went on to write

for the New York dailies. ~~The most important~~ With the help of

~~Mariann Leifsen, the editor of the paper, I spent three years~~

~~learning what~~ how to write ~~without seeking the approval of a nun a~~

~~sentence withou~~ with a goal other than just ~~seeking the approval~~ *Winning*

~~of a nun.~~

move up

~~The first that I~~ The ~~Park Slope News~~ *paper* was the first place my

writing ever appeared with a by-line; thanks to a young editor who

seen ~~something~~ a spark of talent ~~aught up in the~~ somewhere in the

good up to here

rubble

~~words~~ of an overwritten piece. Reading it again,   some 17 years

later, I notice two important things: It needs triming, to be

sure, but it has a constant theme running through it, ~~it~~ *I* touches on

an important subject that would later be written about over and

over again/ gentrification. ~~The piece talks about~~ ''It could

drive the Puerto Ricans, who have taken the place of the Irish, off

of 17th Street. They can't go mahh further without reaching

Greenwood Cemetery.''

At sixteen, I dropped out of high school and went to work down

in Quaker Maid, a gray, prison ~~facterey~~-like factory on the Brook-

lyn waterfront. I spent ~~most of~~ my teenage years working in

factories like this, running up and down the hard slats of wooden

floors as I tryed to keep up withthe race of conveyer belts that

around?

surrounded me. Formal education may have been over for me, but the

part of me that ~~ala~~ always wanted to be a writer ~~was~~ was just ~~begin-~~ *starting*

beginning

~~ning~~ to ~~look at~~ stir ~~to life~~, ~~I never believed that~~ as I looked

this?

around ~~u~~ at people who had spent most of their life working in the

bleakness of Brooklyn's waterfront factories.   ~~Like desparate~~

~~characters in an Arthur Miller play~~

I spent all my free time reading, reading on the Hamilton

Avenue Bus as it bounced doen Prospect Avenue ~~in th~~ heading towards the ~~factories~~ *Industry City*, reading up on the *hot tar* roofs of the tenements of ~~our neighborhood~~ *17 Street*, down on the long bays of the beaches of Coney

Island. I read thi*n*gs like Harold Robbins, ''A Stone For Danny

Fisher'' (called junk by most litery critcs, but to me it had a sort *in the fifties*

of Brooklyn *P*athos to it.) ~~When I could I~~ ~~++The Amboy Dukes novels of street gangs~~

''The Amboy Dukes'', and occaisonely something truly great like

Alfred Kazins ''A Walker In The City.'' I remember buying the book

by accident because I liked the line drawings inside of it of

~~s~~-elevated train stations, wash flying like flags ~~in~~ ~~the poverty of~~ tenement

yards; the very props that ~~made up my own life were back stage in my~~ *flags of poverty*

~~own life.~~ *were part of the stage of my own life.*

~~Eventually, my reading~~ Slowly my reading ~~drifted~~ *Built up* ~~graduated up~~ ov~~er~~ to

more sophisticated writing. I startedto read colections of New

Yorker Magazine stories, which was filled with stories by Eudora *brilliant*

Wetly, J.D. Sallenger, Saul Bellow and V.S. Pritchett. When I ~~fou~~

discovered a favorite, one with a style ^*that* ~~put life in the writing for~~

~~me.~~ I would go down to the librarey and try to read all ~~their works~~ *of them*.

xx

My head was full of words that would help me explain some of the *in the factories*

swells of emotion I felt ~~when I looked around I looked back at some~~

~~of the factories I workkd in~~ but when I tryed to get them down on paper I just couldn't make the connection of mind to page. In the

beginning I thought it should come more easly to me. I was afraid to

take chances, afraid to move away from the comfortable qliques

that were set in my mind by the nuns of Holy Name. There were two

significant incidents in my life ~~that would efect my writing and~~ *that changed this*

~~help me find a sense of style~~. One happened by accident. One day I

was up in the great books section of the New York Public Library on

5th Avenue and I saw something that amazed me. I looked at the

actual, rough drafts of the poet Walt Whitman's Leaves of Grass,

and I saw that it was filled with the same false starts, the same

cross-outs, and the same write-ins that coverd my own writing.

The other inceident was getting my first by-line in a Brooklyn

weekly newspaper. *the Park Slope News* , a local newspaper that was

known to have worked with several Brooklyn writers who went on to

write for New York dailies. I t was here that I learned to think an

articœle out. I learned to write under a deadline, ~~where you just~~

~~can't anounce where you~~ no longer have the luxurey of   which

forces you to rush forward into ~~the story.~~ a story. ~~Most beginning~~

~~writers make the mistake of mulling over a story too much, like a~~

~~bather slipping slowly into cold water too long. Like a bather~~

~~slippipping,~~ *f* *all* forces you to get it down on paper so you can see what you have. Most beginning writers make the mistake of mulling over the opening paragraph of a story too long; they loose the chance of having three or four paragtaphs in front of them which presents *To choose from?* choices. ~~It presents a chance to move up one of the new paragraphs which may result in a more dramatic opening~~ They loose the choice to move up one of the new paragraphs, which may result in a more dramatic opening.

Thanks to a young editor on the Park Slope News, Marion Leifsen, who seen a spark of talent in the rubble of an overwritten piecex ~~It was invited to write write more stories for the paper.~~ *I showed her?* ~~mailed out of the Iris~~ written in the Irsh tenements of Brooklyn, I was invited to write more stories for the paper. With her help, I spent the next three years learning how to write a sentence with a goal other than just winning the approval of a nun. I wrote about what I knew best. My world, *which* was made up of ~~earning wages in factor-~~ *growing up in Brooklyn?* ~~ies, bar-fights~~, swing shifts in bleak factories, sounds of garbage landing in tenement backyards, junkmen, and ~~long-hours~~ ~~pushing cabs through the~~ weekends where *life was celebrated* ~~you shoved your arm into~~ celebrated life over pitchers of beer at chrisenings *and* ~~commu-~~ ~~nions held in vast~~ and weddings in brightly lit American Legion Halls.

The *southern?*
politician?

The night that George Wallace was shot, I received a phone call from Marriann Leifsen asking me to come down to the paper's office, which was in Bay Ridge, and do a piece on my reaction to it. They were closing out the weeks issue, so I would have to write it on deadline. This would be the first time I ever ~~write~~ *wrote* anything with someone urging me to finish it quickly. If I had known what ~~it~~ *that* was like, I probably would have never shown up.

I useuly did my first drafts *in long-hand* on long, yellow legal pads, (I still use them a lot to work out tough paragraphs.) but I knew they would want me to do it right off of the typewriter. ''Don't woory'', Marion told me. ''I'll give you a hand if you get stuck.'' The most nerve wracking part~~,was~~was, every five minutes the ~~editor~~ owner of the paper would stick his head out of his office and yell, ''for Christ sakes,hasn't he got it yet?'' The finished piece, ~~turned out to be s~~ ''A Gut Reaction To The Wallace Shoot-
? wound up as?
ing'', turned out to be one of the more lasting pieces that I did for the Park Slope News. It taught me ~~that~~ not to be afriad of coming
More than that,
up empty when I write. ~~I~~t taught me that sometimes you have to force
yourself
it out,you have to reach inside of ~~yoorself~~ and take chances.

Working on a weekly newspaper gives you a knowledge you could
never learn up at Columbia Journalisem School. ~~One of the first~~
~~things you learn is that words should be considered very carefully~~
they're
~~before their committed to paper, few learn that words are power.~~
~~They draw reaction, change sometimes not friendly, change~~ You
learn that when you sit down ~~to a~~ at a typewriter, your no differnt
than a ~~musician getting ready to tune up~~ musician getting ready to
play a fine song, an actor getting ready to ca   a mood, a nuance.

After three years of interviewing local celebrities, ~~(one
of my most profoundest interviews was a guy from Bay Ridge who had
invented a baseball bat with a hole in it. He claimed it would help
to develop your swing. xx Over his picture which ran on the front
page, a two inch headline read. ''MURDER VICTIM FOUND ON 70th
STREET,''~~)

The Park Slope News was a place to spend time finding a style, a
place to come out of. I interviewd local celebrities, covered
beauty contests in Bay Ridge, wrote about politicians, food, bar
fights, and growing up on i7th Street, which was once the hub of
one of the greatest Irish working-class sections of Brooklyn. One

night, after covering a story down at the Brooklyn Navy Yard,

where the writer Pete Hamill's movie, Badge 373, was being filmed,

~~his brother Brian invited me back to their house for a beer with~~
his brother
Brian Hamill and Denis ~~Hamill~~ invited me back to their house for a

beer. Denis told me that Charlie Monaghan, a local editor, had

read one of my stories, ~~on~~ ''A Night At Ryan's Bar'', and wanted to
speak
~~talk~~ to me about it. He pushed me to call Moanaghan, ~~which lead~~ to
who set up an
an interview with, Byron Dobell, the editor of New York Magazine.

in New York Magazine

This led to publication of, ''Confessions Of A Working

Stiff'', a long autobographical story that really should have

been a book. Eventully, because I was ~~al~~mostly writing about the

people I knew when I was growing up in Brooklyn's Irsh tenements,

I was identified as a working-claas writer. It's important for you
tudent   thats not the worst
of writing to know, as a ~~beginning writer~~, that ~~know~~writing about what you

know best will give your writing strenght. Orweel pbobaly said

it best in ''Why I Write'': ''It's his job, no doubt, to discipline
avoid
his temperament and ~~avld~~ getting stuck at some immature stage;

or in some perverse mood; but if he escapes from his early influ-

ences altogether, he will have killed his impulse to write. For

me, that was the single, most imporatnt lesson I ~~lea~~ ever learned

about writing.

~~After years of trying to puzzle the whole thing out. I could~~

Over the years I've done radio shwos and television, spoke at colleges, all the while perfection my own writing by reading what other writers have to say about style. There are times when writing a simple sentence becomes so difficult, the sheer effort of it leaves me so drained, I feel I have no right to call myself a writer. ~~It's at those times that I call up memories of pieces where essays I've written that caught moods, other times, as if I relived them.~~ I'm constantly learning to look at writing in new ways, learning how to bust out of a blank spot on the page, *Sometimes* when words escape me; like a prize fighter busting out from the ropes with a flurry of punches—hoping one of them will land on target.

The writer, Pete Hamill, once ~~told me in a letter~~ ~~advised me~~ in *Said to me that* . Writers, in a sense, are a lot like actors—they do the thing over and over again until the right ~~mood is there~~ emotion is there; the right nuance that captures mood is there. ~~Not having any formal schooling in writing turned out to be an asset for me, not a hadny cap~~ ~~You may think that not having any formal schooling turned ou was a handycap for me. Actually in writing was a handycap~~ *to* ~~for me.~~ *It was hardly that* ~~Actually it turned out to be an asset~~ *Not having a formal education* . ~~It~~ forced me to go out to the libraries ~~and learn on my own~~ and think out for myself

what the great writers ~~had learned.~~ were saying

        like you, I was

    At first ~~I was like you~~ uncertain who I was trying to make con-

tact with, who I was writing for. Soon I realized that the ~~only~~

~~person you can write~~ strongest writing comes from ~~wrighting for~~

~~yourself.~~ When you write for yourself, Not when you just write what you think others want to read.

~~I taught over what Orwell had to say in his essay, ''Why I Write'',~~

~~and I asked myself~~ I taught over the importance of what George

Orwell had to say in his essay, ''Why I Write.'' I read all his

essays studying their crisp style, their ability to take the

most simplest of themes and to ~~build on th em bring the reader along~~

~~with him~~ build on them until the reader understood their was an

important message coming. I studied the Nick Adams stories of

Hemingway to learn about the short sentences. I read all of James

Thurber's books and found that they were a gift for much more than

               fine way

~~the humor they~~ humor. He had a ~~fine way of writing about~~ capturing

         The life of everyday people

~~life~~ in small town America that was equal to the talent Norman

Rockwell gave us in his painting. One theme ran through all the

great books for me, ~~one lesson, each~~ writer ~~had spoken looked at~~

life ~~in a way that had a~~ that was new. I still try to do that

I still read a lot of newspapers, books, magazines, and my head is alawys full of stories that have impressed me. ~~I still use writing as a weapon, not so much to keep me alive, but to make me feel alive~~. Writing still comes to hard to me, I'm still crosing out, writing notes to myself. I have thought about ''why I write'', and the answer I come up with is quiet simple: It ~~makes me feel more~~
It makes me feel alive, alive as I did when I —
of ~~a part of a fall day when I can describe the birth~~ of feelings
whenever I think that my fear might be getting in the way of my
~~that comes with it. It makes me wonder about life~~.
Writing honestly I think of a day when I first started writing for the

Revising the Essay

How did Patrick Fenton revise his essay "A Style of My Own"?
The author recalls, "When this draft was done, it confused me. I was so caught up with different thoughts that it was like trying to hold onto a team of horses pulling me in different directions. I had to stop and ask what do I have here? I realized I had brainstormed the thing out and that now I had to revise it. I then rewrote the essay and added the last paragraph. I think a first draft is a rock that you have to chip away at to get the statue out."

Comparing the two drafts, we see that he deleted his original introductory paragraph because it was not unified; it tried to do too much. His final draft begins with what was originally his second paragraph, and this paragraph, in addition to being more unified, puts the essay into a more general context at the very beginning.

In his first draft, he introduced Marian Leifsen, the editor of the *Park Slope News*, in the third paragraph. In the final draft, he consolidates mention of her by eliminating it at this point and discussing her later (page 133). He also eliminates the other paragraph on page 137 that mentions his work with that newspaper, and we also find that the mention of the *Park Slope News* on page 143 of the rough draft is moved to the end of the revised draft, and a paragraph has been added to introduce it. The effect of these revisions is to focus on his struggles with writing before moving to his success with the paper.

Also on page 143, he eliminates two paragraphs because mention of the Columbia School of Journalism and the anecdote about interviewing local celebrities detract from his story; they are side issues to his development as a writer.

The original conclusion of the essay has been deleted because it was rambling and repetitive. The conclusion he substitutes is much more effective for several reasons. First, he uses "Confessions of a Working Stiff" as the springboard to what he is doing now. Second, he looks at the subject from a slightly different perspective by mentioning the letter from Alfred Kazin. Also, he again mentions his guilt about his sloppy writing, and this distribution of a theme he introduced at the beginning of the essay reinforces the unity of the essay.

In his first draft, as he says, he was brainstorming or writing freely with no concern for grammar, spelling, or punctuation. Mr. Fenton feels strongly that you should not be concerned with correcting grammar at this point in the writing process because this could block your thinking. In his final draft, on the other hand, he has been careful to write correctly.

Revising the essay.
In order to focus and unify a piece of writing, writers will adopt one or more of several revision strategies. They may add, delete, rearrange, substitute, consolidate, or distribute.

Adding means that material—a word, sentence, or paragraph—is inserted to clarify the subject.

Deleting means that material that distracts from what is being said about the subject is cut.

Rearranging means that parts are moved around in order to make the organization more effective.

Substituting means that material—a word, sentence, or paragraph—is changed to make the meaning clearer.

Consolidating means that because too many references to an aspect of the subject detract from the importance of that aspect or destroy the overall unity of the subject, all material on that aspect is brought together in one part of the essay.

Distributing is the opposite of consolidating. It means that an aspect of the subject which in the original was mentioned only once is now mentioned throughout because of its importance for creating unity.

Procedures for revising your essay.
Whether you used freewriting in starting to compose your first draft or tried to write an already organized piece of writing, you might consider whether your essay would benefit from any of the revision strategies. If you work in

groups, your group members may give you feedback as well.

1. Has important information or transitional material been left out that you might add now?
2. Does every sentence and every paragraph contribute directly to your subject, or should some material be deleted?
3. Do your points follow in a logical order such as least important to most important or, as in a narrative, from beginning to end, or should they be rearranged for a greater impact?
4. Paragraphs that often need substitutions are the introduction and conclusion. Are you happy with yours, or might you substitute better ones?
5. Have you scattered references to an important aspect of your subject throughout the essay, thus reducing its impact or mentioning it before it is effective to do so? If so, you might consolidate your discussion in one part of the essay.
6. Have you mentioned an important theme and then dropped it? Or have you neglected to introduce a theme that you should have mentioned from the very beginning? If so, you will want to distribute mention of this theme throughout the essay.

HANA WEHLE

The Return

Hana Wehle (b. 1917) was born in Prague, Czechoslovakia. She spent several years in Terezin (Theresienstadt), Birkenau-Auschwitz, and Stutthof. Her first husband was killed by the SS in Terezin. When she returned to Prague after the defeat of the Nazis in 1945, she met and married a fellow survivor. Wehle is now living in New York and has published several essays about her experiences in the concentration camps. As you read ''The Return,'' compare reactions you have had to returning to a place you haven't seen for a long time with those of the author.

The air raid sirens are quiet, the bombers are grounded, the bowels of the crematoria furnaces are covered with human ashes—the war is over.

My face presses against the cool windowpane of the train carrying repatriates from various parts of Europe. My destination: Prague, Czechoslovakia. As the black engine hisses through the German countryside, the cities of the Reich stare at me from under the ashes and ruins. I plunge again into the nightmare of the recent past, to be awakened occasionally by the penetrating sound of the engine whistle.

"QUARANTINE"—the big letters obstruct my view. I am lying among the many half-corpses on the wooden planks. My body is tossing restlessly with typhoid fever. My lips are parched, my eyes are searching for water. Unconsciously, my head is turning toward the slowly opening door of the barracks. I see my mother's pale, frightened face. She forces a smile as she nods. She has come to say goodbye before I die. Or—is it she who is parting from me? With glassy eyes I am trying desperately to send her a smile. The monotonous sound of the clattering wheels overshadows the mirage of my mother's face. The wheels are turning on the shiny rails as the train crawls around a bend. My hollowed-out soul struggles to separate my thoughts of the bottomless pit of death from the sounds of whistle and clatter. . . .

The engine puffs out the last cloud of steam and the train comes to a stop. Clutching my shabby bundle of belongings, I uncertainly descend the steps of the train. Soon I am swallowed up by the once so familiar noise and smell of the railroad station. My legs march with the crowds. Once I belonged to them as they belonged to me. There was a balance and harmony in which everyone was both himself and a part of others. Today, a strange, invisible wall of loneliness and fear separates me from them. I never knew that the arrival would be as hard as the departure. In the camps, freedom had seemed so unattainable, glorious and beautiful!

Now I am not marching as I dreamed I would. My body is filling up mercilessly with pain. I see the Square of Saint Wenceslas, the beautiful center of the city of Prague, as it unfolds in front of me. Its pavement, it seems, still reverberates with the sound of marching boots; the frozen eyes, half hidden under the caps of the SS uniforms, form a net of hatred. They pierce the Star of David, no longer fastened on my coat but still scorching my heart.

The sky is gray. The fine drizzle is wetting the roofs of the city. I stand in front of the National Museum, waiting for a trolley car. I feel the moisture mixing with the tears rolling down my cheeks. Twenty-two years ago, I stood here with my mother and my sister, Helen. Then also we waited for a trolley car to come. We were on our way to visit our grandmother. Holding onto our mother's hands, we laughed as I mischievously pulled on Helen's blond braids. The brightly painted cars announced their coming and going with chimelike bells. It was Eastertime. The air was full of holiday mood and the smell of spring. The aroma of the golden chicken soup, lovingly prepared by our grandmother, filled my imagination. The little dumplings moved playfully around the floating rings of fat in the hot liquid which steamed from the fine china designed with a blue onion pattern.

From the bend of a side street, a rattling sound draws my attention. I am forced to emerge from the state of elation, in which everything in me has melted with happiness. In front of me a faded trolley car stops with a squeak. I board the half-empty car mechanically. I feel alone, so alone! As through a veil, my eyes slide from one passenger to another, my body sways from side to side with the music of the wheels. Did my sister survive? Will I find her under the same address? When I left her, three years ago, she was protected by her non-Jewish husband. Did he divorce her? And what about their children? What do I tell them all? How can it be told! Who will believe that I survived my own death? Why me, while our mother, father, and brother had to die? Can they understand? I survived and I have a message from the dead. But what words will I choose to tell it all?

The downpour of thoughts cuts through the silence around me. Yes, I have arrived at my destination. A sudden jerk of the trolley car brings me to my feet. As if in a daze, I walk the familiar street—tracing the gray building in front of me. Here is my sister's house! I need to loosen the stranglehold around my heart as I slowly mount the twisting staircase in the dark hallway. I inhale the collective aromas of the dinners, slipping through and around the many apartment doors in the hall. A small rectangular label shines on a door. This is unmistakably Helen's place! My shaky hand timidly presses the little doorbell. A click of the lock; a slow movement of the opening door lets a wedge of light into the dark hall. . . . Two happy shouts echo through the building. My sister and I look at each other in amazement. We both sense a miracle—we both survived! The invisible wall thrust between us through the Nuremberg Laws* can no longer separate us.

Helen's and my faces are drenched with tears of happiness and sorrow as we cling together in the open doorway. This mixture, streaming down our cheeks, suddenly forms the unspoken words I have been so anxiously searching for. There is one kind of knowledge: we both are together again, we each have a different story to tell. . . .

*In 1939, the Reichs Protector of Bohemia and Moravia placed the Jews under German jurisdiction in accordance with the so-called Nuremberg Laws, adopted by the German parliament (Reichstag) in 1935. These comprehensive decrees defined the status of the Jews and limited their rights, thus establishing anti-Semitism in law.

PROBING FOR MEANING

1. Hana Wehle tells us near the end of her essay that her mother died in the concentration camp. Where does the author give the first evidence of her possible death? Explain.

2. The memories of the author constantly overwhelm her. At how many points in the essay does she succumb to them? What scenes in the past do these thoughts revive?

3. Why does the author feel the arrival is "as hard as the departure"? Why is her present freedom not as "glorious and beautiful" as she had thought it would be while she was in the concentration camp?

4. Why does the author believe that the Nazis might not have sent her sister to a camp? Why is she nevertheless not sure that her sister survived?

5. Why does the author fear that she will not know how to tell her sister about her experience in the concentration camp? Why do their tears at the end form "the unspoken words" she has been "so anxiously searching for"?

PROBING FOR METHOD

1. The author uses the past tense ("I belonged to them") in relating some of her memories, but she uses the progressive tense ("I am lying") in relating others. Why doesn't she use the past tense throughout? What function does the progressive tense fulfill?

2. Why is it significant that the sky is gray and that it is drizzling? What other details take on symbolic overtones?

3. What is the function of flashbacks in this particular narrative?

BRENT STAPLES

A Brother's Murder

Brent Staples (b. 1951) is from Chester, Pennsylvania. He has a Ph.D. in psychology from the University of Chicago and is currently an editor of the New York Times Book Review. *"A Brother's Murder" was first published in the "About Men" column of the* New York Times. *As you read his essay, speculate as to his purpose in addressing this particular audience.*

It has been more than two years since my telephone rang with the news that my younger brother Blake—just 22 years old—had been murdered. The young man who killed him was only 24. Wearing a ski mask, he emerged from a car, fired six times at close range with a massive .44 Magnum, then fled. The two had once been inseparable friends. A senseless rivalry—beginning, I think, with an argument over a girlfriend—escalated from posturing, to threats, to violence, to murder. The way the two were living, death could have come to either of them from anywhere. In fact, the assailant had already survived multiple gunshot wounds from an incident much like the one in which my brother lost his life.

As I wept for Blake I felt wrenched backward into events and circumstances that had seemed light-years gone. Though a decade apart, we both were raised in

Chester, Pa., an angry, heavily black, heavily poor, industrial city southwest of Philadelphia. There, in the 1960's, I was introduced to mortality, not by the old and failing, but by beautiful young men who lay wrecked after sudden explosions of violence. The first, I remember from my 14th year— Johnny, brash lover of fast cars, stabbed to death two doors from my house in a fight over a pool game. The next year, my teenage cousin, Wesley, whom I loved very much, was shot dead. The summers blur. Milton, an angry young neighbor, shot a crosstown rival, wounding him badly. William, another teen-age neighbor, took a shotgun blast to the shoulder in some urban drama and displayed his bandages proudly. His brother, Leonard, severely beaten, lost an eye and donned a black patch. It went on.

I recall not long before I left for college, two local Vietnam veterans—one from the Marines, one from the Army—arguing fiercely, nearly at blows about which outfit had done the most in the war. The most killing, they meant. Not much later, I read a magazine article that set that dispute in a context. In the story, a noncommissioned officer—a sergeant, I believe—said he would pass up any number of affluent, suburban-born recruits to get hard-core soldiers from the inner city. They jumped into the rice paddies with "their manhood on their sleeves," I believe he said. These two items—the veterans arguing and the sergeant's words—still characterize for me the circumstances under which black men in their teens and 20's kill one another with such frequency. With a touchy paranoia born of living battered lives, they are desperate to be *real* men. Killing is only *machismo* taken to the extreme. Incursions to be punished by death were many and minor, and they remain so: they include stepping on the wrong toe, literally; cheating in a drug deal; simply saying "I dare you" to someone holding a gun; crossing territorial lines in a gang dispute. My brother grew up to wear his manhood on his sleeve. And when he died, he was in that group—black, male and in its teens and early 20's—that is far and away the most likely to murder or be murdered.

I left the East Coast after college, spent the mid- and late-1970's in Chicago as a graduate student, taught for a time, then became a journalist. Within 10 years of leaving my hometown, I was overeducated and "upwardly mobile," ensconced on a quiet, tree-lined street where voices raised in anger were scarcely ever heard. The telephone, like some grim umbilical, kept me connected to the old world with news of deaths, imprisonings and misfortune. I felt emotionally beaten up. Perhaps to protect myself, I added a psychological dimension to the physical distance I had already achieved. I rarely visited my hometown. I shut it out.

As I fled the past, so Blake embraced it. On Christmas of 1983, I traveled from Chicago to a black section of Roanoke, Va., where he then lived. The desolate public housing projects, the hopeless, idle young men crashing against one another—these reminded me of the embittered town we'd grown up in. It was a place where once I would have been comfortable, or at least sure of myself. Now, hearing of my brother's forays into crime, his scrapes with police and street thugs, I was scared, unsteady on foreign terrain.

I saw that Blake's romance with the street life and the hustler image had flowered dangerously. One evening that late December, standing in some Roanoke dive among drug dealers and grim, hair-trigger losers, I told him I feared for his life. He had affected the image of the tough he wanted to be. But behind the dark glasses and the swagger, I glimpsed the baby-faced toddler I'd once watched over. I nearly wept. I wanted desperately for him to live. The young think themselves immortal, and a dangerous light shone in his eyes as he spoke laughingly of making fools of the policemen who had raided his apartment looking for drugs. He cried out as I took his right hand. A line of stitches lay between the thumb and index finger. Kickback from a shotgun, he explained, nothing serious. Gunplay had become part of his life.

I lacked the language simply to say: Thousands have lived this for you and died. I fought the urge to lift him bodily and shake him. This place and the way you are living smells of death to me, I said. Take some time away, I said. Let's go downtown tomorrow and buy a plane ticket anywhere, take a bus trip, anything to get away and cool things off. He took my alarm casually. We arranged to meet the following night—an appointment he would not keep. We embraced as though through glass. I drove away.

As I stood in my apartment in Chicago holding the receiver that evening in February 1984, I felt as though part of my soul had been cut away. I questioned myself then, and I still do. Did I not reach back soon or earnestly enough for him? For weeks I awoke crying from a recurrent dream in which I chased him, urgently trying to get him to read a document I had, as though reading it would protect him from what had happened in waking life. His eyes shining like black diamonds, he smiled and danced just beyond my grasp. When I reached for him, I caught only the space where he had been.

PROBING FOR MEANING

1. What do we learn about Blake's way of life from the first paragraph of the essay?

2. What examples does Staples give in paragraph two to convey that he "was introduced to mortality, not by the old and failing, but by beautiful young men who lay wrecked after sudden explosions of violence"?

3. Why does Staples include the argument between the Vietnam veterans? How does it add to your understanding of his thesis that "killing is only *machismo* taken to the extreme"? Do you agree with him? Why or why not?

4. How did the narrator escape the fate of the other young men in the ghetto of Chester, Pennsylvania? Does the fact that he made it alter your opinion of those who didn't? Explain.

5. "As I fled the past, so Blake embraced it." How does this choice affect the relationship of the two brothers?

6. In the concluding paragraph, Staples reveals that he is still haunted by his brother's death as well as guilty about what he could have done. Are his guilt

feelings justified? Do you think anything he could have done would have altered his brother's destiny? Explain.

PROBING FOR METHOD

1. Staples records his personal anguish about his brother's death, but he also focuses on the plight of a whole generation growing up in the ghetto. Do you think his purpose was primarily to inform his audience or was he also trying to influence his readers? Cite evidence from the essay to support your point of view. What effect did the essay have on you?

2. How do techniques such as flashbacks enable Staples to place his brother's murder in a larger context? What other effective narrative techniques does he use?

3. Staples tries to maintain an objective tone in his essay. Are there points at which his tone becomes more personal? What, for example, is the effect of concluding the essay with his recurrent dreams?

4. Does Staples convey his attitude toward the young black men for whom gunplay had become a way of life? Explain your answer.

ALICE WALKER

Beauty: When the Other Dancer Is the Self

Alice Walker (b. 1944) was born in Georgia and graduated from Sarah Lawrence College in 1965. She has taught at several colleges and received many awards and honors. Her published fiction includes In Love and Trouble: Stories of Black Women *(1973),* Meridian *(1976), and* The Color Purple *(1982), for which she was awarded the Pulitzer Prize. As you read "Beauty: When the Other Dancer Is the Self," think about Walker's purpose in writing about this traumatic childhood experience.*

It is a bright summer day in 1947. My father, a fat, funny man with beautiful eyes and a subversive wit, is trying to decide which of his eight children he will take with him to the county fair. My mother, of course, will not go. She is knocked out from getting most of us ready: I hold my neck stiff against the pressure of her knuckles as she hastily completes the braiding and then beribboning of my hair.

My father is the driver for the rich old white lady up the road. Her name is Miss Mey. She owns all the land for miles around, as well as the house in which we live. All I remember about her is that she once offered to pay my mother thirty-five cents for cleaning her house, raking up piles of her magnolia leaves, and washing her family's clothes, and that my mother—she of no money, eight children, and a chronic earache—refused it. But I do not think of this in 1947. I am two and a half years old. I want to go everywhere my daddy goes. I am excited at the prospect of riding in a car. Someone has told me fairs are fun. That there is room in the car for only three of us doesn't faze me at all. Whirling happily in my starchy frock, showing off my biscuit-polished patent-leather shoes and lavender socks, tossing my head in a way that makes my ribbons bounce, I stand, hands on hips, before my father. "Take me, Daddy," I say with assurance; "I'm the prettiest!"

Later, it does not surprise me to find myself in Miss Mey's shiny black car, sharing the back seat with the other lucky ones. Does not surprise me that I thoroughly enjoy the fair. At home that night I tell the unlucky ones all I can remember about the merry-go-round, the man who eats live chickens, and the teddy bears, until they say: that's enough, baby Alice. Shut up now, and go to sleep.

It is Easter Sunday, 1950. I am dressed in a green, flocked, scalloped-hem dress (handmade by my adoring sister, Ruth) that has its own smooth satin petticoat and tiny hot-pink roses tucked into each scallop. My shoes, new T-strap patent leather, again highly biscuit-polished. I am six years old and have learned one of the longest Easter speeches to be heard that day, totally unlike the speech I said when I was two: "Easter lilies/pure and white/blossom in/the morning light." When I rise to give my speech I do so on a great wave of love and pride and expectation. People in the church stop rustling their new crinolines. They seem to hold their breath. I can tell they admire my dress, but it is my spirit, bordering on sassiness (womanishness), they secretly applaud.

"That girl's a little *mess*," they whisper to each other, pleased.

Naturally I say my speech without stammer or pause, unlike those who stutter, stammer, or, worst of all, forget. This is before the word "beautiful" exists in people's vocabulary, but "Oh, isn't she the *cutest* thing!" frequently floats my way. "And got so much sense!" they gratefully add . . . for which thoughtful addition I thank them to this day.

It was great fun being cute. But then, one day, it ended.

I am eight years old and a tomboy. I have a cowboy hat, cowboy boots, checkered shirt and pants, all red. My playmates are my brothers, two and four years older than I. Their colors are black and green, the only difference in the way we are dressed. On Saturday nights we all go to the picture show, even my mother; Westerns are her favorite kind of movie. Back home, "on the ranch," we pretend we are Tom Mix, Hopalong Cassidy, Lash LaRue (we've even named one of our dogs Lash LaRue); we chase each other for hours rustling cattle, being outlaws, delivering damsels from distress. Then my parents decide to buy my brothers guns. These are not "real" guns. They shoot "BB"'s, copper pellets my brothers say will kill birds. Because I am a girl, I do not get a gun. Instantly I am relegated to the position of Indian. Now there appears a great distance between us. They shoot and shoot at everything with their new guns. I try to keep up with my bow and arrows.

One day while I am standing on top of our makeshift "garage"—pieces of tin nailed across some poles—holding my bow and arrow and looking out toward the fields, I feel an incredible blow in my right eye. I look down just in time to see my brother lower his gun.

Both brothers rush to my side. My eye stings, and I cover it with my hand. "If you tell," they say, "we will get a whipping. You don't want that to happen, do you?" I do not. "Here is a piece of wire," says the older brother, picking it up from the roof; "say you stepped on one end of it and the other flew up and hit you." The pain is beginning to start. "Yes," I say. "Yes, I will say that is what happened." If I do not say this is what happened, I know my brothers will find ways to make me wish I had. But now I will say anything that gets me to my mother.

Confronted by our parents we stick to the lie agreed upon. They place me on a bench on the porch and I close my left eye while they examine the right. There is a tree growing from underneath the porch that climbs past the railing to the roof. It is the last thing my right eye sees. I watch as its trunk, its branches, and then its leaves are blotted out by the rising blood.

I am in shock. First there is intense fever, which my father tries to break using lily leaves bound around my head. Then there are chills: my mother tries to get me to eat soup. Eventually, I do not know how, my parents learn what has happened. A week after the "accident" they take me to see a doctor. "Why did you wait so long to come?" he asks, looking into my eye and shaking his head. "Eyes are sympathetic," he says. "If one is blind, the other will likely become blind too."

This comment of the doctor's terrifies me. But it is really how I look that bothers me most. Where the BB pellet struck there is a glob of whitish scar tissue, a hideous cataract, on my eye. Now when I stare at people—a favorite pastime, up to now—they will stare back. Not at the "cute" little girl, but at her scar. For six years I do not stare at anyone, because I do not raise my head.

Years later, in the throes of a mid-life crisis, I ask my mother and sister whether I changed after the "accident." "No," they say, puzzled. "What do you mean?"

What do I mean?

I am eight, and, for the first time, doing poorly in school, where I have been something of a whiz since I was four. We have just moved to the place where the "accident" occurred. We do not know any of the people around us because this is a different county. The only time I see the friends I knew is when we go back to our old church. The new school is the former state penitentiary. It is a large stone building, cold and drafty, crammed to overflowing with boisterous, ill-disciplined children. On the third floor there is a huge circular imprint of some partition that has been torn out.

"What used to be here?" I ask a sullen girl next to me on our way past it to lunch.

"The electric chair," says she.

At night I have nightmares about the electric chair, and about all the people reputedly "fried" in it. I am afraid of the school, where all the students seem to be budding criminals.

"What's the matter with your eye?" they ask, critically.

When I don't answer (I cannot decide whether it was an "accident" or not), they shove me, insist on a fight.

My brother, the one who created the story about the wire, comes to my rescue. But then brags so much about "protecting" me, I become sick.

After months of torture at the school, my parents decide to send me back to our old community, to my old school. I live with my grandparents and the teacher they board. But there is no room for Phoebe, my cat. By the time my grandparents decide there *is* room, and I ask for my cat, she cannot be found. Miss Yarborough, the boarding teacher, takes me under her wing, and begins to teach me to play the piano. But soon she marries an African—a "prince," she says—and is whisked away to his continent.

At my old school there is at least one teacher who loves me. She is the teacher who "knew me before I was born" and bought my first baby clothes. It is she who makes life bearable. It is her presence that finally helps me turn on the one child at the school who continually calls me "one-eyed bitch." One day I simply grab him by his coat and beat him until I am satisfied. It is my teacher who tells me my mother is ill.

My mother is lying in bed in the middle of the day, something I have never seen. She is in too much pain to speak. She has an abscess in her ear. I stand looking down on her, knowing that if she dies, I cannot live. She is being treated with warm oils and hot bricks held against her cheek. Finally a doctor comes. But I must go back to my grandparent's house. The weeks pass but I am hardly aware of it. All I know is that my mother might die, my father is not so jolly, my brothers still have their guns, and I am the one sent away from home.

"You did not change," they say.

Did I imagine the anguish of never looking up?

I am twelve. When relatives come to visit I hide in my room. My cousin Brenda, just my age, whose father works in the post office and whose mother is a nurse, comes to find me. "Hello," she says. And then she asks, looking at my recent school picture, which I did not want taken, and on which the "glob," as I think of it, is clearly visible, "You still can't see out of that eye?"

"No," I say, and flop back on the bed over my book.

That night, as I do almost every night, I abuse my eye. I rant and rave at it, in front of the mirror. I plead with it to clear up before morning. I tell it I hate and despise it. I do not pray for sight. I pray for beauty.

"You did not change," they say.

I am fourteen and baby-sitting for my brother Bill, who lives in Boston. He is my favorite brother and there is a strong bond between us. Understanding my feelings of shame and ugliness he and his wife take me to a local hospital, where the "glob" is removed by a doctor named O. Henry. There is still a small bluish crater where the scar tissue was, but the ugly white stuff is gone. Almost immediately I become a different person from the girl who does not raise her head. Or so I think. Now that I've raised my head I win the boyfriend of my dreams. Now that I've raised my head I have plenty of friends. Now that I've raised my head classwork comes from my lips as faultlessly as Easter speeches did, and I leave high school as valedictorian, most popular student, and *queen*, hardly believing my luck. Ironically, the girl who was voted most beautiful in our class (and was) was later shot twice through the chest by a male companion, using a "real" gun, while she was pregnant. But that's another story in itself. Or is it?

"You did not change," they say.

It is now thirty years since the "accident." A beautiful journalist comes to visit and to interview me. She is going to write a cover story for her magazine that focuses on my latest book. "Decide how you want to look on the cover," she says. "Glamorous, or whatever."

Never mind "glamorous," it is the "whatever" that I hear. Suddenly all I can think of is whether I will get enough sleep the night before the photography session: if I don't, my eye will be tired and wander, as blind eyes will.

At night in bed with my lover I think up reasons why I should not appear on the cover of a magazine. "My meanest critics will say I've sold out," I say. "My family will now realize I write scandalous books."

"But what's the real reason you don't want to do this?" he asks.

"Because in all probability," I say in a rush, "my eye won't be straight."

"It will be straight enough," he says. Then, "Besides, I thought you'd made your peace with that."

And I suddenly remember that I have.

I remember:

I am talking to my brother Jimmy, asking if he remembers anything unusual about the day I was shot. He does not know I consider that day the last time my father, with his sweet home remedy of cool lily leaves, chose me, and that I suffered and raged inside because of this. "Well," he says, "all I remember is standing by the side of the highway with Daddy, trying to flag down a car. A white man stopped, but when Daddy said he needed somebody to take his little girl to the doctor, he drove off."

I remember:
I am in the desert for the first time. I fall totally in love with it. I am so overwhelmed by its beauty, I confront for the first time, consciously, the meaning of the doctor's words years ago: "Eyes are sympathetic. If one is blind, the other will likely become blind too." I realize I have dashed about the world madly, looking at this, looking at that, storing up images against the fading of the light. *But I might have missed seeing the desert!* The shock of that possibility—and gratitude for over twenty-five years of sight—sends me literally to my knees. Poem after poem comes—which is perhaps how poets pray.

ON SIGHT

I am so thankful I have seen
The Desert
And the creatures in the desert
And the desert Itself.

The desert has its own moon
Which I have seen
With my own eye.
There is no flag on it.

Trees of the desert have arms
All of which are always up
That is because the moon is up
The sun is up
Also the sky
The stars
Clouds
None with flags.

If there *were* flags, I doubt
the trees would point.
Would you?

But mostly, I remember this:
I am twenty-seven, and my baby daughter is almost three. Since her birth I have worried about her discovery that her mother's eyes are different from other people's. Will she be embarrassed? I think. What will she say? Every day she watches a television program called "Big Blue Marble." It begins with a picture of the earth as it appears from the moon. It is bluish, a little battered-looking, but full of light, with whitish clouds swirling around it. Every time I see it I weep with love, as if it is a picture of Grandma's house. One day when I am putting Rebecca down for her nap, she suddenly focuses

on my eye. Something inside me cringes, gets ready to try to protect myself. All children are cruel about physical differences, I know from experience, and that they don't always mean to be is another matter. I assume Rebecca will be the same.

But no-o-o-o. She studies my face intently as we stand, her inside and me outside her crib. She even holds my face maternally between her dimpled little hands. Then, looking every bit as serious and lawyerlike as her father, she says, as if it may just possibly have slipped my attention: "Mommy, there's a *world* in your eye." (As in, "Don't be alarmed, or do anything crazy.") And then, gently, but with great interest: "Mommy, where did you *get* that world in your eye?"

For the most part, the pain left then. (So what, if my brothers grew up to buy even more powerful pellet guns for their sons and to carry real guns themselves. So what, if a young "Morehouse man" once nearly fell off the steps of Trevor Arnett Library because he thought my eyes were blue.) Crying and laughing I ran to the bathroom, while Rebecca mumbled and sang herself off to sleep. Yes indeed, I realized, looking into the mirror. There *was* a world in my eye. And I saw that it was possible to love it: that in fact, for all it had taught me of shame and anger and inner vision, I *did* love it. Even to see it drifting out of orbit in boredom, or rolling up out of fatigue, not to mention floating back at attention in excitement (bearing witness, a friend has called it), deeply suitable to my personality, and even characteristic of me.

That night I dream I am dancing to Stevie Wonder's song "Always" (the name of the song is really "As," but I hear it as "Always"). As I dance, whirling and joyous, happier than I've ever been in my life, another bright-faced dancer joins me. We dance and kiss each other and hold each other through the night. The other dancer has obviously come through all right, as I have done. She is beautiful, whole and free. And she is also me.

PROBING FOR MEANING

1. What do you learn about Walker and her family in the first three paragraphs of the essay?

2. Why does she include Easter Sunday, 1950?

3. How does the traumatic event of 1954 affect her appearance? Her concept of herself? Her behavior? What, for example, is the significance of the repeated references to her raising her head at different stages in her life?

4. Do you think the shooting was an accident? Why or why not? Why does Walker emphasize this aspect of the essay?

5. Why does she include the poem in her essay? How did it affect you?

6. Explain the significance of the essay's title.

7. What insights does Walker gain through this experience? What role does her daughter play?

PROBING FOR METHOD

1. What is the effect of Walker's beginning with the present tense to narrate her experience?

2. Read over the italicized statements. What is their impact on the narrative?

3. How does repeating "you did not change" affect the account of her experience?

4. How do the title and the concluding paragraph contribute to the unity of the essay?

5. How would you characterize Walker's purpose in recalling this childhood experience? Explain your answer.

ADRIENNE RICH

Trying to Talk with a Man

Adrienne Rich (b. 1928) is an American poet who received the National Book Award in 1974 for her collection Diving into the Wreck. *Her poetry expresses the conflicts that she confronted as she sought to express herself artistically while struggling with her roles as wife and mother, and later as a feminist and lesbian. Her keen insights on the changing world around her are revealed in such volumes as* Snapshots of a Daughter-in-law *(1962),* Necessities of Life *(1966), and* And a Wild Patience Has Taken Me Thus Far *(1981). As you read "Trying to Talk With A Man," compare the poet's experience with the opposite sex with your own.*

Out in this desert we are testing bombs,

that's why we came here.

Sometimes I feel an underground river
forcing its way between deformed cliffs
an acute angle of understanding
moving itself like a locus of the sun
into this condemned scenery.

What we've had to give up to get here—
whole LP collections, films we starred in

playing in the neighborhoods, bakery windows

full of dry, chocolate-filled Jewish cookies,
the language of love-letters, of suicide notes,
afternoons on the riverbank
pretending to be children

Coming out to this desert
we meant to change the face of
driving among dull green succulents
walking at noon in the ghost town
surrounded by a silence

that sounds like the silence of the place
except that it came with us
and is familiar
and everything we were saying until now
was an effort to blot it out—
Coming out here we are up against it

Out here I feel more helpless
with you than without you
You mention the danger
and list the equipment
we talk of people caring for each other
in emergencies—laceration, thirst—
but you look at me like an emergency

Your dry heat feels like power
your eyes are stars of a different magnitude
they reflect lights that spell out: EXIT
when you get up and pace the floor

talking of the danger
as if it were not ourselves
as if we were testing anything else.

PROBING FOR MEANING

1. At what point do you realize the poem is meant symbolically and not as a literal journey to a desert testing site? What is actually happening in the poem?

2. What do the things they've "had to give up to get here" represent?

3. In what sense did the "silence of the place" come with them? Why is conversation often an attempt to blot out silence? Why are they "up against it" in the desert?

4. Why does she feel more helpless with him than without him? Why does she say he looks at her "like an emergency"?

5. How do their reactions to their conversation differ? Do they succeed in the purpose of the journey?

PROBING FOR METHOD

1. What is the speaker's mood at the beginning of the poem? Does her mood fluctuate at all? Explain your answer.

2. What function does the title play? How does it affect your response to the poem?

3. The poem is based on an extended metaphor, that of the desert testing site. How many images in the poem actually form part of this metaphor? What do they mean in each case?

KATE CHOPIN

The Story of an Hour

Kate Chopin (1851−1904) was born and lived most of her life in St. Louis, Missouri. She married and had six children and did not begin writing until after her husband died in 1883. Her most famous novel, The Awakening *(1899), was described by critics as the story of "a sensuous woman who follows her inclinations" and it was banned from libraries. Chopin was rediscovered in the 1950s and is now regarded as a somewhat revolutionary woman writer. As you read "The Story of An Hour," think about your reactions to Chopin's portrayal of marriage.*

Knowing that Mrs. Mallard was afflicted with a heart trouble, great care was taken to break to her as gently as possible the news of her husband's death.

It was her sister Josephine who told her, in broken sentences; veiled hints that revealed in half concealing. Her husband's friend Richards was there, too, near her. It was he who had been in the newspaper office when intelligence of the railroad disaster was received, with Brently Mallard's name leading the list of "killed." He had only taken the time to assure himself of its truth by a second telegram, and had hastened to forestall any less careful, less tender friend in bearing the sad message.

She did not hear the story as many women have heard the same, with a paralyzed inability to accept its significance. She wept at once, with sudden, wild abandonment, in her sister's arms. When the storm of grief had spent itself she went away to her room alone. She would have no one follow her.

There stood, facing the open window, a comfortable, roomy armchair. Into this she sank, pressed down by a physical exhaustion that haunted her body and seemed to reach into her soul.

She could see in the open square before her house the tops of trees that were all aquiver with the new spring life. The delicious breath of rain was in the air. In the street below a peddler was crying his wares. The notes of a distant song which some one was singing reached her faintly, and countless sparrows were twittering in the eaves.

There were patches of blue sky showing here and there through the clouds that had met and piled one above the other in the west facing her window.

She sat with her head thrown back upon the cushion of the chair, quite motionless, except when a sob came up into her throat and shook her, as a child who has cried itself to sleep continues to sob in its dreams.

She was young, with a fair, calm face, whose lines bespoke repression and even a certain strength. But now there was a dull stare in her eyes, whose gaze was fixed away off yonder on one of those patches of blue sky. It was not a glance of reflection, but rather indicated a suspension of intelligent thought.

There was something coming to her and she was waiting for it, fearfully. What was it? She did not know; it was too subtle and elusive to name. But she felt it, creeping out of the sky, reaching toward her through the sounds, the scents, the color that filled the air.

Now her bosom rose and fell tumultuously. She was beginning to recognize this thing that was approaching to possess her, and she was striving to beat it back with her will—as powerless as her two white slender hands would have been.

When she abandoned herself a little whispered word escaped her slightly parted lips. She said it over and over under her breath: "free, free, free!" The vacant stare and the look of terror that had followed it went from her eyes. They stayed keen and bright. Her pulses beat fast, and the coursing blood warmed and relaxed every inch of her body.

She did not stop to ask if it were or were not a monstrous joy that held her. A clear and exalted perception enabled her to dismiss the suggestion as trivial.

She knew that she would weep again when she saw the kind, tender hands folded in death; the face that had never looked save with love upon her, fixed and gray and dead. But she saw beyond that bitter moment a long procession of years to come that would belong to her absolutely. And she opened and spread her arms out to them in welcome.

There would be no one to live for her during those coming years; she would live for herself. There would be no powerful will bending hers in that blind persistence with which men and women believe they have a right to impose a private will upon a fellow-creature. A kind intention or a cruel intention made the act seem no less a crime as she looked upon it in that brief moment of illumination.

And yet she had loved him—sometimes. Often she had not. What did it matter! What could love, the unsolved mystery, count for in face of this possession of self-assertion which she suddenly recognized as the strongest impulse of her being!

"Free! Body and soul free!" she kept whispering.

Josephine was kneeling before the closed door with her lips to the keyhole, imploring for admission. "Louise, open the door! I beg; open the door— you will make yourself ill. What are you doing, Louise? For heaven's sake open the door."

"Go away. I am not making myself ill." No; she was drinking in a very elixir of life through that open window.

Her fancy was running riot along those days ahead of her. Spring days, and summer days, and all sorts of days that would be her own. She breathed a quick prayer that life might be long. It was only yesterday she had thought with a shudder that life might be long.

She arose at length and opened the door to her sister's importunities. There was a feverish triumph in her eyes, and she carried herself unwittingly like a goddess of Victory. She clasped her sister's waist, and together they descended the stairs. Richards stood waiting for them at the bottom.

Some one was opening the front door with a latchkey. It was Brently Mallard who entered, a little travel-stained, composedly carrying his grip-sack and umbrella. He had been far from the scene of accident, and did not even know there had been one. He stood amazed at Josephine's piercing cry; at Richards's quick motion to screen him from the view of his wife.

But Richards was too late.

When the doctors came they said she had died of heart disease—of joy that kills.

PROBING FOR MEANING

1. What do you learn about Mrs. Mallard in the first three paragraphs?

2. What changes occur in the next four paragraphs?

3. Explain the statement in paragraph 8: "It was not a glance of reflection, but rather indicated a suspension of intelligent thought."

4. What is the dominant emotion she feels after her husband's death? What do you learn about her husband and their marriage in paragraph 13? Was she unhappy? Did he treat her unkindly?

5. Explain the statement in paragraph 15: "What could love, the unsolved mystery, count for in face of this possession of self-assertion which she suddenly recognized as the strongest impulse of her being!"

6. What is the meaning of the last two lines of the story?

PROBING FOR METHOD

1. Chopin's story was published in 1894. Do you think the reaction of her audience then might have been different from your reaction now? Explain your answer.

2. How would you characterize the narrator's tone? Does she convey any attitude toward Mrs. Mallard or toward marriage?

3. How does Chopin use nature to reflect the changing reactions of her protagonist?

4. How does the title of the story reflect Chopin's method of narrating the story?

WRITING TOPICS

Generating Ideas on an Experience

Freewrite, perhaps in your journal in response to one of the following. Use the journalist's questions (who, how, why, when, where, what) where appropriate.

No day comes back again; an inch of time is worth a foot of jade.

Zen Proverb

In creating, the only hard thing's to begin.

James Russell Lowell

Parting is all we know of heaven and all we need of Hell.

Emily Dickinson

Out here I feel more hopeless with you than without you.

Adrienne Rich

As I dance, whirling and joyous, happier than I've ever been in my life, another bright-faced dancer joins me. . . . The other dancer has obviously come through all right, as I have done. She is beautiful, whole and free. And she is also me.

Alice Walker

Only the curious have, if they live, a tale worth telling at all.

Alastair Reid

Education is hanging around until you've caught on.

Robert Frost

Pain invents its own language. With this tongue, we others are not conversant. Never mind, we shall know it in our time.

Richard Selzer

I feel alone, so alone!

Hana Wehle

Free, free, free!

Kate Chopin

In our play we reveal what kind of people we are.

Ovid

The greatest difficulty in education is to get experience out of ideas.

George Santayana

Topics for Essays on an Experience

1. Most writers of narratives choose events and experiences that are of value to their readers. If you have witnessed an event or had an experience that other people can learn from, write an essay in which you relate that event in chronological order, including the insight you obtained from that experience that you want to share. Use the journalist's questions to generate details.

2. Choose an experience you have had—dating, school, camping, traveling—and form a conclusion about that experience that can be of value to other people. For example, you might conclude that dating many different types of people is an education itself. Using your conclusion as a thesis statement, write an essay in which you use your own experience to supply details and examples in developing your essay. Try to analyze your experience rather than relating it in chronological order.

3. Look over what you have written on the statement you chose from Generating Ideas. Consider whether this material can be revised into an essay or whether any one of your thoughts can now be expanded into a formal piece of writing. In either case, develop an essay on the topic.

4. Past experiences—their own or others—play an important role in the essays of Staples and Wehle. Does the fact that each essay is concerned with an ethnic group have any relevance to the writer's purpose? Is there an experience you have had as a member of an ethnic group that could be valuable to record? If so, write an essay about it.

5. Brent Staples, Hana Wehle, Alice Walker, and Kate Chopin concern themselves with the passage of time and the changes that this brings. Write an essay in which you compare the attitudes any two of these authors take toward the passage of time. How is their concept of time similar to or different from yours?

6. "The Story of an Hour" and "Trying to Talk with a Man" dramatize the man-woman relationship. Write an essay in which you examine an aspect of this relationship that the selections have in common. How do they differ? To what extent is the point of view in each similar to yours?

7. Hana Wehle, Brent Staples, and Alice Walker endure an agonizing experience to learn an important truth. In an essay, analyze their experiences and the insights they gained as a result. How did their experiences affect you?

8. In some of the selections in this chapter, the meaning of the narrative is rendered symbolically. Discuss in an essay how symbolic images convey information about an event or an experience in selections by Wehle, Selzer, Rich, or Chopin.

9. Find a windowless room and stay in it for a while. Make some notes on how the experience affects you. Are your reactions similar to or different from Selzer's? Analyze the experience in an essay that focuses on visually re-creating the room for the reader as well as on your responses to it.

PART TWO

THE WRITER'S I AND THE PUBLIC WORLD

Although most of us probably prefer to think and write about our own lives—the people we have known, the places we have been in, the experiences we have had—much of our thinking and writing has to be directed outward—toward the institutions we live with, such as work, marriage, education; toward questions of public life, such as the ethics of sports, relationships between ethnic groups, differences in lifestyles, attitudes toward nature and the environment, the rewards and drawbacks of materialism; toward philosophical questions such as loneliness and privacy, the search for truth, the nature of language, the meaning of death. Writing for school requires writing about these subjects.

The essays collected in Part 2 are still first-person essays. Although they are no longer primarily personal or autobiographical or inward-looking, as in Part 1, the writers in Part 2 also use their own experiences and ideas in developing their themes. The difference is in purpose: The writers do not wish to express their personal feelings but to explore subjects of concern to the reader, who may be one person, a group of people, or the whole society. The emphasis is placed on the subject, not the writer; the focus is also on the reader to the extent that only those personal experiences that explain the subject to the reader are included.

Some writers in Part 2 project their shadows over their writing more than others; some write personal narratives, as in Part 1, simultaneously drawing general significance from them. The essays of Jim Fusilli, Steve Tesich, George Orwell, Gloria Naylor, Loren Eiseley,

Richard Rodriguez, and Anne Morrow Lindbergh are among the many examples of the personal narrative used to make a universal point. Other writers use their own experiences simply as a framework for their essays and draw on examples from other people and from society as a whole in making their points: Pete Hamill, Anne Taylor Fleming, Henry David Thoreau, and E. M. Forster build this personal frame around their essays.

The shadows of still other writers can be found in their essays only to the extent that they use the personal pronoun and convey a recognizably personal attitude toward the subject: Gloria Steinem, Bertrand Russell, Lewis Thomas, and Plato have withdrawn their shadows to this extent.

Why have these writers chosen not to disappear altogether? Their purposes were not to write objectively, but to use the force of personality and the honesty that comes from precision of thought and language to communicate their subjects to their audience and at times even to attempt to persuade them of their point of view. Gloria Steinem, Pete Hamill, Steve Tesich, Bertrand Russell, and Richard Rodriguez are among those whose desire to explain is mingled with a desire to persuade.

William Zinsser, author of *On Writing Well*, cites several reasons for writing in the first person even when we are not writing about ourselves primarily, when we are looking outward. Even though we have always been cautioned to be impersonal because to be so appears to be more dignified, Zinsser says we should not worry that we will lose our dignity. Moreover, he says, "we have become a society fearful of revealing who we are. . . . Americans are suddenly uncertain of what they think and unwilling to go out on a limb—an odd turn of events for a nation famous for the 'rugged individualist.' " Even when "I" is not permitted—as in reports, research papers, newspaper articles, or textbooks—he says, "It's still possible to convey a sense of I-ness. . . . Good writers are always visible just behind their words. If you aren't allowed to use 'I,' at least think 'I' while you write, or write the first draft in the first person and then take the 'I's out. It will warm up your impersonal style."

As you read the essays, stories, and poems in Part 2, decide, just as you did in Part 1, what personality or aspect of personality the writer is projecting and how able the writer has been to convey the truth of her own experiences. Where the writer has pulled her shadow back from her writing, what personal involvement with the subject can you still discern?

In concentrating on the subject instead of on the self, the writer uses a different process for completing the essay. While the journal may still supply ideas for writing—see Thoreau and Lindbergh—the memory and the imagination play less important roles. More formal methods of generating ideas may be helpful; for example, asking yourself the classical questions may help you locate and develop ideas. These questions, many of which originated with Aristotle, include "What is it?" "What caused it?" "What did it cause?" "What is it like?" "What is it unlike?" "What has been said about it?" "What examples are there of it?" and "What is its general significance?" In Chapters 5 and 6, after the first and second essays we discuss how the professional writers have utilized these questions. We also use their essays as examples of how to organize the answers to the questions, again in Chapter 6.

Since you will want to consider your readers' attitudes and interests in presenting your subject, we discuss your obligations to your reader in Chapter 7, as well as his obligations to you in reading and understanding what you have written. Finally, in Chapter 8, we discuss how consideration of your reader may lead you to revisions in style.

CHAPTER FIVE

Goals:
Generating Ideas
Generalizing about Observations
Observing To Support Generalizations

"All you need is love," sang John Lennon two decades ago. "The answer is blowing in the wind," strummed his contemporary Bob Dylan. But Bruce Springsteen in a lyric of the 80s urges, "Talk about a dream, try to make it real." During this decade, our society has, in fact, become increasingly concerned about formulating goals in careers, relationships, possessions, and even in play. "Go for it" has replaced "Let it be."

The writers in this chapter explore the issue of goals: their importance and their limitations. Pete Hamill, for example, is convinced that we have become too competitive and too afraid of losing. Steve Tesich writes that human relationships are not aerobics and that "you can't go to a gym and pump marriage." Gloria Steinem urges valuing work for personal as well as pragmatic rewards, Robert Pirsig extols the old-fashioned notion of "gumption," and Jim Fusilli disputes the popular notion that one can "have it all."

In a poem, Gwendolyn Brooks expresses her confidence that her child will always be a risk taker, and, in a short story, Doris Lessing's protagonist, despite her ambition, loses her "capital."

A discussion of how to generate ideas through generalizing follows Gloria Steinem's essay on pages 181–182. How to generate ideas through observing is discussed on pages 187–188.

GLORIA STEINEM

The Importance of Work

Gloria Steinem (b. 1934) was born in Toledo, Ohio, and graduated from Smith College in 1956. She has been involved with the women's movement since 1968, and in 1972 became founder and editor of MS *magazine. As you read "The Importance of Work," which was included in her latest book* Outrageous Acts and Everyday Rebellions *(1985), think about the points you agree and/ or disagree with on this vital subject.*

Toward the end of the 1970s, *The Wall Street Journal* devoted an eight-part, front-page series to "the working woman"—that is, the influx of women into the paid-labor force—as the greatest change in American life since the Industrial Revolution.

Many women readers greeted both the news and the definition with cynicism. After all, women have always worked. If all the productive work of human maintenance that women do in the home were valued at its replacement cost, the gross national product of the United States would go up by 26 percent. It's just that we are now more likely than ever before to leave our poorly rewarded, low-security, high-risk job of homemaking (though we're still trying to explain that it's a perfectly good one and that the problem is male society's refusal both to do it and to give it an economic value) for more secure, independent, and better-paid jobs outside the home.

Obviously, the real work revolution won't come until all productive work is rewarded—including child rearing and other jobs done in the home—and men are integrated into so-called women's work as well as vice versa. But the radical change being touted by the *Journal* and other media is one part of that long integration process: the unprecedented flood of women into salaried jobs, that is, into the labor force as it has been male-defined and previously occupied by men. We are already more than 41 percent of it—the highest proportion in history. Given the fact that women also make up a whopping 69 percent of the "discouraged labor force" (that is, people who need jobs but don't get counted in the unemployment statistics because they've given up looking), plus an official female unemployment rate that is substantially higher than men's, it's clear that we could expand to become fully half of the national work force by 1990.

Faced with this determination of women to find a little independence and to be paid and honored for our work, experts have rushed to ask: "Why?" It's a question rarely directed at male workers. Their basic motivations of survival and personal satisfaction are taken for granted. Indeed, men are regarded as "odd" and therefore subjects for sociological study and journalistic reports only when they *don't* have work, even if they are rich and don't need jobs or are poor and can't find them. Nonetheless, pollsters and sociologists have gone to great expense to prove that women work outside the home because of dire financial need, or if we persist despite the presence of a wage-earning male, out of some desire to buy "little extras" for our families, or even out of good old-fashioned penis envy.

Job interviewers and even our own families may still ask salaried women the big "Why?" If we have small children at home or are in some job regarded as "men's work," the incidence of such questions increases. Condescending or accusatory versions of "What's a nice girl like you doing in a place like this?" have not disappeared from the workplace.

How do we answer these assumptions that we are "working" out of some pressing or peculiar need? Do we feel okay about arguing that it's as natural for us to have salaried jobs as for our husbands—whether or not we have young children at home? Can we enjoy strong career ambitions without worrying about being thought "unfeminine"? When we confront men's growing resentment of women competing in the work force (often in the form of such guilt-producing accusations as "You're taking men's jobs away" or "You're damaging your children"), do we simply state that a decent job is a basic human right for everybody?

I'm afraid the answer is often no. As individuals and as a movement, we tend to retreat into some version of a tactically questionable defense: "Women workbecausewehaveto." The phrase has become one word, one key on the typewriter—an economic form of the socially "feminine" stance of passivity and self-sacrifice. Under attack, we still tend to present ourselves as creatures of economic necessity and familial devotion. "Womenworkbecausewehaveto" has become the easiest thing to say.

Like most truisms, this one is easy to prove with statistics. Economic need *is* the most consistent work motive—for women as well as men. In 1976, for instance, 43 percent of all women in the paid-labor force were single, widowed, separated, or divorced, and working to support themselves and their dependents. An additional 21 percent were married to men who had earned less than ten thousand dollars in the previous year, the minimum then required to support a family of four. In fact, if you take men's pensions, stocks, real estate, and various forms of accumulated wealth into account, a good statistical case can be made that there are more women who "have" to work (that is, who have neither the accumulated wealth, nor husbands whose work or wealth can support them for the rest of their lives) than there are men with the same need. If we were going to ask one group "Do you really need this job?", we should ask men.

But the first weakness of the whole "have to work" defense is its deceptiveness. Anyone who has ever experienced dehumanized life on welfare or any other confidence-shaking dependency knows that a paid job may be preferable to the dole, even when the handout is coming from a family member. Yet the will and self-confidence to work on one's own can diminish as dependency and fear increase. That may explain why—contrary to the "have to" rationale—wives of men who earn less than three thousand dollars a year are actually *less* likely to be employed than wives whose husbands make ten thousand dollars a year or more.

Furthermore, the greatest proportion of employed wives is found among families with a total household income of twenty-five to fifty thousand dollars a year. This is the statistical underpinning used by some sociologists to prove that women's work is mainly important for boosting families into the middle or upper middle class. Thus, women's incomes are largely used for buying "luxuries" and "little extras": a neat double-whammy that renders us secondary within our families, and makes our jobs expendable in hard times. We may even go along with this interpretation (at least, up to the point of getting fired so a male can have our job). It preserves a husbandly ego-need to be seen as the primary breadwinner, and still allows us a safe "feminine" excuse for working.

But there are often rewards that we're not confessing. As noted in *The Two-Career Couple,* by Francine and Douglas Hall: "Women who hold jobs by choice, even blue-collar routine jobs, are more satisfied with their lives than are the full-time housewives."

In addition to personal satisfaction, there is also society's need for all its members' talents. Suppose that jobs were given out on only a "have to work" basis to both women and men—one job per household. It would be unthinkable to lose the unique abilities of, for instance, Eleanor Holmes Norton, the distinguished chair of the Equal Employment Opportunity Commission. But would we then be forced to question the important work of her husband, Edward Norton, who is also a distinguished lawyer? Since men earn more than twice as much as women on the average, the wife in most households would be more likely to give up her job. Does that mean the nation could do as well without millions of its nurses, teachers, and secretaries? Or that the rare man who earns less than his wife should give up his job?

It was this kind of waste of human talents on a society-wide scale that traumatized millions of unemployed or underemployed Americans during the Depression. Then, a one-job-per-household rule seemed somewhat justified, yet the concept was used to displace women workers only, create intolerable dependencies, and waste female talent that the country needed. That Depression experience, plus the energy and example of women who were finally allowed to work during the manpower shortage created by World War II, led Congress to reinterpret the meaning of the country's full-employment goal in its Economic Act of 1946. Full employment was officially defined as "the employment of those who want to work, without regard to whether their employment is, by some definition, necessary. This goal applies equally to men and to women." Since bad economic times are again creating a resentment of employed women—as well as creating more need for women to be employed—we need such a goal more than ever. Women are again being caught in a tragic double bind: We are required to be strong and then punished for our strength.

Clearly, anything less than government and popular commitment to this 1946 definition of full employment will leave the less powerful groups, whoever they may be, in danger. Almost as important as the financial penalty paid by the powerless is the suffering that comes from being shut out of paid and recognized work. Without it, we lose much of our self-respect and our ability to prove that we are alive by making some difference in the world. That's just as true for the suburban woman as it is for the unemployed steel worker.

But it won't be easy to give up the passive defense of "weworkbecause wehaveto."

When a woman who is struggling to support her children and grandchildren on welfare sees her neighbor working as a waitress, even though that neighbor's husband has a job, she may feel resentful; and the waitress (of course, not the waitress's husband) may feel guilty. Yet unless we establish the obligation to provide a job for everyone who is willing and able to work, that welfare woman may herself be penalized by policies that give out only one public-service job per household. She and her daughter will have to make a painful and divisive decision about which of them gets that precious job, and the whole household will have to survive on only one salary.

A job as a human right is a principle that applies to men as well as women. But women have more cause to fight for it. The phenomenon of the "working woman" has been held responsible for everything from an increase in male impotence (which turned out, incidently, to be attributable to medication for high blood pressure) to the rising cost of steak (which was due to high energy costs and beef import restrictions, not women's refusal to prepare the cheaper, slower-cooking cuts). Unless we see a job as part of every citizen's right to autonomy and personal fulfillment, we will continue to be vulnerable to someone else's idea of what "need" is, and whose "need" counts the most.

In many ways, women who do not have to work for simple survival, but who choose to do so nonetheless, are on the frontier of asserting this right for all women. Those with well-to-do husbands are dangerously easy for us to resent and put down. It's easier still to resent women from families of inherited wealth, even though men generally control and benefit from that wealth. (There is no Rockefeller Sisters Fund, no J. P. Morgan & Daughters, and sons-in-law may be the ones who really sleep their way to power.) But to prevent a woman whose husband or father is wealthy from earning her own living, and from gaining the self-confidence that comes with that ability, is to keep her needful of that unearned power and less willing to disperse it. Moreover, it is to lose forever her unique talents.

Perhaps modern feminists have been guilty of a kind of reverse snobbism that keeps us from reaching out to the wives and daughters of wealthy men;

yet it was exactly such women who refused the restrictions of class and financed the first wave of feminist revolution.

For most of us, however, "womenworkbecausewehaveto" is just true enough to be seductive as a personal defense.

If we use it without also staking out the larger human right to a job, however, we will never achieve that right. And we will always be subject to the false argument that independence for women is a luxury affordable only in good economic times. Alternatives to layoffs will not be explored, acceptable unemployment will always be used to frighten those with jobs into accepting low wages, and we will never remedy the real cost, both to families and to the country, of dependent women and a massive loss of talent.

Worse of all, we may never learn to find productive, honored work as a natural part of ourselves and as one of life's basic pleasures.

PROBING FOR MEANING

1. What points is Steinem making regarding changes in looking at "the working woman"?

2. Do you agree or disagree with Steinem's view that women in general defend their working as something they have to do rather than something to take pride in?

3. Why, according to Steinem, are there more women working in homes where the family income is high?

4. What is your response to the definition of full employment passed by Congress in 1946? Should it be revised for today's world? Why or why not?

5. Steinem regards women who are working not because they have to but because they choose to as pioneers paving the way for all women. Does her view make sense to you or would you qualify it in any way?

6. What do you think of Steinem's conclusion that work may be "one of life's basic pleasures"?

PROBING FOR METHOD

1. Steinem's essay was originally published in 1979. Do you think her point of view is more acceptable to an audience in the mid-80s? Why or why not? Is Steinem writing only to women or does she also have something to say to men? Explain your answer.

2. Steinem's purpose is obviously not only to inform but also to persuade. To what extent did she convince you about the relationship for women between work and individual growth?

3. What other arguments of Steinem did you find persuasive? What factual support did she base her arguments on?

4. How would you describe the tone of Steinem's essay? Is it consistent?

5. The writer's "I" appears only once. How personal is Steinem's use of "we"? To what extent is this a personal essay?

Generalizing About Observations

What generalizations does Steinem arrive at in "The Importance of Work"?
Gloria Steinem begins by quoting an article in the *Wall Street Journal* on
the "working woman" and the effect on American life of the influx of
women into the labor force. She cites many statistics to indicate the scope
of this influx. She says that because men are very curious as to why
women are working in such apparently unprecedented numbers—are
seeking a generalization to explain the phenomenon—her purpose in
writing is to arrive at one.

She begins with the "truism" (a generalization the truth of which
cannot be disputed) that "Womenworkbecausewehaveto." While statistics prove this to be indeed true, she calls this is "passive defense" and
cites examples of women who work because they want to, because they
have chosen to do so (a second generalization). She also cites society's
need for the talents of all citizens (a third generalization). She concludes
with the major generalization she has been seeking—that work is "a natural part of ourselves and . . . one of life's basic pleasures."

Steinem begins with observations—a newspaper article and
statistics—and experience—women she has talked to, her own life—and
seeks to arrive at a generalization that will explain them.

Making generalizations.
Every time something happens to us or we observe it happening to others, we draw conclusions (or generalizations) about its meaning and significance. Often, we link experiences together under a common generalization. Generalizing is how we make sense of our lives.

When we narrate an experience, as we saw in the last chapter, we
indicate to the reader what conclusions we have drawn about the significance of that event. If we have had several similar experiences, we generalize about what links them together. Perhaps we also group them into
categories and find subgeneralizations for each of these categories. For
example, in her essay, Gloria Steinem moves through several subgeneralizations before finding the generalization she is seeking.

Finding an adequate generalization for an experience or a group of
experiences is not always easy. We are not always sure what interpretation is the correct one; perhaps we generalize with too little experience—
too hastily—to really have understood the meaning, as Gloria Steinem
says people do who think "womenworkbecausetheyhaveto." Or perhaps
we ignore—or do not know what to do with—contradictory experiences.
Steinem, for example, knows that some women work because they want
to, and says this fact should not be ignored by those who think women
have to work. If we are to begin to make sense of our experiences, and if,
as writers, we are not to bewilder our readers, we must make the attempt
to draw accurate conclusions about our subject matter.

Procedures to follow in making generalizations.

A. When narrating an experience or a series of experiences, indicate to the reader what you think the significance or meaning of your subject matter is. This generalization, as we have seen, will become the thesis of your essay.
B. If working with a series of experiences, you might want to group them according to categories and indicate why you have grouped them thus through a series of subgeneralizations. This second set of generalizations may become the topic sentences of your paragraphs.
C. Test your generalizations for validity. Have you used too few experiences to justify your conclusion? Have you taken into account any experiences that contradict your conclusion?

PETE HAMILL

Winning Isn't Everything

Pete Hamill (b. 1935) was born in Brooklyn, New York, and attended Pratt Institute. He has had many careers, beginning as a sheet metal worker in the Brooklyn Navy Yard and then as a reporter with the Saturday Evening Post. *During the Vietnam War, he was a correspondent in South Vietnam and received many awards for his outstanding reporting. Hamill's writings include* Irrational Ravings *(1971),* The Gift *(1973), and numerous screenplays. He is currently a free-lance writer who contributes to* Esquire, New York Times Magazine, *and other periodicals. As you read "Winning Isn't Everything," compare your ideas of winning and losing with those of the author.*

One of the more widely accepted maxims of modern American life was uttered on a frozen winter afternoon during the early sixties. The late Vince Lombardi, who coached the Green Bay Packers when they were the greatest team in football, said it. "Winning isn't everything," he declared. "It's the only thing."

Vince Lombardi's notion was immediately appropriated by an extraordinary variety of American males: presidents and lesser politicians, generals, broadcasters, political columnists, Little League coaches, heads of corporations, and probably millions of others. In fact, it sometimes seems that Lombardi's words have had greater impact than any sentence uttered by an American since Stephen Decatur's "our country, right or wrong."

That's surprising on many levels, beginning with the obvious: It's a deceptively simple premise. Winning *isn't* "the only thing." Such an idea muddles the idea of competition, not simply in sports, but in all aspects of our lives. We've learned the hard way in this century that the world is a complex place; it's certainly not the National Football League. Winning isn't the only thing in love, art, marriage, commerce, or politics; it's not even the only thing in sports.

In sports, as in so many other areas of our national life, we've always cherished gallant losers. I remember one afternoon in the fall of 1956 when Sal Maglie was pitching for the Brooklyn Dodgers against the hated Yankees. Maglie was an old man that year, as age is measured in sports. But this was the World Series, and he hauled his thirty-nine-year-old body to the mound, inning after inning, gave everything he had, held the Yankees to a few scattered hits and two runs—and lost. That day Don Larsen pitched his perfect game: no runs, no hits, no errors. Yet, to me, the afternoon belonged to Maglie—tough, gallant, and a loser.

There was an evening in Manila when Joe Frazier went up against Muhammad Ali for the third and final time. That night, Frazier brought his workman's skills into combat against the magic of the artist, called on his vast reservoir of courage and will, and came up empty at the end of fourteen rounds. Frazier was the loser, but that evening, nobody really lost. Because of that fight, Joe Frazier can always boast with honor that he made Muhammad Ali a great fighter. He was the test, the implacable force who made Ali summon all of his own considerable reserves of skill, heart, and endurance for a final effort. The contest consumed them both. Neither was ever again a good fighter. But during their violent confrontation, winning or losing was, in the end, a marginal concern; that all-consuming effort was everything.

There are hundreds of similar examples of losers who showed us how to be more human, and their performances make the wide acceptance of Lombardi's notions even more mystifying. Lombardi's thesis, in fact, represented something of a shift in the nation's popular thought. Americans had been the people who remembered the Alamo or Pearl Harbor; we blew taps over the graves of those who lost at the Battle of the Bulge or Anzio or the Yalu Basin. Those soldiers had all been defeated, but we honored them for their display of a critical human quality: courage.

Ernest Hemingway once defined courage as grace under pressure, and that's always struck me as an eminently useful definition. The best professional athletes not only possess that kind of courage but, more important, are willing to display it to strangers. Baseball's Reggie Jackson or Richard ("Goose") Gossage, for instance, function most completely as athletes and as men when appearing before gigantic crowds under pressure: bases loaded, late innings, a big game. They come to their tasks with gladness and absolute focus, neither whimpering, complaining nor shirking when doing their job; they just try their best to get that job done. And, of course, sometimes they fail. Gossage gives up a single and his team loses. Jackson strikes out. No matter. The important thing is that such men keep their appointments with confidence and grace. Courage has become so deep a part of their character that they don't even think about it. (They certainly *want* to win. Sometimes they absolutely lust for victory. But they know that winning isn't everything. All a man can do is his best.)

Competition isn't really a problem for Americans. All sports, in one way or another, are competitive. But an individual's primary competition is with himself and all his attendant weaknesses. That's obviously true of boxing, where fear must be dominated and made to work to the fighter's benefit. Yet it's also true for team sports, as well as such solitary endeavors as golf, where a player must learn control before anything else. The problem isn't competition, which is a part of life; it's in the notion of the necessity of triumph. A man can lose but still win. And the point of competition in sports is an old and not very fashionable one: It builds character.

That's especially true of prizefighters, the athletes I've known best. Outside the ring, almost all fighters are the gentlest of men. They carry themselves with the dignity of those who have little to prove, either to others or themselves. They're never bullies, rarely use their dangerous skills against ordinary citizens and avoid pointless confrontations. When a fighter hears that a colleague has been involved in a bar brawl or a swingout with a cop, he dismisses that fighter as a cowardly bum. Most of the boxers I know are honest, generous, funny. Yet they also know that as good as they are, there might be someone down the line who has their number. Again, they would prefer to be winners. But they're aware that losing, if a courageous effort is made, is never a disgrace. The highest compliment one fighter can pay another is to say that he has "heart."

There are lessons to be learned from such athletes that can be applied to how we live our lives. In the long run, we'll all come up losers because there's no greater loss than death. And since primitive man first began to think, we humans have devised strategies to deal with dying. Religion is the most obvious one, usually demanding that we adhere to a moral code on earth in exchange for a serene existence after death. Ideologies offer secular versions of the same instinct, insisting that we sacrifice now, directing our lives toward the ideal of a better future, with each man becoming an architect of his own utopia. Patriotism and nationalism carry some of the same fearful baggage.

An athlete's goals are less cosmic, his field of struggle less grandiose and therefore more applicable to ordinary citizens. Great athletes teach us that life is a series of struggles, not one giant effort. Just when we appear to have triumphed, we must stop like Sisyphus and again begin rolling the boulder up that mountain. The true athlete teaches us that winning isn't everything, but struggle is—the struggle to simply get up in the morning or to see hope through the minefields of despair.

Viewed that way, a marriage, or any relationship with another human being, is an ongoing struggle. The mastering of a skill or craft doesn't end with the granting of a diploma; it goes on for life. The relationship between parents and children doesn't end when the children turn eighteen. The running of a corporation isn't a one-shot affair, measured by a single year's statements of profits and losses; it's a continuing process, accomplished by human beings who learn from mistakes, plunge fearlessly into the struggle, take risks and prepare for the future.

It's probably no accident that American capitalism, with its often permanently infantile male executives, experienced a decline that coincided with the period when Vince Lombardi's values received their widest acceptance. The results are visible everywhere. Sit on a plane with American businessmen and they'll be chattering about the Pittsburgh Steelers. Join a group of Japanese businessmen and they'll be discussing twenty-first-century technology. One group is trapped in a philosophy that demands winning as its goal; the other cares more about patient, long-term growth—and for the moment at least, the latter is winning.

Another great maxim of the years of America's triumphs also came from the sports pages via the writer Grantland Rice. "It matters not who won or lost," declared the esteemed chonicler of the prewar years, "but how they played the game." By the time Vince Lombardi came along, such sentiments were being sneered at. We had then become a superpower, capable of blowing up the world. The man of grace, courage, endurance, and compassion was replaced in the public imagination by the swaggering macho blowhard; Humphrey Bogart gave way to John Wayne. With such attitudes dominating the landscape, we were certain to get into trouble, and we did. Vietnam and Watergate underscored the idea of winning at all costs. Yet today we seem incapable of admitting that an obsession with winning often leads to the most squalid of defeats.

Solid marriages are often built upon the experience of disastrous ones. Politicians who lose elections become tempered for the contests that follow, sometimes going on to solid, useful careers. Painters, playwrights, novelists, and other artists often learn as much from their failures as they do from those rare moments when vision, craft, and ambition come together to produce masterpieces. It's also that way in sports.

I remember a night when my friend José Torres, then a middleweight, was boxing Florentino Fernandez in Puerto Rico. I couldn't go to the fight, so I spent the night tuning in and out of the all-news radio stations, anxious about the result because Florentino was a great puncher. About three in the morning, Torres called.

"Oh, Pete," he said, close to tears. "I'm so sorry."

"What happened?"

"I got knocked out," Torres replied, his voice brimming with emotion, since he'd never lost as a professional. We started discussing what had happened. Emotions cooled; the talk became technical. Torres explained that he had learned some things about himself, about boxing. He now understood some of his flaws, and thought he could correct them. We talked for an hour. Then I asked what he was going to do next.

"Go to the gym," he said. "I'm going to be champion of the world."

Two years later, Torres *was* the world's light-heavyweight champion. He didn't quit after his first defeat. That night in San Juan he didn't say winning was the only thing, that it was time to pack it in. He had learned something from defeat, and knew that one violent night, somewhere down the line, he would show the world what he had learned. And that was precisely what he did. But he was aware of something else too: Sooner or later, someone might come along who was better than he was, for at least one evening. After all, even champions are human. Even champions eventually lose. That happened to José Torres as well. But then it didn't really matter. José Torres, like the rest of us, had learned that winning wasn't everything. Living was all, and in life, defeat and victory are inseparable brothers.

PROBING FOR MEANING

1. What is your reaction to Hamill's point that winning has been overemphasized in our society?

2. Why does Hamill think that in sports courage is more important than winning? Do you agree with his reasons? Why or why not?

3. "An individual's primary competition is with himself and all his attendant weaknesses." What point is Hamill making? Do you agree with him? Explain why.

4. Hamill suggests that the most important thing a true athlete can teach us about life is not the importance of winning but the necessity of struggling. How do you respond to this idea?

5. Does Hamill downplay the importance of winning or does he expand our concepts of it by examining other ways of looking at the issue?

PROBING FOR METHOD

1. What is Hamill's purpose in writing this essay? Is he seeking primarily to convince his readers that "winning isn't everything"?

2. On what does he base his opinion? What effective examples does he offer to support his point of view? To what extent did he influence your ideas about winning?

3. For what audience was Hamill writing? Do you think his essay would appeal to people interested in sports? Why or why not?

4. What effect does including his own experience with José Torres have on his argument? Does generalizing from this example make his conclusion more convincing? Why or why not?

Observing To Support Generalizations

What observations does Pete Hamill use to support his generalizations in "Winning Isn't Everything"?
Hamill works with two famous but contradictory sports "maxims" or generalizations: Vince Lombardi's "Winning isn't everything. It's the only thing" from the 1960s and a pre—World War II saying "It matters not who won or lost, but how they played the game." He turns to his own experience and that of other Americans to see which maxim makes the most sense.

First of all, he says Lombardi's saying has had greater influence on American life than almost any other utterance; he blames Watergate and Vietnam on the attitude expressed by Lombardi. He finds that much of our experience contradicts it, however. Our admiration for Sal Maglie and Joe Frazier in sports and for the Alamo and Pearl Harbor shows that we once cherished gallant losers. Even today, athletes like Reggie Jackson value courage more than winning. Hamill's experience with sports and sports figures as well as other human relationships like marriage has shown him that Lombardi's saying doesn't apply to everyone or to every situation.

He knows that American businessmen have forged their philosophies from Lombardi's attitude toward winning and believes our economy will lose further ground to Japan because we refuse to learn from our mistakes over the long run while the Japanese, who do not value the immediate victory, are willing to plan carefully for the future.

Hamill concludes by telling us of the experience of the boxer José Torres, who learned from a defeat rather than packing it in and went on to win the world's light-heavyweight championship.

Hamill finds evidence in American life that supports two contradictory generalizations about winning but cites from his own experience and observations evidence that shows one philosophy to be superior.

Using experience and observations to support generalizations.
The writer who wishes his or her points to be taken seriously—or even to be understood—must seek support for them from his or her own experience and observations. This support can come from many sources: from personal experience or that of other people, from books, newspapers,

magazines, from television and films, from instructors, lecturers, coaches, employers, friends. This support can be included in many forms: as a story, as a fact, as a statistic, as a survey, as a quotation, as an analogy, as an illustration.

As we have seen in studying Gloria Steinem's essay "The Importance of Work," some generalizations are broader than others: They take in several categories of experience, each of which may have its own generalization or subgeneralization. Steinem, for example, supports her generalization that work is one of life's basic pleasures with the subgeneralations that some women work because they have to, others work because they want to, and society needs the talents of all citizens. In Pete Hamill's essay, his generalization is his thesis statement, "Winning Isn't Everything." A subgeneralization is that we have always cherished gallant losers, even in sports. Another subgeneralization is that all relationships with human beings require struggle, not victory. His other points—about the Frazier-Ali fight, about the Alamo and Pearl Harbor, about Reggie Jackson or Richard "Goose" Gossage, about marriage, parents, and children, and about business executives—are observations that support his subgeneralizations, just as his subgeneralizations support his generalizations. A good essay, like a good paragraph, builds on subordination.

Observations themselves can also be classified as more or less general: Some observations are more specific than others. The story of an AIDS victim is more specific than statistics about AIDS. In his essay, Pete Hamill uses Sal Maglie to support his subgeneralization about gallant losers. He supports this observation with more specific observations about the game Maglie pitched against the Yankees in the 1956 World Series. As we saw in Chapter 2, your purpose and audience will help you determine how specific to be, when to use statistics, and when to tell stories (or recount games). Generally speaking, most audiences prefer a good tory—even if only a paragraph long—because, if appropriate, it gives dramatic support to your generalization.

Procedures to follow in supporting generalizations.

1. Consider what you have heard, read, or seen that will support your generalization. Collect as many observations as you can think of. Do research if necesary to locate material: Ask friends, classmates, and instructors, read newspapers and magazines, consult periodical indexes and the card catalog in the library.
2. Reflect on your own observations—personal experience and that of others—for additional support. Reread your journal or try freewriting, if necessary, to help you recall these experiences.
3. Find support for each subgeneralization supporting your central thesis.

ROBERT PIRSIG

Gumption

Robert Pirsig (b. 1928) is from Minneapolis, Minnesota. He has taught English at Montana State College, and in 1974 he received a Guggenheim Fellowship. "Gumption" is taken from Pirsig's autobiography Zen and The Art of Motorcycle Maintenance: An Inquiry Into Values *(1974). As you read his essay, compare his definition of gumption with yours.*

I like the word "gumption" because it's so homely and so forlorn and so out of style it looks as if it needs a friend and isn't likely to reject anyone who comes along. It's an old Scottish word, once used a lot by pioneers, but which, like "kin," seems to have all but dropped out of use. I like it also because it describes exactly what happens to someone who connects with Quality. He gets filled with gumption.

The Greeks called it *enthousiasmos*, the root of "enthusiasm," which means literally "filled with *theos*," or God, or Quality. See how that fits?

A person filled with gumption doesn't sit around dissipating and stewing about things. He's at the front of the train of his own awareness, watching to see what's up the track and meeting it when it comes. That's gumption. . . .

The gumption-filling process occurs when one is quiet long enough to see and hear and feel the real universe, not just one's own stalled opinions about it. But it's nothing exotic. That's why I like the word.

You see it often in people who return from long, quiet fishing trips. Often they're a little defensive about having put so much time to "no account" because there's no intellectual justification for what they've been doing. But the returned fisherman usually has a peculiar abundance of gumption, usually for the very same things he was sick to death of a few weeks before. He hasn't been wasting time. It's only your limited cultural viewpoint that makes it seem so.

If you're going to repair a motorcycle, an adequate supply of gumption is the first and most important tool. If you haven't got that you might as well gather up all the other tools and put them away, because they won't do you any good.

Gumption is the psychic gasoline that keeps the whole thing going. If you haven't got it there's no way the motorcycle can possibly be fixed. But if you *have* got it and know how to keep it there's absolutely no way in this whole world that motorcycle can *keep* from getting fixed. It's bound to happen. Therefore the thing that must be monitored at all times and preserved before anything else is the gumption.

This paramount importance of gumption solves a problem of format of this Chautauqua. The problem has been how to get off the generalities. If the Chautauqua gets into the actual details of fixing one individual machine the chances are overwhelming that it won't be your make and model and the information will be not only useless but dangerous, since information that fixes one model can sometimes wreck another. For detailed information of an objective sort, a separate shop manual for the specific make and model of machine must be used. In addition, a general shop manual such as *Audel's Automotive Guide* fills in the gaps.

But there's another kind of detail that no shop manual goes into but that is common to all machines and can be given here. This is the detail of the Quality relationship, the gumption relationship, between the machine and the mechanic, which is just as intricate as the machine itself. Throughout the process of fixing the machine things always come up, low-quality things, from a dusted knuckle to an accidentally ruined "irreplaceable" assembly. These drain off gumption, destroy enthusiasm and leave you so discouraged you want to forget the whole business. I call these things "gumption traps."

There are hundreds of different kinds of gumption traps, maybe thousands, maybe millions. I have no way of knowing how many I don't know. I know it *seems* as though I've stumbled into every kind of gumption trap imaginable. What keeps me from thinking I've hit them all is that with every job I discover more. Motorcycle maintenance gets frustrating. Angering. Infuriating. That's what makes it interesting. . . .

What I have in mind now is a catalog of "Gumption Traps I Have Known." I want to start a whole new academic field, gumptionology, in which these traps are sorted, classified, structured into hierarchies and interrelated for the edification of future generations and the benefit of all mankind.

Gumptionology 101—An examination of affective, cognitive and psychomotor blocks in the perception of Quality relationships—3cr, VII, MWF. I'd like to see that in a college catalog somewhere.

In traditional maintenance gumption is considered something you're born with or have acquired as a result of good upbringing. It's a fixed commodity. From the lack of information about how one acquires this gumption one might assume that a person without any gumption is a hopeless case.

In nondualistic maintenance gumption isn't a fixed commodity. It's variable, a reservoir of good spirits that can be added to or subtracted from. Since it's a result of the perception of Quality, a gumption trap, consequently, can be defined as anything that causes one to lose sight of Quality, and thus lose one's enthusiasm for what one is doing. As one might guess from a definition as broad as this, the field is enormous and only a beginning sketch can be attempted here.

As far as I can see there are two main types of gumption traps. The first type is those in which you're thrown off the Quality track by conditions that arise from external circumstances, and I call these "setbacks." The second type is traps in which you're thrown off the Quality track by conditions that are primarily within yourself. These I don't have any generic name for—"hang-ups," I suppose. . . .

PROBING FOR MEANING

1. What are some reasons Pirsig offers for liking the word "gumption"? Is it a word you are familiar with or use often? What words could you substitute for gumption?

2. "Gumption is the psychic gasoline that keeps the whole thing going." How does Pirsig apply this to life in general rather than only to motorcycles?

3. How do you react to Pirsig's new academic field of gumptionology? Is he being serious or humorous? Explain your answer.

4. Can you offer from reading the essay a definition of a "Chautauqua"?

PROBING FOR METHOD

1. In his discussion of gumption, Pirsig includes in his definition what gumption is not. Is this an effective device? Why or why not?

2. What is Pirsig's purpose in writing about gumption? Does he succeed in convincing you that gumption is a quality we should all seek? Why or why not?

3. How would you describe Pirsig's style? Is it accessible to a general audience? Why or why not?

4. Compare Pirsig's use of concrete observations with that of the other writers in this chapter. How does his treatment differ? What effect does his approach have on the reader?

JIM FUSILLI

A Wall Street Rocker

Jim Fusilli (b. 1954) is a graduate of St. Peter's College in Jersey City with a B.A. in English. In addition to his position at Dow Jones, he composes lyrics and is a free-lance writer whose work has appeared in the Wall Street Journal *among other publications. He has also written a novel scheduled for publication in 1988. He wrote "Wall Street Rocker" because he "wanted to publish a first-person essay and the topic seemed to have the broadest appeal." As you read Fusilli's essay, record your thoughts about what he is trying to accomplish.*

"Who says you can't have it all?" asks the beer commercial. "Who says you can't have pin stripes and rock 'n' roll?" Me. I say you can't have it all. I try, so I know. Five days a week I write and edit employee newsletters and do a variety of other corporate tasks. Two nights a week, I sing and play guitar in a rock'n' roll band. The two aren't compatible. Not even close.

Other people with full-blown careers play instruments. Richard Nixon plays the piano, Johnny Carson the drums; Sherlock Holmes played the violin. But playing in the band is not like that. It's not a once-in-a-while thing. You don't sit at home and pluck the strings for yourself. That's fun. There's no pressure.

But with a band, especially one that's serious about its business, you have to put up with all the ancillary activity that goes with the turf. There's the interaction with group members— in my case, five other guys, three of whom are full-time music makers, all with artistic idiosyncrasies. There are endless rehearsals and conferences. If you write your own songs, as we do, there are musical and vocal arrangements to work out. Sometimes you have to defend your material, and sometimes you have to play a song you don't like.

That may sound like a typical day at the office to you. But for me, it comes *after* a day at the office, and there's a giant mind-shift that has to take place. I take the E-train to an uptown New York rehearsal hall, and if I don't feel and think like a musician by the time I get there, I'm sunk. The practicality of business life doesn't apply. Progress comes slowly, if at all. There's little tangible evidence of achievement, except for the cassettes I make at each rehearsal. Frustration is acute. We practice the same number for a solid month. Not even accountants work on the same number every day.

And I think like a businessman now. I'm no longer interested in playing just for fun. I look at the bottom line; so far, I've lost time and money. I want schedules; I work best on deadline. I want the band's goals defined.

My goal is to get good tapes and send them out. It would be swell to get a song on the next album Quincy Jones produces and pull in a few million bucks in royalties. Accordingly, once we perform a song I've written and get a quality recording of it, I ask that we drop it from our repertory. Sometimes I ask the other guys what they want out of it. When they answer "I like to play," I don't understand.

And there are other problems: I'm the only guy who shows up at the rehearsal hall in a suit. Think of how you'd look if you showed up at the office with a sleeveless T-shirt, black studded jeans and leather gloves. My hair—standard Wall Street issue—looks fine at the office, ridiculous at rock clubs. I'm constantly dieting. Rockers are either thin or extremely fat, and I'm neither. I used to be able to jump from the piano top into a split. Now I have to sit to tie my shoes.

We are frequently the oldest band on the bill. We get booked in places designed for people trying to make it. People our age—I'm 32— who haven't yet made it and have solid day jobs usually give up. At one gig, I sat in the dressing room and watched a kid I was certain was a girl change into costume.

When the kid turned around, I saw he was just a very young boy. Then he said "excuse me" as he walked by. I was thankful he didn't add "dad" to the sentence's end.

I recently asked Van Morrison if he ever felt too old to live the rock 'n' roll life. "No way," he said adamantly but then described all the problems getting older in the rock world bring. Don't tell me Paul McCartney is 43, Dylan 44, Chuck Berry 59. Age isn't a dilemma if you've made it and can look back on the mayhem. If your troubles are before you, it's another thing altogether. Remember, Michael Jackson is 27, and he made some $70 million from his last album. And John Lennon's son is now a pop star.

The obvious question is, "Why not walk away?" There's plenty of satisfaction in my Wall Street career, in writing and editing. I'm not leaving it. I certainly don't want to try to hustle a job as a guitarist or a singer in New York. There are more of those than newsletter editors.

When I was in high school, there were four reasons to form a rock band: to meet girls, have fun, show off in public while getting paid for it and because we were crazy for the music. Reason 1 is definitely dead: The only ladies I'm interested in are my wife and our 2-year-old daughter.

Number 2: Fun dribbles in, but sometimes not for weeks at a time. "Then you shouldn't do it if you feel that way," retorts our keyboard player. Two minutes later he says, "You aren't going to quit, are you?" "No," I say, "I'm not going to quit."

As for the in-public part, I truly enjoy performing. Leaving aside the pain of it—carting my own heavy equipment around, staying up until 4 A.M., arguing over who gets guest passes—it's still terrific to play in front of an audience, particularly a New York crowd that refuses to applaud unless you're good. We get a good reception. We're skilled technically and we maintain high energy, a rare combination, as far as I can tell. My material is well-received, my voice is stronger than ever and, on guitar, I cut my parts with little difficulty. I do O.K.

That leaves the music, which has something to do, I think, with a dream. In this case, it's the dream that I have something to say. It's cloaked in a four-minute song with maybe five chords and a pretty neat modulation. It's probably been said before, but this is how I say it, and I want it heard.

Bruce Springsteen—he's 36—writes: "Talk about a dream, try to make it real." That sounds about right. I think you've got to go after it and give it your best shot until the dream is dead. When I complete a song, lyric and medley, and perform it, it's a wonderful feeling. I get butterflies and my skin tingles. It's actually thrilling. There's nothing like it. And that doesn't sound like a dead dream to me.

PROBING FOR MEANING

1. What specific examples from his own experience does Fusilli cite to support his thesis that "you can't have it all"?

2. What does Fusilli want out of playing with the band? Why does that some-times put him in conflict with the other members?

3. What point does Fusilli make about chronology and the life of a rock and roll musician? Do you agree with him that "age isn't a dilemma if you've made it"?

4. What does Fusilli get out of performing? Do you think many people would pay his price to continue as "a Wall Street rocker"? Would you? Why or why not?

PROBING FOR METHOD

1. Why are Fusilli's introduction and conclusion so effective? What technique do both have in common?

2. Fusilli's essay was published originally in the "About Men" column of the *New York Times Magazine*. Who reads the *Times*? Why do you think he chose this particular audience? Can you think of another audience who would also be responsive to his essay? How did it affect you?

3. Fusilli has arrived at an original generalization based entirely on his own expe-riences. Many writers begin with generalizations and use their experiences to support them (see Pete Hamill's "Winning Isn't Everything"). What kind of topics might be most effectively treated by Fusilli's approach? By Hamill's?

STEVE TESICH

An Amateur Marriage

Steve Tesich (b. 1943) was born in Yugoslavia and came to America as an adolescent. He is a writer of plays and screenplays and in 1979 won the Academy Award for "Breaking Away." He is also a frequent contributor to periodicals, including the "About Men" column published weekly in The New York Times Magazine. *In an 1980 interview Tesich stated: "I don't like the image of myself as a busy writer and in some ways I wish all of these things weren't happening at once. . . . I like to have hours to think and I wish things had spaced themselves out more." While reading Tesich's essay on marriage, think about how his attitude toward it is similar to or different from yours.*

Everyone told me that when I turned 16 some great internal change would occur. I truly expected the lights to go down on my former life and come up again on a new, far more enchanting one. It didn't work. Nothing happened.

When asked by others, I lied and said that, yes, I did feel a great change had taken place. They lied and told me that they could see it in me.

They lied again when I turned 18. There were rumors that I was now a "man." I noticed no difference, but I pretended to have all the rumored symptoms of manhood. Even though these mythical milestones, these rituals of passage, were not working for me, I still clung to the belief that they should, and I lied and said they were.

My 21st birthday was the last birthday I celebrated. The rituals weren't working, and I was tired of pretending I was changing. I was merely growing—adding on rooms for all the kids who were still me to live in. At 21, I was single but a family man nevertheless.

All these birthday celebrations helped to prepare me for the greatest myth of all: marriage. Marriage comes with more myths attached to it than a six-volume set of ancient Greek history. Fortunately for me, by the time I decided to get married I didn't believe in myths anymore.

It was a very hot day in Denver, and I think Becky and I decided to get married because we knew the city hall was air-conditioned. It was a way of hanging around a cool place for a while. I had forgotten to buy a wedding ring, but Becky was still wearing the ring from her previous marriage, so we used that one. It did the job. She had to take it off and then put it back on again, but it didn't seem to bother anyone. The air-conditioners were humming.

I felt no great change take place as I repeated our marriage vows. I did not feel any new rush of "commitment" to the woman who was now my wife, nor did I have any plans to be married to her forever. I did love her, but I saw no reason why I should feel that I had to love her forever. I would love her for as long as I loved her. I assumed she felt the same way. The women I saw on my way out of city hall, a married man, did not look any less beautiful than the women I saw on my way in. It was still hot outside. We walked to our car carrying plastic bags containing little samples of mouthwash, toothpaste, shampoo and aspirin, gifts from the Chamber of Commerce to all newlyweds.

And so my marriage began—except that I never really felt the beginning. I had nothing against transforming myself into a married man, but I felt no tidal pull of change. I assumed Becky had married me and not somebody else, so why should I become somebody else? She married a family of kids of various ages, all of them me, and I married a family of kids of various ages, all of them her. At one time or another I assumed some of them were bound to get along.

Marriage, I was told, required work. This sounded all wrong to me from the start. I couldn't quite imagine the kind of "work" it required, what the hours were, what the point was. The very idea of walking into my apartment and "working" on my marriage seemed ludicrous. My apartment was a place where I went to get away from work. The rest of life was full of work. If marriage required "work," I would have to get another apartment just for myself where I could go and rest. Since I couldn't afford that at the time, I said nothing to Becky about working on our marriage. She said nothing about it herself. We were either very wise or very lazy.

We are led to believe that the harder we try, the better we get. This "aerobic dancing theory" of life may apply to certain things, but I don't think marriage is one of them. You can't go to a gym and pump marriage. It can't be tuned-up like a car. It can't be trained like a dog. In this century of enormous scientific breakthroughs, there have been no major marriage breakthroughs that I know of.

Progress junkies find this a frustrating state of affairs. They resist the notion that marriage is essentially an amateur endeavor, not a full-time profession, and they keep trying to work on their marriages and make them better. The only way to do that is to impose a structure on the marriage and then fiddle and improve the structure. But that has nothing to do with the way you feel when the guests have left the house and it's just the two of you again. You are either glad you're there with that person or you're not. I've been both.

This need to improve, the belief that we can improve everything, brings to mind some of my friends who are constantly updating their stereo equipment until, without being aware of it, they wind up listening to the equipment and not to the music. You can do the same thing to friendship, to marriage, to life in general. Let's just say I have chosen to listen to the music, such as it is, on the equipment on hand.

The best trips that I have taken were always last-minute affairs, taken as a lark. When I've sent off for brochures and maps, the trips always turned into disappointments. The time I invested in planning fed my expectations, and I traveled to fulfill my expectations rather than just to go somewhere I hadn't been. I consider my marriage one of those trips taken as a lark. I have become rather fond of the sheer aimlessness of the journey. It's a choice. I know full well that people do plan journeys to the Himalayas, they hire guides, they seek advice, and when they get there, instead of being disappointed, they experience a kind of exhilaration that I never will. My kind of marriage will never reach Mount Everest. You just don't go there as a lark, nor do you get there by accident.

I'm neither proud nor ashamed of the fact that I've stayed married for 13 years. I don't consider it an accomplishment of any kind. I have changed; my wife has changed. Our marriage, however, for better or worse, is neither better nor worse. It has remained the same. But the climate has changed.

I got married on a hot day a long time ago, because it was a way of cooling off for a while. Over the years, it's also become a place where I go to warm up when the world turns cold.

PROBING FOR MEANING

1. Why does Tesich begin by mentioning his sixteenth, eighteenth, and twenty-first birthdays?

2. How do you react to his statement that he "saw no reason why I should feel

that I had to love her forever"? Is this a cynical or just a realistic view of marriage?

3. Tesich reacts very strongly to society's idea that marriage is work. Are the reasons he offers for resisting this concept convincing? Did he convince you?

4. What are the implications of Tesich's remarks about "progress junkies"? Is he making a point about our society apart from marriage?

5. What point is Tesich making about his marriage by relating it to the fact that the best trips he took were last minute rather than carefully planned?

6. What is the significance of the essay's title?

PROBING FOR METHOD

1. Tesich's essay was originally published in the "About Men" column of the *New York Times Magazine*. Is his essay one that would appeal primarily to a male audience? Explain your answer.

2. Like Francke (Chapter 7), Tesich uses humor to enhance his meaning. Which examples of humor do you find most effective.

3. Tesich uses the image of a journey to present his subject. Why is this use of figurative language effective?

4. Tesich's view of marriage is obviously controversial. What was his purpose in writing the essay? Do you think he was only stating his opinion or was he also trying to influence his readers?

5. Tesich arrives at a generalization from his own experience. What other generalizations might he have arrived at? What in his experience could he use to support these other generalizations? Why does he choose this one?

GWENDOLYN BROOKS

Life for My Child Is Simple, and Is Good

Gwendolyn Brooks (b. 1917) is an American poet who was raised in the slums of Chicago—a setting she later used for many of her poems, which focus on contemporary black life. Her volumes include A Street in Bronzeville *(1949),* Annie Allen *(1949), for which she won a Pulitzer Prize, and* The Bean Eaters *(1960). She has also influenced a generation of younger black writers through writing workshops that she conducted in Chicago. As you read her poem about her aspirations for her son, compare her hopes for him with those you have for your child or for yourself.*

Life for my child is simple, and is good.
He knows his wish. Yes, but that is not all.
Because I know mine too.
And we both want joy of undeep and unabiding things,
Like kicking over a chair or throwing blocks out of a window
Or tipping over an icebox pan
Or snatching down curtains or fingering an electric outlet
Or a journey or a friend or an illegal kiss.
No. There is more to it than that.
It is that he has never been afraid.
Rather, he reaches out and lo the chair falls with a beautiful crash,
And the blocks fall, down on the people's heads,
And the water comes slooshing sloopily out across the floor.
And so forth.
Not that success, for him, is sure, infallible.
But never has he been afraid to reach.
His lesions are legion.
But reaching is his rule.

PROBING FOR MEANING

1. How are the examples of the joys of "unabiding things" similar?
2. What is the relationship between the son's being "unafraid" and "reaching"?
3. Explain in your own words the line "his lesions are legion." Does that line contradict the first line of the poem? Why or why not?
4. How are the poet's goals for her son similar to or different from yours?

PROBING FOR METHOD

1. What is the impact on the poem's meaning of the transitional line "there is more to it than that"?

2. What is the poet's purpose in writing the poem?

3. Characterize the poet's audience. Is she writing for parents? For children? Both?

DORIS LESSING

Notes for a Case History

Doris Lessing (b. 1919) was born in Iran and at age six moved with her parents to a farm in Southern Rhodesia. Her intense commitment to socialism and other causes, including the women's movement, is expressed in many of her works, including her autobiographical Children of Violence *(1950–1969) and* The Golden Notebook *(1962). In recent work, she has turned to science fiction as a mode for expressing her strong sense of moral responsibility. As you read "Notes for a Case History," compare Maureen to other ambitious people you have known.*

Maureen Watson was born at 93 Nelson's Way, N.1., in 1942. She did not remember the war, or rather, when people said "The War," she thought of Austerity: couponed curtains, traded clothes, the half pound of butter swapped for the quarter of tea. (Maureen's parents preferred tea to butter.) Further back, at the roots of her life, she *felt* a movement of fire and shadow, a leaping and a subsidence of light. She did not know whether this was a memory or a picture she had formed, perhaps from what her parents had told her of the night the bomb fell two streets from Nelson's Way and they had all stood among piles of smoking rubble for a day and night, watching firemen hose the flames. This feeling was not only of danger, but of fatality, of being helpless before great impersonal forces; and was how she most deeply felt, saw, or thought an early childhood which the social viewer would describe perhaps like this: "Maureen Watson, conceived by chance on an unexpected granted-at-the-last-minute leave, at the height of the worst war in history, infant support of a mother only occasionally upheld (the chances of war deciding) by a husband she had met in a bomb shelter during an air raid: poor baby, born into a historical upheaval which destroyed forty million and might very well have destroyed her."

As for Maureen, her memories and the reminiscences of her parents made her dismiss the whole business as boring, and nothing to do with her.

It was at her seventh birthday party she first made this clear. She wore a mauve organdy frock with a pink sash, and her golden hair was in ringlets. One of the mothers said: "This is the first unrationed party dress my Shirley has had. It's a shame, isn't it?" And her own mother said: "Well of course these war children don't know what they've missed." At which Maureen said: "*I* am not a war child." "What are you then, love?" said her mother, fondly exchanging glances.

"I'm Maureen," said Maureen.

"And I'm Shirley," said Shirley, joining cause.

Shirley Banner was Maureen's best friend. The Watsons and the Banners were better than the rest of the street. The Watsons lived in an end house, at higher weekly payments. The Banners had a sweets-paper-and-tobacco shop.

Maureen and Shirley remembered (or had they been told?) that once Nelson's Way was a curved terrace of houses. Then the ground-floor level had broken into shops: a grocer's, a laundry, a hardware, a baker, a dairy. It seemed as if every second family in the street ran a shop to supply certain defined needs of the other families. What other needs were there? Apparently none; for Maureen's parents applied for permission to the Council, and the ground floor of their house became a second grocery shop, by way of broken-down walls, new shelves, a deepfreeze. Maureen remembered two small rooms, each with flowered curtains where deep shadows moved and flickered from the two small fires that burned back to back in the centre wall that divided them. These two rooms disappeared in clouds of dust from which sweet-smelling planks of wood stuck out. Strange but friendly men paid her compliments on her golden corkscrews and asked her for kisses, which they did not get. They gave her sips of sweet tea from their canteens (filled twice a day by her mother) and made her bracelets of the spiralling fringes of yellow wood. Then they disappeared. There was the new shop. Maureen's Shop. Maureen went with her mother to the sign shop to arrange for these two words to be written in yellow paint on a blue ground.

Even without the name, Maureen would have known that the shop was connected with hopes for her future; and that her future was what her mother lived for.

She was pretty. She had always known it. Even where the shadows of fire and dark were, they had played over a pretty baby. "You were such a pretty baby, Maureen." And at the birthday parties: "Maureen's growing really pretty, Mrs. Watson." But all babies and little girls are pretty, she knew that well enough . . . no, it was something more. For Shirley was plump, dark—pretty. Yet their parents'—or rather, their mothers'—talk had made it clear from the start that Shirley was not in the same class as Maureen.

When Maureen was ten there was an episode of importance. The two mothers were in the room above Maureen's Shop and they were brushing their little girls' hair out. Shirley's mother said: "Maureen could do really well for herself, Mrs. Watson." And Mrs. Watson nodded, but sighed deeply. The sigh annoyed Maureen, because it contradicted the absolute certainty that she felt (it had been bred into her) about her future. Also because it had to do with the *boring* era which she remembered, or thought she did, as a tiger-striped movement of fire. *Chance:* Mrs. Watson's sigh was like a prayer to the gods of Luck: it was the sigh of a small helpless thing being tossed about by big seas and gales. Maureen made a decision, there and then, that she had nothing in common with the little people who were prepared to be helpless and tossed about. For she was going to be quite different. She was already different. Not only The War but the shadows of war had long gone, except for talk in the newspapers which had nothing to do with her. The shops were full of everything. The Banners' sweets-tobacco-paper shop had just been done up; and Maureen's was short of nothing. Maureen and Shirley, two pretty little girls in smart mother-made dresses, were children of plenty, and knew it, because their parents kept saying (apparently they did not care how tedious they were): "These kids don't lack for anything, do they? They don't know what it can be like, do they?" This, with the suggestion that they ought to be grateful for not lacking anything, always made the children sulky, and they went off to flirt their full many-petticoated skirts where the neighbours could see them and pay them compliments.

Eleven years. Twelve years. Already Shirley had subsided into her role of pretty girl's plainer girl friend, although of course she was not plain at all. Fair girl, dark girl, and Maureen by mysterious birthright was the "pretty one," and there was no doubt in either of their minds which girl the boys would try first for a date. Yet this balance was by no means as unfair as it seemed. Maureen, parrying and jesting on street corners, at bus stops, knew she was doing battle for two, because the boys she discarded Shirley got: Shirley got far more boys than she would have done without Maureen who, for her part, needed— more, *had* to have—a foil. Her role demanded one.

They both left school at fifteen, Maureen to work in the shop. She was keeping her eyes open: her mother's phrase. She wore a slim white overall, pinned her fair curls up, was neat and pretty in her movements. She smiled calmly when customers said: "My word, Mrs. Watson, your Maureen's turned out, hasn't she?"

About that time there was a second moment of consciousness. Mrs. Watson was finishing a new dress for Maureen, and the fitting was taking rather long. Maureen fidgeted and her mother said: "Well, it's your capital, isn't it? You've got to see that, love." And she added the deep unconscious sigh. Maureen said: "Well don't go on about it, it's not very nice, is it?" And what she meant was, not that the idea was not very nice, but that she had gone beyond needing to be reminded about it; she was feeling the irritated embarrassment of a child when it is reminded to clean its teeth after this habit has become second nature. Mrs. Watson saw and understood this, and sighed again; and this time it was the maternal sigh which means: Oh dear, you are growing up fast! "Oh *Mum*," said Maureen, "sometimes you just make me tired, you do really."

Sixteen. She was managing her capital perfectly. Her assets were a slight delicate prettiness, and a dress sense that must have been a gift from God, or more probably because she had been reading the fashion magazines since practically before consciousness. Shirley had put in six months of beehive hair, pouting scarlet lips, and an air of sullen disdain; but Maureen's sense of herself was much finer. She modelled herself on film stars, but with an understanding of how far she could go—of what was allowable to Maureen. So the experience of being Bardot, Monroe, or whoever it was, refined her: she took from it an essence, which was learning to be a vehicle for othe people's fantasies. So while Shirley had been a dozen stars, but really *been* them, in violent temporary transmogrifications, from which she emerged (often enough with a laugh) Shirley—plump, good-natured, and herself—Maureen remained herself through every role, but creating her appearance, like an alter ego, to meet the expression in people's eyes.

Round about sixteen, another incident: prophetic. Mrs. Watson had a cousin who worked in the dress trade, and this man, unthought-of for many years, was met at a wedding. He commented on Maureen, a vision in white gauze. Mrs Watson worked secretly on this slender material for some weeks; then wrote to him: Could Maureen be a model? He had only remote connections with the world of expensive clothes and girls, but he dropped into the shop with frankly personal aims. Maureen in a white wrapper was still pretty, very; but her remote air told this shrewd man that she would certainly not go out with him. She was saving herself; he knew that air of self-esteem very well from other exemplars. Such girls do not go out with middle-aged cousins, except as a favour or to get something. However, he told Mrs. Watson that Maureen was definitely model material, but that she would have to do something about her voice. (He meant her accent of course; and so Mrs. Watson understood him. He left addresses and advice, and Mrs. Watson was in a state of quivering ambition. She said so to Maureen: "This is your chance, girl. Take it." What Maureen heard was: "This is *my* chance."

Maureen, nothing if not alert for her Big Chance, for which her whole life had prepared her, accepted her mother's gift of a hundred pounds (she did not thank her, no thanks were due) and actually wrote to the school where she would be taught voice training.

Then she fell into sullen withdrawal, which she understood so little that a week had gone by before she said she must be sick—or something. She was rude to her mother: very rare, this. Her father chided her for it: even rarer. But he spoke in such a way that Maureen understood for the first time that this drive, this push, this family effort to gain her a glamorous future, came from her mother, her father was not implicated. For him, she was a pretty-enough girl, spoiled by a silly woman.

Maureen slowly understood she was not sick, she was growing up. For one thing: if she changed her "voice" so as to be good enough to mix with new people, she would no longer be part of this street, she would no longer be *Our Maureen*. What would she be then? Her mother knew: she would marry a duke and be whisked off to Hollywood. Maureen examined her mother's ideas for her and shrank with humiliation. She was above all no fool, but she had been very foolish. For one thing: when she used her eyes, with the scales of illusion off them, she saw that the million streets of London blossomed with girls as pretty as she. What, then, had fed the illusion in herself and in other people? What accounted for the special tone, the special looks that always greeted her? Why, nothing more than that she, Maureen, because of her mother's will behind her, had carried herself from childhood as something special, apart, destined for a great future.

Meanwhile (as she clearly saw) she was in 93 Nelson's Way, serving behind the counter of Maureen's Shop. (She now wondered what the neighbours had thought—before they got used to it—about her mother's fondness so terribly displayed.) She was dependent on nothing less than that a duke or a film producer would walk in to buy a quarter of tea and some sliced bread.

Maureen sulked. So her father said. So her mother complained. Maureen was—thinking? Yes. But more, a wrong had been done her, she knew it, and the sulking was more of a protective silence while she grew a scab over a wound.

She emerged demanding that the hundred pounds should be spent on sending her to secretarial school. Her parents complained that she could have learned how to be a secretary for nothing if she had stayed on at school another year. She said: "Yes, but you didn't have the sense to make me, did you? What did you think—I was going to sell butter like you all my life?" Unfair, on the face of it; but deeply fair, in view of what they had done to her. In their different ways they knew it. (Mr. Watson knew in his heart, for instance, that he should never have allowed his wife to call the shop "Maureen's.") Maureen went, then, to secretarial school for a year. Shirley went with her: she had been selling cosmetics in the local branch of a big chain store. To raise the hundred pounds was difficult for Shirley's parents: the shop had done badly, had been bought by a big firm; her father was an assistant in it. For that matter, it wasn't all that easy for the Watsons: the hundred pounds was the result of small savings and pinchings over years.

This was the first time Maureen had thought of the word capital in connection with money, rather than her own natural assets: it was comparatively easy for the Watsons to raise money, because they had capital: the Banners had no capital. (Mrs. Watson said the Banners had had *bad luck*.) Maureen strengthened her will; and as a result the two families behaved even more as if the girls would have different futures—or, to put it another way, that while the two sums of a hundred pounds were the same, the Watsons could be expected to earn more on theirs than the Banners.

This was reflected directly in the two girls' discussions about boys. Shirley would say: "I'm more easygoing than you."

Maureen would reply: "*I* only let them go so far."

Their first decisions on this almighty subject had taken place years before, when they were thirteen. Even then Shirley went further ("let them go further") than Maureen. It was put down, between them, to Shirley's warmer temperament—charitably; for both knew it was because of Maureen's higher value in the market.

At the secretarial school they met boys they had not met before. Previously boys had been from the street or the neighbourhood, known from birth, and for this reason not often gone out with—that would have been boring (serious, with possibilities of marriage). Or boys picked up after dances or at the pictures. But now there were new boys met day after day in the school. Shirley went out with one for weeks, thought of getting engaged, changed her mind, went out with another. Maureen went out with a dozen, chosen carefully. She knew what she was doing—and scolded Shirley for being so *soft*. "You're just stupid, Shirl—I mean, you've got to get on. Why don't you do like me?"

What Maureen did was to allow herself to be courted, until she agreed at least, as a favour, to be taken out. First, lunch—a word she began to use now. She would agree to go out to lunch two or three times with one boy, while she was taken out to supper (dinner) by another. The dinner partner, having been rewarded by a closed-mouth kiss for eight, ten, twelve nights, got angry or sulky or reproachful, according to his nature. He dropped her, and the lunch partner was promoted to dinner partner.

Maureen ate free for the year of her training. It wasn't that she planned it like this: but when she heard others girls say they paid their way or liked to be independent, it seemed to Maureen wrong-headed. To pay for herself would be to let herself be undervalued: even the idea of it made her nervous and sulky.

At the end of the training Maureen got a job in a big architect's office. She was a junior typist. She stuck out for a professional office because the whole point of the training was to enable her to meet a better class of people. Of course she had already learned not to use the phrase, and when her mother did snubbed her with: "I don't know what you mean, better *class*, but it's not much point my going into that hardware stuck upstairs in an office by myself if I can get a job where there's some life about."

Shirley went into a draper's shop where there was one other typist (female) and five male assistants.

In Maureen's place there were six architects, out most of the time, or invisible in large offices visited only by the real secretaries; a lower stratum of young men in training, designers, draftsmen, managers, etc., and a pool of typists.

The young men were mostly of her own class. For some months she ate and was entertained at their expense; and at each week's end there was a solemn ceremony, the high point of the week, certainly the most exciting moment in it, when she divided her wage. It was seven pounds (rising to ten in three years) and she allocated two pounds for clothes, four for the post office, and one pound for the week's odd expenses.

At the end of a year she understood two things. That she had saved something like two hundred pounds. That there was not a young man in the office who would take her out again. They regarded her, according to their natures, with resentment or with admiration for her cool management of them. But there was nothing doing *there*—so they all knew.

Maureen thought this over. If she were not taken out to meals and entertainment, she must pay for herself and save no money, or she must never go out at all. If she was going to be taken out, then she must give something in return. What she gave was an open mouth, and freedom to the waist. She calculated that because of her prettiness she could give much less than other girls.

She was using her *capital* with even more intelligence than before. A good part of her time—all not spent in the office or being taken out—went in front of her looking glass, or with the better-class fashion magazines. She studied them with formidable concentration. By now she knew she could have gone anywhere in these islands, except for her voice. Whereas, months before, she had sulked in a sort of fright at the idea of cutting herself off from her street and the neighbours, now she softened and shaped her voice, listening to the clients and the senior architects in the office. She knew her voice had changed when Shirley said: "You're talking nice, Maureen, much nicer than me."

There was a boy in the office who teased her about it. His name was Tony Head. He was in training to be an accountant for the firm, and was very much from her own background. After having taken her out twice to lunch, he had never asked her again. She knew why: he had told her. "Can't afford you, Maureen," he said. He earned not much more than she did. He was nineteen, ambitious, serious, and she liked him.

Then she was nineteen. Shirley was engaged to one of the assistants in her shop, and would be married next Christmas.

Maureen took forty pounds out of her savings and went on a tour to Italy. It was her first time out of England. She hated it: not Italy, but the fact that half the sixty people on the tour were girls, like herself, looking for a good time, and the other half elderly couples. In Rome, Pisa, Florence, Venice, the Italians mooned over Maureen, courted her with melting eyes, while she walked past them, distant as a starlet. They probably thought she was one. The courier, a sharp young man, took Maureen out to supper one night after he had finished his duties, and made it clear that her mouth, even if opened, and her breasts, were not enough. Maureen smiled at him sweetly through the rest of the trip. No one paid for her odd coffees, ices and drinks. On the last night of the trip, in a panic because the forty-pound investment had yielded so little, she went out with an Italian boy who spoke seven words of English. She thought him crude, and left him after an hour.

But she had learned a good deal for her forty pounds. Quietly, in her lunch hour, she went off to the National Gallery and to the Tate. There she looked, critical and respectful, at pictures, memorising their subjects, or main colours, learning names. When invited out, she asked to be taken to "foreign" films, and when she got back home wrote down the names of the director and the stars. She looked at the book page of the *Express* (she made her parents buy it instead of the *Mirror*) and sometimes bought a recommended book, if it was a best seller.

Twenty. Shirley was married and had a baby. Maureen saw little of her—both girls felt they had a new world of knowledge the other couldn't appreciate.

Maureen was earning ten pounds a week, and saved six.

There came to the office, as an apprentice architect, Stanley Hunt, from grammar school and technical college. Tallish, well-dressed, fair, with a small moustache. They took each other's measure, knowing they were the same kind. It was some weeks before he asked her out. She knew, by putting herself in his place, that he was looking for a wife with a little money or a house of her own, if he couldn't get a lady. (She smiled when she heard him using this word about one of the clients.) He tried to know clients socially, to be accepted by them as they accepted the senior architects. All this Maureen watched, her cool little face saying nothing.

One day, after he had invited a Miss Plast (Chelsea, well-off, investing money in houses) to coffee, and been turned down, he asked Maureen to join him in a sandwich lunch. Maureen thanked him delightfully, but said she already had an engagement. She went off to the National Gallery, sat on the steps, froze off wolves and pickups, and ate a sandwich by herself.

A week later, invited to lunch by Stanley, she suggested the Trattoria Siciliana which was more expensive, as she knew quite well, than he had expected. But this meal was a success. He was impressed with her, though he knew (how could he not, when his was similar?) her background.

She was careful to be engaged for two weeks. Then she agreed to go the the pictures—"a foreign film, if you don't mind, I think the American films are just boring." She did not offer to pay, but remarked casually that she had nearly six hundred pounds in the post office. "I'm thinking of buying a little business, sometime. A dress shop. I've got a cousin in the trade."

Stanley agreed that "with your taste" it would be a sure thing.

Maureen no longer went to the Palais, or similar places (though she certainly did not conceal from Stanley that she had "once"), but she loved to dance. Twice they went to the West End together and danced at a Club which was "a nice place." They danced well together. On the second occasion she offered to pay her share, for the first time in her life. He refused, as she had known he would, but she could see he liked her for offering: more, was relieved; in the office they said she was mean, and he must have heard them. On that night, taken home lingeringly, she opened her mouth for him and let his hands go down to her thighs. She felt a sharp sexuality which made her congratulate herself that she had never, like Shirley, gone "half-way" before. Well of course, girls were going to get married to just anybody if they let themselves be all worked up every time they were taken out!

But Stanley was not at all caught. He was too cool a customer, as she was. He was still looking for something better.

He would be an architect in a couple of years; he would be in a profession; he was putting down money for a house; he was good-looking, attractive to women, and with these assets he ought to do better than marry Maureen. Maureen agreed with him.

But meanwhile he took her out. She was careful often to be engaged elsewhere. She was careful always to be worth taking somewhere expensive. When he took her home, while she did not go so far as "nearly the whole way," she went "everything but"; and she was glad she did not like him better, because otherwise she would have been lost. She knew quite well she did not really like him, although her mind was clouded by her response to his hands, his moustache, his clothes and his new car.

She knew, because meanwhile a relationship she understood very well, and regretted, had grown up with Tony. He, watching this duel between the well-matched pair, would grin and drop remarks at which Maureen coloured and turned coldly away. He often asked her out—but only for a "Dutch treat"—expecting her to refuse. "How's your savings account, Maureen? I can't save, you girls get it all spent on you." Tony took out a good many girls: Maureen kept a count of them. She hated him; yet she liked him, and knew she did. She relied on him above all for this grinning, honest understanding of her: he did not approve of her, but perhaps (she felt in her heart) he was right? During this period she several times burst into tears when alone, without apparent reason; afterwards she felt that life had no flavour. Her future was narrowing down to Stanley; and at these times she viewed it through Tony Head's eyes.

One night the firm had a party for the senior members of the staff. Stanley was senior, Maureen and Tony were not. Maureen knew that Stanley had previously asked another girl to go, and when he asked herself, was uncertain whether she could make it until the very last moment: particularly as his inviting her, a junior, meant that he was trying out on the senior members the idea of Maureen as a wife. But she acquitted herself very well. First, she was the best-looking woman in the room by far, and the best-dressed. Everyone looked at her and commented: they were used to her as a pretty typist; but tonight she was using all her will to make them look at her, to make her face and body reflect what they admired. She made no mistakes. When the party was over Stanley and two of the younger architects suggested they drive out to London airport for breakfast, and they did. The two other girls were middle-class. Maureen kept silent for the most part, smiling serenely. She had been to Italy, she remarked, when a plane rose to go to Italy. Yes, she had liked it, though she thought the Italians were too noisy; what she had enjoyed best was the Sistine Chapel and a boat trip on the Adriatic. She hadn't cared for Venice much, it was beautiful, but the canals smelled, and there were far too many people; perhaps it would be better to go in winter? She said all this, having a right to it, and it came off. As she spoke she remembered Tony, who had once met her on her way to the National Gallery. "Getting yourself an education, Maureen? That's right, it'll pay off well, that will."

She knew, thinking it all over afterwards, that the evening had been important for her with Stanley. Because of this, she did not go out with him for a week, she said she was busy talking to her cousin about the possibilities of a dress shop. She sat in her room thinking about Stanley, and when thoughts of Tony came into her mind, irritatedly pushed them away. If she could succeed with Stanley, why not with someone better? The two architects from that evening had eyed her all the following week: they did not, however, ask her out. She then found that both were engaged to marry the girls they had been with. It was bad luck: she was sure that otherwise they would have asked her out. How to meet more like them? Well, that was the trouble—the drive to the airport was a bit of a fluke; it was the first time she had actually met the seniors socially.

Meanwhile Stanley showed an impatience in his courtship—and for the first time. As for her, she was getting on for twenty-one, and all the girls she had grown up with were married and had their first or even their second babies.

She went out with Stanley to a dinner in the West End at an Italian restaurant. Afterwards they were both very passionate. Maureen, afterwards, was furious with herself: some borderline had been crossed (she supposed she still could be called a virgin?) and now decisions would have to be made.

Stanley was in love with her. She was in love with Stanley. A week later he proposed to her. It was done with a violent moaning intensity that she knew was due to his conflicts over marrying her. She was not good enough. He was not good enough. They were second-best for each other. They writhed and moaned and bit in the car, and agreed to marry. Her eight hundred pounds would make it easier to buy the house in a good suburb. He would formally meet her parents next Sunday.

"So you're engaged to Stanley Hunt?" said Tony.

"Looks like, it doesn't it?"

"Caught him—good for you!"

"He's caught me, more like it!"

"Have it your way."

She was red and angry. He was serious.

"Come and have a bite?" he said. She went.

It was a small restaurant, full of office workers eating on luncheon vouchers. She ate fried plaice ("No chips, please") and he ate steak-and-kidney pudding. He joked, watched her, watched her intently, said finally: "Can't you do better than that?" He meant, and she knew it, better in the sense she would use herself, in her heart: he meant *nice*. Like himself. But did that mean that Tony thought *she* was nice? Unlike Stanley? She did not think she was, she was moved to tears (concealed) that he did. "What's wrong with him then?" she demanded, casual. "What's wrong with *you*? You need your head examined." He said it seriously, and they exchanged a long look. The two of them sat looking goodbye at each other: the extremely pretty girl at whom everyone in the room kept glancing and remarking on, and the good-looking, dark, rather fat young accountant who was brusque and solemn with disappointment in her. With love for her? Very likely.

She went home silent, thinking of Tony. When she thought of him she needed to cry. She also needed to hurt him.

But she told her parents she was engaged to Stanley, who would be an architect. They would have their own house, in (they thought) Hemel Hampstead. He owned a car. He was coming to tea on Sunday. Her mother forgot the dukes and the film producers before the announcement ended: her father listened judiciously, then congratulated her. He had been going to a football match on Sunday, but agreed, after persuasion, that this was a good-enough reason to stay home.

Her mother then began discussing, with deference to Maureen's superior knowledge, how to manage next Sunday to best advantage. For four days she went on about it. But she was talking to herself. Her husband listened, said nothing. And Maureen listened, critically, like her father. Mrs. Watson began clamouring for a definite opinion on what sort of cake to serve on Sunday. But Maureen had no opinion. She sat, quiet, looking at her mother, a largish ageing woman, her ex-fair hair dyed yellow, her flesh guttering. She was like an excited child, and it was not attractive. *Stupid, stupid, stupid*—that's all you are, thought Maureen.

As for Maureen, if anyone had made the comparison, she was "sulking" as she had before over being a model and having to be drilled out of her "voice." She said nothing but: "It'll be all right, Mum, don't get so worked up." Which was true, because Stanley knew what to expect: he knew why he had not been invited to meet her parents until properly hooked. He would have done the same in her place. He *was* doing the same: she was going to meet his parents the week after. What Mrs. Watson, Mr. Watson, wore on Sunday; whether sandwiches or cake were served; whether there were fresh or artificial flowers—none of it mattered. The Watsons were part of the bargain: what he was paying in return for publicly owning the most covetable woman anywhere they were likely to be; and for the right to sleep with her after the public display.

Meanwhile Maureen said not a word. She sat on her bed looking at nothing in particular. Once or twice she examined her face in the mirror, and even put cream on it. And she cut out a dress, but put it aside.

On Sunday Mrs. Watson laid tea for four, using her own judgement since Maureen was too deeply in love (so she told everyone) to notice such trifles. At four Stanley was expected, and at 3:55 Maureen descended to the living room. She wore: a faded pink dress from three summers before; her mother's cretonne overall used for housework; and a piece of cloth tied round her hair that might very well have been a duster. At any rate, it was a faded grey. She had put on a pair of her mother's old shoes. She could not be called plain; but she looked like her own faded elder sister, dressed for a hard day's spring cleaning.

Her father, knowledgeable, said nothing: he lowered the paper, examined her, let out a short laugh, and lifted it again. Mrs. Watson, understanding at last that this was a real crisis, burst into tears. Stanley arrived before Mrs. Watson could stop herself crying. He nearly said to Mrs. Watson: "I didn't know Maureen had an older sister." Maureen sat listless at one end of the table; Mr. Watson sat grinning at the other, and Mrs. Watson sniffed and wiped her eyes between the two.

Maureen said: "Hello, Stanley, meet my father and mother." He shook their hands and stared at her. She did not meet his eyes: rather, the surface of her blue gaze met the furious, incredulous, hurt pounce of his glares at her. Maureen poured tea, offered him sandwiches and cake, and made conversation about the weather, and the prices of food, and the dangers of giving even good customers credit in the shop. He sat there, a well-set-up young man, with his brushed hair, his brushed moustache, his checked brown cloth jacket, and a face flaming with anger and affront. He said nothing, but Maureen talked on, her voice trailing and cool. At five o'clock, Mrs. Watson again burst into tears, her whole body shaking, and Stanley brusquely left.

Mr. Watson said: "Well, why did you lead him on, then?" and turned on the television. Mrs. Watson went to lie down. Maureen, in her own room, took off the various items of her disguise, and returned them to her mother's room. "Don't cry, Mum. What are you carrying on like that for? What's the matter?" Then she dressed extremely carefully in a new white linen suit, brown shoes, beige blouse. She did her hair and her face, and sat looking at herself. The last two hours (or week) hit her, and her stomach hurt so that she doubled up. She cried; but the tears smeared her makeup, and she stopped herself with the side of a fist against her mouth.

It now seemed to her that for the last week she had simply not been Maureen; she had been someone else. What had she done it for? Why? Then she knew it was for Tony: during all that ridiculous scene at the tea table, she had imagined Tony looking on, grinning, but understanding her.

She now wiped her face quite clear of tears, and went quietly out of the house so as not to disturb her father and mother. There was a telephone booth at the corner. She stepped calm and aloof along the street, her mouth held (as it always was) in an almost smile. Bert from the grocer's shop said: "Hey, Maureen, that's a smasher. Who's it for?" And she gave him the smile and the toss of the head that went with the street and said: "You, Bert, it's all for you." She went to the telephone booth thinking of Tony. She felt as if he already knew what had happened. She would say: "Let's go and dance, Tony." He would say: "Where shall I meet you?" She dialed his number, and it rang and it rang and it rang. She stood holding the receiver, waiting. About ten minutes— more. Slowly she replaced it. *He had let her down.* He had been telling her, in words and without, to be something, to stay something, and now he did not care, he had let her down.

Maureen quietened herself and telephoned Stanley.

All right then, if that's how you want it, she said to Tony.

Stanley answered, and she said amiably: "Hello."

Silence. She could hear him breathing, fast. She could see his affronted face.

"Well, aren't you going to say anything?" She tried to make this casual, but she could hear the fear in her voice. Oh yes, she could lose him and probably had. To hide the fear she said: "Can't you take a joke, Stanley?" and laughed.

"A joke!"

She laughed. Not bad, it sounded all right.

"I thought you'd gone off your nut, clean off your rocker. . . ." He was breathing in and out, a rasping noise. She was reminded of his hot breathing down her neck and her arms. Her own breath quickened, even while she thought: I don't like him, I really don't like him at all . . . and she said softly: "Oh Stan, I was having a bit of a giggle, that's all."

Silence. Now, this was the crucial moment.

"Oh Stan, can't you see—I thought it was all just boring, that's all it was." She laughed again.

He said: "Nice for your parents, I don't think."

"Oh they don't mind—they laughed after you'd left, though first they were cross." She added hastily, afraid he might think they were laughing at him: "They're used to me, that's all it is."

Another long silence. With all her willpower she insisted that he should soften. But he said nothing, merely breathed in and out, into the receiver.

"Stanley, it was only a joke, you aren't really angry, are you, Stanley?" The tears sounded in her voice now, and she judged it better that they should.

He said, after hesitation: "Well, Maureen, I just didn't like it, I don't like that kind of thing, that's all." She allowed herself to go on crying, and after a while he said, forgiving her in a voice that was condescending and irritated: "Well, all right, all right, there's no point in crying, is there?"

He was annoyed with himself for giving in, she knew that, because she would have been. He had given her up, thrown her over, during the last couple of hours: he was pleased, really, that something from outside had forced him to give her up. Now he could be free for the something better that would turn up—someone who would not strike terror into him by an extraordinary performance like this afternoon's.

"Let's go off to the pictures, Stan. . . ."

Even now, he hesitated. Then he said, quick and reluctant: "I'll meet you at Leicester Square, outside the Odeon, at seven o'clock." He put down the receiver.

Usually he came to pick her up in the car from the corner of the street.

She stood smiling, the tears running down her face. She knew she was crying because of the loss of Tony, who had let her down. She walked back to her house to make up again, thinking that she was in Stanley's power now: there was no balance between them, the advantage was all his.

PROBING FOR MEANING

1. Characterize Maureen. What is she like as a child? As a teenager? As a young adult? What is her goal in life? When does she first begin to formulate this goal?

2. Describe Maureen's relationship with her parents. How do Maureen's mother and father view her differently?

3. The story takes place in London, just after World War II. What role does "The War" play in the story? Why does Maureen insist that she is not a "war child"?

4. What significance do Maureen's moods of "sullen withdrawal" have? What is their cause and effect?

5. Why would Maureen consider spending £100 (about $200) to improve her "voice"? What attempts at self-education does Maureen make? With what success? In general, what role does social class play in the story?

6. Compare and contrast Stanley and Tony. How do Maureen's relationships with these men differ?

7. Why does Maureen behave as she does when Stanley visits her parents' house?

8. What is the significance of the last line of the story?

PROBING FOR METHOD

1. What is the symbolism of "Maureen's Shop"? In this connection, what is Maureen's "capital" throughout the story? Why is this a particularly appropriate description of her "assets"?

2. At one point, the author comments, "Maureen . . . needed—more, *had* to have—a foil. Her role demanded one." In what ways is Shirley a "foil" for Maureen? In other words, how does the author use Shirley as a contrast to the heroine to tell us something about Maureen? Why does Maureen herself feel she needs a foil?

3. What is a "case history"? Who might write a case history? In what way does the style of the story reflect a case history? In this connection, how are the transitions between the parts of Maureen's life presented?

4. Why does the story end as it does? In other words, what is implied by ending the case history at this point in Maureen's life?

WRITING TOPICS
Generating Ideas on a Goal

Freewrite, perhaps in your journal, in response to one of the following:

> Winning isn't everything. It's the only thing.
>
> *Vince Lombardi*

> Success is counted sweetest by those who ne'er succeed.
>
> *Emily Dickinson*

> Youth is given, age is achieved.
>
> *May Swenson*

> Ask not what your country can do for you; ask what you can do for your country.
>
> *John Fitzgerald Kennedy*

> All I wanted was to go somewhere, all I wanted was a change.
>
> *Mark Twain*

> Everyday life has such poverty. . . . with writing or another art you have a shield against life as well as an integrating force.
>
> *Mario Puzo*

> A person filled with gumption doesn't sit around dissipating and stewing about things. He's at the front of the train of his own awareness, watching to see what's up the track and meeting it when it comes.
>
> *Robert Pirsig*

> Living was all, and in life, defeat and victory are inseparable brothers.
>
> *Pete Hamill*

> A job as a human right is a principle that applies to men as well as women. But women have more cause to fight for it.
>
> *Gloria Steinem*

> Marriage comes with more myths attached to it than a six-volume set of ancient Greek history.
>
> *Steve Tesich*

> But I have promises to keep, and miles to go before I sleep.
>
> *Robert Frost*

> Work is a necessity for man. Man invented the alarm clock.
>
> *Pablo Picasso*

I learn by going where I have to go.

Theodore Roethke

Nobody loses all the time.

e. e. cummings

Writing Topics

1. Pirsig in "Gumption" discusses the importance of individual initiative. Write an essay discussing your views on taking the initiative, giving examples from your own experience or that of someone you know.

2. Hamill warns against being too competitive. What are your views on competition? Are they similar to or different from those of your parents? From Hamill's? In what areas of life do you consider yourself least or most competitive? Write an essay on the subject of competition.

3. Steinem talks about the importance of fulfilling work. How would you characterize your goals with regard to work? Do you think being ambitious is more important than enjoying work? Can you imagine doing both? Write an essay defining your attitudes toward work, indicating the factors that influenced them.

4. Fusilli works on Wall Street by vocation and is a writer and musician by avocation. If you had to make a similar choice, how can you imagine fulfilling both goals? Does Fusilli have "gumption"? What other qualities would a person need to accomplish all that he does? Write an essay on the ingredients of success.

5. Read over what you have written for Generating Ideas. Can you revise what you have written for an essay, or is there an idea there that you can expand for a fully developed piece of writing?

6. Hamill writes that "struggle" is important in every area of our lives including human relationships, while Tesich is opposed to the concept of "working" at a marriage. Write an essay discussing your goals with respect to human relationships. To what extent are they similar to or different from those of Hamill and Tesich?

7. Maureen in "Notes for a Case History" is ambitious and wants to use her "capital," yet at the end of the story she knows she has lost her advantage with Stanley. Write an essay analyzing why, despite her goals, Maureen was a loser. What would you have done differently? Could she have made another choice?

8. Parents often have expectations for their children. Write an essay analyzing your response to Gwendolyn Brooks's hopes that her son will never be afraid of "reaching out" or of "taking risks," despite the fact that in so doing life may be more difficult for him. Discuss in your essay the extent to which you think life might also be more interesting if one is more daring.

CHAPTER SIX

Emotions:
Generating Ideas, Planning the Essay
Asking Questions
Arranging the Answers

While we experience our emotions individually, as members of society we often have feelings that others share. Social forces influence us just as do individual people, places, and events. For example, many of the writers in this chapter believe that sometimes factors in our society can cause us to feel maritally and/or sexually frustrated, prejudiced, revengeful, alienated, lonely, and afraid. They attempt to analyze these emotions we share with one another, hoping to ease our isolation by helping us to better understand their complexity.

Bertrand Russell, for example, is concerned with "what conditions seem on the whole to make for happiness in marriage and what for unhappiness;" Gloria Naylor evaluates a painful experience of prejudice she encountered in third grade; George Orwell discusses the futility of revenge; Maxine Hong Kingston gives the reasons for her alienation as a Chinese immigrant in an American classroom; and Anne Taylor Fleming analyzes the causes and effects of being afraid of loneliness.

In her poem "Wild Nights, Wild Nights," Emily Dickinson captures a moment of passion, and in his short story Sherwood Anderson reveals the cruelty of society toward a sensitive individual.

A discussion of "classical" questions for generating ideas follows George Orwell's essay on pages 219–221, and a discussion of how to organize the answers follows Gloria Naylor's essay on pages 225–226.

GEORGE ORWELL

Revenge Is Sour

George Orwell (1903–1950) was an English novelist, essayist, and critic born in India. He was considered to be a free-thinking socialist, and his works are largely comprised of studies of working-class life and culture. Orwell's essays deal directly with the question of human freedom, and his best known novels Animal Farm *(1946) and* 1984 *(1949) are both horrifying journeys into the world of totalitarianism. As you read "Revenge Is Sour," think about how your ideas on the subject are similar to or different from Orwell's.*

Whenever I read phrases like "war guilt trials," "punishment of war criminals," and so forth, there comes back into my mind the memory of something I saw in a prisoner-of-war camp in South Germany, earlier this year.

Another correspondent and myself were being shown round the camp by a little Viennese Jew who had been enlisted in the branch of the American army which deals with the interrogation of prisoners. He was an alert, fair-haired, rather good-looking youth of about twenty-five, and politically so much more knowledgeable than the average American officer that it was a pleasure to be with him. The camp was on an airfield, and, after we had been round the cages, our guide led us to a hangar where various prisoners who were in a different category from the others were being "screened."

Up at one end of the hangar about a dozen men were lying in a row on the concrete floor. These, it was explained, were SS officers who had been segregated from the other prisoners. Among them was a man in dingy civilian clothes who was lying with his arm across his face and apparently asleep. He had strangely and horribly deformed feet. The two of them were quite symmetrical, but they were clubbed out into an extraordinary globular shape which made them more like a horse's hoof than anything human. As we approached the group the little Jew seemed to be working himself up into a state of excitement.

"That's the real swine!" he said, and suddenly he lashed out with his heavy army boot and caught the prostrate man a fearful kick right on the bulge of one of his deformed feet.

"Get up, you swine!" he shouted as the man started out of sleep, and then repeated something of the kind in German. The prisoner scrambled to his feet and stood clumsily to attention. With the same air of working himself into a fury—indeed he was almost dancing up and down as he spoke—the Jew told us the prisoner's history. He was a "real" Nazi: his party number indicated that he had been a member since the very early days, and he had held a post corresponding to a General in the political branch of the SS. It could be taken as quite certain that he had had charge of concentration camps and had presided over tortures and hangings. In short, he represented everything that we had been fighting against during the past five years.

Meanwhile, I was studying his appearance. Quite apart from the scrubby, unfed, unshaven look that a newly captured man generally has, he was a disgusting specimen. But he did not look brutal or in any way frightening: merely neurotic and, in a low way, intellectual. His pale, shifty eyes were deformed by powerful spectacles. He could have been an unfrocked clergyman, an actor ruined by drink, or a spiritualist medium. I have seen very similar people in London common lodging houses, and also in the Reading Room of the British Museum. Quite obviously he was mentally unbalanced—indeed, only doubtfully sane, though at this moment sufficiently in his right mind to be frightened of getting another kick. And yet everything that the Jew was telling me of his history could have been true, and probably was true! So the Nazi torturer of one's imagination, the monstrous figure against whom one had struggled for so many years, dwindled to this pitiful wretch, whose obvious need was not for punishment, but for some kind of psychological treatment.

Later, there were further humiliations. Another SS officer, a large, brawny man, was ordered to strip to the waist and show the blood-group number tattooed on his under-arm; another was forced to explain to us how he had lied about being a member of the SS and attempted to pass himself off as an ordinary soldier of the Wehrmacht. I wondered whether the Jew was getting any real kick out of this newfound power that he was exercising. I concluded that he wasn't really enjoying it, and that he was merely—like a man in a brothel, or a boy smoking his first cigar, or a tourist traipsing round a picture gallery— *telling* himself that he was enjoying it, and behaving as he had planned to behave in the days when he was helpless.

It is absurd to blame any German or Austrian Jew for getting his own back on the Nazis. Heaven knows what scores this particular man may have had to wipe out; very likely his whole family had been murdered; and, after all, even a wanton kick to a prisoner is a very tiny thing compared with the outrages committed by the Hitler régime. But what this scene, and much else that I saw in Germany, brought home to me was that the whole idea of revenge and punishment is a childish day-dream. Properly speaking, there is no such thing as revenge. Revenge is an act which you want to commit when you are powerless and because you are powerless: as soon as the sense of impotence is removed, the desire evaporates also.

Who would not have jumped for joy, in 1940, at the thought of seeing SS officers kicked and humiliated? But when the thing becomes possible, it is merely pathetic and disgusting. It is said that when Mussolini's corpse was exhibited in public, an old woman drew a revolver and fired five shots into it, exclaiming, "Those are for my five sons!" It is the kind of story that the newspapers make up, but it might be true. I wonder how much satisfaction she got out of those five shots, which, doubtless, she had dreamed years earlier of firing. The condition of her being able to get near enough to Mussolini to shoot at him was that he should be a corpse.

In so far as the big public in this country is responsible for the monstrous peace settlement now being forced on Germany, it is because of a failure to see in advance that punishing an enemy brings no satisfaction. We acquiesced in crimes like the expulsion of all Germans from East Prussia—crimes which in some cases we could not prevent but might at least have protested against—because the Germans had angered and frightened us, and therefore we were certain that when they were down we should feel no pity for them. We persist in these policies, or let others persist in them on our behalf, because of a vague feeling that, having set out to punish Germany, we ought to go ahead and do it. Actually there is little acute hatred of Germany left in this country, and even less, I should expect to find, in the army of occupation. Only the minority of sadists, who must have their "atrocities" from one source or another, take a keen interest in the hunting-down of war criminals and quislings. If you ask the average man what crime Goering, Ribbentrop and the rest are to be charged with at their trial, he cannot tell you. Somehow the punishment of these monsters ceases to seem attractive when it becomes possible: indeed, once under lock and key, they almost cease to be monsters.

Unfortunately, there is often need of some concrete incident before one can discover the real state of one's feelings. Here is another memory from Germany. A few hours after Stuttgart was captured by the French army, a Belgian journalist and myself entered the town, which was still in some disorder. The Belgian had been broadcasting throughout the war for the European Service of the BBC, and, like nearly all Frenchmen or Belgians, he had a very much tougher attitude towards "the Boche" than an Englishman or an American would have. All the main bridges into the town had been blown up, and we had to enter by a small footbridge which the Germans had evidently made efforts to defend. A dead German soldier was lying supine at the foot of the steps. His face was a waxy yellow. On his breast someone had laid a bunch of the lilac which was blossoming everywhere.

The Belgian averted his face as we went past. When we were well over the bridge he confided to me that this was the first time he seen a dead man. I suppose he was thirty-five years old, and for four years he had been doing war propaganda over the radio. For several days after this, his attitude was quite different from what it had been earlier. He looked with disgust at the bomb-wrecked town and the humiliations the Germans were undergoing, and even on one occasion intervened to prevent a particularly bad bit of looting. When he left, he gave the residue of the coffee we had brought with us to the Germans on whom we were billeted. A week earlier he would probably have been scandalised at the idea of giving coffee to a "Boche." But his feelings, he told me, had undergone a change at the sight of "ce pauvre mort" beside the bridge: it had suddenly brought home to him the meaning of war. And yet, if we had happened to enter the town by another route, he might have been spared the experience of seeing even one corpse out of the—perhaps—twenty million that the war has produced.

PROBING FOR MEANING

1. Why does the Viennese Jew react with such fury to the prisoner whom he calls "the real swine"? What effect does the prisoner's appearance have on Orwell?

2. What does Orwell mean when he writes, "Properly speaking, there is no such thing as revenge"?

3. What is it, according to Orwell, that causes the English to persist in carrying out policies of revenge against Germany? Do you agree with his argument that the punishment of Nazi war criminals "ceases to seem attractive when it becomes possible"?

4. What does the incident in Stuttgart help the Belgian journalist to discover about his feelings? How does this incident clarify Orwell's feelings?

PROBING FOR METHOD

1. What does the story of the woman who shot Mussolini's corpse add to our understanding of the effects of revenge? Why did Orwell include this story?

2. Orwell writes that "there is often need of some concrete incident before one can discover the real state of one's feelings." In what sense does this statement underscore the organizational principle of the essay? In what sense does it represent a central theme?

3. What is Orwell's tone? How objectively does he analyze his own feelings? What purpose motivates him to write this essay?

Asking Questions

What questions has Orwell asked in "Revenge is Sour"?
In order to generate ideas for his essay about his experience in a prisoner-of-war camp in postwar Germany, Orwell has asked himself several questions.

1. What is the significance of the "war guilt trials"?
2. What associations do I have with these trials?
3. What happened when the Viennese Jew and I saw the SS officer?
4. Who was he? What should I write about him?
5. How did the Jew seek revenge?
6. Why did he seek revenge?
7. What other acts of revenge took place in the camp?

8. What effect did these acts of revenge have on those who committed them?
9. What happened outside Stuttgart just after the British captured it?
10. Who was involved?
11. How did it happen?
12. Why did it happen?
13. What effect did it have on those involved?
14. How does the effect of revenge compare with the expected effect?

Orwell is relating several stories, so he uses the "journalist's questions," which, as we saw in Chapter 3, are very useful when narrating an event: who, where, when, how, and what. In addition, he asks several "classical" questions, useful for any topic: what is the significance of, what associations do I have with, what are the causes of (what are the reasons for, why), what is the effect of (result of), how does this compare (or contrast) with that?

Asking Questions.
There are several sets of questions that the writer can ask about his or her subject as a way of generating material and making sure that all necessary information is supplied. The most useful are the journalist's questions and the classical questions. The journalist's questions are discussed in Chapter 3. The classical questions include the following:

1. What is it?
2. What is it like? Unlike?
3. What caused it? What will it cause?
4. What examples are there of it? (See Chapter 5.)
5. What significance does it have? (See Chapter 5.)
6. What has been said about it?
7. What does it look like?
8. What classes are there of it? Into what classification does it fall?
9. What can be done about it?
10. What process does it go through?

Both the journalist's and the classical questions can be asked as simple questions and also as complex queries, having several parts. In analyzing the causes of an effect, the writer must be careful to ask if the causes he or she suggests actually did create the effect. Did B come about because of A? For example, would it be correct to say that the high divorce rate in America was caused by women's liberation?

In predicting the effects of a situation, the writer must also ask if the effect will necessarily follow. If there is A, in other words, will there necessarily be B? For example, would it be correct to say that the easing of divorce laws leads necessarily to the disintegration of marriage?

Also, you must be sure to ask what all the major causes of an effect are. If women's liberation is only one cause of the disintegration of marriage, then there must be others. While B might exist without A, it would surely exist with a combination of A1, A2, and A3. It might be fair to say that women's liberation, the easing of divorce laws, and the peculiar demands placed upon marriage in our time lead to the disintegration of marriage.

Just as you must ask about all causes, you must also analyze all effects. How many B's are there? The easing of divorce laws may contribute to the disintegration of marriage, but that may not be the only effect. Such a change will also allow people who cannot live together to find happiness apart.

Procedures to follow in asking questions.

A. Experiment with asking the journalist's questions about any subject. While these questions apply easily to events, they also work well with other topics. If you were writing about a job you applied for, for example, you might discuss who you would be working for, where the job would be located, what you would be doing, how the work would be performed, and when you would have vacations.

B. The classical questions are more analytical, and they should be used to complement the journalist's queries. For the essay on the job you applied for, you might ask why you applied for it, what effect this position will have on your financial status or your career plans, what type (or class) of job it is, how it compares and contrasts with previous jobs you have had, and the process you will have to go through in order to land it.

C. Since most of these questions have several parts, particularly questions asking for causes and effects, make sure to ask all the related questions.

GLORIA NAYLOR

What's in a Name?

Gloria Naylor (b. 1950) is a graduate of Brooklyn College of the City University of New York and has done graduate work at Yale University. Her first novel, The Women of Brewster Place, *was published in 1982, followed in 1985 by*

Linden Hills. Her essay "What's In A Name?" published in the "Hers" col-
umn of the New York Times, *examines how cultural differences affect the con-*
notation of words. As you read Naylor's essay, write down the connotations
you think of to the "names" she refers to in her essay.

Language is the subject. It is the written form with which I've managed to keep
the wolf away from the door and, in diaries, to keep my sanity. In spite of this,
I consider the written word inferior to the spoken, and much of the frustration
experienced by novelists is the awareness that whatever we manage to capture
in even the most transcendent passages falls far short of the richness of life.
Dialogue achieves its power in the dynamics of a fleeting moment of sight,
sound, smell and touch.

I'm not going to enter the debate here about whether it is language that
shapes reality or vice versa. That battle is doomed to be waged whenever we
seek intermittent reprieve from the chicken and egg dispute. I will simply take
the position that the spoken word, like the written word, amounts to a nonsen-
sical arrangement of sounds or letters without a consensus that assigns "meaning." And building from the meanings of what we hear, we order reality.
Words themselves are innocuous; it is the consensus that gives them true
power.

I remember the first time I heard the word nigger. In my third-grade
class, our math tests were being passed down the rows, and as I handed the
papers to a little boy in back of me, I remarked that once again he had received
a much lower mark than I did. He snatched his test from me and spit out that
word. Had he called me a nymphomaniac or a necrophiliac, I couldn't have
been more puzzled. I didn't know what a nigger was, but I knew that whatever it meant, it was something he shouldn't have called me. This was verified
when I raised my hand, and in a loud voice repeated what he had said and
watched the teacher scold him for using a "bad" word. I was later to go home
and ask the inevitable question that every black parent must face—"Mommy,
what does 'nigger' mean?"

And what exactly did it mean? Thinking back, I realize that this could not
have been the first time the word was used in my presence. I was part of a
large extended family that had migrated from the rural South after World War
II and formed a close-knit network that gravitated around my maternal grandparents. Their ground-floor apartment in one of the buildings they owned in
Harlem was a weekend mecca for my immediate family, along with countless
aunts, uncles and cousins who brought along assorted friends. It was a bus-
tling and open house with assorted neighbors and tenants popping in and out
to exchange bits of gossip, pick up an old quarrel or referee the ongoing check-
ers game in which my grandmother cheated shamelessly. They were all there

to let down their hair and put up their feet after a week of labor in the factories, laundries and shipyards of New York.

Amid the clamor, which could reach deafening proportions—two or three conversations going on simultaneously, punctuated by the sound of a baby's crying somewhere in the back rooms or out on the street—there was still a rigid set of rules about what was said and how. Older children were sent out of the living room when it was time to get into the juicy details about "you-know-who" up on the third floor who had gone and gotten herself "p-r-e-g-n-a-n-t!" But my parents, knowing that I could spell well beyond my years, always demanded that I follow the others out to play. Beyond sexual misconduct and death, everything else was considered harmless for our young ears. And so among the anecdotes of the triumphs and disappointments in the various workings of their lives, the word nigger was used in my presence, but it was set within contexts and inflections that caused it to register in my mind as something else.

In the singular, the word was always applied to a man who had distinguished himself in some situation that brought their approval for his strength, intelligence or drive:

"Did Johnny *really* do that?"

"I'm telling you, that nigger pulled in $6,000 of overtime last year. Said he got enough for a down payment on a house."

When used with a possessive adjective by a woman—"my nigger"—it became a term of endearment for husband or boyfriend. But it could be more than just a term applied to a man. In their mouths it became the pure essence of manhood—a disembodied force that channeled their past history of struggle and present survival against the odds into a victorious statement of being: "Yeah, that old foreman found out quick enough—you don't mess with a nigger."

In the plural, it became a description of some group within the community that had overstepped the bounds of decency as my family defined it: Parents who neglected their children, a drunken couple who fought in public, people who simply refused to look for work, those with excessively dirty mouths or unkempt households were all "trifling niggers." This particular circle could forgive hard times, unemployment, the occasional bout of depression—they had gone through all of that themselves—but the unforgivable sin was a lack of self-respect.

A woman could never be a "nigger" in the singular, with its connotation of confirming worth. The noun girl was its closest equivalent in that sense, but only when used in direct address and regardless of the gender doing the addressing. "Girl" was a token of respect for a woman. The one-syllable word was drawn out to sound like three in recognition of the extra ounce of wit, nerve or daring that the woman had shown in the situation under discussion.

"G-i-r-l, stop. You mean you said that to his face?"

But if the word was used in a third-person reference or shortened so that it almost snapped out of the mouth, it always involved some element of communal disapproval. And age became an important factor in these exchanges. It was only between individuals of the same generation, or from an older person to a younger (but never the other way around), that "girl" would be considered a compliment.

I don't agree with the argument that use of the word nigger at this social stratum of the black community was an internalization of racism. The dynamics were the exact opposite: the people in my grandmother's living room took a word that whites used to signify worthlessness or degradation and rendered it impotent. Gathering there together, they transformed "nigger" to signify the varied and complex human beings they knew themselves to be. If the word was to disappear totally from the mouths of even the most liberal of white society, no one in that room was naïve enough to believe it would disappear from white minds. Meeting the word head-on, they proved it had absolutely nothing to do with the way they were determined to live their lives.

So there must have been dozens of times that the word "nigger" was spoken in front of me before I reached the third grade. But I didn't "hear" it until it was said by a small pair of lips that had already learned it could be a way to humiliate me. That was the word I went home and asked my mother about. And since she knew that I had to grow up in America, she took me in her lap and explained.

PROBING FOR MEANING

1. What is Naylor saying about language in the first two paragraphs of the essay? What does she mean by her statement "Words themselves are innocuous; it is the consensus that gives them true power?"

2. What do we learn about Naylor's family? Why does she include them?

3. What distinctions does Naylor go on to make about the differences in the connotations of "nigger" in black and white culture? Is the word always used favorably within black culture? Explain your answer.

4. What point does Naylor make about "nigger" in the next-to-last paragraph of her essay? Describe your reaction to it.

5. What is the meaning of the concluding paragraph? What does Naylor imply about America in her last sentence?

6. Is Naylor's experience one with which you can empathize? Why or why not?

PROBING FOR METHOD

1. Naylor begins her essay with the generalization "Language is the subject." What technique does she then use to get to her major generalization as thesis statement

in paragraph 3? Would her essay have been more effective had she reversed the paragraphs? Why or why not?

2. What is the tone of Naylor's essay? Neutral? Angry? Sad? Does it remain consistent throughout? If it changes, where and how does it change?

3. Discuss Naylor's purpose in writing this essay. Is she merely informing or is she also trying to persuade her readers? How in general did the essay affect you?

4. Does Naylor give credence to her definition of "nigger" by using examples from her own family or does this method make her essay too subjective? Why or why not?

5. Naylor asks, "What does 'nigger' mean?" What other questions did she ask herself about her subject as she wrote the essay?

Arranging the Answers

How does Naylor arrange the answers to the questions she has asked?
Naylor asks, "What are the similarities and differences between speech and writing?" "What happened the first time I heard the word 'nigger'?" "What does 'nigger' mean to black people?" "How, by implication, does that compare to the meaning white people give the word?" "How does the use of the word 'nigger' compare to that of the word 'girl'?" "What effect did my being called a nigger have on my mother?" Her questions call, then, for arrangement patterns of comparison and contrast, narration, definition, and cause and effect.

In comparing and contrasting writing and speech, she first points out their differences and then discusses their similarities. In contrasting black and white definitions of "nigger," she refers to the white definition, assuming her readers know it, and then discusses the black definition. In comparing and contrasting the definitions of the words "nigger" and "girl," she points out their differences (gender of person addressed and person doing the addressing, age of person doing the addressing, form of address), then their similarities (approval, disapproval depending on context). Her arrangement varies from pointing out similarities and then differences or vice versa to presenting one subject for comparison and then the other.

In answering the question, "What happened?" the author follows an A–Z chronological order (see Chapter 3). In answering the question, "What effect did it have on my mother?" she presents the effect and the cause as having a relationship in which A necessarily leads to B.

In defining "nigger," she asks a series of subquestions: "What does the word mean in the singular?" "What does it mean with a possessive adjective?" "What does it mean in the plural?" "What does 'nigger' not mean to black people?" She also asks two questions about "girl":

"What does it mean as a form of direct address?" "What does it mean when used in a third-person reference?" She arranges each answer to include an example of each use of the words.

Arranging answers.
As we saw in Chapter 3, several arrangement patterns are possible for narrating an event: a straight chronological A—Z arrangement or variations on a flashback Z—A—Z pattern.

Cause and effect questions also call for several possible organizations: a listing of causes, a listing of effects, a chain pattern of cause/effect/cause/effect, or a listing of primary causes and then secondary causes (or effects), if such a distinction is made.

In organizing a comparison-and-contrast essay, the writer may take one of three approaches: whole by whole, part by part, or a combination of the two. In the first method, the writer looks at all aspects of one item first and then examines all aspects of the other item or items, in the way that Naylor does in defining "nigger" and implicitly contrasting it with the white definition.

In a part-by-part structure, the writer looks at one aspect of the first item and compares it to a corresponding aspect of the other item, and so on, working back and forth between the two items until all aspects have been covered. Naylor uses this method in comparing and contrasting writing and speech.

In the combination method, the writer fully presents one item and then compares and contrasts items one and two part by part. Bertrand Russell uses this method in his essay "Marriage."

In arranging a definition, various patterns are possible, depending on the questions the writer has chosen to ask. Naylor devotes a paragraph to answering each of her questions. Generalized patterns might include a historical survey of the meanings a word has been given, the denotations a word has, followed by its connotations, and meanings, followed by illustrations of these meanings.

In organizing any answer, the writer seeks an internal logic based on his or her material (see the discussion in Chapter 2 on Organizing an Essay).

Procedures for arranging answers.

A. Determine what type of arrangement pattern each answer requires: narration, description, definition, comparison and contrast, cause and effect, and so forth.

B. Choose or create an arrangement pattern that most logically presents your material.

BERTRAND RUSSELL

Marriage

Bertrand Russell (1872–1970) was an English mathematician and philosopher who was also a social reformer interested in education and pacifism. A voluminous writer, he was awarded the Nobel Prize for Literature in 1950. His works include Marriage and Morals *(1929),* History of Western Philosophy *(1945), and* Human Society in Ethics and Politics *(1954). As you read "Marriage," written almost thirty years ago, think about how Russell's ideas on the subject would be received today. How do they compare to yours?*

I propose to discuss marriage without reference to children, merely as a relation between men and women. Marriage differs, of course, from other sex relations by the fact that it is a legal institution. It is also in most communities a religious institution, but it is the legal aspect which is essential. The legal institution merely embodies a practice which exists not only among primitive men but among apes and various other animals. Animals practice what is virtually marriage, whenever the cooperation of the male is necessary to the rearing of the young. As a rule, animal marriages are monogamic, and according to some authorities this is the case in particular amongst the anthropoid apes. It seems, if these authorities are to be believed, that these fortunate animals are not faced with the problems that beset human communities, since the male, once married, ceases to be attracted to any other female, and the female, once married, ceases to be attractive to any other male. Among the anthropoid apes, therefore, although they do not have the assistance of religion, sin is unknown, since instinct suffices to produce virtue. There is some evidence that among the lowest races of savages a similar state of affairs exists. Bushmen are said to be strictly monogamous, and I understand that the Tasmanians (now extinct) were invariably faithful to their wives. Even in civilized mankind faint traces of monogamic instinct can sometimes be perceived. Considering the influence of habit over behavior, it is perhaps surprising that the hold of monogamy on instinct is not stronger than it is. This, however, is an example of the mental peculiarity of human beings, from which spring both their vices and their intelligence, namely the power of imagination to break up habits and initiate new lines of conduct.

It seems probable that what first broke up primitive monogamy was the intrusion of the economic motive. This motive, wherever it has any influence upon sexual behavior, is invariably disastrous, since it substitutes relations of slavery or purchase for relations based upon instinct. In early agricultural and pastoral communities both wives and children were an economic asset to a man. The wives worked for him, and the children, after the age of five or six, began to be useful in the fields or in tending beasts. Consequently the most powerful men aimed at having as many wives as possible. Polygamy can seldom be the general practice of a community, since there is not as a rule a great excess of females; it is the prerogative of chiefs and rich men. Numerous wives and children form a valuable property, and will therefore enhance the already privileged position of their owners. Thus the primary function of a wife comes to be that of a lucrative domestic animal, and her sexual function becomes subordinated. At this level of civilization it is as a rule easy for a man to divorce his wife, though he must in that case restore to her family any dowry that she may have brought. It is, however, in general impossible for a wife to divorce her husband.

The attitude of most semi-civilized communities towards adultery is of a piece with this outlook. At a very low level of civilization adultery is sometimes tolerated. The Samoans, we are told, when they have to go upon a journey, fully expect their wives to console themselves for their absence.* At a slightly higher level, however, adultery in women is punished with death or at best with very severe penalties. Mungo Park's account of Mumbo Jumbo used to be well known when I was young, but I have been pained in recent years to find highbrow Americans alluding to Mumbo Jumbo as a god of the Congo. He was in fact neither a god nor connected with the Congo. He was a pretense demon invented by the men of the upper Niger to terrify women who had sinned. Mungo Park's account of him so inevitably suggests a Voltairean view as to the origins of religion that it has tended to be discreetly suppressed by modern anthropologists, who cannot bear the intrusion of rational scoundrelism into the doings of savages. A man who had intercourse with another man's wife was, of course, also a criminal, but a man who had intercourse with an unmarried woman did not incur any blame unless he diminished her value in the marriage market.

With the coming of Christianity this outlook was changed. The part of religion in marriage was very greatly augmented, and infractions of the marriage law came to be blamed on grounds of taboo rather than of property. To have intercourse with another man's wife remained, of course, an offense against that man, but to have any intercourse outside marriage was an offense against God, and this, in the view of the Church, was a far graver matter. For the same reason divorce, which had previously been granted to men on easy terms, was declared inadmissible. Marriage became a sacrament and therefore lifelong.

Was this a gain or a loss to human happiness? It is very hard to say.

*Margaret Mead, "Coming of Age in Samoa," 1928, p.104ff.

Among peasants the life of married women has always been a very hard one, and on the whole it has been hardest among the least civilized peasants. Among most barbarous peoples a woman is old at twenty-five, and cannot hope at that age to retain any traces of beauty. The view of women as a domestic animal was no doubt very pleasant for men, but for women it meant a life of nothing but toil and hardship. Christianity, while in some ways it made the position of women worse, especially in the well-to-do classes, did at least recognize their theological equality with men, and refused to regard them as absolutely the property of their husbands. A married woman had not, of course, the right to leave her husband for another man, but she could leave him for a life of religion. And on the whole progress towards a better status for women was easier, in the great bulk of the population, from the Christian than from the pre-Christian standpoint.

When we look round the world at the present day and ask ourselves what conditions seem on the whole to make for happiness in marriage and what for unhappiness, we are driven to a somewhat curious conclusion, that the more civilized people become the less capable they seem of lifelong happiness with one partner. Irish peasants, although until recent times marriages were decided by the parents, were said by those who ought to know them to be on the whole happy and virtuous in their conjugal life. In general, marriage is easiest where people are least differentiated. When a man differs little from other men, and a woman differs little from other women, there is no particular reason to regret not having married some one else. But people with multifarious tastes and pursuits and interests will tend to desire congeniality in their partners, and to feel dissatisfied when they find that they have secured less of it than they might have obtained. The Church, which tends to view marriage solely from the point of view of sex, sees no reason why one partner should not do just as well as another, and can therefore uphold the indissolubility of marriage without realizing the hardship that this often involves.

Another condition which makes for happiness in marriage is paucity of unowned women and absence of social occasions when husbands meet other women. If there is no possibility of sexual relations with any women other than one's wife, most men will make the best of the situation and, except in abnormally bad cases, will find it quite tolerable. The same thing applies to wives, especially if they never imagine that marriage should bring much happiness. That is to say, a marriage is likely to be what is called happy if neither party ever expected to get much happiness out of it.

Fixity of social custom, for the same reason tends to prevent what are called unhappy marriages. If the bonds of marriage are recognized as final and irrevocable, there is no stimulus to the imagination to wander outside and consider that a more ecstatic happiness might have been possible. In order to secure domestic peace where this state of mind exists, it is only necessary that neither the husband nor the wife should fall outrageously below the commonly recognized standard of decent behavior, whatever this may be.

Among civilized people in the modern world none of these conditions for what is called happiness exist, and accordingly one finds that very few marriages after the first few years are happy. Some of the causes of unhappiness are bound up with civilization, but others would disappear if men and women were more civilized than they are. Let us begin with the latter. Of these the most important is bad sexual education, which is a far commoner thing among the well-to-do than it can ever be among peasants. Peasant children early become accustomed to what are called the facts of life, which they can observe not only among human beings but among animals. They are thus saved from both ignorance and fastidiousness. The carefully educated children of the well-to-do, on the contrary, are shielded from all practical knowledge of sexual matters, and even the most modern parents, who teach children out of books, do not give them that sense of practical familiarity which the peasant child early acquires. The triumph of Christian teaching is when a man and woman marry without either having had previous sexual experience. In nine cases out of ten where this occurs, the results are unfortunate. Sexual behavior among human beings is not instinctive, so that the inexperienced bride and bridegroom, who are probably quite unaware of this fact, find themselves overwhelmed with shame and discomfort. It is little better when the woman alone is innocent but the man has acquired his knowledge from prostitutes. Most men do not realize that a process of wooing is necessary after marriage, and many well-brought-up women do not realize what harm they do to marriage by remaining reserved and physically aloof. All this could be put right by better sexual education, and is in fact very much better with the generation now young than it was with their parents and grandparents. There used to be a widespread belief among women that they were morally superior to men on the ground that they had less pleasure in sex. This attitude made frank companionship between husbands and wives impossible. It was, of course, in itself quite unjustifiable, since failure to enjoy sex, so far from being virtuous, is a mere physiological or psychological deficiency, like a failure to enjoy food, which also a hundred years ago was expected of elegant females.

Other modern causes of unhappiness in marriage are, however, not so easily disposed of. I think that uninhibited civilized people, whether men or women, are generally polygamous in their instincts. They may fall deeply in love and be for some years entirely absorbed in one person, but sooner or later sexual familiarity dulls the edge of passion, and then they begin to look elsewhere for a revival of the old thrill. It is, of course, possible to control this impulse in the interests of morality, but it's very difficult to prevent the impulse from existing. With the growth of women's freedom there has come a much greater opportunity for conjugal infidelity than existed in former times. The opportunity gives rise to the thought, the thought gives rise to the desire, and in the absence of religious scruples the desire gives rise to the act.

Women's emancipation has in various ways made marriage more difficult. In old days the wife had to adapt herself to the husband, but the husband did not have to adapt himself to the wife. Nowadays many wives, on grounds of woman's right to her own individuality and her own career, are unwilling to adapt themselves to their husbands beyond a point, while men who still hanker after the old tradition of masculine domination see no reason why they should do all the adapting. This trouble arises especially in connection with infidelity. In the old days the husband was occasionally unfaithful, but as a rule his wife did not know of it. If she did, he confessed that he had sinned and made her believe that he was penitent. She, on the other hand, was usually virtuous. If she was not, and the fact came to her husband's knowledge, the marriage broke up. Where, as happens in many modern marriages, mutual faithfulness is not demanded, the instinct of jealously nevertheless survives, and often proves fatal to the persistence of any deeply rooted intimacy even where no overt quarrels occur.

There is another difficulty in the way of modern marriage, which is felt especially by those who are most conscious of the value of love. Love can flourish only as long as it is free and spontaneous; it tends to be killed by the thought that it is a duty. To say that it is your duty to love so-and-so is the surest way to cause you to hate him or her. Marriage as a combination of love with legal bonds thus falls between two stools. Shelley says:

> I never was attached to that great sect
> Whose doctrine is, that each one should select
> Out of the crowd a mistress or a friend,
> And all the rest, though fair and wise, commend
> To cold oblivion, though it is in the code
> Of modern morals, and the beaten road
> Which those poor slaves with weary footsteps tread,
> Who travel to their home among the dead
> By the broad highway of the world, and so
> With one chained friend, perhaps a jealous foe,
> The dreariest and the longest journey go.

There can be no doubt that to close one's mind on marriage against all the approaches of love from elsewhere is to diminish receptivity and sympathy and the opportunities of valuable human contacts. It is to do violence to something which, from the most idealistic standpoint, is in itself desirable. And like every kind of restrictive morality it tends to promote what one may call a policeman's outlook upon the whole of human life—the outlook, that is to say, which is always looking for an opportunity to forbid something.

For all these reasons, many of which are bound up with things undoubtedly good, marriage has become difficult, and if it is not to be a barrier to happiness it must be conceived in a somewhat new way. One solution often suggested, and actually tried on a large scale in America, is easy divorce. I hold, of course, as every humane person must, that divorce should be granted on more grounds than are admitted in the English law, but I do not recognize in easy divorce a solution of the troubles of marriage. Where a marriage is childless, divorce may be often the right solution, even when both parties are doing their best to behave decently; but where there are children the stability of marriage is to my mind a matter of considerable importance. I think that where a marriage is fruitful and both parties to it are reasonable and decent the expectation ought to be that it will be lifelong, but not that it will exclude other sex relations. A marriage which begins with passionate love and leads to children who are desired and loved ought to produce so deep a tie between a man and woman that they will feel something infinitely precious in their companionship, even after sexual passion has decayed, and even if either or both feels sexual passion for some one else. This mellowing of marriage has been prevented by jealousy, but jealousy, though it is an instinctive emotion, is one which can be controlled if it is recognized as bad, and not supposed to be the expression of a just moral indignation. A companionship which has lasted for many years and through many deeply felt events has a richness of content which cannot belong to the first days of love, however delightful these may be. And any person who appreciates what time can do to enhance values will not lightly throw away such companionship for the sake of new love.

It is therefore possible for a civilized man and woman to be happy in marriage, although if this is to be the case a number of conditions must be fulfilled. There must be a feeling of complete equality on both sides; there must be no interference with mutual freedom; there must be the most complete physical and mental intimacy; and there must be a certain similarity in regard to standards of values. (It is fatal, for example, if one values only money while the other values only good work.) Given all these conditions, I believe marriage to be the best and most important relation that can exist between two human beings. If it has not often been realized hitherto, that is chiefly because husband and wife have regarded themselves as each other's policeman. If marriage is to achieve its possibilities, husbands and wives must learn to understand that whatever the law may say, in their private lives they must be free.

PROBING FOR MEANING

1. Why, according to Russell, do apes and savages practice monogamy while civilized man does not?

2. What influence in Russell's view did economic factors have on primitive monogamy historically? On adultery?

3. What influence, according to the author, did Christianity have on monogamy? On the role of women? What causes does Russell cite for the success of monogamy under Christianity?

4. According to Russell, what are the causes of unhappy marriages in our contemporary, highly civilized world?

5. Why is divorce not the answer in Russell's view? Why does he believe in marriage? Under what conditions does he believe marriage can succeed?

6. Do you agree that marriage should be continued as an institution of society? Do you agree with Russell's conditions for its continuance? Would you propose other solutions to the problems that marriage poses?

PROBING FOR METHOD

1. What tone does Russell adopt in his essay? Does he maintain the same tone throughout? Explain.

2. After studying carefully his style, describe the level of audience for whom Russell is writing.

3. What pattern of organization does he use in the essay?

4. Russell typically makes an assertion and then illustrates it or comments about it, sometimes for the next several paragraphs. Find a place in the essay where he states a major idea and then uses the paragraphs immediately following to expand and illustrate that one idea.

5. In what way does the last paragraph sound final? What aspects of its tone and message qualify it to serve as conclusion?

MAXINE HONG KINGSTON

The Misery of Silence

Maxine Hong Kingston (b. 1940) was born in Stockton, California, and is a graduate of The University of California. Her autobiographies The Woman Warrior *(1976) and* China Men *(1980) focus on her experiences as a first-generation American in a Chinese immigrant community. As you read "The Misery of Silence," compare Kingston's experiences at school with your own.*

When I went to kindergarten and had to speak English for the first time, I became silent. A dumbness—a shame—still cracks my voice in two, even when I want to say "hello" casually, or ask an easy question in front of the check-out counter, or ask directions of a bus driver. I stand frozen, or I hold up the line with the complete, grammatical sentence that comes squeaking out at impossible length. "What did you say?" says the cab driver, or "Speak up," so I have to perform again, only weaker the second time. A telephone call makes my throat bleed and takes up that day's courage. It spoils my day with self-disgust when I hear my broken voice come skittering out into the open. It makes people wince to hear it. I'm getting better, though. Recently I asked the postman for special-issue stamps; I've waited since childhood for postmen to give me some of their own accord. I am making progress, a little every day.

My silence was thickest—total—during the three years that I covered my school paintings with black paint. I painted layers of black over houses and flowers and suns, and when I drew on the blackboard, I put a layer of chalk on top. I was making a stage curtain, and it was the moment before the curtain parted or rose. The teachers called my parents to school, and I saw they had been saving my pictures, curling and cracking, all alike and black. The teachers pointed to the pictures and looked serious, talked seriously too, but my parents did not understand English. ("The parents and teachers of criminals were executed," said my father.) My parents took the pictures home. I spread them out (so black and full of possibilities) and pretended the curtains were swinging open, flying up, one after another, sunlight underneath, mighty operas.

During the first silent year I spoke to no one at school, did not ask before going to the lavatory, and flunked kindergarten. My sister also said nothing for three years, silent in the playground and silent at lunch. There were other quiet Chinese girls not of our family, but most of them got over it sooner than we did. I enjoyed the silence. At first it did not occur to me I was supposed to talk or to pass kindergarten. I talked at home and to one or two of the Chinese kids in class. I made motions and even made some jokes. I drank out of a toy saucer when the water spilled out of the cup, and everybody laughed, pointing at me, so I did it some more. I didn't know that Americans don't drink out of saucers.

I liked the Negro students (Black Ghosts) best because they laughed the loudest and talked to me as if I were a daring talker too. One of the Negro girls had her mother coil braids over her ears Shanghai-style like mine; we were Shanghai twins except that she was covered with black like my paintings. Two Negro kids enrolled in Chinese school, and the teachers gave them Chinese names. Some Negro kids walked me to school and home, protecting me from the Japanese kids, who hit me and chased me and stuck gum in my ears. The Japanese kids were noisy and tough. They appeared one day in kindergarten, released from concentration camp, which was a tic-tac-toe mark, like barbed wire, on the map.

It was when I found out I had to talk that school became a misery, that the silence became a misery. I did not speak and felt bad each time that I did not speak. I read aloud in first grade, though, and heard the barest whisper with little squeaks come out of my throat.

"Louder," said the teacher, who scared the voice away again. The other Chinese girls did not talk either, so I knew the silence had to do with being a Chinese girl.

Reading out loud was easier than speaking because we did not have to make up what to say, but I stopped often, and the teacher would think I'd gone quiet again. I could not understand "I." The Chinese "I" has seven strokes, intricacies. How could the American "I," assuredly wearing a hat like the Chinese, have only three strokes, the middle so straight? Was it out of politeness that this writer left off strokes the way a Chinese has to write her own name small and crooked? No, it was not politeness; "I" is a capital and "you" is lower-case. I stared at that middle line and waited so long for its black center to resolve into tight strokes and dots that I forgot to pronounce it. The other troublesome word was "here," no strong consonant to hang on to, and so flat, when "here" is two mountainous ideographs. The teacher, who had already told me every day how to read "I" and "here," put me in the low corner under the stairs again, where the noisy boys usually sat.

When my second grade class did a play, the whole class went to the auditorium except the Chinese girls. The teacher, lovely and Hawaiian, should have understood about us, but instead left us behind in the classroom. Our voices were too soft or nonexistent, and our parents never signed the permission slips anyway. They never signed anything unnecessary. We opened the door a crack and peeked out, but closed it again quickly. One of us (not me) won every spelling bee, though.

I remember telling the Hawaiian teacher, "We Chinese can't sing 'land where our fathers died.' " She argued with me about politics, while I meant because of curses. But how can I have that memory when I couldn't talk? My mother says that we, like the ghosts, have no memories.

After American school, we picked up our cigar boxes, in which we had arranged books, brushes, and an inkbox neatly, and went to Chinese school, from 5:00 to 7:30 P.M. There we chanted together, voices rising and falling, loud and soft, some boys shouting, everybody reading together, reciting together and not alone with one voice. When we had a memorization test, the teacher let each of us come to his desk and say the lesson to him privately, while the rest of the class practiced copying or tracing. Most of the teachers were men. The boys who were so well behaved in the American school played tricks on them and talked back to them. The girls were not mute. They screamed and yelled during recess, when there were no rules; they had fist-fights. Nobody was afraid of children hurting themselves or of children hurting school property. The glass doors to the red and green balconies with the gold joy symbols were left wide open so that we could run out and climb the fire escapes. We played capture-the-flag in the auditorium, where Sun Yat-sen and Chiang Kai-shek's pictures hung at the back of the stage, the Chinese flag on their left and the American flag on their right. We climbed the teak ceremonial chairs and made flying leaps off the stage. One flag headquarters was behind the glass door and the other on stage right. Our feet drummed on the hollow stage. During recess the teachers locked themselves up in their office with the shelves of books, copybooks, inks from China. They drank tea and warmed their hands at a stove. There was no play supervision. At recess we had the school to ourselves, and also we could roam as far as we could go—downtown, Chinatown stores, home—as long as we returned before the bell rang.

At exactly 7:30 the teacher again picked up the brass bell that sat on his desk and swung it over our heads, while we charged down the stairs, our cheering magnified in the stairwell. Nobody had to line up.

Not all of the children who were silent at American school found a voice at Chinese school. One new teacher said each of us had to get up and recite in front of the class, who was to listen. My sister and I had memorized the lesson perfectly. We said it to each other at home, one chanting, one listening. The teacher called on my sister to recite first. It was the first time a teacher had called on the second-born to go first. My sister was scared. She glanced at me and looked away; I looked down at my desk. I hoped that she could do it because if she could, then I would have to. She opened her mouth and a voice came out that wasn't a whisper, but it wasn't a proper voice either. I hoped that she would not cry, fear breaking up her voice like twigs underfoot. She sounded as if she were trying to sing though weeping and strangling. She did not pause or stop to end the embarrassment. She kept going until she said the last word, and then she sat down. When it was my turn, the same voice came out, a crippled animal running on broken legs. You could hear splinters in my voice, bones rubbing jagged against one another. I was loud, though. I was glad I didn't whisper.

How strange that the emigrant villagers are shouters, hollering face to face. My father asks, "Why is it I can hear Chinese from blocks away? Is it that I understand the language? Or is it they talk loud?" They turn the radio up full blast to hear the operas, which do not seem to hurt their ears. And they yell over the singers that wail over the drums, everybody talking at once, big arm gestures, spit flying. You can see the disgust on American faces looking at women like that. It isn't just the loudness. It is the way Chinese sounds, ching-chong ugly, to American ears, not beautiful like Japanese sayonara words with the consonants and vowels as regular as Italian. We make guttural peasant noise and have Ton Duc Thang names you can't remember. And the Chinese can't hear Americans at all; the language is too soft and western music unhearable. I've watched a Chinese audience laugh, visit, talk-story, and holler during a piano recital, as if the musician could not hear them. A Chinese-American, somebody's son, was playing Chopin, which has no punctuation, no cymbals, no gongs. Chinese piano music is five black keys. Normal Chinese women's voices are strong and bossy. We American-Chinese girls had to whisper to make ourselves American-feminine. Apparently we whispered even more softly than the Americans. Once a year the teachers referred my sister and me to speech therapy, but our voices would straighten out, unpredictably normal, for the therapists. Some of us gave up, shook our heads, and said nothing, not one word. Some of us could not even shake our heads. At times shaking my head no is more self-assertion than I can manage. Most of us eventually found some voice, however faltering. We invented an American-feminine speaking personality.

PROBING FOR MEANING

1. In the first paragraph of the essay Kingston reveals her agony about speaking English. What is the relationship between her silence in school and the paintings she did in kindergarten?

2. What does she reveal about her school experience through her portrayal of the other students in paragraph 4? Was her experience in any way similar to yours? How?

3. What does Kingston's portrayal of her American teachers suggest? Is it one with which you identify? Why or why not?

4. What was the main reason for the difference in the children's behavior in Chinese school as opposed to American school? Why did Kingston include this comparison in her essay?

5. What distinctions does she make between Chinese and American speech patterns in the last paragraph? What is your reaction to her point that "We American-Chinese girls had to whisper to make ourselves American-feminine?

6. Is Kingston's experience one with which you can empathize? Why or why not?

PROBING FOR METHOD

1. What is Kingston's thesis statement? Where in the essay does this generalization occur?

2. Read over the introduction and conclusion of the essay. Is her technique of moving from the particular to the general effective? How does her method differ from Naylor's? Which do you prefer and why?

3. What was Kingston's purpose in recording this experience?

4. How effectively does Kingston support the generalizations in her topic sentences? Are the examples that she cites convincing to you? Why or why not? How effectively do they support the thesis of her essay?

5. In addition to discussing the causes of her silence in school, Kingston records her impressions of other ethnic groups as well as their cultural differences. How does this affect the unity and coherence of her essay? Explain your answer.

6. What questions has the author asked in generating ideas for this essay? How has she organized the answers?

ANNE TAYLOR FLEMING

The Fear of Being Alone

Anne Taylor Fleming is a free-lance writer living in Los Angeles. She writes most regularly for the New York Times Magazine, *does weekly radio commentary for CBS, and contributes essays to the "MacNeil/Lehrer NewsHour."*

Her writing career began shortly after she graduated from the University of California at Santa Cruz in 1971 with Highest Honors in Political Philosophy. Returning to her native Los Angeles, she began a free-lance career and over the next decade wrote a number of "My Turn" essays for Newsweek.

At the end of this past summer I had plans to go away for a week, simply a week, without my husband. It was the first time in three years that I was making such a solo pilgrimage, and I was frightened. As I walked down the long corridor to the plane, I looked straight ahead, turning a bottle of tranquilizers over and over in my pocket. I felt like a child lost in a department store; my palms were sweaty and my face was flushed. I tried to remember other solitary departures when I had been similarly discomfited: the walk to the first day of school; the bus ride to Girl Scout camp when I was 9 and my sister, who was also on the bus, was 10 and suddenly wanted nothing to do with me; the first midnight jet to college.

Of what was I so afraid? I was afraid of being by myself, of being wholly quiet, of being with people who did not know my name and did not care. I was afraid of being liked by strangers and of not being liked by strangers. Mostly I was afraid of being alone again, even for so short a time. After four and a half years of marriage I had simply lost the habit.

Marriage is not the culprit, though it is an obvious protective mantle against aloneness. The fear of being alone is not reserved for the married just as it is not reserved for women. I have heard stories like mine from young boys and have seen the same childlike fear in the faces of middle-aged men. Nor is this fear the special property of Americans. But we seem, in this country, to fan the fear of being alone. We are raised and in turn raise our children in clumps, in groups, in auditoriums and car pools and locker rooms and scout dens. Great emphasis is placed on how sociable we are as children, on how popular we are with our peers. Great emphasis is also placed on how well children mix in their own families. Despite the alleged falling apart of the American family, the dialogue about familial relations is constant, binding. If only in talk, parents and children do not leave each other much alone. Great nostalgic emphasis is still placed on the ritual togetherness of the family meal.

A solitary eater, anytime, anywhere, conjures up one of those sad, empty, too well-lighted diners of an Edward Hopper painting.

And when for children there is no meal to attend, no group activity, no distraction planned by a weekend father, there is the constant company of the people on TV. A child need never be alone, need never know silence except when asleep. Even then, for urban and suburban children, there are the nonceasing nighttime noises of cars, of neighbors, of arguing or partying parents. To be away from the noise, away from the group—parents or peers—becomes a scary thing and aloneness becomes confused and synonymous with loneliness.

I used to think that the worst thing I could say to my husband when lying next to him was, "I'm lonely." That, I thought, was very wounding, a reflection on his inability to be company to me. I think now that it's a reflection on me, on my inability to be gracefully alone even in the presence of someone I love. We all marry, in part, to avoid being alone; many of us divorce when we find we can be just as alone in marriage as before, and sometimes more so. Often, women in crumbling marriages conceive babies not to try to hold a man, as the cliché goes, but to guarantee themselves some company—even that of an infant—when that man is gone. After the divorce, for a man or woman, comes the frantic search for a replacement, a new lover, a dog, a singles club, a stronger drink or drug. Waking next to strangers in strange beds—surely, the loneliest habit— is considered preferable to being alone.

Of this random bedding there has been much written lately, especially by a handful of philosopher-journalists who blame such "promiscuity" on what they call the New Narcissism, the inward-turning, selfish, self-absorption of the American people. Each one of us, their lament goes, is "into" his or her own jollies—the pursuit of happiness having become the pursuit of hedonism—our faces resolutely turned away from the world and its problems. But this is the oddest of narcissisms then, the insecure narcissism of people who do not like to be alone. The ant-narcissists point to the prodigious number and variety of soul searchers—est devotees, Aricans, Moonies, meditators and Rolfers—as proof of the neurotic self-celebration of Americans. But even these soul searchings go on in huge groups; they are orgies of mass psyche scratching. Hundreds of people writhe together on auditorium floors in an attempt to soothe their individual wounds. They jog together and ride bicycles together and walk the most beautiful country roads together in an effort to slim their individual thighs.

So even if Americans are involved in a manic and somewhat selfish pursuit of psychic and physical fitness, it is a collective not a private pursuit. Everyone is holding hands; they're one long daisy chain of self-improvement. This is, at best, a symbiotic narcissism, the narcissism of people very dependent on one another, of people afraid or bored to be alone, of people homogenizing into one sex—it is less scary and less lonely, perhaps, to bed with a body that looks and feels more like one's own—of people who need to see reflected in the water not only their own faces but countless other faces as well.

I do not mean to advertise the advantages of being alone. Many have done that with more conviction than I could. I regard aloneness not as a pleasure so much as an accident that, if one is to be at all happy, must be survived. Nor do I mean to put down narcissism. On the contrary, I find no fault with a certain healthy narcissism. Few among us would undertake the saving of other souls until we first have a stab of saving our own.

The point is simply that narcissism is not the point and that in many ways it's a misnomer. A true narcissist is a true loner and most of us, raised as we are, make lousy loners. We share each other's beds somewhat freely not out of boldness but out of timidity, out of the fear of being alone. We hunt for gurus not out of self-love, or narcissism, but out of self-doubt. If we are to be even mildly happy and therefore generous of spirit—as the anti-narcissists would have us be—then what we need is more narcissism, more privatism, not less. What we need instead of soul-searching sessions are classes on how to be alone: Aloneness 1A, Intermediary Aloneness, Advanced Aloneness. The great joy of these new classes is that attendance would not only not be required, it would be forbidden.

PROBING FOR MEANING

1. According to Fleming, what causes Americans to fear being alone? What effects does this fear have on them?

2. What is the "New Narcissism" to which Fleming refers in paragraph 6?

3. Why does she think it is incorrect to blame the "promiscuity" of contemporary life on narcissism?

4. In what way, according to Fleming, might learning to cope better with being alone improve the quality of life in America? Do you agree with her analysis? Why or why not?

PROBING FOR METHOD

1. List the effects of loneliness Fleming describes in paragraphs 1 and 2. How does her consideration, then rejection, of two alleged causes of loneliness strengthen her analysis when she later reveals the "real" cause?

2. What evidence does Fleming offer to prove that Americans are trained to regard aloneness as loneliness?

3. In what sense is Fleming's conclusion paradoxical or ironic? Find other examples of paradox in the essay.

EMILY DICKINSON

Wild Nights, Wild Nights

Emily Dickinson (1830–1886) was an American poet whose reclusive life in Amherst, Massachusetts, contrasted sharply with her radical thoughts about human life and emotions. Although few of her thousand poems were published in her lifetime, she is now regarded as an important influence in modern poetry. As you read "Wild Nights, Wild Nights," jot down your response to this powerful love poem written by a supposedly sedate New England woman.

Wild Nights—Wild Nights!
Were I with thee
Wild Nights should be
Our luxury!

Futile—the Winds—
To Heart in port—
Done with the Compass—
Done with the Chart!

Rowing in Eden—
Ah, the Sea!
Might I but moor—Tonight—
In Thee!

PROBING FOR MEANING

1. Explain the first four lines. Why does Dickinson use "should" in line 3?
2. What is the significance of the poet's wishing to dispense with the "compass" and the "chart"?
3. What is the effect on the poem's meaning of going from "Eden" in line 9 to "Thee" in line 12?
4. State the poem's theme in a sentence.

PROBING FOR METHOD

1. Dashes, exclamation points, and the capitalization of many nouns are three of Emily Dickinson's trademarks. What effect does each device produce?
2. Dickinson uses the metaphor of the sea in describing her emotional associations with "wild nights." Why is this technique effective?

SHERWOOD ANDERSON

Hands

Sherwood Anderson (1878—1941) was an American novelist and short story writer whose collection of short stories Winesburg, Ohio *(1919), reflecting life in a small midwestern town, brought him instant recognition. Anderson was convinced that the growth of urban centers would result in the disintegration of the personal life. As you read "Hands," consider how Wing would have been treated today in your home town.*

Upon the half decayed veranda of a small frame house that stood near the edge of a ravine near the town of Winesburg, Ohio, a fat little old man walked nervously up and down. Across a long field that had been seeded for clover but that had produced only a dense crop of yellow mustard weeds, he could see the public highway along which went a wagon filled with berry pickers returning from the fields. The berry pickers, youths and maidens, laughed and shouted boisterously. A boy clad in a blue shirt leaped from the wagon and attempted to drag after him one of the maidens, who screamed and protested shrilly. The feet of the boy in the road kicked up a cloud of dust that floated across the face of the departing sun. Over the long field came a thin girlish voice. "Oh, you Wing Biddlebaum, comb your hair, it's falling into your eyes," commanded the voice to the man, who was bald and whose nervous little hands fiddled about the bare white forehead as though arranging a mass of tangled locks.

Wing Biddlebaum, forever frightened and beset by a ghostly band of doubts, did not think of himself as in any way a part of the life of the town where he had lived for twenty years. Among all the people of Winesburg but one had come close to him. With George Willard, son of Tom Willard, the proprietor of the New Willard House, he had formed something like a friendship. George Willard was the reporter on the "Winesburg Eagle" and sometimes in the evenings he walked out along the highway to Wing Biddlebaum's house. Now as the old man walked up and down on the veranda, his hands moving nervously about, he was hoping that George Willard would come and spend the evening with him. After the wagon containing the berry pickers had passed, he went across the field through the tall mustard weeds and climbing a rail fence peered anxiously along the road to the town. For a moment he stood thus, rubbing his hands together and looking up and down the road, and then, fear overcoming him, ran back to walk again upon the porch on his own house.

In the presence of George Willard, Wing Biddlebaum, who for twenty years had been the town mystery, lost something of his timidity, and his shadowy personality, submerged in a sea of doubts, came forth to look at the world. With the young reporter at his side, he ventured in the light of day into Main Street or strode up and down on the rickety front porch of his own house, talking excitedly. The voice that had been low and trembling became shrill and loud. The bent figure straightened. With a kind of wriggle, like a fish returned to the brook by the fisherman, Biddlebaum the silent began to talk, striving to put into words the ideas that had been accumulated by his mind during long years of silence.

Wing Biddlebaum talked much with his hands. The slender expressive fingers, forever active, forever striving to conceal themselves in his pockets or behind his back, came forth and became the piston rods of his machinery of expression.

The story of Wing Biddlebaum is a story of hands. Their restless activity, like unto the beating of the wings of an imprisoned bird, had given him his name. Some obscure poet of the town had thought of it. The hands alarmed their owner. He wanted to keep them hidden away and looked with amazement at the quiet inexpressive hands of other men who worked beside him in the fields, or passed, driving sleepy teams on country roads.

When he talked to George Willard, Wing Biddlebaum closed his fists and beat with them upon a table or on the walls of his house. The action made him more comfortable. If the desire to talk came to him when the two were walking in the fields, he sought out a stump or the top board of a fence and with his hands pounding busily talked with renewed ease.

The story of Wing Biddlebaum's hands is worth a book in itself. Sympathetically set forth it would tap many strange, beautiful qualities in obscure men. It is a job for a poet. In Winesburg the hands had attracted attention merely because of their activity. With them Wing Biddlebaum had picked as high as a hundred and forty quarts of strawberries in a day. They became his distinguishing feature, the source of his fame. Also they made more grotesque an already grotesque and elusive individuality. Winesburg was proud of the hands of Wing Biddlebaum in the same spirit in which it was proud of Banker White's new stone house and Wesley Moyer's bay stallion, Tony Tip, that had won the two-fifteen trot at the fall races in Cleveland.

As for George Willard, he had many times wanted to ask about the hands. At times an almost overwhelming curiosity had taken hold of him. He felt that there must be a reason for their strange activity and their inclination to keep hidden away and only a growing respect for Wing Biddlebaum kept him from blurting out the questions that were often in his mind.

Once he had been on the point of asking. The two were walking in the fields on a summer afternoon and had stopped to sit upon a grassy bank. All afternoon Wing Biddlebaum had talked as one inspired. By a fence he had stopped and beating like a giant woodpecker upon the top board had shouted at George Willard, condemning his tendency to be too much influenced by the people about him. "You are destroying yourself," he cried. "You have the inclination to be alone and to dream and you are afraid of dreams. You want to be like others in town here. You hear them talk and you try to imitate them."

On the grassy bank Wing Biddlebaum had tried again to drive his point home. His voice became soft and reminiscent, and with a sigh of contentment he launched into a long rambling talk, speaking as one lost in a dream.

Out of the dream Wing Biddlebaum made a picture for George Willard. In the picture men lived again in a kind of pastoral golden age. Across a green open country came clean-limbed young men, some afoot, some mounted upon horses. In crowds the young men came to gather about the feet of an old man who sat beneath a tree in a tiny garden and who talked to them.

Wing Biddlebaum became wholly inspired. For once he forgot the hands. Slowly they stole forth and lay upon George Willard's shoulders. Something new and bold came into the voice that talked. "You must try to forget all you have learned," said the old man. "You must begin to dream. From this time on you must shut your ears to the roaring of the voices."

Pausing in his speech, Wing Biddlebaum looked long and earnestly at George Willard. His eyes glowed. Again he raised the hands to caress the boy and then a look of horror swept over his face.

With a convulsive movement of his body, Wing Biddlebaum sprang to his feet and thrust his hands deep into his trousers pockets. Tears came to his eyes. "I must be getting along home. I can talk no more with you," he said nervously.

Without looking back, the old man had hurried down the hillside and across a meadow, leaving George Willard perplexed and frightened upon the grassy slope. With a shiver of dread the boy arose and went along the road toward town. "I'll not ask him about his hands," he thought, touched by the memory of the terror he had seen in the man's eyes. "There's something wrong, but I don't want to know what it is. His hands have something to do with his fear of me and of everyone."

And George Willard was right. Let us look briefly into the story of the hands. Perhaps our talking of them will arouse the poet who will tell the hidden wonder story of the influence for which the hands were but fluttering pennants of promise.

In his youth Wing Biddlebaum had been a school teacher in a town in Pennsylvania. He was not then known as Wing Biddlebaum, but went by the less euphonic name of Adolph Myers. As Adolph Myers he was much loved by the boys of his school.

Adolph Myers was meant by nature to be a teacher of youth. He was one of those rare, little-understood men who rule by a power so gentle that it passes as a lovable weakness. In their feeling for the boys under their charge such men are not unlike the finer sort of women in their love of men.

And yet that is but crudely stated. It needs the poet there. With the boys of his school, Adolph Myers had walked in the evening or had sat talking until dusk upon the schoolhouse steps lost in a kind of dream. Here and there went his hands, caressing the shoulders of the boys, playing about the tousled heads. As he talked his voice became soft and musical. There was a caress in that also. In a way the voice and the hands, the stroking of the shoulders and the touching of the hair were a part of the school-master's effort to carry a dream into the young minds. By the caress that was in his fingers he expressed himself. He was one of those men in whom the force that creates life is diffused, not centralized. Under the caress of his hands doubt and disbelief went out of the minds of the boys and they began also to dream.

And then the tragedy. A half-witted boy of the school became enamored of the young master. In his bed at night he imagined unspeakable things and in the morning went forth to tell his dreams as facts. Strange, hideous accusations fell from his loose-hung lips. Through the Pennsylvania town went a shiver. Hidden, shadowy doubts that had been in men's minds concerning Adolph Myers were galvanized into beliefs.

The tragedy did not linger. Trembling lads were jerked out of bed and questioned. "He put his arms about me," said one. "His fingers were always playing in my hair," said another.

One afternoon a man of the town, Henry Bradford, who kept a saloon, came to the schoolhouse door. Calling Adolph Myers into the school yard he began to beat him with his fists. As his hard knuckles beat down into the frightened face of the schoolmaster, his wrath became more and more terrible. Screaming with dismay, the children ran here and there like disturbed insects. "I'll teach you to put your hands on my boy, you beast," roared the saloon keeper, who, tired of beating the master, had begun to kick him about the yard.

Adolph Myers was driven from the Pennsylvania town in the night. With lanterns in their hands a dozen men came to the door of the house where he lived alone and commanded that he dress and come forth. It was raining and one of the men had a rope in his hands. They had intended to hang the schoolmaster, but something in his figure, so small, white, and pitiful, touched their hearts and they let him escape. As he ran away into the darkness they repented of their weakness and ran after him, swearing and throwing sticks and great balls of soft mud at the figure that screamed and ran faster and faster into the darkness.

For twenty years Adolph Myers had lived alone in Winesburg. He was but forty but looked sixty-five. The name of Biddlebaum he got from a box of goods seen at a freight station as he hurried through an eastern Ohio town. He had an aunt in Winesburg, a black-toothed old woman who raised chickens, and with her he lived until she died. He had been ill for a year after the experience in Pennsylvania, and after his recovery worked as a day laborer in the fields, going timidly about and striving to conceal his hands. Although he did not understand what had happened he felt that the hands must be to blame.

Again and again the fathers of the boys had talked of the hands. "Keep your hands to yourself," the saloon keeper had roared, dancing with fury in the schoolhouse yard.

Upon the veranda of his house by the ravine, Wing Biddlebaum continued to walk up and down until the sun had disappeared and the road beyond the field was lost in the grey shadow. Going into his house he cut slices of bread and spread honey upon them. When the rumble of the evening train that took away the express cars loaded with the day's harvest of berries had passed and restored the silence of the summer night, he went again to walk upon the veranda. In the darkness he could not see the hands and they became quiet. Although he still hungered for the presence of the boy, who was the medium through which he expressed his love of man, the hunger became again a part of his loneliness and his waiting. Lighting a lamp, Wing Biddlebaum washed the few dishes soiled by his simple meal and, setting up a folding cot by the screen door that led to the porch, prepared to undress for the night. A few stray white bread crumbs lay on the cleanly washed floor by the table; putting the lamp upon a low stool he began to pick up the crumbs, carrying them to his mouth one by one with unbelievable rapidity. In the dense blotch of light beneath the table, the kneeling figure looked like a priest engaged in some service of his church. The nervous expressive fingers, flashing in and out of the light, might well have been mistaken for the fingers of the devotee going swiftly through decade after decade of his rosary.

PROBING FOR MEANING

1. What do you learn about George Willard and Wing Biddlebaum from the first three paragraphs of the story?

2. What does Anderson mean by his statement "The story of Wing Biddlebaum is a story of hands"? Why is telling his story "a job for a poet"?

3. What is the author suggesting about human nature in the scene where Adolph Myers is driven from the town? Would people tend to react the same way today? What is your reaction to their behavior?

4. In spite of what happened to him, why does Wing want George to listen to his dreams instead of to other people in the town? What is your response to Wing's advice?

5. Explain the meaning of the story's last paragraph.

6. State the theme of the story in one or two sentences.

PROBING FOR METHOD

1. What does the narrator accomplish through his description of the setting in paragraph one?

2. The author uses "hands" both literally and symbolically in the story. How does their symbolism relate to the story's theme? Give examples.

3. What is the author's purpose in including George Willard? Does his presence reinforce the story's meaning? Why or why not?

4. How would you describe the tone of the story? Is the narrator detached or involved?

5. Discuss the narrator's use of poetic language. Where is it most effective? How does it enhance the story's theme?

WRITING TOPICS

Generating Ideas on an Emotion

Freewrite or write a journal entry in response to one of the following:

Give all to love, obey thy heart.

Ralph Waldo Emerson

The heart has its reasons which reason knows nothing of.

Blaise Pascal

Degradation of anger. Anger at a child. How shall I learn to absorb the violence and make explicit only the caring?

Adrienne Rich

They love each other. There is no loneliness like theirs.

James Wright

It was when I found out I had to talk that school became a misery, that the silence became a misery.

Maxine Hong Kingston

So there must have been dozens of times that the word "nigger" was spoken in front of me before I reached the third grade. But I didn't "hear" it until it was said by a small pair of lips that had already learned it could be a way to humiliate me.

Gloria Naylor

We do not need to reveal ourselves to others, but only to those we love. For then we are no longer revealing ourselves in order to seem but in order to give.

Albert Camus

We cling to a time and a place because without them man is lost, not only man but life.

Loren Eiseley

When I don't feel hurt, I hope they bury me.

Bernard Malamud

Love is a universal language.

Robert Graves

Topics for Essays on an Emotion

1. Read over Naylor's essay and write your reaction to her statement that "Words themselves are innocuous; it is the consensus that gives them true power." Using a word that has powerful emotional connotations for you, write an essay defining that word as consensus has defined it and analyzing your emotional reactions to it.

2. Russell and Dickinson write about two emotionally charged subjects: sex and marriage. Write an essay discussing your emotional associations with one or both of these topics.

3. Orwell, Naylor, and Anderson write about different kinds of prejudice. If you have personally been the victim of prejudice, write an essay analyzing the emotions that were part of this experience.

4. Kingston experiences alienation as a Chinese-American student grappling with English in an American school. If you have also experienced alienation in a similar or in a different situation, write an essay focusing on your emotional reactions to it.

5. Read over what you have written on the statement from the Generating Ideas section. Can you revise it for an essay or can you expand on one of your ideas to create a fully developed piece of writing? If so, complete the assignment.

6. Individuality is said to be part of the American philosophy of life, yet in our culture those who dare to be nonconformists are often ridiculed or penalized. Write an essay analyzing your emotional reactions, favorable or unfavorable, to individuality and/or nonconformity.

7. Sometimes we act in what seems to be an irrational manner. Yet the emotions that cause us to act this way are often understandable. Discuss in an essay what one or more selections reveal about the causes of irrational behavior.

8. Many of the authors in this section attempt to evaluate highly emotional situations from a detached, objective, analytical point of view. Write an essay in which you compare the effect upon you of the most objective writer with the effect of the least objective writer. Explain why you find one writer more objective than the other.

9. To what extent do you identify with Fleming's opening description of one of her "solitary departures"? Recall a similar experience you had, either as a chld or as an adult. Offer your own analysis of the emotional effect such a solitary departure produce in you.

10. John Coleman (Chapter 1) describes how he felt being called a "boy" by a waitress in the restaurant in which he was working. Gloria Naylor discusses the connotation of calling a woman "girl." Write an essay discussing the implications of being called a "boy" or a "girl" as opposed to a "man" or a "woman" in the circumstances described by both Naylor and Coleman.

CHAPTER SEVEN

Choices:
Reading the Essay
The Writer's Responsibility
The Reader's Responsibility

"Man is the only being who refuses to be what he is," writes Albert Camus, who believes that we can choose to become "fully human"—loving and peaceful—if we wish to do so. Other thinkers say our environment so shapes us that our freedom to choose that path is limited; if we are violent and unloving, environmental influences may prevent our breaking out of that pattern to something better.

Although our ability to choose may not be limitless, the selections in this chapter present many choices open to us. Martin Krovetz chooses mobility rather than settling down in one place; Henry David Thoreau goes off to the woods in search of a simpler way of life; Richard Rodriguez makes a deliberate decision not to take advantage of affirmative action; Linda Bird Francke finally enjoys a room of her own; and Loren Eiseley releases a sparrow hawk he had intended to capture.

In "A Moral Exigency," Mary Wilkins Freeman's protagonist makes an unusual choice for a friend, and in his poem "Curiosity," Alastair Reid contrasts people who choose the curiosity of cats to those who choose the complacency of dogs.

What is your philosophy about making choices? Do you prefer to think that fate governs our destinies or do you agree with Camus that we do have some freedom of choice? Analyze the choices you have made. How have they affected your life? A discussion of the writer's responsibility in making an essay understandable follows Martin Krovetz's "Going My Way" on pages 252–254. A discussion of the reader's responsibility follows Henry David Thoreau's essay on pages 260–263.

MARTIN KROVETZ

Going My Way

When Martin Krovetz wrote this article for the "My Turn" column of News-week *magazine in 1975, he was assistant principal of Carmel High School in Carmel-by-the-Sea, California. After reading "Going My Way," you will not be surprised that we cannot reach him in Carmel. He has moved on. How many times have you moved to a new place? Do you expect to move during your lifetime? Krovetz discusses here the effects of moving and of staying.*

We live in an age of change and mobility. The person who has had the same job for twenty years and has lived in the same house for that time may have trouble understanding my thoughts expressed here.

Until I was 15 years old I lived in Rochester, N.Y. During that time I attended three elementary schools, one junior high school and one high school. My last two years of high school were in Miami Beach. I then attended a large state university for four years to earn my B.A., followed by four more years at a second large university where I earned my Ph.D. I spent no more than four years at any one of these eight schools. I am employed in my third major job. I left the other two voluntarily after three years each and went on to something new. Now after two years in my present position I'm actively considering what should come next.

Everything has come in two-, three- or four-year cycles. No roots here, no roots there. Upward mobility is the theme. What's next, what's right to get there, thinking more of the future than the present. . . .

I was an excellent student in school. My Phi Beta Kappa key reminds me that I played by most of the rules. I realize now, as many people do, that most of the book learning has slipped my mind, but the messages given by the teachers all those years still ring loud and strong. Elementary school prepares you for junior high school. Junior high school prepares you for high school. High school prepares you for college. College prepares you for graduate school. Graduate school prepares you for a job. (There are a lot of Ph.D.'s unemployed these days, I hear.) If you work hard enough at the first job, the second job will offer more prestige, power and pay. If you work hard at the second job. . . . The endless cycle of a prosperous and *worthwhile* life. What better example of Marshall McLuhan's "the medium is the message."

Somewhere a part of me has been lost. There have been many whos at each stop, but it gets harder and harder to give of myself to others when I know that the relationship will be shortlived, based on the life-style I have chosen for myself to date. I tell myself that the next stop may not be lasting, but it will be longer. The next stop is where the roots will grow and flourish. I

251 MARTIN L. KROVETZ

sound too much like the aspiring law student who plans to play by all the rules until he is president of the General Motors Corp. and will then change the world.

Every year, I try to get back to Florida to visit with my father, sister, grandparents, nieces and nephew, aunts and uncles and two people who have been my closest friends since the first days of college. Two weeks out of 52 my extended family is a reality. A couple of times a year I correspond with friends from graduate school. We are spread all over North America now, but over the last four years I have seen several of them once or twice during someone's vacation.

At the same time, if I'm not moving, someone else probably is. As an educator, I have become close friends with many of my past students. Their lives too are spent in two-, three- and four-year cycles. They too are now spread all over North America.

Needless to say, I'm not sure that I want to change my life-style. I have an advantage that reportedly a majority of Americans do not have: I like my work. Each change of jobs has been stimulating and has caused me to grow as a person. I am away from my extended family, but I spend a lot of time with my nuclear family and find my relationship with my wife and three children to be very rewarding. I have made friends all along the way. I have hated to leave any of them, but I have enjoyed watching us change and grow with each move and with each new group of friends. Life is a learning process and by living in a number of places in the United States I have come to recognize and appreciate the pluralism within this country. Also, intellectually at least, I allow myself to think that I am somewhat of a free thinker, a person who will take risks and state his views even if it happens to endanger his job security; I pride myself on this, in fact.

The dilemma facing me is at least somewhat clear. Do I choose the professional and personal satisfaction that I perceive comes from a life-style characterized by mobility, or do I choose the shelter and satisfaction that come from choosing a more stable life-style and then try to find ways to achieve the other satisfactions? I notice as I write this that the ingrained biases are evident to me; I cringed slightly as I wrote the word "shelter." Protection and shelter have negative connotations for me; strength, power and fame are positive. I am not at all sure that these ideas are mutually exclusive; I know that the valences are questionable, but I will need to reevaluate my value system in order to be able to make a valid judgment.

I suppose that I see the world as made up of "them guys" who choose to not take chances, to work 40 hours a week at a boring job, drink lots of beer and watch "Let's Make a Deal" on television; and "us guys" who are willing to take chances, speak up, move, drink wine, eat cheese and read lots of newsmagazines. Along the way a number of "them guys" have been my friends, and they have admitted that they are jealous of the way I choose to approach life. I now wonder if I'm a little jealous of some of what they have as well.

I suspect that I will allow this dilemma to be waged inside me for a few more years and perhaps through several more moves. At some point, however,

I shall choose to at least try to look at my new house and new community as *home*. In the long run I still might choose to remain there for only three or four years; but once at least I should allow myself to think that the soil is rich and permit my roots to grow.

PROBING FOR MEANING

1. Summarize the major point of the essay in a sentence.

2. For what reasons—social, economic, and personal—has Krovetz moved so often? Cite examples from the essay for each category.

3. What are the positive effects of his mobility? The negative? Do you think one outweighs the other?

4. What solution does he propose to his dilemma? Do you think he will change his life-style? Why or why not?

PROBING FOR METHOD

1. "Going My Way" was originally published in *Newsweek*. For what kind of audience was Krovetz writing?

2. Analyze the tone of his essay. Does he, for example, feel superior to "them guys" whom he mentions toward the end?

3. Krovetz switches from the plural pronoun "we" of the first sentence to "I." Is the use of the plural pronoun justified, that is, is Krovetz the representative of a group of Americans?

Reading an Essay: The Writer's Responsibility

How does Krovetz address his reader?

Krovetz has chosen a rather specific audience for his essay. By writing for a particular magazine, *Newsweek*, he limits his readership to those who read newsmagazines. He more or less describes this readership in his essay as " 'us guys' who are willing to take chances, speak up, move, drink wine, eat cheese and read lots of newsmagazines." By studying "Going My Way," we can make other assumptions about his audience: They are educated (know what a Phi Beta Kappa key is; know who Marshall McLuhan was and what "the medium is the message" means), are upwardly mobile, and "appreciate the pluralism within this country." By extension, we can say they are any age over 22, are probably male, are moderate to liberal in their political views, may be of any religious persuasion, are from the middle to upper-middle class, and are of any profession that encourages its members to be mobile.

Krovetz also indicates who his audience is not. In the second sentence of his essay, he says, "The person who has had the same job for twenty years and has lived in the same house for that time may have trouble understanding my thoughts expressed here." He adds later, "I suppose that I see the world as made up of 'them guys' who choose not to take chances, to work 40 hours a week at a boring job, drink lots of beer and watch 'Let's Make a Deal' on television" as a way of further categorizing whom he is not addressing.

Krovetz establishes a somewhat ambivalent relationship with his reader through assuming alternating roles, one as the teller of a cautionary tale, and the other as an advocate of mobility. His voice also varies as he alternates between the uneasy voice reflecting his role as the carrier of possible bad tidings and the self-satisfied, even superior voice of one supporting his and his readers' life-style. How would his role and voice have to be changed were he to address "them guys"?

Addressing the reader.
The writer must assume his share of the responsibility for the reading of a piece of writing. If he is writing for a specific audience, he must know who that audience is, what their interests are, what their educational level is, what social and economic class they are from, how much they know about the subject—a fairly detailed profile, in other words. If he does not have a specific audience in mind, then he should attempt to create that audience through an approach that makes consistent demands on the reader's education, knowledge, social and religious perspectives— that creates a profile of the desired reader, in other words.

The writer must also adopt a role for himself and a voice that reflects that role so that the reader has a sense of who the writer is and what relationship he wishes to establish between them. A writer need not limit herself to one role or voice if she is ambivalent about her subject matter, but since writers usually have a consistent attitude toward their subjects, they usually elect to fulfill one role and speak in one voice.

Procedures to follow for addressing your reader.

A. Establish or create a profile of your reader. Whether you know who your reader will be or not, you will find it helpful to determine one or more of the following:
   1. Age, sex, ethnic background
   2. Education and career interests
   3. Social and economic class
   4. Religious beliefs
   5. What your reader knows about your subject
B. Based on the above profile, you should be able to determine what the reader's attitude toward your subject is. If it is similar to yours, then you can adopt a role and voice that assumes agreement. If it is different, then you will want to adopt a role and voice that will bridge the gap.

HENRY DAVID THOREAU

Simplicity

Henry David Thoreau (1817–1862) was an American essayist and poet who was part of the American romantic literary movement. In 1845 he built a cabin at Walden Pond in Massachusetts, where he lived for the next two years. In Walden *(1854), he describes his daily experiences. A nonconformist, Thoreau was imprisoned for failing to pay his taxes and recorded the episode in his essay "Civil Disobedience." He is recognized today not only for his prose style but also for his individualism, which not only challenged the social status quo of his contemporaries but challenges ours today as well. His belief in passive resistance influenced Gandhi and Martin Luther King, Jr. As you read his essay from* Walden *about simplifying life, make a note of his suggestions that you consider feasible and add some of your own.*

I went to the woods because I wished to live deliberately, to front only the essential facts of life, and see if I could not learn what it had to teach, and not, when I came to die, discover that I had not lived. I did not wish to live what was not life, living is so dear; nor did I wish to practice resignation, unless it was quite necessary. I wanted to live deep and suck out all the marrow of life, to live so sturdily and Spartan-like as to put to rout all that was not life, to cut a broad swath and shave close, to drive life into a corner, and reduce it to its lowest terms, and, if it proved to be mean, why then to get the whole and genuine meanness of it, and publish its meanness to the world; or if it were sublime, to know it by experience, and be able to give a true account of it in my next excursion. For most men, it appears to me, are in a strange uncertainty about it, whether it is of the devil or of God, and have *somewhat hastily* concluded that it is the chief end of man here to "glorify God and enjoy him forever."

Still we live meanly, like ants; though the fable tells us that we were long ago changed into men; like pygmies we fight with cranes;[1] it is error upon error, and clout upon clout, and our best virtue has for its occasion a superfluous and evitable wretchedness. Our life is frittered away by detail. An honest man has hardly need to count more than his ten fingers, or in extreme cases he

---

[1]In an ancient Greek fable, the god Zeus transformed ants into men to populate a kingdom. In the Greek epic poem *The Iliad*, the poet Homer compares the Trojan army with cranes fighting against pygmies.

may add his ten toes, and lump the rest. Simplicity, simplicity, simplicity! I say, let your affairs be as two or three, and not a hundred or a thousand; instead of a million count half a dozen, and keep your accounts on your thumb nail. In the midst of this chopping sea of civilized life, such are the clouds and storms and quicksands and thousand-and-one items to be allowed for, that a man has to live, if he would not founder and go to the bottom and not make his port at all, by dead reckoning, and he must be a great calculator indeed who succeeds. Simplify, simplify. Instead of three meals a day, if it be necessary eat but one; instead of a hundred dishes, five; and reduce other things in proportion.

Our life is like a German Confederacy,[2] made up of petty states, with its boundary forever fluctuating, so that even a German cannot tell you how it is bounded at any moment. The nation itself, with all its so-called internal improvements, which, by the way are all external and superficial, is just such an unwieldy and overgrown establishment, cluttered with furniture and tripped up by its own traps, ruined by luxury and heedless expense, by want of calculation and a worthy aim, as the million households in the land; and the only cure for it as for them is in a rigid economy, a stern and more than Spartan simplicity of life and elevation of purpose. It lives too fast. Men think that it is essential that the *Nation* have commerce, and export ice, and talk through a telegraph, and ride thirty miles an hour, without a doubt, whether *they* do or not; but whether we should live like baboons or like men, is a little uncertain. If we do not get our sleepers, and forge rails, and devote days and nights to the work, but go to tinkering upon our *lives* to improve *them*, who will build railroads? And if railroads are not built, how shall we get to heaven in season? But if we stay at home and mind our business, who will want railroads? We do not ride on the railroad; it rides upon us. Did you ever think what those sleepers are that underlie the railroad? Each one is a man, an Irishman, or a Yankee man. The rails are laid on them, and they are covered with sand, and the cars run smoothly over them. They are sound sleepers, I assure you. And every few years a new lot is laid down and run over; so that, if some have the pleasure of riding on a rail, others have the misfortune to be ridden upon. And when they run over a man that is walking in his sleep, a supernumerary sleeper in the wrong position, and wake him up, they suddenly stop the cars, and make a hue and cry about it, as if this were an exception. I am glad to know that it takes a gang of men for every five miles to keep the sleepers down and level in their beds as it is, for this is a sign that they may sometime get up again.

Why should we live with such hurry and waste of life? We are determined to be starved before we are hungry. Men say that a stitch in time saves nine, and so they take a thousand stitches to-day to save nine to-morrow. As

[2]At the time Thoreau wrote, Germany consisted of many different kingdoms.

for *work*, we haven't any of any consequence. We have the Saint Vitus' dance, and cannot possibly keep our heads still. If I should only give a few pulls at the parish bell-rope, as for a fire, that is, without setting the bell, there is hardly a man on his farm in the outskirts of Concord, notwithstanding that press of engagements which was his excuse so many times this morning, nor a boy, nor a woman, I might almost say, but would forsake all and follow that sound, not mainly to save property from the flames, but, if we will confess the truth, much more to see it burn, since burn it must, and we, be it known, did not set it on fire,—or to see it put out, and have a hand in it, if that is done as handsomely; yes, even if it were the parish church itself. Hardly a man takes a half hour's nap after dinner, but when he wakes he holds up his head and asks, "What's the news?" as if the rest of mankind had stood his sentinels. Some give directions to be waked every half hour, doubtless for no other purpose; and then, to pay for it, they tell what they have dreamed. After a night's sleep the news is as indispensable as the breakfast. "Pray tell me anything new that has happened to a man anywhere on this globe,"—and he reads it over his coffee and rolls, that a man has had his eyes gouged out this morning on the Wachito River;[3] never dreaming the while that he lives in the dark unfathomed mammoth cave of this world, and has but the rudiment of an eye himself.

For my part, I could easily do without the post-office. I think that there are very few important communications made through it. To speak critically, I never received more than one or two letters in my life—I wrote this some years ago—that were worth the postage. The penny-post is, commonly, an institution through which you seriously offer a man that penny for his thoughts which is so often safely offered in jest. And I am sure that I never read any memorable news in a newspaper. If we read of one man robbed, or murdered, or killed by accident, or one house burned, or one vessel wrecked, or one steamboat blown up, or one cow run over on the Western Railroad, or one mad dog killed, or one lot of grasshoppers in the winter,—we never need read of another. One is enough. If you are acquainted with the principle, what do you care for a myriad instances and applications? To a philosopher all *news*, as it is called, is gossip, and they who edit and read it are old women over their tea. Yet not a few are greedy after this gossip. There was such a rush, as I hear, the other day at one of the offices to learn the foreign news by the last arrival, that several large squares of plate glass belonging to the establishment were broken by the pressure,—news which I seriously think a ready wit might write a twelvemonth or twelve years beforehand with sufficient accuracy. As for Spain, for instance, if you know how to throw in Don Carlos and the Infanta, and Don Pedro and Seville and Granada, from time to time in the right proportions,—they may have changed the names a little since I saw the papers,—and serve up a bull-fight when other entertainments fail, it will be

---

[3] A river in Arkansas.

true to the letter, and give us as good an idea of the exact state or ruin of things in Spain as the most succinct and lucid reports under this head in the newspapers: and as for England, almost the last significant scrap of news from that quarter was the revolution of 1649;[4] and if you have learned the history of her crops for an average year, you never need attend to that thing again, unless your speculations are of a merely pecuniary character. If one may judge who rarely looks into the newspapers, nothing new does ever happen in foreign parts, a French revolution not excepted.[5]

What news! how much more important to know what that is which was never old! "Kieou-he-yu (great dignitary of the state of Wei) sent a man to Khoung-tseu to know his news. Khoung-tseu caused the messenger to be seated near him, and questioned him in these terms: What is your master doing? The messenger answered with respect: My master desires to diminish the number of his faults, but he cannot come to the end of them. The messenger being gone, the philosopher remarked: What a worthy messenger! What a worthy messenger!"[6] The preacher, instead of vexing the ears of drowsy farmers on their day of rest at the end of the week,—for Sunday is the fit conclusion of an ill-spent week, and not the fresh and brave beginning of a new one, —with this one other draggle-tail of a sermon, should shout with thundering voice,—"Pause! Avast! Why so seeming fast, but deadly slow?"

Shams and delusions are esteemed for soundest truths, while reality is fabulous. If men would steadily observe realities only, and not allow themselves to be deluded, life, to compare it with such things as we know, would be like a fairy tale and the Arabian Nights' Entertainments.[7] If we respected only what is inevitable and has a right to be, music and poetry would resound along the streets. When we are unhurried and wise, we perceive that only great and worthy things have any permanent and absolute existence,—that petty fears and petty pleasures are but the shadow of the reality. This is always exhilarating and sublime. By closing the eyes and slumbering, and consenting to be deceived by shows, men establish and confirm their daily life of routine and habit everywhere, which still is built on purely illusory foundations. Children, who play life, discern its true law and relations more clearly than men, who fail to live it worthily, but who think that they are wiser by experience, that is, by failure. I have read in a Hindoo book, that "there was a king's son, who, being expelled in infancy from his native city, was brought up by a for-

---

[4]When King Charles I was beheaded and the Puritans under Oliver Cromwell assumed control of the government.

[5]Several French revolutions had occurred in the sixty years before Thoreau wrote: 1789, 1830, and 1848, the latter while Thoreau was writing *Walden,* the book in which this essay appeared.

[6]Quoted from Confucius, *Analects,* XIV.

[7]The *Thousand and One Nights,* a collection of exotic stories including those about Sindbad the Sailor and Ali Baba and the Forty Thieves.

ester, and, growing up to maturity in that state, imagined himself to belong to the barbarous race with which he lived. One of his father's ministers having discovered him, revealed to him what he was, and the misconception of his character was removed, and he knew himself to be a prince. So soul," continues the Hindoo philosopher, "from the circumstances in which it is placed, mistakes its own character, until the truth is revealed to it by some holy teacher, and then it knows itself to be *Brahme*."[8] I perceive that we inhabitants of New England live this mean life that we do because our vision does not penetrate the surface of things. We think that that *is* which *appears* to be. If a man should walk through this town and see only the reality, where, think you, would the "Milldam"[9] go to? If he should give us an account of the realities he beheld there, we should not recognize the place in his description. Look at a meeting-house, or a courthouse, or a jail, or a shop, or a dwelling-house, and say what that thing really is before a true gaze, and they would all go to pieces in your account of them. Men esteem truth remote, in the outskirts of the system, behind the farthest star, before Adam and after the last man. In eternity there is indeed something true and sublime. But all these times and places and occasions are now and here. God himself culminates in the present moment, and will never be more divine in the lapse of all the ages. And we are enabled to apprehend at all what is sublime and noble only by the perpetual instilling and drenching of the reality that surrounds us. The universe constantly and obediently answers to our conceptions; whether we travel fast or slow, the track is laid for us. Let us spend our lives in conceiving then. The poet or the artist never yet had so fair and noble a design but some of his posterity at least could accomplish it.

Let us spend one day as deliberately as Nature, and not be thrown off the track by every nutshell and mosquito's wing that falls on the rails. Let us rise early and fast, or break fast, gently and without perturbation; let company come and let company go, let the bells ring and the children cry,—determined to make a day of it. Why should we knock under and go with the stream? Let us not be upset and overwhelmed in that terrible rapid and whirlpool called a dinner, situated in the meridian shallows. Weather this danger and you are safe, for the rest of the way is down hill. With unrelaxed nerves, with morning vigor, sail by it, looking another way, tied to the mast like Ulysses.[10] If the engine whistles, let it whistle till it is hoarse for its pains. If the bell rings, why should we run? We will consider what kind of music they are like.

Let us settle ourselves, and work and wedge our feet downward through

---

[8]The soul (after Brahma, the Hindu god.)

[9]Main street in Concord, Thoreau's hometown.

[10]Ulysses, the hero of Homer's other epic poem, *The Odyessey*, ties himself to the mast of his ship rather than respond to the alluring song of the Sirens, for to do so would send him to his death. Thoreau compares eating dinner to responding to the Sirens.

the mud and slush of opinion, and prejudice, and tradition, and delusion, and appearance, that alluvion which covers the globe, through Paris and London, through New York and Boston and Concord, through church and state, through poetry and philosophy and religion, till we come to a hard bottom and rocks in place, which we can call *reality*, and say, This is, and no mistake; and then begin, having a *point d'appui*,[11] below freshet and frost and fire, a place where you might found a wall or a state, or set a lamppost safely, or perhaps a gauge, not a Nilometer,[12] but a Realometer, that future ages might know how deep a freshet of shams and appearances had gathered from time to time. If you stand right fronting and face to face to a fact, you will see the sun glimmer on both its surfaces, as if it were a cimeter,[13] and feel its sweet edge dividing you through the heart and marrow, and so you will happily conclude your mortal career. Be it life or death, we crave only reality. If we are really dying, let us hear the rattle in our throats and feel cold in the extremities; if we are alive, let us go about our business.

Time is but the stream I go a-fishing in. I drink at it; but while I drink I see the sandy bottom and detect how shallow it is. Its thin current slides away, but eternity remains. I would drink deeper; fish in the sky, whose bottom is pebbly with stars. I cannot count one. I know not the first letter of the alphabet. I have always been regretting that I was not as wise as the day I was born. The intellect is a cleaver; it discerns and rifts its way into the secret of things. I do not wish to be any more busy with my hands than is necessary. My head is hands and feet. I feel all my best faculties concentrated in it. My instinct tells me that my head is an organ for burrowing, as some creatures use their snout and forepaws, and with it I would mine and burrow my way through these hills. I think that the richest vein is somewhere hereabouts; so by the divining rod and thin rising vapors I judge; and here I will begin to mine.

PROBING FOR MEANING

1. Summarize the major point of Thoreau's essay in a sentence.

2. What is Thoreau criticizing in the second paragraph? Why does he dislike railroads? Do you think his point of view is reactionary?

3. "Why should we live with such hurry and waste of life?" What examples does Thoreau cite? What additional instances would you offer?

4. Thoreau thinks that being preoccupied with news is a form of distraction. What is your reaction to his point of view? Is it practical for today's world? Why or why not?

---

[11]French expression meaning "point of support" or foundation.

[12]A gauge used in ancient Egypt for measuring the depth of the Nile.

[13]A scimitar, a curved sword used by Arabs and Turks.

5. Why does Thoreau quote from Confucius? Does he make his point of view more convincing as a result? Why or why not?

6. State your reaction to his essay in one or two sentences.

PROBING FOR METHOD

1. Read over Thoreau's journal entry for July 5 that appears in Chapter 1. Of what significance might be his encounter with the saw-miller's family for the ideas of "Simplicity"?

2. What ideas does he incorporate into the essay from his July 6 entry (also in Chapter 1)? How similar is the language he uses to express these ideas? In what other ways has he revised the July 6 entry in writing his essay? Why do you think he made these revisions? (Note that Thoreau has written extensively on the issue of slavery elsewhere in *Walden* and in his famous essay "On Civil Disobedience.")

3. For what audience is Thoreau writing? What is the significance of his beginning and ending the essay with "I," and then changing to "we" and "you" in the middle part?

4. How would you characterize the tone of voice of this essay? Notice that it changes in the first and last paragraphs. How do these changes affect the meaning of the essay?

5. What is Thoreau's purpose in writing "Simplicity"? Is he seeking to inform his readers or does he want to influence them? Give evidence for your point of view.

Reading an Essay: The Reader's Responsibility

What is the reader's responsibility in reading Thoreau's essay?
The twentieth-century reader may very well ask how he should read an essay written for a nineteenth-century reader, as writing styles have changed considerably. Not only are Thoreau's paragraphs very long (we have even subdivided some of them), but also his sentences are long, his language more formal than we are used to, and he often makes reference to literary works that we seldom read today. Furthermore, we may ask why we should read anything not from our own time. Is the effort worth it? What can someone living in the past tell us that is worthwhile? These are legitimate questions, certainly, to ask about Thoreau's essay.

First, how should we read "Simplicity"? Our first glance has told us that his paragraphs are long and therefore that the reading will be difficult. We also notice many footnotes, which indicates that the ideas will be difficult also. Before plunging in or turning away in despair, we should ask what else a preview indicates. The title "Simplicity" may seem a bit ironic, given our first impression, but is cause for some hope. Perhaps the essay isn't as complex as it seems. Looking at the first phrase is also encouraging and even interesting: "I went to the woods. . . ." What indeed could be more simple than going to the woods? And while most of us live in cities or suburbs, we also have a fascination for "getting away from it all." We too like to go "to the woods."

What then is Thoreau going to say? Is he in fact going to talk about getting away from it all? Is he going to talk about how to make our lives more simple? How can someone in nineteenth-century New England have worried about being surrounded by people and cares and responsibilities? Did people then have something in common with people now? What other questions come to mind as you begin to think about what your preview has revealed?

Skim through the essay at this point, reading the first and second sentences in each paragraph. This method will give you an indication of where Thoreau is taking you. You will no doubt be surprised at how contemporary Thoreau's ideas seem to be: Our lives too are frittered away by detail, we too hurry and waste our lives, perhaps we too should try to do without the post office, should look beneath the surface appearances of people and ideas to find reality. Having discovered what the essay is about, you may be more hopeful and interested as you begin to read. Most important, you may know now why you should read the essay: Thoreau is going to suggest how we can live with less anxiety, with more confidence that we know what life is all about.

Once you have read the essay to fill in the details and examples with which Thoreau supports his topic sentences, record your main impressions of what you have read, perhaps in your journal or in your notebook. What were Thoreau's main ideas? How did he support them? What is your reaction to what Thoreau is saying? What other books or films or songs that you are familiar with make a similar point? What effect has the idea of "Simplicity" had on society since it was published along with the other essays in *Walden*?

Next, write a second journal entry or notebook page in which you review all that you have learned about the essay. This second entry will ensure that you have understood what you read as well as its implications and will be particularly helpful in studying for a test.

The reader's responsibility.
Any reader faced with a difficult text, whether because it was written in a previous era or because it was written for a highly educated or technical audience, has responsibilities to herself and to the author to understand what she is reading. These responsibilities involve discovering how to read the text and why it should be read. Sometimes, one has to learn how to read a piece of writing before one can work up much enthusiasm for wanting to read it. In other instances, one may be motivated to read before knowing quite how to go about doing so.

In either case, previewing a piece of writing first will give you some ideas about it, perhaps enough ideas to motivate you to want to read further. Thinking about what type of writing this is, about the title, about the writer's name, about any headings, about footnotes, about length of paragraphs, about any other features of the text that stand out gives you a foundation on which to build. Then, asking questions about it based on your preview will add further incentive. Skimming for main ideas is a final stage in this prereading process.

After reading the text through, writing down what has been learned encourages the reader to record the main ideas, mull over the issues raised, and fit the writer's thesis into what she knows about the subject in general.

Procedures to follow in fulfilling the reader's responsibility.

A. Before reading the text:
   1. Preview—ask yourself the following questions:
      a. What type of writing is this: an essay or article, a story, a textbook chapter, a report, a set of instructions? What do I know about the typical structure of this type of writing?
      b. What are the title and subtitle, if any? What do they suggest to me that I already know about?
      c. Have I heard of the author before? If so, what do I know about him or her? If not, who does he or she seem to be—is there a title included, such as M.D., or is a brief biography included?
      d. What does the text itself look like? Are there headings, footnotes, illustrations? What do they suggest to me?
   2. Question—based on your preview, ask yourself questions about the text, questions that you want to know the answers to, questions that will help you understand the text, and questions that will help you relate the text to your previous reading and experience. These questions might include specific versions of the following general questions:
      a. What is this text about?
      b. Who is the author writing for?
      c. What does he/she want the reader to understand?
      d. How does this text relate to what I know about the subject already, either from my reading or from my experience?

At this point, you should also be able to answer the question, "Why should I read this text?" If your answer is simply that you must fulfill an assignment, ask yourself the question again to see if you can't find a motivation that engages you more deeply, one that would encourage you to continue even if you were not assigned to do so.

B. Read the text.
   1. Skim the text to see where it's going by reading the first and second senten-
      ces of each paragraph.
   2. Read the text to determine how the writer supports each of her or his topic
      sentences.
C. After reading:
   1. Study what you have read by writing the answers to your questions in your
      journal or notebook, or discuss them with members of your class.
   2. Review what you have read by writing the answers again.

LOREN EISELEY

Sparrow Hawks

Loren Eiseley (1907−1977) was an American educator, anthropologist, poet, and
author born in Lincoln, Nebraska. He was best known for his ability to combine
a poetic style with scientific subject matter. He believed that reason by itself,
without vision and imagination, would destroy mankind. His best-known works
are The Immense Journey *(1957),* Darwin's Century *(1958), and* The
Unexpected Universe *(1969). As you read "Sparrow Hawks," consider how*
you may have acted in Eiseley's place.

I joined some colleagues heading into a remote windy tableland where huge
bones were reputed to protrude like boulders from the turf. . . . There had
been talk of birds in connection with my duties. Birds are intense, fast-living
creatures—reptiles, I suppose one might say, that have escaped out of the
heavy sleep of time, transformed fairy creatures dancing over sunlit meadows.
It is a youthful fancy, no doubt, but because of something that happened up
there among the escarpments of that range, it remains with me a lifelong impression. I can never bear to see a bird imprisoned.

   We came into that valley through the trailing mists of a spring night. It
was a place that looked as though it might never have known the foot of man,
but our scouts had been ahead of us and we knew all about the abandoned
cabin of stone that lay far up on one hillside. It had been built in the land rush

of the last century and then lost to the cattlemen again as the marginal soils failed to take to the plow.

There were spots like this all over that country. Lost graves marked by unlettered stones and old corroding rim-fire cartridge cases lying where somebody had made a stand among the boulders that rimmed the valley. They are all that remain of the range wars; the men are under the stones now. I could see our cavalcade winding in and out through the mist below us: torches, the reflection of the truck lights on our collecting tins, and the far-off bumping of a loose dinosaur thigh bone in the bottom of a trailer. I stood on a rock a moment looking down and thinking what it cost in money and equipment to capture the past.

We had, in addition, instructions to lay hands on the present. The word had come through to get them alive—birds, reptiles, anything. A zoo somewhere abroad needed restocking. It was one of those reciprocal matters in which science involves itself. Maybe our museum needed a stray ostrich egg and this was the payoff. Anyhow, my job was to help capture some birds and that was why I was there before the trucks.

The cabin had not been occupied for years. We intended to clean it out and live in it, but there were holes in the roof and the birds had come in and were roosting in the rafters. You could depend on it in a place like this where everything blew away, and even a bird needed some place out of the weather and away from coyotes. A cabin going back to nature in a wild place draws them till they come in, listening at the eaves, I imagine, pecking softly among the shingles till they find a hole and then suddenly the place is theirs and man is forgotten. . . .

I got the door open softly and I had the spotlight all ready to turn on and blind whatever birds there were so they couldn't see to get out through the roof. I had a short piece of ladder to put against the far wall where there was a shelf on which I expected to make the biggest haul. I had all the information I needed just like any skilled assassin. I pushed the door open, the hinges squeaking only a little. A bird or two stirred—I could hear them—but nothing flew and there was a faint starlight through the holes in the roof.

I padded across the floor, got the ladder up and the light ready, and slithered up the ladder till my head and arms were over the shelf. Everything was dark as pitch except for the starlight at the little place back of the shelf near the eaves. With the light to blind them, they'd never make it. I had them. I reached my arm carefully over in order to be ready to seize whatever was there and I put the flash on the edge of the shelf where it would stand by itself when I turned it on. That way I'd be able to use both hands.

Everything worked perfectly except for one detail—I didn't know what kinds of birds were there. I never thought about it at all, and it wouldn't have mattered if I had. My orders were to get something interesting. I snapped on the flash and sure enough there was a great beating and feathers flying, but instead of my having them, they, or rather he, had me. He had my hand, that is, and for a small hawk not much bigger than my fist he was doing all right. I heard him give one short metallic cry when the light went on and my hand descended on the bird beside him; after that he was busy with his claws and his beak was sunk in my thumb. In the struggle I knocked the lamp over on the shelf, and his mate got her sight back and whisked neatly through the hole in the roof and off among the stars outside. It all happened in fifteen seconds and you might think I would have fallen down the ladder, but no, I had a professional assassin's reputation to keep up, and the bird, of course, made the mistake of thinking the hand was the enemy and not the eyes behind it. He chewed my thumb up pretty effectively and lacerated my hand with his claws, but in the end I got him, having two hands to work with.

He was a sparrow hawk and a fine young male in the prime of life. I was sorry not to catch the pair of them, but as I dripped blood and folded his wings carefully, holding him by the back so that he couldn't strike again, I had to admit the two of them might have been more than I could have handled under the circumstances. The little fellow had saved his mate by diverting me, and that was that. He was born to it, and made no outcry now, resting in my hand hopelessly, but peering toward me in the shadows behind the lamp with a fierce, almost indifferent glance. He neither gave nor expected mercy and something out of the high air passed from him to me, stirring a faint embarrassment.

I quit looking into that eye and managed to get my huge carcass with its fist full of prey back down the ladder. I put the bird in a box too small to allow him to injure himself by struggle and walked out to welcome the arriving trucks. It had been a long day, and camp still to make in the darkness. In the morning that bird would be just another episode. He would go back with the bones in the truck to a small cage in a city where he would spend the rest of his life. And a good thing, too. I sucked my aching thumb and spat out some blood. An assassin has to get used to these things. I had a professional reputation to keep up.

In the morning, with the change that comes on suddenly in that high country, the mist that had hovered below us in the valley was gone. The sky was a deep blue, and one could see for miles over the high outcroppings of stone. I was up early and brought the box in which the little hawk was imprisoned out onto the grass where I was building a cage. A wind as cool as a mountain spring ran over the grass and stirred my hair. It was a fine day to be alive. I looked up and all around and at the hole in the cabin roof out of which the other little hawk had fled. There was no sign of her anywhere that I could see.

"Probably in the next county by now," I thought cynically, but before beginning work I decided I'd have a look at my last night's capture.

Secretively, I looked again all around the camp and up and down and opened the box. I got him right out in my hand with his wings folded properly and I was careful not to startle him. He lay limp in my grasp and I could feel his heart pound under the feathers but he only looked beyond me and up.

I saw him look that last look away beyond me into a sky so full of light that I could not follow his gaze. The little breeze flowed over me again, and nearby a mountain aspen shook all its tiny leaves. I suppose I must have had an idea then of what I was going to do, but I never let it come up into consciousness. I just reached over and laid the hawk on the grass.

He lay there a long minute without hope, unmoving, his eyes still fixed on that blue vault above him. It must have been that he was already so far away in heart that he never felt the release from my hand. He never even stood. He just lay with his breast against the grass.

In the next second after that long minute he was gone. Like a flicker of light, he had vanished with my eyes full on him, but without actually seeing even a premonitory wing beat. He was gone straight into that towering emptiness of light and crystal that my eyes could scarcely bear to penetrate. For another long moment there was silence. I could not see him. The light was too intense. Then from far up somewhere a cry came ringing down.

I was young then and had seen little of the world, but when I heard that cry my heart turned over. It was not the cry of the hawk I had captured; for, by shifting my position against the sun, I was now seeing further up. Straight out of the sun's eye, where she must have been soaring restlessly above us for untold hours, hurtled his mate. And from far up, ringing from peak to peak of the summits over us, came a cry of such unutterable and ecstatic joy that it sounds down across the years and tingles among the cups on my quiet breakfast table.

I saw them both now. He was rising fast to meet her. They met in a great soaring gyre that turned to a whirling circle and a dance of wings. Once more, just once, their two voices, joined in a harsh wild medley of question and response, struck and echoed against the pinnacles of the valley. Then they were gone forever somewhere into those upper regions beyond the eyes of men.

PROBING FOR MEANING

1. Why had Eiseley come to capture the birds?

2. Do you think you would have freed the bird after being attacked by it as Eiseley was? Why or why not?

3. "I was young then and had seen little of the world, but when I heard that cry my heart turned over." Do you think Eiseley would have reacted in the same way had he been older? Should he have been more concerned about fulfilling his professional responsibilities?

4. Was freeing the bird a sentimental act? Is a sentimental act bad? Good? Sometimes bad, sometimes good? Explain.

5. What is your overall response to the essay?

PROBING FOR METHOD

1. What clue does Eiseley give in the first paragraph that foreshadows the decision he will make later?

2. What is the significance of Eiseley's referring to himself as an "assassin" in paragraphs 6, 8, and 10?

3. For what audience is Eiseley writing?

4. What is his purpose in recalling this experience?

5. Look up the meaning of "epiphany." Why is that an appropriate term to describe Eiseley's experience in paragraphs 17 and 18? What was your reaction to his description of his experience?

6. To what senses does Eiseley appeal in his use of figurative language? Cite examples from the essay that you found effective.

RICHARD RODRIGUEZ

None of This Is Fair

Richard Rodriguez (b. 1944) is a Mexican-American writer who grew up in Sacramento, California. As a child, Rodriguez struggled in parochial school with the task of learning his "public" language—English. He subsequently studied at Stanford and did graduate work at Columbia, the Warburg Institute in London, and the University of California at Berkeley. In 1981 he wrote Hunger of Memory: The Education of Richard Rodriguez, *in which he describes the complexities and contradictions—personal and political—of growing up bilingual in America. As you read "None of This Is Fair," make a list of the points with which you agree and disagree.*

My plan to become a professor of English—my ambition during long years in college at Stanford, then in graduate school at Columbia and Berkeley—was complicated by feelings of embarrassment and guilt. So many times I would see other Mexican-Americans and know we were alike only in race. And yet, simply because our race was the same, I was, during the last years of my schooling, the beneficiary of their situation. Affirmative Action programs had made it all possible. The disadvantages of others permitted my promotion; the absence of many Mexican-Americans from academic life allowed my designation as a "minority student."

For me opportunities had been extravagant. There were fellowships, summer research grants, and teaching assistantships. After only two years in graduate school, I was offered teaching jobs by several colleges. Invitations to Washington conferences arrived and I had the chance to travel abroad as a "Mexican-American representative." The benefits were often, however, too gaudy to please. In three published essays, in conversations with teachers, in letters to politicians and at conferences, I worried the issue of Affirmative Action. Often I proposed contradictory opinions. Though consistent was the admission that—because of an early, excellent education—I was no longer a principal victim of racism or any other social oppression. I said that but still I continued to indicate on applications for financial aid that I was a Hispanic-American. It didn't really occur to me to say anything else, or to leave the question unanswered.

Thus I complied with and encouraged the odd bureaucratic logic of Affirmative Action. I let government officials treat the disadvantaged condition of many Mexican-Americans with my advancement. Each fall my presence was noted by Health, Education, and Welfare department statisticians. As I pursued advanced literary studies and learned the skill of reading Spenser and Wordsworth and Empson, I would hear myself numbered among the culturally disadvantaged. Still, silent, I didn't object.

But the irony cut deep. And guilt would not be evaded by averting my glance when I confronted a face like my own in a crowd. By late 1975, nearing the completion of my graduate studies at Berkeley, I was so wary of the benefits of Affirmative Action that I feared my inevitable success as an applicant for a teaching position. The months of fall—traditionally that time of academic job-searching—passed without my applying to a single school. When one of my professors chanced to learn this in late November, he was astonished, then furious. He yelled at me: Did I think that because I was a minority student jobs would just come looking for me? What was I thinking? Did I realize that he and several other faculty members had already written letters on my behalf? Was I going to start acting like some other minority students he had known? They struggled for success and then, when it was almost within reach, grew strangely afraid and let it pass. Was that it? Was I determined to fail?

I did not respond to his questions. I didn't want to admit to him, and thus to myself, the reason I delayed.

I merely agreed to write to several schools. (In my letter I wrote: "I cannot claim to represent disadvantaged Mexican-Americans. The very fact that I am in a position to apply for this job should make that clear.") After two or three days, there were telegrams and phone calls, invitations to interviews, then airplane trips. A blur of faces and the murmur of their soft questions. And, over someone's shoulder, the sight of campus buildings shadowing pictures I had seen years before when I leafed through Ivy League catalogues with great expectations. At the end of each visit, interviewers would smile and wonder if I had any questions. A few times I quietly wondered what advantage my race had given me over other applicants. But that was an impossible question for them to answer without embarrassing me. Quickly, several persons insisted that my ethnic identity had given me no more than a "foot inside the door"; at most, I had a "slight edge" over other applicants. "We just looked at your dossier with extra care and we like what we saw. There was never any question of having to alter our standards. You can be certain of that."

In the early part of January, offers arrived on stiffly elegant stationery. Most schools promised terms appropriate for any new assistant professor. A few made matters worse—and almost more tempting—by offering more: the use of university housing; an unusually large starting salary; a reduced teaching schedule. As the stack of letters mounted, my hesitation increased. I started calling department chairmen to ask for another week, then 10 more days—"more time to reach a decision"—to avoid the decision I would need to make.

At school, meantime, some students hadn't received a single job offer. One man, probably the best student in the department, did not even get a request for his dossier. He and I met outside a classroom one day and he asked about my opportunities. He seemed happy for me. Faculty members beamed. They said they had expected it. "After all, not many schools are going to pass up getting a Chicano with a Ph.D. in Renaissance literature," somebody said laughing. Friends wanted to know which of the offers I was going to accept. But I couldn't make up my mind. February came and I was running out of time and excuses. (One chairman guessed my delay was a bargaining ploy and increased his offer with each of my calls.) I had to promise a decision by the 10th; the 12th at the very latest.

On the 18th of February, late in the afternoon, I was in the office I shared with several other teaching assistants. Another graduate student was sitting across the room at his desk. When I got up to leave, he looked over to say in an uneventful voice that he had some big news. He had finally decided to accept a position at a faraway university. It was not a job he especially wanted, he admitted. But he had to take it because there hadn't been any other offers. He felt trapped, and depressed, since his job would separate him from his young daughter.

I tried to encourage him by remarking that he was lucky at least to have found a job. So many others hadn't been able to get anything. But before I finished speaking I realized that I had said the wrong thing. And I anticipated his next question.

"What are your plans?" he wanted to know. "Is it true you've gotten an offer from Yale?"

I said that it was. "Only, I still haven't made up my mind."

He stared at me as I put on my jacket. And smiling, then unsmiling, he asked if I knew that he too had written to Yale. In his case, however, no one had bothered to acknowledge his letter with even a postcard. What did I think of that?

He gave me no time to answer.

"Damn!" he said sharply and his chair rasped the floor as he pushed himself back. Suddenly, it was to *me* that he was complaining. "It's just not right, Richard. None of this is fair. You've done some good work, but so have I. I'll bet our records are just about equal. But when we look for jobs this year, it's a different story. You get all of the breaks."

To evade his criticism, I wanted to side with him. I was about to admit the injustice of Affirmative Action. But he went on, his voice hard with accusation. "It's all very simple this year. You're a Chicano. And I am a Jew. That's the only real difference between us."

His words stung me: there was nothing he was telling me that I didn't know. I had admitted everything already. But to hear someone else say these things, and in such an accusing tone, was suddenly hard to take. In a deceptively calm voice, I responsed that he had simplified the whole issue. The phrases came like bubbles to the tip of my tongue: "new blood"; "the importance of cultural diversity"; "the goal of racial integration." These were all the arguments I had proposed several years ago—and had long since abandoned. Of course the offers were unjustifiable. I knew that. All I was saying amounted to a frantic self-defense. I tried to find an end to a sentence. My voice faltered to a stop.

"Yeah, sure," he said. "I've heard all that before. Nothing you say really changes the fact that Affirmative Action is unfair. You see that, don't you? There isn't any way for me to compete with you. Once there were quotas to keep my parents out of certain schools; now there are quotas to get you in and the effect on me is the same as it was for them."

I listened to every word he spoke. But my mind was really on something else. I knew at that moment that I would reject all of the offers. I stood there silently surprised by what an easy conclusion it was. Having prepared for so many years to teach, having trained myself to do nothing else, I had hesitated out of practical fear. But now that it was made, the decision came with relief. I immediately knew I had made the right choice.

My colleague continued talking and I realized that he was simply right. Affirmative Action programs *are* unfair to white students. But as I listened to him assert his rights, I thought of the seriously disadvantaged. How different they were from white, middle-class students who come armed with the testimony of their grades and aptitude scores and self-confidence to complain about the unequal treatment they now receive. I listen to them. I do not want to be careless about what they say. Their rights are important to protect. But inevitably when I hear them or their lawyers, I think about the most seriously disadvantaged, not simply Mexican-Americans, but of all those who do not ever imagine themselves going to college or becoming doctors: white, black, brown. Always poor. Silent. They are not plaintiffs before the court or against the misdirection of Affirmative Action. They lack the confidence (my confidence!) to assume their right to a good education. They lack the confidence and skills a good primary and secondary education provides and which are prerequisites for informed public life. They remain silent.

The debate drones on and surrounds them in stillness. They are distant, faraway figures like the boys I have seen peering down from freeway overpasses in some other part of town.

PROBING FOR MEANING

1. Why did Rodriguez feel "embarrassment and guilt" about becoming a college professor?

2. Why was his teacher so angry at Rodriguez's failure to apply for jobs? In your opinion, was his anger justified?

3. What happens when he finally sends out applications? Why does he feel uneasy about all the offers he received? How do you think you would have reacted in his situation?

4. "You're a Chicano. And I am a Jew. That's the only real difference between us." Why does Rodriguez include this statement in his essay? Do you agree with the graduate student who states that affirmative action is unfair to whites? Why or why not?

5. What do you think of Rodriguez's decision to turn down all his offers? Would you have acted as he did?

6. Which group of people does Rodriguez think needs affirmative action? What prevents these people from receiving its benefits? Do you agree with him? Why or why not?

PROBING FOR METHOD

1. For what audience is Rodriguez writing?

2. What is his purpose in discussing his views on affirmative action? Is he trying to convince his readers that "none of this is fair"?

3. Characterize the tone of his essay. Is it consistent?

4. Rodriguez waits until the end of his essay to mention the "seriously disadvantaged" who need affirmative action. Would his point have had more impact had he mentioned it earlier? Should he have used a special example as he did with the job application? Why or why not?

5. Read over the conclusion of the essay. Is it more effective to end the essay using figurative language, as Rodriguez has, or should he have concluded the essay with "They remain silent" at the end of the next-to-the-last paragraph. Explain your answer.

LINDA BIRD FRANCKE

A Bedroom of One's Own

Linda Bird Francke (b. 1939) was born in New York City and attended Bradford Junior College. She is a nonfiction writer who focuses on issues related to women. Her writings include The Ambivalence of Abortion *(1978) and* Growing Up Divorced *(1983). In 1984 she collaborated with Rosalynn Carter in* First Lady of Plains *(1984) and most recently with Jehan Sadat on* An Egyptian Woman. *Francke is also a frequent contributor to the "Hers" column of the* New York Times, *addressing subjects by and about women. Francke has written that she takes "great pleasure and pride in being a woman in contemporary America. In my lifetime, a woman's horizons have expanded to include possibilities my mother's generation never imagined." As you read "A Bedroom of One's Own" (the title refers to Virginia Woolf's feminist essay, "A Room of One's Own"), notice how Francke infuses humor into her essay to enhance meaning.*

One of the things I achieved in my thirty-ninth year was the incomprehensible luxury of regaining not only my own bedroom but my own bed as well. It was startling how much the regaining of lost nocturnal turf meant to me.

For more years than I comfortably cared to remember, I had shared both bedroom and bed with more people than I also comfortably cared to remember. Whether bedroom coupling was caused by lack of space, a dearth of funds or the marital premise that twin beds are the first sign of a failing marriage and that separate bedrooms signal the drafting of a separation agreement, I had lain beside someone else's snores for a score and fifteen years.

As a little girl, my first roommate was my older sister, who perversely and persistently shined a flashlight on the ceiling over my side of the room, then slowly lowered her hand over the beam until the giant claw tore at the fine edge of my control. Then, for three years there was a merciful period when she went off to boarding school and I claimed the bedroom as my own, having the unembarrassed space to chat myself to sleep every night, pretending on alternate evenings that I was Nancy Drew solving every conceivable mystery on Larkspur Lane, or Heidi nestled in a bed of fresh hay, waiting for Peter the Goatherd to bring me my morning mug of frothy goat's milk.

But then it came my turn to start the boarding school/college cycle, and in the next five years I escalated into one, two and finally three roommates. My private chats with myself were replaced by counting the breaths of my adenoidal sleepmates and trying hard not to listen to the radios several of them played all night under their pillows, the discovery of which by the pumpkin-breasted housemother would have meant instant expulsion from the school and possibly death.

It didn't get any better after we were daisy-chained into the greater world. And after an overshared apartment with four friends, and three years of trying to sort out laundry, bills and lamb chops, I was desperate. Marriage, I thought. That will do it. Then I'll finally have my own place. But I had overlooked one thing. The husband gets to live there, too. So not only did I lose the fantasy of my own bedroom at the altar, I irretrievably lost my own bed as well. Amid piles of wedding-present queen-sized sheets from Porthault and color-coordinated towels with my new initials on them (for I had lost my own name as well), I embarked on the next fifteen years of shared bedroom life.

Now, for those of the togetherness school, a warm body to snuggle up against on a cold night or when the occasional terrors strike is one of the elixirs of married life. But the operative word is "occasional." Though some very pleasant things do occur in bed or on the living-room floor, there is no compelling reason to spin that pleasure into eight hours of shared sleep. And it was that every-night sharing that caused me to start couch-hopping around our New York apartment, sleeping one night in the living room, another in the dining room, and even several, inexplicably comfortable, on the bathroom floor. I was not avoiding my husband, who is a lovely man, but searching for some long-lost pocket of privacy where the scientific principle of cause and effect concerned only me.

If I woke up freezing cold, it was not because someone else had wrestled the quilt onto his side or kicked out the plug on the electric blanket. In the bitter nights of winter, I could climb into the feathers wearing ski socks and various layers of the morning's clothes without hearing justified snickers of incredulity. It was a joy to find some time and space that was not reactive, and though it occasionally puzzled my husband, my children saw nothing strange in my emerging from the dining room in the morning with my blanket over my shoulder.

Exploring cautiously with other women my new discovery of sleeping alone, I soon found that after their initial reluctance to admit to such marital blasphemy, they too found solace in those nights when their husbands were away traveling or in the summer city while the women tended to the country rentals.

"I go to bed with some trashy novel and a bag of Doritos," admitted one such friend in East Hampton, "and I practically wag my tail with the pleasure of it. Then Sam comes on the weekend and he says, 'Ugh, how can you read that trash, and you know I can't sleep with the light on, and what are all these crumbs in the bed?' He's right, of course, but those nights are worth anything." Another friend thinks her marriage has been saved by the fact that her husband now spends week nights in the city and returns to Connecticut on the weekends.

"When we all lived in New York he'd come home, drink a couple of martinis to relax, then get into bed with cheese and crackers and watch television," the now weekend wife said. "Of course he'd fall asleep and I'd end up crumbing his chest into the 'silent butler' just like I was cleaning up during a cocktail party. This way of life is better."

Though I hesitate to pull the mattress pad out from under the marriage counselor industry, which professes that sleeping together is staying together, I can't believe more relationships wouldn't survive if bedroom sharing were an elective rather than the required course. As children we dreamed of gaining the life stage of having our own rooms and our own things and we all wrote angry cardboard signs which read PRIVAT—KEPE OUT AND THIS MEANS U! So where is it written that having successfully attained adulthood, we no longer have that same need for privacy?

But now, during an experimental year of country living during which my husband joins me on weekends, that traditional barrier has been broken. I now sink into my own bed in my own bedroom each week night, making a little guilt-free nest in the comfortable clutter of clean laundry, and half-read books and newspapers while shooing away the dog, who believes strongly in nightly togetherness. I read late or not at all, watch 3 A.M. television or turn off the light at 8:30. Solo sleeping is an eight-hour holiday of private indulgence that leaves me slightly more willing to serve the family and worldly good in the morning. And besides, I'm told on long-term authority that I was the one who did the snoring anyway.

PROBING FOR MEANING

1. What does Francke find so appealing about a bed of her own? What specific examples did you find most effective?

2. What details does she give to support her point that married couples should sleep in the same bed only occasionally? How do you react to her point of view?

3. What is Francke's purpose in writing her essay? Is it only to amuse her readers or is she also making a point? Did she convince you? Why or why not?

PROBING FOR METHOD

1. Francke's essay was originally published in the "Hers" column of the *New York Times*. Does her essay appeal primarily to women? Why or why not?

2. Characterize the tone of the essay. How does she use humor to enhance meaning?

3. In addition to citing examples from her own experience, Francke also includes examples from her friends' experiences. Is this an effective way of supporting her thesis? Why or why not?

ALASTAIR REID

Curiosity

*Alastair Reid (b. 1926) is a poet, translator, essayist, and author of books for
children. Born in Scotland, he currently lives in Spain. He has taught at Sarah
Lawrence College and published several volumes of poetry, including*
Weathering: New and Selected Poems *(1978). Reid contributes frequently to
the* Atlantic Monthly, Encounter, *and the* New Yorker. *As you read
"Curiosity," write down your reaction to his comment that "Only the curious
have, if they live, a tale worth telling at all."*

Curiosity
may have killed the cat; more likely
the cat was just unlucky, or else curious
to see what death was like, having no cause
to go on licking paws, or fathering
litter on litter of kittens, predictably.

Nevertheless, to be curious
is dangerous enough. To distrust
what is always said, what seems,
to ask odd questions, interfere in dreams,
leave home, smell rats, have hunches
do not endear cats to those doggy circles
where well-smelt baskets, suitable wives, good lunches
are the order of things, and where prevails
much wagging of incurious heads and tails.

Face it. Curiosity
will not cause us to die—
only lack of it will.
Never to want to see
the other side of the hill
or that improbable country
where living is an idyll
(although a probable hell)
would kill us all.
Only the curious
have, if they live, a tale
worth telling at all.

Dogs say cats love too much, are irresponsible,
are changeable, marry too many wives,
desert their children, chill all dinner tables
with tales of their nine lives.
Well, they are lucky. Let them be
nine-lived and contradictory,
curious enough to change, prepared to pay
the cat price, which is to die
and die again and again,
each time with no less pain.
A cat minority of one
is all that can be counted on
to tell the truth. And what cats have to tell
on each return from hell
is this: that dying is what the living do,
that dying is what the loving do,
and that dead dogs are those who do not know
that dying is what, to live, each has to do.

PROBING FOR MEANING

1. The poet finds many instances in which to apply the old saying "curiosity killed the cat" to human life. What kind of people are cats? Why is curiosity dangerous for people?

2. Why does the poet state, "only the curious/ have, if they live, a tale/worth telling at all"?

3. What kind of people are dogs? What criticism do they have of cats? Why does the poet say dogs are dead? What does living entail?

4. The poet uses paradox when he says, "dying is what the living do." What does this paradox mean?

PROBING FOR METHOD

1. What is the tone of the poem? How does the tone contribute to the meaning?

2. The title of the poem also serves as the first line. Why might the poet choose to structure the poem in this way?

3. How does the line structure contribute to the poem's statement?

MARY E. WILKINS FREEMAN

A Moral Exigency

Mary E. Wilkins Freeman (1852–1930) was an American writer who lived most of her life in small towns in Massachusetts and Vermont. She began writing in her early twenties with a collection of children's poetry, Decorative Plaques *(1883). She published her first short story for adults in 1882 and subsequently produced several collections, including* A New England Nun and Other Stories *(1892). As you read "A Moral Exigency," one of Freeman's many stories about single women in New England, think about how you might have acted in Eunice's situation.*

At five o'clock, Eunice Fairweather went up-stairs to dress herself for the sociable and Christmas-tree to be given at the parsonage that night in honor of Christmas Eve. She had been very busy all day, making preparations for it. She was the minister's daugher, and had, of a necessity, to take an active part in such affairs.

She took it, as usual, loyally and energetically, but there had always been seasons from her childhood—and she was twenty-five now—when the social duties to which she had been born seemed a weariness and a bore to her. They had seemed so to-day. She had patiently and faithfully sewed up little lace bags with divers-colored worsteds, and stuffed them with candy. She had strung pop-corn, and marked the parcels which had been pouring in since daybreak from all quarters. She had taken her prominent part among the corps of indefatigable women always present to assist on such occasions, and kept up her end of the line as minister's daughter bravely. Now, however, the last of the zealous, chattering women she had been working with had bustled home, with a pleasant importance in every hitch of her shawled shoulders, and would not bustle back again until half-past six or so; and the tree, fully bedecked, stood in unconscious impressiveness in the parsonage parlor.

Eunice had come up-stairs with the resolution to dress herself directly for the festive occasion, and to hasten down again to be in readiness for new exigencies. Her mother was delicate, and had kept to her room all day in order to prepare herself for the evening, her father was inefficient at such times, there was no servant, and the brunt of everything came on her.

But her resolution gave way; she wrapped herself in an old plaid shawl and lay down on her bed to rest a few minutes. She did not close her eyes, but lay studying idly the familiar details of the room. It was small, and one side ran in under the eaves; for the parsonage was a cottage. There was one window, with a white cotton curtain trimmed with tasselled fringe, and looped up on an old porcelain knob with a picture painted on it. That knob, with its tiny bright landscape, had been one of the pretty wonders of Eunice's childhood. She looked at it even now with interest, and the marvel and the beauty of it had not wholly departed her eyes. The walls of the little room had a scraggly-patterned paper on them. The first lustre of it had departed, for that too was one of the associates of Eunice's childhood, but in certain lights there was a satin sheen and a blue line visible. Blue roses on a satin ground had been the original pattern. It had never been pretty, but Eunice had always had faith in it. There was an ancient straw matting on the floor, a homemade braided rug before the cottage bedstead, and one before the stained pine bureau. There were a few poor attempts at adornment on the walls; a splint letter-case, a motto worked in worsteds, a gay print of an eminently proper little girl hold-ing a faithful little dog.

This last, in its brilliant crudeness, was not a work of art, but Eunice believed in it. She was a conservative creature. Even after her year at the semi-nary, for which money had been scraped together five years ago, she had the same admiring trust in all the revelations of her childhood. Her home, on her return to it, looked as fair to her as it had always done; no old ugliness which familiarity had caused to pass unnoticed before gave her a shock of surprise.

She lay quietly, her shawl shrugged up over her face, so only her steady, light-brown eyes were visible. The room was drearily cold. She never had a fire; one in a sleeping-room would have been sinful luxury in the poor minis-ter's family. Even her mother's was only warmed from the sitting-room.

In sunny weather Eunice's room was cheerful, and its look, if not actually its atmosphere, would warm one a little, for the windows faced southwest. But to-day all the light had come through low, gray clouds, for it had been threat-ening snow ever since morning, and the room had been dismal.

A comfortless dusk was fast spreading over everything now. Eunice rose at length, thinking that she must either dress herself speedily or go down-stairs for a candle.

She was a tall, heavily-built girl, with large, well-formed feet and hands. She had a full face, and a thick, colorless skin. Her features were coarse, but their combination affected one pleasantly. It was a staunch, honest face, with a suggestion of obstinacy in it.

She looked unhappily at herself in her little square glass, as she brushed out her hair and arranged it in a smooth twist at the top of her head. It was not becoming, but it was the way she had always done it. She did not admire the effect herself when the coiffure was complete, neither did she survey her ap-pearance complacently when she had gotten into her best brown cashmere dress, with its ruffle of starched lace in the neck. But it did not occur to her that any change could be made for the better. It was her best dress, and it was the way she did up her hair. She did not like either, but the simple facts of them ended the matter for her.

After the same fashion she regarded her own lot in life, with a sort of resigned disapproval.

On account of her mother's ill-health, she had been encumbered for the last five years with the numberless social duties to which the wife of a poor country minister is liable. She had been active in Sunday-school picnics and church sociables, in mission bands and neighborhood prayer-meetings. She was a church member and a good girl, but the *role* did not suit her. Still she accepted it as inevitable, and would no more have thought of evading it than she would have thought of evading life altogether. There was about her an almost stubborn steadfastness of onward movement that would forever keep her in the same rut, no matter how disagreeable it might be, unless some influence outside of herself might move her.

When she went down-stairs, she found her mother seated beside the sitting-room stove, also arrayed in her best—a shiny black silk, long in the shoulder-seams, the tops of the sleeves adorned with pointed caps trimmed with black velvet ribbon.

She looked up at Eunice as she entered, a complacent smile on her long, delicate face; she thought her homely, honest-looking daughter charming in her best gown.

A murmur of men's voices came from the next room, whose door was closed.

"Father's got Mr. Wilson in there," explained Mrs. Fairweather, in response to Eunice's inquiring glance. "He came just after you went up-stairs. They've been talking very busily about something. Perhaps Mr. Wilson wants to exchange."

Just at that moment, the study door opened and the two men came out, Eunice's father, tall and round-shouldered, with grayish sandy hair and beard, politely allowing his guest to precede him. There was a little resemblance between the two, though there was no relationship. Mr. Wilson was a younger man by ten years; he was shorter and slighter; but he had similarly sandy hair and beard, though they were not quite so gray, and something the same cast of countenance. He was settled over a neighboring parish; he was a widower with four young children; his wife had died a year before.

He had spoken to Mrs. Fairweather on his first entrance, so he stepped directly toward Eunice with extended hand. His ministerial affability was slightly dashed with embarrassment, and his thin cheeks were crimson around the roots of his sandy beard.

Eunice shook the proffered hand with calm courtesy, and inquired after his children. She had not a thought that his embarrassment betokened anything, if, indeed, she observed it at all.

Her father stood by with an air of awkward readiness to proceed to action, waiting until the two should cease the interchanging of courtesies.

When the expected pause came he himself placed a chair for Mr. Wilson. "Sit down, Brother Wilson," he said, nervously, "and I will consult with my daughter concerning the matter we were speaking of. Eunice, I would like to speak with you a moment in the study."

"Certainly sir," said Eunice. She looked surprised, but she followed him into the study "Tell me as quickly as you can what it is, father," she said, "for it is nearly time for people to begin coming, and I shall have to attend to them."

She had not seated herself, but stood leaning carelessly against the study wall, questioning her father with her steady eyes.

He stood in his awkward height before her. He was plainly trembling. "Eunice," he said, in a shaking voice, "Mr. Wilson came—to say—he would like to marry you, my dear daughter."

He cleared his throat to hide his embarrassment. He felt a terrible constraint in speaking to Eunice of such matters; he looked shamefaced and distressed.

Eunice eyed him steadily. She did not change color in the least. "I think I would rather remain as I am, father," she said quietly.

Her father roused himself then. "My dear daughter," he said, with restrained eagerness, "don't decide this matter too hastily, without giving it all the consideration it deserves. Mr. Wilson is a good man; he would make you a worthy husband, and he needs a wife sadly. Think what a wide field of action would be before you with those four little motherless children to love and care for! You would have a wonderful opportunity to do good."

"I don't think," said Eunice, bluntly, "that I should care for that sort of an opportunity."

"Then," her father went on, "you will forgive me if I speak plainly, my dear. You—are getting older; you have not had any other visitors. You would be well provided for in this way—"

"Exceedingly well," replied Eunice, slowly. "There would be six hundred a year and a leaky parsonage for a man and woman and four children, and— nobody knows how many more." She was almost coarse in her slow indignation, and did not blush at it.

"The Lord would provide for his servants."

"I don't know whether he would or not. I don't think he would be under any obligation to if his servant deliberately encumbered himself with more of a family than he had brains to support."

Her father looked so distressed that Eunice's heart smote her for her forcible words. "You don't want to get rid of me, surely, father," she said, in a changed tone.

Mr. Fairweather's lips moved uncertainly as he answered: "No, my dear daughter; don't ever let such a thought enter your head. I only—Mr. Wilson is a good man, and a woman is best off married, and your mother and I are old. I have never laid up anything. Sometimes—Maybe I don't trust the Lord enough, but I have felt anxious about you, if anything happened to me." Tears were standing in his light-blue eyes, which had never been so steady and keen as his daughter's.

There came a loud peal of the door-bell. Eunice started. "There! I must go," she said. "We'll talk about this another time. Don't worry about it, father dear."

"But, Eunice, what shall I say to him?"

"Must something be said to-night?"

"It would hardly be treating him fairly otherwise."

Eunice looked hesitatingly at her father's worn, anxious face. "Tell him," said at length, "that I will give him his answer in a week."

Her father looked gratified. "We will take it to the Lord, my dear."

Eunice's lip curled curiously, but she said, "Yes, sir" dutifully, and hastened from the room to answer the door-bell.

The fresh bevies that were constantly arriving after that engaged her whole attention. She could do no more than give a hurried "Good-evening" to Mr. Wilson when he came to take leave, after a second short conference with her father in the study. He looked deprecatingly hopeful.

The poor man was really in a sad case. Six years ago, when he married, he had been romantic. He would never be again. He was not thirsting for love and communion with a kindred spirit now, but for a good, capable woman who would take care of his four clamorous children without a salary.

He returned to his shabby, dirty parsonage that night with, it seemed to him, quite a reasonable hope that his affairs might soon be changed for the better. Of course he would have preferred that the lady should have said yes directly; it would both have assured him and shortened the time until his burdens should be lightened; but he could hardly have expected that, when his proposal was so sudden, and there had been no preliminary attention on his part. The week's probation, therefore, did not daunt him much. He did not really see why Eunice should refuse him. She was plain, was getting older; it probably was her first, and very likely her last, chance of marriage. He was a clergyman in good standing, and she would not lower her social position. He felt sure that he was now about to be relieved from the unpleasant predicament in which he had been ever since his wife's death, and from which he had been forced to make no effort to escape, for decency's sake, for a full year. The year, in fact, had been up five days ago. He actually took credit to himself for remaining quiescent during those five days. It was rather shocking, but there was a good deal to be said for him. No wife and four small children, six hundred dollars a year, moderate brain, and an active conscience, are a hard combination of circumstances for any man.

To-night, however, he returned thanks to the Lord for his countless blessings with pious fervor, which would have been lessened had he known of the state of Eunice's mind just at that moment.

The merry company had all departed, the tree stood dismantled in the parlor, and she was preparing for bed, with her head full, not of him, but another man.

Standing before her glass, combing out her rather scanty, lustreless hair, her fancy pictured to her, beside her own homely, sober face, another, a man's, blond and handsome, with a gentle, almost womanish smile on the full red lips, and a dangerous softness in the blue eyes. Could a third person have seen the double picture as she did, he would have been struck with a sense of the incongruity, almost absurdity, of it. Eunice herself, with her hard, uncompromising common-sense, took the attitude of a third person in regard to it, and at length blew her light out and went to bed, with a bitter amusement in her heart at her own folly.

There had been present that evening a young man who was a comparatively recent acquisition to the village society. He had been in town about three months. His father, two years before, had purchased one of the largest farms in the vicinity, moving there from an adjoining state. This son had been absent at the time; he was reported to be running a cattle ranch in one of those distant territories which seem almost fabulous to New-Englanders. Since he had come home he had been the cynosure of the village. He was thirty and a little over, but he was singularly boyish in his ways, and took part in all the town frolics with gusto. He was popularly supposed to be engaged to Ada Harris, Squire Harris's daughter, as she was often called. Her father was the prominent man of the village, lived in the best house, and had the loudest voice in public matters. He was a lawyer, with rather more pomposity than abililty, perhaps, but there had always been money and influence in the Harris family, and these warded off all criticism.

The daughter was a pretty blonde of average attainments, but with keen wits and strong passions. She had not been present at the Christmas-tree, and her lover, either on that account, or really from some sudden fancy he had taken to Eunice, had been at her elbow the whole evening. He had a fashion of making his attentions marked: he did on that occasion. He made a pretense of assisting her, but it was only a pretence, and she knew it, though she thought it marvellous. She had met him, but had not before exchanged two words with him. She had seen him with Ada Harris, and he had seemed almost as much out of her life as a lover in a book. Young men of his kind were unknown quantities heretofore to this steady, homely young woman. They seemed to belong to other girls.

So his devotion to her through the evening, and his asking permission to call when he took leave, seemed to her well-nigh incredible. Her head was not turned, in the usual acceptation of the term—it was not an easy head to turn—but it was full of Burr Mason, and every thought, no matter how wide a starting-point it had, lost itself at last in the thought of him.

Mr. Wilson's proposal weighed upon her terribly through the next week. Her father seemed bent upon her accepting it; so did her mother, who sighed in secret over the prospect of her daughter's remaining unmarried. Either through unworldliness, or their conviction of the desirability of the marriage in itself, the meagreness of the financial outlook did not seem to influence them in the least.

Eunice did not once think of Burr Mason as any reason for her reluctance, but when he called the day but one before her week of probation was up, and when he took her to drive the next day, she decided on a refusal of the minister's proposal easily enough. She had wavered a little before.

So Mr. Wilson was left to decide upon some other worthy, reliable woman as a subject for his addresses, and Eunice kept on with her new lover.

How this sober, conscientious girl could reconcile to herself the course she was now taking, was a question. It was probable she did not make the effort; she was so sensible that she would have known its futility and hypocrisy beforehand.

She knew her lover had been engaged to Ada Harris; that she was encouraging him in cruel and dishonorable treatment of another woman; but she kept steadily on. People even came to her and told her that the jilted girl was breaking her heart. She listened, her homely face set in an immovable calm. She listened quietly to her parents' remonstrance, and kept on.

There was an odd quality in Burr Mason's character. He was terribly vacillating, but he knew it. Once he said to Eunice, with the careless freedom that would have been almost insolence in another man: "Don't let me see Ada Harris much, I warn you, dear. I mean to be true to you, but she has such a pretty face, and I meant to be true to her, but you have—I don't know just what, but something she has not."

Eunice knew the truth of what he said perfectly. The incomprehensibleness of it all to her, who was so sensible of her own disadvantages, was the fascination she had for such a man.

A few days after Burr Mason had made that remark, Ada Harris came to see her. When Eunice went into the sitting-room to greet her, she kept her quiet, unmoved face, but the change in the girl before her was terrible. It was not wasting of flesh or pallor that it consisted in, but something worse. Her red lips were set so hard that the soft curves in them were lost, her cheeks burned feverishly, her blue eyes had a fierce light in them, and, most pitiful thing of all for another woman to see, she had not crimped her pretty blond hair, but wore it combed straight back from her throbbing forehead.

When Eunice entered, she waited for no preliminary courtesies, but sprang forward, and caught hold of her hand with a strong, nervous grasp, and stood so, her pretty, desperate face confronting Eunice's calm, plain one.

"Eunice!" she cried, "Eunice! why did you take him away from me? Eunice! Eunice!" Then she broke into a low wail, without any tears.

Eunice released her hand, and seated herself. "You had better take a chair, Ada," she said, in her slow, even tones. "When you say *him*, you mean Burr Mason, I suppose."

"You know I do. Oh, Eunice, how could you? how could you? I thought you were so good!"

"You ask me why *I* do this and that, but don't you think he had anything to do with it himself?"

Ada stood before her, clinching her little white hands. "Eunice Fairweather, you know Burr Mason, and I know Burr Mason. You know that if you gave him up, and refused to see him, he would come back to me. You know it."

"Yes, I know it."

"You know it; you sit there and say you know it, and yet you do this cruel thing—you, a minister's daughter. You understood from the first how it was. You knew he was mine, that you had no right to him. You knew if you shunned him ever so little, that he would come back to me. And yet you let him come and make love to you. You knew it. There is no excuse for you: you knew it. It is no better for him. You have encouraged him in being false. You have dragged him down. You are a plainer girl than I, and a soberer one, but you are no better. You will not make him a better wife. You cannot make him a good wife after this. It is all for yourself—yourself!"

Eunice sat still.

Then Ada flung herself on her knees at her side, and pleaded, as for her life. "Eunice, O Eunice, give him up to me! It is killing me! Eunice, dear Eunice, say you will!"

As Eunice sat looking at the poor, dishevelled golden head bowed over her lap, a recollection flashed across her mind, oddly enough, of a certain recess at the village school they two had attended years ago, when she was among the older girls, and Ada a child to her: how she had played she was her little girl, and held her in her lap, and that golden head had nestled on her bosom.

"Eunice, O Eunice, he loved me first. You had better have stolen away my own heart. It would not have been so wicked or so cruel. How could you? O Eunice, give him back to me, Eunice, *won't* you?"

"No."

Ada rose, staggering, without another word. She moaned a little to herself as she crossed the room to the door. Eunice accompanied her to the outer door, and said good-bye. Ada did not return it. Eunice saw her steady herself by catching hold of the gate as she passed through.

Then she went slowly up-stairs to her own room, wrapped herself in a shawl, and lay down on her bed, as she had that Christmas Eve. She was very pale, and there was a strange look almost of horror, on her face. She stared, as she lay there, at all the familiar objects in the room, but the most common and insignificant of them had a strange and awful look to her. Yet the change was in herself, not in them. The shadow that was over her own soul overshadowed them and perverted her vision. But she felt also almost a fear of all those inanimate objects she was gazing at. They were so many reminders of a better state with her, for she had gazed at them all in her unconscious childhood. She was sickened with horror at their dumb accusations. There was the little glass she had looked in before she had stolen another woman's dearest wealth away from her, the chair she had sat in, the bed she had lain in.

At last Eunice Fairweather's strong will broke down before the accusations of her own conscience, which were so potent as to take upon themselves material shapes.

Ada Harris, in her pretty chamber, lying worn out on her bed, her face buried in the pillow, started at a touch on her shoulder. Some one had stolen into the room unannounced—not her mother, for she was waiting outside. Ada turned her head, and saw Eunice. She struck at her wildly with her slender hands. "Go away!" she screamed.

"Ada!"

"Go away!"

"Burr Mason is down-stairs. I came with him to call on you."

Ada sat upright, staring at her, her hand still uplifted.

"I am going to break my engagement with him."

"Oh, Eunice! Eunice! you blessed—"

Eunice drew the golden head down on her bosom, just as she had on that old school-day.

"Love me all you can, Ada," she said. "I want—something."

PROBING FOR MEANING

1. An "exigency" is something that demands immediate attention. Why is the story's title appropriate?

2. What portrait emerges of Eunice in the first few paragraphs of the essay? Explain the significance of the statement "She was a church member and a good girl, but the *role* did not suit her."

3. Eunice very directly refuses the minister's offer of marriage. Did her frank response to her father surprise you? Why or why not?

4. What is your reaction to Ada Harris?

5. How would you characterize Burr Mason? Is Eunice's relationship with him worthwhile? Do you think Eunice should have given him up? Would you have done the same thing? Why or why not?

6. Explain the last line of the story.

PROBING FOR METHOD

1. Freeman's story was written more than sixty years ago. Do you think it might have had more audience appeal then? Explain your answer.

2. What role does setting play in the story?

3. What techniques does Freeman use to portray the changes that take place in Eunice as the narrative progresses?

4. What is the tone of the narrative? Is the narrator objective, or does she evaluate the characters? Explain your answer.

WRITING TOPICS
Generating Ideas on a Choice

Freewrite, or write a journal entry in response to one of the following:

I am learning that if I just go on accepting the framework for life that others have given me, if I fail to make my own choices, the reason for my life will be missing. I will be unable to recognize that which I have the power to change. I refuse to spend my life regretting the things I failed to do.

Liv Ullmann

To be nobody—but—myself—in a world which is doing its best, night and day, to make you like everybody else— means to fight the hardest battle which any human being can fight, and never stop fighting.

e. e. cummings

Two roads diverged in a wood, and I—I took the one less traveled by, and that has made all the difference.

Robert Frost

Protection and shelter have negative connotations for me; strength, power and fame are positive.

Martin Krovetz

Though I hesitate to pull the mattress pad out from under the marriage counselor industry, which professes that sleeping together is staying together, I can't believe more relationships wouldn't survive if bedroom sharing were an elective rather than the required course.

Linda Bird Francke

Women should be pedestals to men.

May Swenson

Nothing you say really changes the fact that Affirmative Action is unfair. You see that, don't you? There isn't any way for me to compete with you. Once there were quotas to keep my parents out of certain schools; now there are quotas to get you in and the effect on me is the same as it was for them.

Richard Rodriguez

You can tell the ideals of a nation by its advertisements.

Norman Douglas

The only thing necessary for the triumph of evil is for good men to do nothing.
                                                        Edmund Burke

Gather ye rosebuds while ye may.

                                                        Robert Herrick

Topics for Essays on a Choice

1. In "Going My Way," Krovetz emphasizes that, unlike many people, he likes his job. Write an essay discussing the choice many must make between a major in college based on the job market or a major based on their own interests and abilities.
2. Affirmative action is a controversial issue in our society. If you are a member of a minority group who could benefit from affirmative action, write an essay citing reasons why your choice to do so is ethical. If you are in a position to be hurt by affirmative action, write an essay giving reasons why affirmative action programs offer unfair choices to minorities. Be as specific as you can.
3. Thoreau feels very strongly about the negative aspects of complicating one's life. Write an essay analyzing the choices you would have to make to simplify your life, including your attitude towards having to make them.
4. Reid and Krovetz both prefer risks to security. Write an essay analyzing the reasons for the choice you would make between the security of the familiar (job, vocation, person) and taking a risk involving the unknown. What factors would influence your choice?
5. Read over what you wrote about the statement under Generating Ideas. Consider if you can revise what you have written for an essay or if there is one idea that you can expand to a fully developed piece of writing.
6. Freeman's protagonist made a compassionate choice which many would view as foolish. Write an essay about a choice you made for ethical reasons that might be regarded as naïve. Analyze the elements of your choice.
7. The tone of Francke's essay is humorous but the point she makes is serious: the importance of having one's own "space." Write an essay analyzing choices which you have made or can imagine making to fulfill your need for privacy.
8. Eiseley's choice results in his experiencing an epiphany. Write an essay about a choice you made that had deep significance for you emotionally and intellectually.

CHAPTER EIGHT

Philosophies:
Revising the Essay
Revising for Coherence
Revising for Style

Plato, in his "Allegory of the Cave," compares man's search for sense and significance in life to his leaving the safe, dark but warm cave of illusions for the blinding light of the sun of truth. Many people prefer to remain in the cave and lead a life patterned for them by others, but some need the greater fulfillment resulting from the search for a personal philosophy of life.

In the view of James Baldwin, however, many black Americans are denied the luxury of a personal philosophy because white Americans not only have refused to grant them the right to their own language but also have failed to recognize how black expressions have enriched American English.

Anne Morrow Lindbergh's quest is more personal—she is trying to find "techniques for living"—while Lewis Thomas encourages us to look at dying differently and "to give up the notion that death is catastrophe, or detestable, or avoidable, or even strange."

Several writers, while searching, turn to nature: E. M. Forster buys property in the country; Anne Morrow Lindbergh visits the seashore; and Daru, in Albert Camus's story, inhabits a barren Algerian plateau.

Each writer's truth is different. Stafford finds significance in freedom; Lindbergh, in simplicity; Camus, in brotherhood; Forster, in self-inspection; Baldwin, in exhortation; Thomas, in acceptance.

The writers describe their philosophies with lucidity. A discussion of revising for greater coherence follows Forster's essay on pages 293–294, and a discussion of revising for a clearer style follows Lindbergh's essay on pages 302–304.

E. M. FORSTER

My Wood

E. M. Forster (1879–1970) was an English novelist and essayist known for his humanistic philosophy expressed in the novel A Passage to India *(1924), which exposes the prejudices and injustices that existed under British domination of colonial India. With subtle irony, he reveals the moral and emotional emptiness of British middle-class life. He believes that the bourgeoisie bury their capacity for passion and intuition and have to recapture those qualities in order to make life vital. He also wrote seven books of literary criticism and in 1951 published a collection of sociological essays entitled* Two Cheers for Democracy. *His essay "My Wood" was first published in 1934 and reflects Forster's point of view on the effect possessions may have on individual freedom. To what extent do you agree with him that "property produces men of weight"?*

A few years ago I wrote a book which dealt in part with the difficulties of the English in India. Feeling that they would have no difficulties in India themselves, the Americans read the book freely. The more they read it the better it made them feel, and a cheque to the author was the result. I bought a wood with the cheque. It is not a large wood—it contains scarcely any trees, and it is intersected, blast it, by a public footpath. Still, it is the first property that I have owned, so it is right that other people should participate in my shame, and should ask themselves, in accents that will vary in horror, this very important question: What is the effect of property upon the character? Don't let's touch economics; the effect of private ownership upon the community as a whole is another question—a more important question, perhaps, but another one. Let's keep to psychology. If you own things, what's their effect on you? What's the effect on me of my wood?

In the first place, it makes me feel heavy. Property does have this effect. Property produces men of weight, and it was a man of weight who failed to get into the Kingdom of Heaven. He was not wicked, the unfortunate millionaire in the parable, he was only stout; he stuck out in front, not to mention behind, and as he wedged himself this way and that in the crystalline entrance and bruised his well-fed flanks, he saw beneath him a comparatively slim camel passing through the eye of a needle and being woven into the robe of God. The Gospels all through couple stoutness and slowness. They point out what is perfectly obvious, yet seldom realized: that if you have a lot of things you cannot move about a lot, that furniture requires dusting, dusters require servants, servants require insurance stamps, and the whole tangle of them makes you think twice before you accept an invitation to dinner or go for a bathe in the Jordan. Sometimes the Gospels proceed further and say with Tolstoy that property is sinful; they approach the difficult ground of asceticism here, where I cannot follow them. But as to the immediate effects of property on people, they just show straightforward logic. It produces men of weight. Men of weight cannot, by definition, move like the lightning from the East unto the West, and the ascent of a fourteen-stone bishop into a pulpit is thus the exact antithesis of the coming of the Son of Man. My wood makes me feel heavy.

In the second place, it makes me feel it ought to be larger.

The other day I heard a twig snap in it. I was annoyed at first, for I thought that someone was blackberrying, and depreciating the value of the undergrowth. On coming nearer, I saw it was not a man who had trodden on the twig and snapped it, but a bird, and I felt pleased. My bird. The bird was not equally pleased. Ignoring the relation between us, it took fright as soon as it saw the shape of my face, and flew straight over the boundary hedge into a field, the property of Mrs. Henessy, where it sat down with a loud squawk. It had become Mrs. Henessy's bird. Something seemed grossly amiss here, something that would not have occurred had the wood been larger. I could not afford to buy Mrs. Henessy out, I dared not murder her, and limitations of this sort beset me on every side. Ahab did not want that vineyard—he only needed it to round off his property, preparatory to plotting a new curve—and all the land around my wood has become necessary to me in order to round off the wood. A boundary protects. But—poor little thing—the boundary ought in its turn to be protected. Noises on the edge of it. Children throw stones. A little more, and then a little more, until we reach the sea. Happy Canute! Happier Alexander! And after all, why should even the world be the limit of possession? A rocket containing a Union Jack, will, it is hoped, be shortly fired at the moon. Mars. Sirius. Beyond which . . . But these immensities ended by saddening me. I could not suppose that my wood was the destined nucleus of universal dominion—it is so very small and contains no mineral wealth beyond the blackberries. Nor was I comforted when Mrs. Henessy's bird took alarm for the second time and flew clean away from us all, under the belief that it belonged to itself.

In the third place, property makes its owner feel that he ought to do something to it. Yet he isn't sure what. A restlessness comes over him, a vague sense that he has a personality to express—the same sense which, without any vagueness, leads the artist to an act of creation. Sometimes I think I will cut down such trees as remain in the wood, at other times I want to fill up the gaps between them with new trees. Both impulses are pretentious and empty. They are not honest movements towards money-making or beauty. They spring from a foolish desire to express myself and from an inability to enjoy what I have got. Creation, property, enjoyment form a sinister trinity in the human mind. Creation and enjoyment are both very, very good, yet they are often unattainable without a material basis, and at such moments property pushes itself in as a substitute, saying, "Accept me instead—I'm good enough for all three." It is not enough. It is, as Shakespeare said of lust, "The expense of spirit in a waste of shame"; it is "Before, a joy proposed; behind, a dream." Yet we don't know how to shun it. It is forced on us by our economic system as the alternative to starvation. It is also forced on us by an internal defect in the soul, by the feeling that in property may lie the germs of self-development and of exquisite or heroic deeds. Our life on earth is, and ought to be, material and carnal. But we have not yet learned to manage our materialism and carnality properly; they are still entangled with the desire for ownership, where (in the words of Dante) "Possession is one with loss."

And this brings us to our fourth and final point: the blackberries.

Blackberries are not plentiful in this meagre grove, but they are easily seen from the public footpath which traverses it, and all too easily gathered. Foxgloves, too—people will pull up the foxgloves, and ladies of an educational tendency even grub for toadstools to show them on the Monday in class. Other ladies, less educated, roll down the bracken in the arms of their gentlemen friends. There is paper, there are tins. Pray, does my wood belong to me or doesn't it? And, if it does, should I not own it best by allowing no one else to walk there? There is a wood near Lyme Regis, also cursed by a public footpath, where the owner has not hesitated on this point. He has built high stone walls each side of the path, and has spanned it by bridges, so that the public circulate like termites while he gorges on the blackberries unseen. He really does own his wood, this able chap. Dives in Hell did pretty well, but the gulf dividing him from Lazarus could be traversed by vision, and nothing traverses it here. And perhaps I shall come to this in time. I shall wall in and fence out until I really taste the sweets of property. Enormously stout, endlessly avaricious, pseudo-creative, intensely selfish, I shall weave upon my forehead the quadruple crown of possession until those nasty Bolshies come and take it off again and thrust me aside into the outer darkness.

PROBING FOR MEANING

1. Why does Forster say that the effect of private ownership upon the community is another, perhaps more important, issue than its effect is upon character?

2. How do the examples Forster uses in his second paragraph illustrate the first effect of property on character? Do you agree that property produces men of weight? Are people more virtuous if they have fewer possessions?

3. Who are Ahab, Canute, and Alexander? From what you know or can learn about their lives, why are they good examples of Forster's second effect? Does ownership always make one more greedy?

4. What effect does the last sentence in the fourth paragraph have on the meaning of the paragraph?

5. "Creation, property, enjoyment form a sinister trinity in the human mind." What does Forster mean by this statement? What examples does he give to explain it? What examples can you add of your own? Is property in your opinion a substitute for creativity?

6. Explain Dante's words, "Possession is one with loss."

7. What point does Forster make with the example of the blackberries? Do you agree that property generally has this effect?

8. Who are the "nasty Bolshies" mentioned in the last paragraph? What does this sentence contribute to the essay?

PROBING FOR METHOD

1. Forster leads into his introduction by commenting that Americans provided him with the money to purchase his wood. For what reason does Forster mention Americans in an introduction to an essay on materialism? What attitude does he have toward them?

2. What attitude toward his wood does Forster have? Do the words "shame" and "horror" used in paragraph 1 describe his tone in any way? How does the last sentence of the essay contribute to tone?

3. Forster's organization is perfectly clear. What devices does he use to convey the movement of the essay? Is this device effective? Why don't all writers mark each section of their essays as clearly?

4. What would the essay have been like without all the examples Forster uses? Would it have been as effective?

5. While Forster's essay uses concrete examples throughout, his thesis is the abstract one that property affects us adversely. Much of his language is also abstract; what, for example, do the words "antithesis," "trinity," "carnality," "avaricious," and "pseudo-creative" mean? How, in each case, do they relate either to his thesis or to his example?

Revising For Coherence

How does Forster achieve coherence?
The various sentences and paragraphs connect to each other and to the thesis of the essay largely through Forster's repetition of key words and phrases. Chief among these, of course, is the phrase "my wood," which the author repeats in all but one paragraph (using "the wood" in that paragraph). He also uses several synonyms for "my wood," including "property," "dominion," and "possession," to refer to it in a symbolic sense, and "this meagre grove" to refer to it physically.

Sentences are linked with sentences and paragraphs with paragraphs as well. Paragraphs are linked very clearly with the introductory phrases "In the first place," "In the second place," "In the third place," and "And this brings us to our fourth and final point. . . . " The sentences within paragraph 2 are linked to each other by various devices. The pronoun "it" in the first sentence obviously refers to "my wood," linking the sentence to the preceding sentence in paragraph 1 and thereby linking the paragraphs as well. The uses of the word "property" in the next two sentences link them together as well as to the first sentence. The "he" of the fourth sentence refers to the "unfortunate millionaire" of sentence 3 and thus is also a linking device. Mention of "the Gospels" in sentence 5 links it with the Gospel parable he has just related. The next few sentences alternate between use of "the Gospels" as linking devices and the pronoun "they," which refers to the Gospels. The final sentences use the synonyms "men of weight" and "makes me feel heavy" to connect with each other and with the topic sentence of the paragraph: "In the first place, it makes me feel heavy" (sentence 1).

Revising for coherence.
Transitions are words and phrases that establish connections between words, sentences, and paragraphs. Through the use of transitions, the writer gives the essay the coherence necessary if the reader is to understand the progression of ideas. The most common form of transition is the conjunction. Conjunctions establish such logical relations between thoughts as addition (*and*), contrast (*but*), comparison (*as*), causation (*for*), choice (*or*), and chronology (*before* and *after*). Transitional phrases can also be used to make similar connections: *in addition, on the other hand, as well as, as a result, after a while.*

A second means of creating connections between thoughts is by repeating key words that refer to the organizing idea (or synonyms or pronouns clearly referring to it). The repetition of key words assures the reader of the unity of the paper, of its development of one organizing idea.

Procedures to follow in revising for coherence.

A. Indicate very clearly to your reader that the various parts of your essay—paragraphs, sentences, and clauses—are connected to each other by repeating the key words of your essay throughout. (Avoid boring repetition by occasionally substituting synonyms and demonstrative adjectives or pronouns.)
B. Connect paragraphs by means of introductory words and phrases to establish chronological order, spatial order, cause-and-effect logic, or whatever principle your organization is built upon.
C. Connect sentences by these same transitional phrases and words. Between clauses and phrases, use conjunctions that clearly establish their relationship.

ANNE MORROW LINDBERGH

Channelled Whelk

Anne Morrow Lindbergh (b. 1906) is an American writer best known for Gift from the Sea *(1955), a unified collection of essays addressed to women from which "Channelled Whelk" was taken.* Gift from the Sea *describes a life recorded first in the author's several volumes of diaries. Reprinted here are two entries from the last volume,* War Within and Without: Diaries and Letters *(1939–44), published in 1980, which foreshadow many of the themes of "Channelled Whelk." Anne Lindbergh also wrote* North to the Orient *(1935), which describes her flight to the Orient with her husband, aviator Charles A. Lindbergh;* The Wave of the Future *(1940), a controversial essay that was regarded as a defense of fascism; a novel,* Dearly Beloved *(1962); and a depiction of the launching of the Apollo moon mission,* Earth Shine *(1969). In an interview in 1969, Mrs. Lindbergh stated that she was convinced "that writing . . . is more than living, . . . it is being conscious of living (since) an experience isn't finished until it's written." Before reading "Channelled Whelk" and her journal entries, you might want to respond briefly in writing to her comment. Must we write about an experience in order to "finish" it?*

The shell in my hand is deserted. It once housed a whelk, a snail-like creature, and then temporarily, after the death of the first occupant, a little hermit crab, who has run away, leaving his tracks behind him like a delicate vine on the sand. He ran away, and left me his shell. It was once a protection to him. I turn the shell in my hand, gazing into the wide open door from which he made his exit. Had it become an encumbrance? Why did he run away? Did he hope to find a better home, a better mode of living? I too have run away, I realize, I have shed the shell of my life, for these few weeks of vacation.

But his shell—it is simple; it is bare, it is beautiful. Small, only the size of my thumb, its architecture is perfect, down to the finest detail. Its shape, swelling like a pear in the center, winds in a gentle spiral to the pointed apex. Its color, dull gold, is whitened by a wash of salt from the sea. Each whorl, each faint knob, each criss-cross vein in its egg-shell texture, is as clearly defined as on the day of creation. My eye follows with delight the outer circumstance of that diminutive winding staircase up which this tenant used to travel.

My shell is not like this, I think. How untidy it has become! Blurred with moss, knobby with barnacles, its shape is hardly recognizable any more. Surely, it had a shape once. It has a shape still in my mind. What is the shape of my life?

The shape of my life today starts with a family. I have a husband, five children and a home just beyond the suburbs of New York. I have also a craft, writing, and therefore work I want to pursue. The shape of my life is, of course, determined by many other things; my background and childhood, my mind and its education, my conscience and its pressures, my heart and its desires. I want to give and take from my children and husband, to share with friends and community, to carry out my obligations to man and to the world as a woman, as an artist, as a citizen.

But I want first of all—in fact, as an end to these other desires—to be at peace with myself. I want a singleness of eye, a purity of intention, a central core to my life that will enable me to carry out these obligations and activities as well as I can. I want, in fact—to borrow from the language of the saints—to live "in grace" as much of the time as possible. I am not using this term in a strictly theological sense. By grace I mean an inner harmony, essentially spiritual, which can be translated into outward harmony. I am seeking perhaps what Socrates asked for in the prayer from the *Phaedrus* when he said, "May the outward and inward man be at one." I would like to achieve a state of inner spiritual grace from which I could function and give as I was meant to in the eye of God.

Vague as this definition may be, I believe most people are aware of periods in their lives when they seem to be "in grace" and other periods when they feel "out of grace," even though they may use different words to describe these states. In the first happy condition, one seems to carry all one's tasks before one lightly, as if borne alone on a great tide; and in the opposite state one can hardly tie a shoestring. It is true that a large part of life consists in learning a technique of tying the shoe-string, whether one is in grace or not. But there are techniques of living too; there are even techniques in the search for grace. And techniques can be cultivated. I have learned by some experience, by many examples, and by the writings of countless others before me, also occupied in the search, that certain environments, certain modes of life, certain rules of conduct are more conducive to inner and outer harmony than others. There are, in fact, certain roads that one may follow. Simplification of life is one of them.

I mean to lead a simple life, to choose a simple shell I can carry easily— like a hermit crab. But I do not. I find that my frame of life does not foster simplicity. My husband and five children must make their way in the world. The life I have chosen as wife and mother entrains a whole caravan of complications. It involves a house in the suburbs and either household drudgery or household help which wavers between scarcity and non-existence for most of us. It involves food and shelter; meals, planning, marketing, bills, and making the ends meet in a thousand ways. It involves not only the butcher, the baker, the candlestickmaker but countless other experts to keep my modern house with its modern "simplifications" (electricity, plumbing, refrigerator, gas-stove, oil-burner, dish-washer, radios, car, and numerous other labor-saving devices) functioning properly. It involves health; doctors, dentists, appointments, medicine, cod-liver oil, vitamins, trips to the drugstore. It involves education, spiritual, intellectual, physical; schools, school conferences, carpools, extra trips for basket-ball or orchestra practice; tutoring; camps, camp equipment and transportation. It involves clothes, shopping, laundry, cleaning, mending, letting skirts down and sewing buttons on, or finding someone else to do it. It involves friends, my husband's, my children's, my own, and endless arrangements to get together; letters, invitations, telephone calls and transportation hither and yon.

For life today in America is based on the premise of ever-widening circles of contact and communication. It involves not only family demands, but community demands, national demands, international demands on the good citizen, through social and cultural pressures, through newspapers, magazines, radio programs, political drives, charitable appeals, and so on. My mind reels with it. What a circus act we women perform every day of our lives. It puts the trapeze artist to shame. Look at us. We run a tight rope daily, balancing a pile of books on the head. Baby-carriage, parasol, kitchen chair, still under control. Steady now!

This is not the life of simplicity but the life of multiplicity that the wise men warn us of. It leads not to unification but to fragmentation. It does not bring grace; it destroys the soul. And this is not only true of my life, I am forced to conclude; it is the life of millions of women in America. I stress America, because today, the American woman more than any other has the privilege of choosing such a life. Woman in large parts of the civilized world has been forced back by war, by poverty, by collapse, by the sheer struggle to survive, into a smaller circle of immediate time and space, immediate family life, immediate problems of existence. The American woman is still relatively free to choose the wider life. How long she will hold this enviable and precarious position no one knows. But her particular situation has a significance far above its apparent economic, national or even sex limitations.

For the problem of the multiplicity of life not only confronts the American woman, but also the American man. And it is not merely the concern of the American as such, but of our whole modern civilization, since life in America today is held up as the ideal of a large part of the rest of the world. And finally, it is not limited to our present civilization, though we are faced with it now in an exaggerated form. It has always been one of the pitfalls of mankind. Plotinus was preaching the dangers of multiplicity of the world back in the third century. Yet, the problem is particularly and essentially woman's. Distraction is, always has been, and probably always will be, inherent in woman's life.

For to be a woman is to have interests and duties, raying out in all directions from the central mother-core, like spokes from the hub of a wheel. The pattern of our lives is essentially circular. We must be open to all points of the compass; husband, children, friends, home, community; stretched out, exposed, sensitive like a spider's web to each breeze that blows, to each call that comes. How difficult for us, then, to achieve a balance in the midst of these contradictory tensions, and yet how necessary for the proper functioning of our lives. How much we need, and how arduous of attainment is that steadiness preached in all rules for holy living. How desirable and distant is the ideal of the contemplative, artist, or saint—the inner inviolable core, the single eye.

With a new awareness, both painful and humorous, I begin to understand why the saints were rarely married women. I am convinced it has nothing inherently to do, as I once supposed, with chastity or children. It has to do primarily with distractions. The bearing, rearing, feeding and educating of children; the running of a house with its thousand details; human relationships with their myriad pulls—woman's normal occupations in general run counter to creative life, or contemplative life, or saintly life. The problem is not merely one of *Woman and Career, Woman and the Home, Woman and Independence*. It is more basically: how to remain whole in the midst of the distractions of life; how to remain balanced, no matter what centrifugal forces tend to pull one off center; how to remain strong, no matter what shocks come in at the periphery and tend to crack the hub of the wheel.

What is the answer? There is no easy answer, no complete answer. I have only clues, shells from the sea. The bare beauty of the channelled whelk tells me that one answer, and perhaps a first step, is in simplification of life, in cutting out some of the distractions. But how? Total retirement is not possible. I cannot shed my responsibilities. I cannot permanently inhabit a desert island. I cannot be a nun in the midst of family life. I would not want to be. The solution for me, surely, is neither in total renunciation of the world, nor in total acceptance of it. I must find a balance somewhere, or an alternating rhythm between these two extremes; a swinging of the pendulum between solitude and communion, between retreat and return. In my periods of retreat, perhaps

I can learn something to carry back into my worldly life. I can at least practice for these two weeks the simplification of outward life, as a beginning. I can follow this superficial clue, and see where it leads. Here, in beach living, I can try.

One learns first of all in beach living the art of shedding; how little one can get along with, not how much. Physical shedding to begin with, which then mysteriously spreads into other fields. Clothes, first. Of course, one needs less in the sun. But one needs less anyway, one finds suddenly. One needs not need a closet-full, only a small suitcase-full. And what a relief it is! Less taking up and down of hems, less mending, and—best of all—less worry about what to wear. One finds one is shedding not only clothes—but vanity.

Next, shelter. One does not need the airtight shelter one has in winter in the North. Here I live in a bare sea-shell of a cottage. No heat, no telephone, no plumbing to speak of, no hot water, a two-burner oil stove, no gadgets to go wrong. No rugs. There were some, but I rolled them up the first day; it is easier to sweep the sand off a bare floor. But I find I don't bustle about with unnecessary sweeping and cleaning here. I am no longer aware of the dust. I have shed my Puritan conscience about absolute tidiness and cleanliness. Is it possible that, too, is a material burden? No curtains. I do not need them for privacy; the pines around my house are enough protection. I want the windows open all the time, and I don't want to worry about rain. I begin to shed my Martha-like anxiety about many things. Washable slipcovers, faded and old—I hardly see them; I don't worry about the impression they make on other people. I am shedding pride. As little furniture as possible; I shall not need much. I shall ask into my shell only those friends with whom I can be completely honest. I find I am shedding hypocrisy in human relationships. What a rest that will be! The most exhausting thing in life, I have discovered, is being insincere. That is why so much of social life is exhausting; one is wearing a mask. I have shed my mask.

I find I live quite happily without those things I think necessary in winter in the North. And as I write these words, I remember, with some shock at the disparity in our lives, a similar statement made by a friend of mine in France who spent three years in a German prison camp. Of course, he said, qualifying his remark, they did not get enough to eat, they were sometimes atrociously treated, they had little physical freedom. And yet, prison life taught him how little one can get along with, and what extraordinary spiritual freedom and peace such simplification can bring. I remember again, ironically, that today more of us in America than anywhere else in the world have the luxury of choice between simplicity and complication of life. And for the most part, we, who could choose simplicity, choose complication. War, prison, survival periods, enforce a form of simplicity on man. The monk and the nun choose it of their own free will. But if one accidentally finds it, as I have for a few days, one finds also the serenity it brings.

Is it not rather ugly, one may ask? One collects material possessions not only for security, comfort or vanity, but for beauty as well. Is your sea-shell house not ugly and bare? No, it is beautiful, my house. It is bare, of course, but the wind, the sun, the smell of the pines blow through its bareness. The unfinished beams in the roof are veiled by cobwebs. They are lovely, I think, gazing up at them with new eyes; they soften the hard lines of the rafters as grey hairs soften the lines on a middle-aged face. I no longer pull out grey hairs or sweep down cobwebs. As for the walls, it is true they looked forbidding at first. I felt cramped and enclosed by their blank faces. I wanted to knock holes in them, to give them another dimension with pictures or windows. So I dragged home from the beach grey arms of driftwood, worn satin-smooth by wind and sand. I gathered trailing green vines with floppy red-tipped leaves. I picked up the whitened skeletons of conchshells, their curious hollowed-out shapes faintly reminiscent of abstract sculpture. With these tacked to walls and propped up in corners, I am satisfied. I have a periscope out to the world. I have a window, a view, a point of flight from my sedentary base.

I am content. I sit down at my desk, a bare kitchen table with a blotter, a bottle of ink, a sand dollar to weight down one corner, a clam shell for a pen tray, the broken tip of a conch, pink-tinged, to finger, and a row of shells to set my thoughts spinning.

I love my sea-shell of a house. I wish I could live in it always. I wish I could transport it home. But I cannot. It will not hold a husband, five children and the necessities and trappings of daily life. I can only carry back my little channelled whelk. It will sit on my desk in Connecticut, to remind me of the ideal of a simplified life, to encourage me in the game I played on the beach. To ask how little, not how much, can I get along with. To say—is it necessary?—when I am tempted to add one more accumulation to my life, when I am pulled toward one more centrifugal activity.

Simplification of outward life is not enough. It is merely the outside. But I am starting with the outside. I am looking at the outside of a shell, the outside of my life—the shell. The complete answer is not to be found on the outside, in an outward mode of living. This is only a technique, a road to grace. The final answer, I know, is always inside. But the outside can give a clue, can help one to find the inside answer. One is free, like the hermit crab, to change one's shell.

Channelled whelk, I put you down again, but you have set my mind on a journey, up an inwardly winding spiral staircase of thought.

PROBING FOR MEANING

1. Why does Lindbergh compare the shell to her life? How is the shell different from the life she is living?

2. What does she mean by "being at peace" with herself? What does it mean to be "out of grace"? How serious a state is the latter?

3. What is the technique for living that she talks about? Do you agree with her that it is a very difficult technique to learn? What has contributed to this difficulty?

4. Do you agree with her that multiplicity leads to fragmentation? What evidence does she cite for this statement?

5. "Distraction is, always has been, and probably always will be, inherent in woman's life." Why is a woman's life more fragmented than a man's? Why is this particularly true in America? Why is it enviable, as Lindbergh claims it is, to be fragmented if fragmentation destroys the soul?

6. She discusses what she calls "the art of shedding." To what is this analogous? Which people have perfected this art? How possible is it for most people to "shed"?

7. What stages in "shedding" does Lindbergh delineate? How did she avoid making shedding ugly?

8. What does she hope to accomplish in her cottage at the seashore? Why does she think her concentration on physical shedding will affect her spiritually or emotionally (in other words, that the "outside" will affect the "inside")?

PROBING FOR METHOD

1. What method does Lindbergh use in introducing her essay? Does her first paragraph include a thesis statement? If so, what is it?

2. What parallel exists between the whelk shell and her life? On how many levels does this parallel work? How does using the shell to refer to her life help convey her point? What other comparisons might she have used?

3. What techniques are employed in the conclusion? How effective is the conclusion?

4. What writing techniques does Lindbergh employ to achieve simplicity of style, thereby underscoring her theme of simplicity in life?

ANNE MORROW LINDBERGH

FROM *War Within and Without: Diaries and Letters (1939–1944)*

Tuesday, April 8th (1941)

Delicious spring day. The top twigs of trees all golden with it. Go up to work on feminist essay. Read over old notes, including my "answer" to my critics. Wish now I had published it—and the thought disturbs my morning. How hard it is to remember "It is not our business to reply to this and that but to set up our love and our indignation against their pity and hate. . . ." [Yeats] But misuse—*misuse* is so hard to bear. Will it ever, I wonder, be washed away from my little book.

Do not write—only notes. Writing is slow and it is hard to live by what I preach and be content with "very little but pure gold." The problem of the woman and her "work" is still so unsolved. It eats at me perpetually. Soeur Lisi is a perfect person for my children, gives them all they should have. And I have the time to write (in the mornings). But it still is not right because I *should* be giving them what she does (and getting from them what she does!). There cannot be two women important to a child. Either you *are* that woman or you are *not*. I know, because I have been that person to Jon—for long periods—and now I am not. To Land I am important, now, still.

It should work but, as it is, it goes somewhat like this: Mornings for work after meals, plans, etc. Afternoons for Husband and exercise and business. From teatime to 7 I see the children, put them to bed, etc. Evenings go to correcting diaries (the ones that are being copied), or writing in present diary. No letter-writing, no reading, people occasionally.

Then the week is interrupted by Soeur Lisi's day off and a day (or afternoon) in town. Can you write a book and have children at the same time? Yes, if you're content to do it very *very* slowly.

I feel pressed and frustrated, as though I were continually failing to get done what I should. This means I am trying to do too much.

I should like to be a full-time Mother and a full-time Artist and a full-time Wife-Companion and also a "Charming Woman" on the side! And to be aware and record it all. I cannot do it all. Something must go—several things probably. The "charming woman" first!

Flying this afternoon with C. at the Long Island Aviation Country Club. I practice landings and figure eights. I am creaky at it, but the discipline is fun and good. I think of Despiau (flying would be good for all artists) saying, "The problem in Art is that of extreme freedom encased in extreme discipline." This is flying, too.

Sunday, August 17th (1941)

Great wind blowing, all blinds flapping. C. and I look for new site for tent, more sheltered.

I walk up on the hill and lie on the ground. The security of it and the beauty make me able to think out all the things I am possessive about. The hanging-on feeling—about life itself and its passing by, of youth and romance, of time itself, of friends, of good repute.

It is easier here to "let go," not to put your heart "where moth and rust doth corrupt." And yet the complete ascetic denies life. "Between assertion and denial" there is a point one must find.

I feel a new life is starting here but I am just now at sea and do not know where it begins.

Revising For Style

How has Lindbergh revised her style from journal entries to essay?
In moving from her several volumes of diaries to "Channelled Whelk,"
Lindbergh revised both style and content because the reason for her writing had changed. While her journals were written for herself alone (in
fact, forty years elapsed between the writing of these entries and their
publication), the essay was intended to be read by others. In revising her
content, then, she eliminated all personal references to events and people
because she wanted her reader to be able to identify with her. She also
developed the analogy between the channelled whelk and her vacation
on the beach by simplifying various events of her life and in order to give
them a coherent meaning. For example, in the second journal entry, she
mentions a tent; in other entries, she refers to a trailer because at various
periods of her life, she used each as a private place on her property in
which to write. Her metamorphosis of tent and trailer into a "bare sea-
shell of a cottage" is more coherent, more picturesque, and more poetic.

She also revises her style. In the journals, just as her life swings on a
pendulum from the private world of writing to the public world of being
a wife and mother, so does her writing swing from calmness to frustration, often within one entry, as the examples here indicate. In the essay,
she lessens the height, in both directions, of the swing of the pendulum.
At the beginning of the essay, when she is exploring the shell as an analogy for her search for simplicity, her word choice reflects this meditative
purpose. Her language is poetic, including connotative words and figures
of speech. The shell of the whelk "is simple; it is bare, it is beautiful." Its
shape, "swelling like a pear in the center, winds in a gentle spiral to the
pointed apex." Its color is "dull gold, . . . whitened by a wash of salt
from the sea."

When her purpose in the essay changes from exploration to explanation, her language changes also. When she is exploring what she would
like her life to be like, her language is poetic and slowly paced. When she
explains the hectic pace that in fact characterizes her life, her language
reflects that pace. She reels off lists of things that must be done, first in
long sentences beginning with "It involves . . ." and then, as though she
is out of breath, in increasingly short sentences ending in "Steady now!"
As she reverts once more to exploring the harmonious life she would like
to live, her language becomes leisurely and poetic again.

Her sense of audience also influences her style. She is writing not
for an educated audience only, but for the general public as well. She
would no doubt like all women with families and careers to read her
essay. As a result, her language is fairly simple. The role she plays is
alternately that of a harried wife and mother who is also a writer and that
of a thoughtful person meditating during a leisurely vacation. Her tone of

voice, correspondingly, is thoughtful, earnest, sincere, serene when she is describing her desire for simplicity, "pressed and frustrated" when she describes her hectic life. She has used the fluctuating roles and voices of the journals but with more deliberation.

Revising for an appropriate style.
In revising your language, you must consider who your audience is, what role and voice you want to establish, and what your purpose is in writing.

Vocabulary levels vary, even among adult audiences; a careful writer will not write "above the head" of the intended reader, nor insult the reader by aiming too low. The writers in this chapter use fairly simple vocabularies, but their occasional use of sophisticated words indicates that they are writing for well-read, although not necessarily college-educated readers. The type of vocabulary used is also influenced by the intended reader: An audience of professionals often responds best to a professional vocabulary, for example. If Lewis Thomas, a physician, had been writing to other physicians, his vocabulary would have been much more technical than that he has used in "Death in the Open."

Next, you must determine what role and voice to establish for your audience and revise accordingly. The writers in this chapter establish various roles: Lewis Thomas chooses the role of teacher and sage; his voice is friendly but not intimate. James Baldwin also adopts the role of teacher, but his voice is angry, the voice of a black intellectual who must constantly try to make white people understand that black English is a legitimate language. Forster chooses the role of perplexed possessor of property, and his voice is whimsical.

After defining your audience, you must decide your purpose in writing. All the authors here wish to provoke the reader to thought, some through exploring their subject, like Lindbergh and Thomas, others with a more persuasive intent, such as Forster, Baldwin, and Plato. How does style reflect purpose? Lindbergh has engaged in a personal exploration, and her language is more emotional and more poetic as a result. Thomas, on the other hand, examines his subject more objectively, as in fact a physician might, and his language is objective, devoid of personal reference and poetic descriptions and figures of speech. Forster and Plato both use poetic language in fulfilling their more persuasive purposes, but the element of emotion found in Lindbergh is missing, indicating they are both more objective about their subjects. Baldwin is both emotional and persuasive. Like Forster and Plato and unlike Baldwin, most persuasive writing attempts to arouse the emotions of the reader, while not necessarily revealing the emotions of the writer.

Language can create both intimacy (Lindbergh) and distance (Plato), objectivity (Thomas) and subjectivity (Baldwin); the writer's chief tools are type of vocabulary (general, technical, professional), the connotations called forth by choice of language (words with strong associations beyond their literal definitions), the use of poetic descriptions and figures of speech, and sentence rhythms.

Procedures to follow in revising for style.

A. Audience considerations
  1. Determine as precisely as possible who your audience will be. Is it your peers, your teacher, another designated reader?
  2. Decide what vocabulary is appropriate for this audience: Do they require a technical vocabulary, do they require the vocabulary of a general readership, or do they require the more sophisticated vocabulary of the college graduate?
B. Role and voice
  1. What role are you assuming as you write: friend, teacher, expert, thinker?
  2. What voice do you want to reflect that role: Are you an angry friend, a humorous teacher, an objective expert? Or are you a sympathetic friend, a friendly teacher, a humorous expert?
  3. As you revise, keep your role and voice in mind, selecting your language to reflect that role and voice consistently.
C. Purpose: What is your purpose in writing—expressing yourself, exploring, explaining, interpreting, or attempting to persuade?
D. In general, observe the following as well if you would write with style:
  1. Be precise in your choice of words. Aim for clarity in considering the connotations of words. Use a thesaurus for ideas, but be careful at the same time not to overwrite by using words you do not fully comprehend. Strive for words that convey your tone consistently and clearly.
  2. Avoid repetitiveness. Vary your vocabulary. Use your thesaurus along with your dictionary to find synonyms for words you use so frequently that they make your style boring.
  3. Avoid wordiness. Be concise. If your essay needs lengthening, add details about your topic, not unnecessary words.

PLATO

The Allegory of the Cave

Plato (427–348 B.C.) was a Greek philosopher, teacher, and writer who became actively involved in the politics of the Athenian city-state. He vehemently protested the corruption that had permeated Athenian democracy, and the death of his teacher and friend Socrates impelled him to search for an alternative lifestyle. In "The Allegory of the Cave," one of his most famous philosophic dialogues, he talks about the human desire for illusion rather than truth. As you read his essay, jot down some notes on the effectiveness of his argument.

Next, said I, here is a parable to illustrate the degrees in which our nature may be enlightened or unenlightened. Imagine the condition of men living in a sort of cavernous chamber underground, with an entrance open to the light and a long passage all down the cave. Here they have been from childhood, chained by the leg and also by the neck, so that they cannot move and can see only what is in front of them, because the chains will not let them turn their heads. At some distance higher up is the light of a fire burning behind them; and between the prisoners and the fire is a track with a parapet built along it, like the screen at a puppet-show, which hides the performers while they show their puppets over the top.

I see, said he.

Now behind this parapet imagine persons carrying along various artificial objects, including figures of men and animals in wood or stone or other materials, which project above the parapet. Naturally, some of these persons will be talking, others silent.

It is a strange picture, he said, and a strange sort of prisoners.

Like ourselves, I replied; for in the first place prisoners so confined would have seen nothing of themselves or of one another, except the shadows thrown by the firelight on the wall of the Cave facing them, would they?

Not if all their lives they had been prevented from moving their heads.

And they would have seen as little of the objects carried past.

Of course.

Now, if they could talk to one another, would they not suppose that their words referred only to those passing shadows which they saw?

Necessarily.

And suppose their prison had an echo from the wall facing them? When one of the people crossing behind them spoke, they could only suppose that the sound came from the shadow passing before their eyes.

No doubt.

In every way, then, such prisoners would recognize as reality nothing but the shadows of those artificial objects.

Inevitably.

Now consider what would happen if their release from the chains and the healing of their unwisdom should come about in this way. Suppose one of them were set free and forced suddenly to stand up, turn his head, and walk with eyes lifted to the light; all these movements would be painful, and he would be too dazzled to make out the objects whose shadows he had been used to see. What do you think he would say, if someone told him that what he had formerly seen was meaningless illusion, but now, being somewhat nearer to reality and turned towards more real objects, he was getting a truer view? Suppose further that he were shown the various objects being carried by and were made to say, in reply to questions, what each of them was. Would he not be perplexed and believe the objects now shown him to be not so real as what he formerly saw?

Yes, not nearly so real.

And if he were forced to look at the fire-light itself, would not his eyes ache, so that he would try to escape and turn back to the things which he could see distinctly, convinced that they really were clearer than these other objects now being shown to him?

Yes.

And suppose someone were to drag him away forcibly up the steep and rugged ascent and not let him go until he had hauled him out into the sun-light, would he not suffer pain and vexation at such treatment, and, when he had come out into the light, find his eyes so full of its radiance that he could not see a single one of the things that he was now told were real?

Certainly he would not see them all at once.

He would need, then, to grow accustomed before he could see things in that upper world. At first it would be easiest to make out shadows, and then the images of men and things reflected in water, and later on the things them-selves. After that, it would be easier to watch the heavenly bodies and the sky itself by night, looking at the light of the moon and stars rather than the Sun and the Sun's light in the daytime.

Yes, surely.

Last of all, he would be able to look at the Sun and contemplate its na-ture, not as it appears when reflected in water or any alien medium, but as it is in itself in its own domain.

No doubt.

And now he would begin to draw the conclusion that it is the Sun that produces the seasons and the course of the year and controls everything in the visible world, and moreover is in a way the cause of all that he and his com-panions used to see.

Clearly he would come at last to that conclusion.

Then if he called to mind his fellow prisoners and what passed for wisdom in his former dwelling-place, he would surely think himself happy in the change and be sorry for them. They may have had a practice of honouring and commending one another, with prizes for the man who had the keenest eye for the passing shadows and the best memory for the order in which they followed or accompanied one another, so that he would make a good guess as to which was going to come next. Would our released prisoner be likely to covet those prizes or to envy the men exalted to honour and power in the Cave? Would he not feel like Homer's Achilles, that he would far sooner be on earth as a hired servant in the house of a landless man or endure anything rather than go back to his old beliefs and live in the old way?

Yes, he would prefer any fate to such a life.

Now imagine what would happen if he went down again to take his former seat in the Cave. Coming suddenly out of the sunlight, his eyes would be filled with darkness. He might be required once more to deliver his opinion on those shadows, in competition with the prisoners who had never been released, while his eyesight was still dim and unsteady; and it might take some time to become used to the darkness. They would laugh at him and say that he had gone up only to come back with his sight ruined; it was worth no one's while even to attempt the ascent. If they could lay hands on the man who was trying to set them free and lead them up, they would kill him.

Yes, they would.

Every feature in this parable, my dear Glaucon, is meant to fit our earlier analysis. The prison dwelling corresponds to the region revealed to us through the sense of sight, and the fire-light within it to the power of the Sun. The ascent to see the things in the upper world you may take as standing for the upward journey of the soul into the region of the intelligible; then you will be in possession of what I surmise, since that is what you wish to be told. Heaven knows whether it is true; but this, at any rate, is how it appears to me. In the world of knowledge, the last thing to be perceived and only with great difficulty is the essential Form of Goodness. Once it is perceived, the conclusion must follow that, for all things, this is the cause of whatever is right and good; in the visible world it gives birth to light and to the lord of light, while it is itself sovereign in the intelligible world and the parent of intelligence and truth. Without having had a vision of this Form no one can act with wisdom, either in his own life or in matters of state.

PROBING FOR MEANING

1. An allegory or parable is a concrete story on one level and an explication of abstract, moral truths on another. Plato explains at the end what each part of his story symbolizes on the moral level. What correspondences does he establish?

2. If we assume that the people in the cave represent humankind, why does Plato call them "prisoners"? Plato is not specific as to who placed the people in chains, but who seems to be the jailer when the freed prisoner returns to free the others?

3. Plato equates making the "ascent to see the things in the upper world" on the story level with gaining knowledge on the abstract level. Why, instead of making the ascent, would people prefer to remain in the cave with illusions of what is real? Do you agree with Plato's analysis of human nature here? Explain.

4. Plato says of the man who returns to the cave after seeing the sun, "If they could lay hands on [him] . . . they would kill him." Are there historical or contemporary situations that fulfill this prediction?

PROBING FOR METHOD

1. Plato's essay is presented as a dialogue between a teacher and a student. What contribution to structure and theme is made by the brief comments of the student?

2. What logical plan of organization can be seen at work within this essay?

3. Why is Plato's language so simple? How does it compare with Lindbergh's in "Channelled Whelk"? What purpose does his language serve?

4. Is Plato's final comment upon the allegory necessary, or would you have been able to fit together its features without his ending? Without his commentary, would you have come up with alternative meanings? Explain.

JAMES BALDWIN

If Black English Isn't a Language, Then Tell Me, What Is?

James Baldwin (b. 1924) was born in Harlem. Much of his writing, including his first novel, Go Tell It on the Mountain *(1953), and his many collections of essays from* Notes of a Native Son *(1955) to the more recent* No Name in the Street, *is autobiographical and concerned with the complexity of the black man and woman's search for identity. In his essay on black English published originally in the* New York Times *in 1979, Baldwin explains the intricate relationship between language and selfhood. As you read his essay, write two or three sentences on your thoughts about the connection of language and self-expression.*

St. Paul De Vence, France—The argument concerning the use, or the status, or the reality, of black English is rooted in American history and has absolutely nothing to do with the question the argument supposes itself to be posing. The argument has nothing to do with language itself but with the *role* of language. Language, incontestably, reveals the speaker. Language, also, far more dubiously, is meant to define the other—and, in this case, the other is refusing to be defined by a language that has never been able to recognize him.

People evolve a language in order to describe and thus control their circumstances, or in order not to be submerged by a reality that they cannot articulate. (And, if they cannot articulate it, they *are* submerged.) A Frenchman living in Paris speaks a subtly and crucially different language from that of the man living in Marseilles; neither sounds very much like a man living in Quebec; and they would all have great difficulty in apprehending what the man from Guadeloupe, or Martinique, is saying, to say nothing of the man from Senegal—although the "common" language of all these areas is French. But each has paid, and is paying, a different price for this "common" language, in which, as it turns out, they are not saying, and cannot be saying, the same things: They each have very different realities to articulate, or control.

What joins all languages, and all men, is the necessity to confront life, in order, not inconceivably, to outwit death: The price for this is the acceptance, and achievement, of one's temporal identity. So that, for example, though it is not taught in the schools (and this has the potential of becoming a political issue) the south of France still clings to its ancient and musical Provençal, which resists being described as a "dialect." And much of the tension in the Basque countries, and in Wales, is due to the Basque and Welsh determination not to allow their languages to be destroyed. This determination also feeds the flames in Ireland for among the many indignities the Irish have been forced to undergo at English hands is the English contempt for their language.

It goes without saying, then, that language is also a political instrument, means, and proof of power. It is the most vivid and crucial key to identity: It reveals the private identity, and connects one with, or divorces one from, the larger, public, or communal identity. There have been, and are, times, and places, when to speak a certain language could be dangerous, even fatal. Or, one may speak the same language, but in such a way that one's antecedents are revealed, or (one hopes) hidden. This is true in France, and is absolutely true in England: The range (and reign) of accents on that damp little island make England coherent for the English and totally incomprehensible for everyone else. To open your mouth in England is (if I may use black English) to "put your business in the street": You have confessed your parents, your youth, your school, your salary, your self-esteem, and, alas, your future.

Now, I do not know what white Americans would sound like if there had never been any black people in the United States, but they would not sound the way they sound. *Jazz*, for example, is a very specific sexual term, as in *jazz me, baby*, but white people purified it into the Jazz Age. *Sock it to me*, which means, roughly, the same thing, has been adopted by Nathaniel Hawthorne's descendants with no qualms or hesitations at all, along with *let it all hang out* and *right on! Beat to his socks*, which was once the black's most total and despairing image of poverty, was transformed into a thing called the Beat Generation, which phenomenon was, largely, composed of *uptight*, middle-class white people, imitating poverty, trying to *get down*, to get *with it*, doing their *thing*, doing their despairing best to be *funky*, which we, the blacks, never dreamed of doing—we *were* funky, baby, like *funk* was going out of style.

Now, no one can eat his cake, and have it, too, and it is late in the day to attempt to penalize black people for having created a language that permits the nation its only glimpse of reality, a language without which the nation would be even more *whipped* than it is.

I say that this present skirmish is rooted in American history, and it is. Black English is the creation of the black diaspora. Blacks came to the United States chained to each other, but from different tribes: Neither could speak the other's language. If two black people, at that bitter hour of the world's history, had been able to speak to each other, the institution of chattel slavery could never have lasted as long as it did. Subsequently, the slave was given, under the eye, and the gun, of his master, Congo Square, and the Bible—or, in other words, and under these conditions, the slave began the formation of the black church, and it is within this unprecedented tabernacle that black English began to be formed. This was not, merely, as in the European example, the adoption of a foreign tongue, but an alchemy that transformed ancient elements into a new language: *A language comes into existence by means of brutal necessity, and the rules of the language are dictated by what the language must convey.*

There was a moment, in time, and in this place, when my brother, or my mother, or my father, or my sister, had to convey to me, for example, the danger in which I was standing from the white man standing just behind me, and to convey this with a speed, and in a language, that the white man could not possibly understand, and that, indeed, he cannot understand, until today. He cannot afford to understand it. This understanding would reveal to him too much about himself, and smash that mirror before which he has been frozen for so long.

Now, if this passion, this skill, this (to quote Toni Morrison) "sheer intelligence," this incredible music, the mighty achievement of having brought a people utterly unknown to, or despised by "history"—to have brought this people to their present, troubled, troubling, and unassailable and unanswerable place—if this absolutely unprecedented journey does not indicate that black English is a language, I am curious to know what definition of language is to be trusted.

A people at the center of the Western world, and in the midst of so hostile a population, has not endured and transcended by means of what is patronizingly called a "dialect." We, the blacks, are in trouble, certainly, but we are not doomed, and we are not inarticulate because we are not compelled to defend a morality that we know to be a lie.

The brutal truth is that the bulk of the white people in America never had any interest in educating black people, except as this could serve white purposes. It is not the black child's language that is in question, it is not his language that is despised: It is his experience. A child cannot be taught by anyone who despises him, and a child cannot afford to be fooled. A child cannot be taught by anyone whose demand, essentially, is that the child repudiate his experience, and all that gives him sustenance, and enter a limbo in which he will no longer be black, and in which he knows that he can never become white. Black people have lost too many black children that way.

And, after all, finally, in a country with standards so untrustworthy, a country that makes heroes of so many criminal mediocrities, a country unable to face why so many of the non-white are in prison, or on the needle, or standing, futureless, in the streets—it may very well be that both the child, and his elder, have concluded that they have nothing whatever to learn from the people of a country that has managed to learn so little.

PROBING FOR MEANING

1. Baldwin distinguishes between the characteristics of a language as opposed to the characteristics of a dialect. What are these characteristics, according to Baldwin, and how do they differ?

2. In Baldwin's view, what is the relationship between language and reality?

3. Characterize your response to Baldwin's comment in paragraph 4 that "language is also a political instrument, means, and proof of power." Has this been true of your experience? How?

4. To what extent do you agree with Baldwin's thesis that language and identity are very closely related?

PROBING FOR METHOD

1. Baldwin's essay originally appeared in the *New York Times*. How would you characterize his intended audience? What evidence would you cite from the essay to support your characterization?

2. Discuss Baldwin's purpose in writing the essay. What methods did he use to influence your point of view on his subject?

3. What is the effect of the italicized words used in the essay? How would their *exclusion* affect the impact of the essay? Explain your answer.

4. Read over the last sentence of the essay. Is it an effective conclusion? Why or why not?

LEWIS THOMAS

Death in the Open

Lewis Thomas (b. 1913) is an American physician, researcher, and essayist, born in Flushing, New York. He is currently director of the Memorial Sloane-Kettering Cancer Center. Thomas's first book, Lives of a Cell *(1974), brought him wide acclaim as an essayist. In addition to writing frequently for the* New England Journal of Medicine, *Thomas has published two other essay collections,* The Medusa and the Snail *(1979) and* The Youngest Science: Notes of a Medicine Watcher *(1983). As you read "Death in the Open," speculate as to the kind of audience Thomas was writing for.*

Most of the dead animals you see on highways near the cities are dogs, a few cats. Out in the countryside, the forms and coloring of the dead are strange; these are the wild creatures. Seen from a car window they appear as fragments, evoking memories of woodchucks, badgers, skunks, voles, snakes, sometimes the mysterious wreckage of a deer.

It is always a queer shock, part sudden upwelling of grief, part unaccountable amazement. It is simply astounding to see an animal dead on a highway. The outrage is more than just the location; it is the impropriety of such visible death, anywhere. You do not expect to see dead animals in the open. It is the nature of animals to die alone, off somewhere, hidden. It is wrong to see them lying out on the highway; it is wrong to see them anywhere.

Everything in the world dies, but we only know about it as a kind of abstraction. If you stand in a meadow, at the edge of a hillside, and look around carefully, almost everything you can catch sight of is in the process of dying, and most things will be dead long before you are. If it were not for the constant renewal and replacement going on before your eyes, the whole place would turn to stone and sand under your feet.

There are some creatures that do not seem to die at all; they simply vanish totally into their own progeny. Single cells do this. The cell becomes two, then four, and so on, and after a while the last trace is gone. It cannot be seen as death; barring mutation, the descendants are simply the first cell, living all over again. The cycles of the slime mold have episodes that seem as conclusive as death, but the withered slug, with its stalk and fruiting body, is plainly the transient tissue of a developing animal; the free-swimming amebocytes use this organ collectively in order to produce more of themselves.

There are said to be a billion billion insects on the earth at any moment, most of them with very short life expectancies by our standards. Someone has estimated that there are 25 million assorted insects hanging in the air over every temperate square mile, in a column extending upward for thousands of feet, drifting through the layers of the atmosphere like plankton. They are dying steadily, some by being eaten, some just dropping in their tracks, tons of them around the earth, disintegrating as they die, invisibly.

Who ever sees dead birds, in anything like the huge numbers stipulated by the certainty of the death of all birds? A dead bird is an incongruity, more startling than an unexpected live bird, sure evidence to the human mind that something has gone wrong. Birds do their dying off somewhere, behind things, under things, never on the wing.

Animals seem to have an instinct for performing death alone, hidden. Even the largest, most conspicuous ones find ways to conceal themselves in time. If an elephant missteps and dies in an open place, the herd will not leave him there; the others will pick him up and carry the body from place to place, finally putting it down in some inexplicably suitable location. When elephants encounter the skeleton of an elephant out in the open, they methodically take up each of the bones and distribute them, in a ponderous ceremony, over neighboring acres.

It is a natural marvel. All of the life of the earth dies, all of the time, in the same volume as the new life that dazzles us each morning, each spring. All we see of this is the odd stump, the fly struggling on the porch floor of the summer house in October, the fragment on the highway. I have lived all my life with an embarrassment of squirrels in my backyard, they are all over the place, all year long, and I have never seen, anywhere, a dead squirrel.

I suppose it is just as well. If the earth were otherwise, and all the dying were done in the open, with the dead there to be looked at, we would never have it out of our minds. We can forget about it much of the time, or think of it as an accident to be avoided, somehow. But is does make the process of dying seem more exceptional than it really is, and harder to engage in at the times when we must ourselves engage.

In our way, we conform as best we can to the rest of nature. The obituary pages tell us of the news that we are dying away, while the birth announcements in finer print, off at the side of the page, inform us of our replacements, but we get no grasp from this of the enormity of scale. There are 3 billion of us on the earth, and all 3 billion must be dead, on a schedule, within this lifetime. The vast mortality, involving something over 50 million of us each year, takes place in relative secrecy. We can only really know of the deaths in our households, or among our friends. These, detached in our minds from all the rest, we take to be unnatural events, anomalies, outrages. We speak of our own dead in low voices; struck down, we say, as though visible death can only occur for cause, by disease or violence, avoidably. We send off for flowers, grieve, make ceremonies, scatter bones, unaware of the rest of the 3 billion on the same schedule. All of that immense mass of flesh and bone and consciousness will disappear by absorption into the earth, without recognition by the transient survivors.

Less than a half century from now, our replacements will have more than doubled the numbers. It is hard to see how we can continue to keep the secret, with such multitudes doing the dying. We will have to give up the notion that death is catastrophe, or detestable, or avoidable, or even strange. We will need to learn more about the cycling of life in the rest of the system, and about our connection to the process. Everything that comes alive seems to be in trade for something that dies, cell for cell. There might be some comfort in the recognition of synchrony, in the formation that we all go down together, in the best of company.

PROBING FOR MEANING

1. Why, according to Thomas, do we feel shocked by the body of a dead animal on a highway?

2. What effects does the animal world's "instinct for performing death alone" have on human beings? How do humans express this instinct?

3. Why does Thomas feel that we will have to give up the notion that death is "catastrophe, or detestable, or avoidable, or even strange"? What effect might giving up this notion have on us?

PROBING FOR METHOD

1. Is there a logic to the order in which Thomas offers examples of how animals perform death alone? What effect does he achieve by pointing to insects, then birds, then elephants? Why does he mention squirrels last?

2. How scientific is the cause-and-effect analysis offered by Thomas? To what degree would you describe his tone as argumentative?

3. For what sort of audience is Thomas writing?

WILLIAM STAFFORD

Freedom

William Stafford (b. 1914) is an American poet and teacher who was a conscientious objector during World War II and has been active since in pacifist movements. He has published poetry in many journals, including Harper's *and the*

New Yorker, *and his collections of poetry include* Traveling Through the Dark *(1963), for which he received the National Book Award. Stafford defines the role of the poet as "finding out what the world is trying to be." As you read "Freedom" (1968), compare Stafford's definition of freedom to yours.*

> Freedom is not following a river.
> Freedom is following a river,
>   though, if you want to.
> It is deciding now by what happens now.
> It is knowing that luck makes a difference.
>
> No leader is free; no follower is free—
>   the rest of us can often be free.
> Most of the world are living by
> creeds too odd, chancey, and habit-forming
>   to be worth arguing about by reason.
>
> If you are oppressed, wake up about
> four in the morning: most places,
> you can usually be free some of the time
>   if you wake up before other people.

PROBING FOR MEANING

1. Explain the first three lines of the poem. Are they in any way contradictory?
2. To what extent do you agree or disagree with lines 6 and 7?
3. What examples can you think of to illustrate Stafford's point in lines 8–10?
4. What is your interpretation of the last four lines of the poem? To what extent have you found them to be true?
5. How does your definition of freedom differ from Stafford's?

PROBING FOR METHOD

1. What is the effect on the poem's meaning of beginning with a definition of what freedom is not? How does this technique affect your response to the poem?
2. Throughout the poem Stafford makes short declarative statements about freedom. To what extent is this technique effective?
3. Characterize the tone of the poem. Is it humorous? Provocative? Persuasive? Explain your answer.

ALBERT CAMUS

The Guest

Albert Camus (1913–1960) was a French novelist, dramatist, essayist, and journalist whose work had a significant impact on his contemporaries. He was a member of the French Resistance movement during World War II and the editor of Combat, *an underground publication. Although he has been identified with existentialism, Camus's profound humanism distinguishes him from many purely existentialist writers. Convinced of the absurdity of life, Camus, nevertheless, in his art and in his life, struggled with the paradoxical aspirations of personal freedom and social justice, solitude and solidarity, and reason and passion. He was awarded the Nobel Prize in 1957 for his philosophical essays, which include "The Myth of Sisyphus" (1942) and "The Rebel" (1953), and for his fiction, which includes* The Stranger *(1942),* The Plague *(1948) and* The Fall *(1957). He was killed in an automobile accident in 1961 at the height of his literary career. In "The Guest," from his collection of short stories* Exile *and* The Kingdom *(1957), his protagonist Daru is forced to grapple with his concept of honor. As you read the story, think about how you might have reacted in Daru's situation.*

The Schoolmaster was watching the two men climb toward him. One was on horseback, the other on foot. They had not yet tackled the abrupt rise leading to the schoolhouse built on the hillside. They were toiling onward, making slow progress in the snow, among the stones, on the vast expanse of the high, deserted plateau. From time to time the horse stumbled. Without hearing anything yet, he could see the breath issuing from the horse's nostrils. One of the men, at least, knew the region. They were following the trail although it had disappeared days ago under a layer of dirty white snow. The schoolmaster calculated that it would take them half an hour to get onto the hill. It was cold; he went back into the school to get a sweater.

He crossed the empty, frigid classroom. On the blackboard the four rivers of France, drawn with four different colored chalks, had been flowing toward their estuaries for the past three days. Snow had suddenly fallen in mid-October afer eight months of drought without the transition of rain, and the twenty pupils, more or less, who lived in the villages scattered over the plateau had stopped coming. With fair weather they would return. Daru now heated only the single room that was his lodging, adjoining the classroom and giving also onto the plateau to the east. Like the class windows, his window looked to the south too. On that side the school was a few kilometers from the point where the plateau began to slope toward the south. In clear weather could be seen the purple mass of the mountain range where the gap opened onto the desert.

Somewhat warmed, Daru returned to the window from which he had first seen the two men. They were no longer visible. Hence they must have tackled the rise. The sky was not so dark, for the snow had stopped falling during the night. The morning had opened with a dirty light which had scarcely become brighter as the ceiling of clouds lifted. At two in the afternoon it seemed as if the day were merely beginning. But still this was better than those three days when the thick snow was falling amidst unbroken darkness with little gusts of wind that rattled the double door of the classroom. Then Daru had spent long hours in his room, leaving it only to go the shed and feed the chickens or get some coal. Fortunately the delivery truck from Tadjid, the nearest village to the north, had brought his supplies two days before the blizzard. It would return in forty-eight hours.

Besides, he had enough to resist a siege, for the little room was cluttered with bags of wheat that the administration left as a stock to distribute to those of his pupils whose families had suffered from the drought. Actually they had all been victims because they were all poor. Every day Daru would distribute a ration to the children. They had missed it, he knew, during these bad days. Possibly one of the fathers or big brothers would come this afternoon and he could supply them with grain. It was just a matter of carrying them over to the next harvest. Now shiploads of wheat were arriving from France and the worst was over. But it would be hard to forget that poverty, that army of ragged ghosts wandering in the sunlight, the plateaus burned to a cinder month after month, the earth shriveled up little by little, literally scorched, every stone bursting into dust under one's foot. The sheep had died then by thousands and even a few men, here and there, sometimes without anyone's knowing.

In contrast with such poverty, he who lived almost like a monk in his remote schoolhouse, nonetheless satisfied with the little he had and with the rough life, had felt like a lord with his whitewashed walls, his narrow couch, his unpainted shelves, his well, and his provision of water and food. And suddenly this snow, without warning, without the foretaste of rain. This is the way the region was, cruel to live in, even without men—who didn't help matters either. But Daru had been born here. Everywhere else, he felt exiled.

He stepped out onto the terrace in front of the schoolhouse. The two men were now halfway up the slope. He recognized the horseman as Balducci, the old gendarme he had known for a long time. Balducci was holding on the end of a rope an Arab who was walking behind him with hands bound and head lowered. The gendarme waved a greeting to which Daru did not reply, lost as he was in contemplation of the Arab dressed in a faded blue jellaba, his feet in sandals but covered with socks of heavy raw wool, his head surmounted by a narrow, short *chèche*. They were approaching. Balducci was holding back his horse in order not to hurt the Arab and the group was advancing slowly.

Within earshot, Balducci shouted: "One hour to do the three kilometers from El Ameur!" Daru did not answer. Short and square in his thick sweater, he watched them climb. Not once had the Arab raised his head. "Hello," said Daru when they got up onto the terrace. "Come in and warm up." Balducci painfully got down from his horse without letting go the rope. From under his bristling mustache he smiled at the schoolmaster. His little dark eyes, deep-set under a tanned forehead, and his mouth surrounded with wrinkles made him look attentive and studious. Daru took the bridle, led the horse to the shed, and came back to the two men, who were now waiting for him in the school. He led them into his room. "I am going to heat up the classroom," he said. "We'll be more comfortable there." When he entered the room again, Balducci was on the couch. He had undone the rope tying him to the Arab, who had squatted near the stove. His hands still bound, the *chèche* pushed back on his head, he was looking toward the window. At first Daru noticed only his huge lips, fat, smooth, almost Negroid; yet his nose was straight, his eyes were dark and full of fever. The *chèche* revealed an obstinate forehead and, under the weathered skin now rather discolored by the cold, the whole face had a restless and rebellious look that struck Daru when the Arab, turning his face toward him, looked him straight in the eyes. "Go into the other room," said the schoolmaster, "and I'll make you some mint tea." "Thanks," Balducci said. "What a chore! How I long for retirement." And addressing his prisoner in Arabic: "Come on, you." The Arab got up and, slowly, holding his bound wrists in front of him, went into the classroom.

With the tea, Daru brought a chair. But Balducci was already enthroned on the nearest pupil's desk and the Arab had squatted against the teacher's platform facing the stove, which stood between the desk and the window. When he held out the glass of tea to the prisoner, Daru hesitated at the sight of his bound hands. "He might perhaps be untied." "Sure," said Balducci. "That was for the trip." He started to get to his feet. But Daru, setting the glass on the floor, had knelt beside the Arab. Without saying anything, the Arab watched him with his feverish eyes. Once his hands were free, he rubbed his swollen wrists against each other, took the glass of tea, and sucked up the burning liquid in swift little sips.

"Good," said Daru. "And where are you headed?"

Balducci withdrew his mustache from the tea. "Here, son."

"Odd pupils! And you're spending the night?"

"No. I'm going back to El Ameur. And you will deliver this fellow to Tinguit. He is expected at police headquarters."

Balducci was looking at Daru with a friendly little smile.

"What's the story?" asked the schoolmaster. "Are you pulling my leg?"

"No, son. Those are the orders."

"The orders? I'm not . . ." Daru hesitated, not wanting to hurt the old Corsican. "I mean, that's not my job."

"What! What's the meaning of that? In wartime people do all kinds of jobs."

"Then I'll wait for the declaration of war!"

Balducci nodded.

"O.K. But the orders exist and they concern you too. Things are brewing, it appears. There is talk of a forthcoming revolt. We are mobilized, in a way."

Daru still had his obstinate look.

"Listen, son," Balducci said. "I like you and you must understand. There's only a dozen of us at El Ameur to patrol throughout the whole territory of a small department and I must get back in a hurry. I was told to hand this guy over to you and return without delay. He couldn't be kept there. His village was beginning to stir; they wanted to take him back. You must take him to Tinguit tomorrow before the day is over. Twenty kilometers shouldn't faze a husky fellow like you. After that, all will be over. You'll come back to your pupils and your comfortable life."

Behind the wall the horse could be heard snorting and pawing the earth. Daru was looking out the window. Decidedly, the weather was clearing and the light was increasing over the snowy plateau. When all the snow was melted, the sun would take over again and once more would burn the fields of stone. For days, still, the unchanging sky would shed its dry light on the solitary expanse where nothing had any connection with man.

"After all," he said, turning around toward Balducci, "what did he do?" And, before the gendarme had opened his mouth, he asked: "Does he speak French?"

"No, not a word. We had been looking for him for a month but they were hiding him. He killed his cousin."

"Is he against us?"

"I don't think so. But you can never be sure."

"Why did he kill?"

"A family squabble, I think. One owed the other grain, it seems. It's not at all clear. In short, he killed his cousin with a billhook. You know, like a sheep, *kreezk*!"

Balducci made the gesture of drawing a blade across his throat and the Arab, his attention attracted, watched him with a sort of anxiety. Daru felt a sudden wrath against the man, against all men with their rotten spite, their tireless hates, their blood lust.

But the kettle was singing on the stove. He served Balducci more tea, hesitated, then served the Arab again, who, a second time, drank avidly. His raised arms made the jellaba fall open and the schoolmaster saw his thin, muscular chest.

"Thanks, kid," Balducci said. "And now, I'm off."

He got up and went toward the Arab, taking a small rope from his pocket.

"What are you doing?" Daru asked dryly.

Balducci, disconcerted, showed him the rope.

"Don't bother."

The old gendarme hesitated. "It's up to you. Of course, you are armed?"

"I have my shotgun."

"Where?"

"In the trunk."

"You ought to have it near your bed."

"Why? I have nothing to fear."

"You're crazy son. If there's an uprising, no one is safe, we're all in the same boat."

"I'll defend myself. I'll have time to see them coming."

Balducci began to laugh, then suddenly the mustache covered the white teeth.

"You'll have time? O.K. That's just what I was saying. You have always been a little cracked. That's why I like you, my son was like that."

At the same time he took out his revolver and put it on the desk.

"Keep it; I don't need two weapons from here to El Ameur."

The revolver shone against the black paint of the table. When the gendarme turned toward him, the schoolmaster caught the smell of leather and horseflesh.

"Listen, Balducci," Daru said suddenly, "every bit of this disgusts me, and first of all your fellow here. But I won't hand him over. Fight, yes, if I have to. But not that."

The old gendarme stood in front of him and looked at him severely.

"You're being a fool," he said slowly. "I don't like it either. You don't get used to putting a rope on a man even after years of it, and you're even ashamed—yes, ashamed. But you can't let them have their way."

"I won't hand him over," Daru said again.

"It's an order, son, and I repeat it."

"That's right. Repeat to them what I've said to you: I won't hand him over."

Balducci made a visible effort to reflect. He looked at the Arab and at Daru. At last he decided.

"No, I won't tell them anything. If you want to drop us, go ahead; I'll not denounce you. I have an order to deliver the prisoner and I'm doing so. And now you'll just sign this paper for me."

"There's no need. I'll not deny that you left him with me."

"Don't be mean with me. I know you'll tell the truth. You're from hereabouts and you are a man. But you must sign, that's the rule."

Daru opened his drawer, took out a little square bottle of purple ink, the red wooden penholder with the "sergeant-major" pen he used for making models of penmanship, and signed. The gendarme carefully folded the paper and put it into his wallet. Then he moved toward the door.

"I'll see you off," Daru said.

"No," said Balducci. "There's no use being polite. You insulted me."

He looked at the Arab, motionless in the same spot, sniffed peevishly, and turned away toward the door. "Good-by, son," he said. The door shut behind him. Balducci appeared suddenly outside the window and then disappeared. His footsteps were muffled by the snow. The horse stirred on the other side of the wall and several chickens fluttered in fright. A moment later Balducci reappeared outside the window leading the horse by the bridle. He walked toward the little rise without turning around and disappeared from sight with the horse following him. A big stone could be heard bouncing down. Daru walked back toward the prisoner, who, without stirring, never took his eyes off him. "Wait," the schoolmaster said in Arabic and went toward the bedroom. As he was going through the door, he had a second thought, went to the desk, took the revolver, and stuck it in his pocket. Then, without looking back, he went into his room.

For some time he lay on his couch watching the sky gradually close over, listening to the silence. It was this silence that had seemed painful to him during the first days here, after the war. He had requested a post in the little town at the base of the foothills separating the upper plateaus from the desert. There, rocky walls, green and black to the north, pink and lavender to the south, marked the frontier of eternal summer. He had been named to a post farther north, on the plateau itself. In the beginning, the solitude and the silence had been hard for him on these wastelands peopled only by stones. Occasionally, furrows suggested cultivation, but they had been dug to uncover a certain kind of stone good for building. The only plowing here was to harvest rocks. Elsewhere a thin layer of soil accumulated in the hollows would be scraped out to enrich paltry village gardens. This is the way it was: bare rock covered three quarters of the region. Towns sprang up, flourished, then disappeared; men came by, loved one another or fought bitterly, then died. No one in this desert, neither he nor his guest, mattered. And yet, outside this desert neither of them, Daru knew, could have really lived.

When he got up, no noise came from the classroom. He was amazed at the unmixed joy he derived from the mere thought that the Arab might have fled and that he would be alone with no decision to make. But the prisoner was there. He had merely stretched out between the stove and the desk. With eyes open, he was staring at the ceiling. In that position, his thick lips were particularly noticeable, giving him a pouting look. "Come," said Daru. The Arab got up and followed him. In the bedroom, the schoolmaster pointed to a chair near the table under the window. The Arab sat down without taking his eyes off Daru.

"Are you hungry?"

"Yes," the prisoner said.

Daru set the table for two. He took flour and oil, shaped a cake in a frying-pan, and lighted the little stove that functioned on bottled gas. While the cake was cooking, he went out to the shed to get cheese, eggs, dates, and condensed milk. When the cake was done he set it on the window sill to cool, heated some condensed milk diluted with water, and beat up the eggs into an omelette. In one of his motions he knocked against the revolver stuck in his right pocket. He set the bowl down, went into the classroom, and put the revolver in his desk drawer. When he came back to the room, night was falling. He put on the light and served the Arab. "Eat," he said. The Arab took a piece of the cake, lifted it eagerly to his mouth, and stopped short.

"And you?" he asked.

"After you. I'll eat too."

The thick lips opened slightly. The Arab hesitated, then bit into the cake determinedly.

The meal over, the Arab looked at the schoolmaster. "Are you the judge?"

"No, I'm simply keeping you until tomorrow."

"Why do you eat with me?"

"I'm hungry."

The Arab fell silent. Daru got up and went out. He brought back a folding bed from the shed, set it up between the table and the stove, perpendicular to his own bed. From a large suitcase which, upright in a corner, served as a shelf for papers, he took two blankets and arranged them on the camp bed. Then he stopped, felt useless, and sat down on his bed. There was nothing more to do or to get ready. He had to look at this man. He looked at him, therefore, trying to imagine his face bursting with rage. He couldn't do so. He could see nothing but the dark yet shining eyes and the animal mouth.

"Why did you kill him?" he asked in a voice whose hostile tone surprised him.

The Arab looked away.

"He ran away. I ran after him."

He raised his eyes to Daru again and they were full of a sort of woeful interrogation. "Now what will they do to me?"

"Are you afraid?"

He stiffened, turning his eyes away.

"Are you sorry?"

The Arab stared at him openmouthed. Obviously he did not understand. Daru's annoyance was growing. At the same time he felt awkward and self-conscious with his big body wedged between the two beds.

"Lie down there," he said impatiently. "That's your bed."

The Arab didn't move. He called to Daru:

"Tell me!"

The schoolmaster looked at him.

"Is the gendarme coming back tomorrow?"

"I don't know."

"Are you coming with us?"

"I don't know. Why?"

The prisoner got up and stretched out on top of the blankets, his feet toward the window. The light from the electric bulb shone straight into his eyes and he closed them at once.

"Why?" Daru repeated, standing beside the bed.

The Arab opened his eyes under the blinding light and looked at him, trying not to blink.

"Come with us," he said.

In the middle of the night, Daru was still not asleep. He had gone to bed after undressing completely; he generally slept naked. But when he suddenly realized that he had nothing on, he hesitated. He felt vulnerable and the temptation came to him to put his clothes back on. Then he shrugged his shoulders; after all, he wasn't a child and, if need be, he could break his adversary in two. From his bed he could observe him, lying on his back, still motionless with his eyes closed under the harsh light. When Daru turned out the light, the darkness seemed to coagulate all of a sudden. Little by little, the night came back to life in the window where the starless sky was stirring gently. The schoolmaster soon made out the body lying at his feet. The Arab still did not move, but his eyes seemed open. A faint wind was prowling around the schoolhouse. Perhaps it would drive away the clouds and the sun would reappear.

During the night the wind increased. The hens fluttered a little and then were silent. The Arab turned over on his side with his back to Daru, who thought he heard him moan. Then he listened for his guest's breathing, become heavier and more regular. He listened to that breath so close to him and mused without being able to go to sleep. In this room where he had been sleeping alone for a year, this presence bothered him. But it bothered him also by imposing on him a sort of brotherhood he knew well but refused to accept in the present circumstances. Men who share the same rooms, soldiers or prisoners, develop a strange alliance as if, having cast off their armor with their clothing, they fraternized every evening, over and above their differences, in the ancient community of dream and fatigue. But Daru shook himself; he didn't like such musings, and it was essential to sleep.

A little later, however, when the Arab stirred slightly, the schoolmaster was still not asleep. When the prisoner made a second move, he stiffened, on the alert. The Arab was lifting himself slowly on his arms with almost the motion of a sleepwalker. Seated upright in bed, he waited motionless without turning his head toward Daru, as if he were listening attentively. Daru did not stir; it had just occurred to him that the revolver was still in the drawer of his desk. It was better to act at once. Yet he continued to observe the prisoner, who, with the same slithery motion, put his feet on the ground, waited again, then began to stand up slowly. Daru was about to call out to him when the Arab began to walk, in a quite natural but extraordinarily silent way. He was heading toward the door at the end of the room that opened into the shed. He lifted the latch with precaution and went out, pushing the door behind him but without shutting it. Daru had not stirred. "He is running away," he merely thought. "Good riddance!" Yet he listened attentively. The hens were not fluttering; the guest must be on the plateau. A faint sound of water reached him, and he didn't know what it was until the Arab again stood framed in the doorway, closed the door carefully, and came back to bed without a sound. Then Daru turned his back on him and fell asleep. Still later he seemed, from the depths of his sleep, to hear furtive steps around the schoolhouse. "I'm dreaming! I'm dreaming!" he repeated to himself. And he went on sleeping.

When he awoke, the sky was clear; the loose window let in a cold, pure air. The Arab was asleep, hunched up under the blankets now, his mouth open, utterly relaxed. But when Daru shook him, he started dreadfully, staring at Daru with wild eyes as if he had never seen him and such a frightened expression that the schoolmaster stepped back. "Don't be afraid. It's me. You must eat." The Arab nodded his head and said yes. Calm had returned to his face, but his expression was vacant and listless.

The coffee was ready. They drank it seated together on the folding bed as they munched their pieces of the cake. Then Daru led the Arab under the shed and showed him the faucet where he washed. He went back into the room, folded the blankets and the bed, made his own bed and put the room in order. Then he went through the classroom and out onto the terrace. The sun was already rising in the blue sky; a soft, bright light was bathing the deserted plateau. On the ridge the snow was melting in spots. The stones were about to reappear. Crouched on the edge of the plateau, the schoolmaster looked at the deserted expanse. He thought of Balducci. He had hurt him, for he had sent him off in a way as if he didn't want to be associated with him. He could still hear the gendarme's farewell and, without knowing why, he felt strangely empty and vulnerable. At that moment, from the other side of the schoolhouse, the prisoner coughed. Daru listened to him almost despite himself and then, furious, threw a pebble that whistled through the air before sinking into the snow. That man's stupid crime revolted him, but to hand him over was contrary to honor. Merely thinking of it made him smart with humiliation. And he cursed at one and the same time his own people who had sent him this Arab and the Arab too who had dared to kill and not managed to get away. Daru got up, walked in a circle on the terrace, waited motionless, and then went back into the schoolhouse.

The Arab, leaning over the cement floor of the shed, was washing his teeth with two fingers. Daru looked at him and said: "Come." He went back into the room ahead of the prisoner. He slipped a hunting-jacket on over his sweater and put on walking-shoes. Standing, he waited until the Arab had put on his *chèche* and sandals. They went into the classroom and the schoolmaster pointed to the exit, saying: "Go ahead." The fellow didn't budge. "I'm coming," said Daru. The Arab went out. Daru went back into the room and made a package of pieces of rusk, dates, and sugar. In the classroom, before going out, he hesitated a second in front of his desk, then crossed the threshold and locked the door. "That's the way," he said. He started toward the east, fol lowed by the prisoner. But, a short distance from the schoolhouse, he thought he heard a slight sound behind them. He retraced his steps and examined the surroundings of the house; there was no one there. The Arab watched him without seeming to understand. "Come on," said Daru.

They walked for an hour and rested beside a sharp peak of limestone. The snow was melting faster and faster and the sun was drinking up the puddles at once, rapidly cleaning the plateau, which gradually dried and vibrated like the air itself. When they resumed walking, the ground rang under their feet. From time to time a bird rent the space in front of them with a joyful cry. Daru breathed in deeply the fresh morning light. He felt a sort of rapture before the vast familiar expanse, now almost entirely yellow under its dome of blue sky. They walked an hour more, descending toward the south. They reached a level height made up of crumbly rocks. From there on, the plateau sloped down, eastward, toward a low plain where there were a few spindly trees and, to the south, toward outcroppings of rock that gave the landscape a chaotic look.

Daru surveyed the two directions. There was nothing but the sky on the horizon. Not a man could be seen. He turned toward the Arab, who was looking at him blankly. Daru held out the package to him. "Take it," he said. "There are dates, bread, and sugar. You can hold out for two days. Here are a thousand francs too." The Arab took the package and the money but kept his full hands at chest level as if he didn't know what to do with what was being given him. "Now look," the schoolmaster said as he pointed in the direction of the east, "there's the way to Tinguit. You have a two-hour walk. At Tinguit you'll find the administration and the police. They are expecting you." The Arab looked toward the east, still holding the package and the money against his chest. Daru took his elbow and turned him rather roughly toward the south. At the foot of the height on which they stood could be seen a faint path. "That's the trail across the plateau. In a day's walk from here you'll find pasturelands and the first nomads. They'll take you in and shelter you according to their law." The Arab had now turned toward Daru and a sort of panic was visible in his expression. "Listen," he said. Daru shook his head: "No, be quiet. Now I'm leaving you." He turned his back on him, took two long steps in the direction of the school, looked hesitantly at the motionless Arab, and started off again. For a few minutes he heard nothing but his own step resounding on the cold ground and did not turn his head. A moment later, however, he turned around. The Arab was still there on the edge of the hill, his arms hanging now, and he was looking at the schoolmaster. Daru felt something rise in his throat. But he swore with impatience, waved vaguely, and started off again. He had already gone some distance when he again stopped and looked. There was no longer anyone on the hill.

Daru hesitated. The sun was now rather high in the sky and was beginning to beat down on his head. The schoolmaster retraced his steps, at first somewhat uncertainly, then with decision. When he reached the little hill, he was bathed in sweat. He climbed it as fast as he could and stopped, out of breath, at the top. The rock-fields to the south stood out sharply against the blue sky, but on the plain to the east a steamy heat was already rising. And in that slight haze, Daru, with heavy heart, made out the Arab walking slowly on the road to prison.

A little later, standing before the window of the classroom, the school-master was watching the clear light bathing the whole surface of the plateau, but he hardly saw it. Behind him on the blackboard, among the winding French rivers, sprawled the clumsily chalked-up words he had just read: "You handed over our brother. You will pay for this." Daru looked at the sky, the plateau, and, beyond, the invisible lands stretching all the way to the sea. In this vast landscape he had loved so much, he was alone.

PROBING FOR MEANING

1. "Cruel to live in" is the way the narrator describes this part of Algeria. What details indicate the truth of the description? Why doesn't Daru leave? Where in the story does he indicate his attitude toward the land?

2. What does Daru think of humanity? What connection exists between his atti-tude toward people and his profession?

3. Describe the relationship between Balducci and Daru. What does this relation-ship further reveal about Daru's attitude toward others?

4. Daru, the French Algerian, must play host to an Arab. What kind of host is he? How would you describe his behavior toward, and thoughts about, the Arab?

5. How does the guest respond to the host? What details of conversation and action indicate this response?

6. "That man's stupid crime revolted him, but to hand him over was contrary to honor." Why does Daru's philosophy make it dishonorable to turn in a murderer?

7. Why does Daru give the Arab a choice, rather than setting him on the path to freedom? Why does the Arab choose to walk to prison? Daru observes the Arab's choice "with heavy heart." Why?

8. "In this vast landscape he had loved so much, he was alone." For what reason does Camus add the ironic touch of the Arab threat scrawled on the blackboard? Was Daru ever not alone? Does he want to be alone?

PROBING FOR METHOD

1. To what extent do we see the action through Daru's eyes? Do we enter the mind of any characters other than Daru? Could the story have been written in the first person? What different effect would a first-person narration create?

2. Why is the natural setting so appropriate for a story dramatizing the author's philosophy that life is meaningless except as people choose to make it meaningful?

3. How do the snowstorm and sunlight—dark and light—serve as an ironic sym-bolic background to the actions of Daru and the Arab?

WRITING TOPICS

Generating Ideas on a Philosophy

Freewrite, brainstorm, or write a journal entry in response to one of the following:

The heart is a lonely hunter.

Carson McCullers

Knowledge is power.

Francis Bacon

Freedom is the right to live among your own kind.

Arthur Miller

Time in the hand is not control of time.

Adrienne Rich

Life in itself is nothing, an empty cup, a flight of uncarpeted stairs.

Edna St. Vincent Millay

Tell all the truth but tell it slant.

Emily Dickinson

You see things; and you say, "Why?" But I dream things that never were; and say, "Why not?"

George Bernard Shaw

I believe that man will not merely endure: he will prevail.

William Faulkner

No leader is free; no follower is free—
  the rest of us can often be free.

William Stafford

The mind is an enchanting thing.

Marianne Moore

We live in freedom by necessity.

W. H. Auden

Beauty is truth, truth beauty.

John Keats

Life ain't all we want, but it's all we get.

Samuel Beckett

A child cannot be taught by anyone who despises him, and a child cannot afford to be fooled.

James Baldwin

Topics for Essays on a Philosophy

1. Property "makes me feel heavy," says Forster in "My Wood." Lindbergh also writes about the complications of materialism. Write an essay discussing their attitudes toward possessions and comparing them to yours.
2. Write an essay defining your ideas about freedom. How are they similar to or different from Stafford's?
3. Lindbergh and Thoreau in Chapter 7 advocate that we "simplify" our lives. Write an essay in which you respond to the feasibility of simplifying.
5. Lewis Thomas advocates that we change our attitudes toward death. Write an essay in which you compare your concept of death to his.
6. Read over what you have written on the statement you chose from the list for Generating Ideas. Consider whether this material can be revised into an essay or if one of your thoughts can now be expanded into a formal piece of writing. In either case, develop an essay on the topic.
7. Using a possession of your own, develop an analogy that, like Forster's use of his wood, illustrates your attitude toward possessions.
8. Plato and Daru in "The Guest," choose to live apart from society, one mentally, the other physically. What are the effects on them of their philosophies of individualism?
9. Write an essay discussing Baldwin's concept that language is the most vivid and crucial key to identity. Include in your essay specific examples from your own experience.
10. Anne Morrow Lindbergh, Wright Morris (Chapter 1), and Patrick Fenton (Chapter 4) are all concerned about the importance of writing in their lives. Is there an art form that you are interested in developing? To what extent do you empathize with their struggle to find time to be creative? Write an essay on the importance of creativity in one's life.
11. Language is a preoccupation of several writers in this anthology including Rodriguez (Chapter 1), Fenton (Chapter 4), Naylor and Kingston (Chapter 6), and Lindbergh and Baldwin (Chapter 8). Write an essay in which you analyze the similarities and differences in their philosophies about language. To what extent have their views been influenced by their cultural differences? Have you modified your philosophy of language as a result of learning about theirs?

1976 by Maxine Hong Kingston. Reprinted by permission of Alfred A. Knopf, Inc.

Anne Taylor Fleming, "The Fear of Being Alone." From *Newsweek,* December 13, 1976. Reprinted by permission of the author.

Emily Dickinson, "Wild Nights, Wild Nights." Reprinted by permission of the publishers and the Trustees of Amherst College from *The Poems of Emily Dickinson,* edited by Thomas H. Johnson, Cambridge, Mass.: The Belknap Press of Harvard University Press, Copyright 1951, 1955, 1979, 1983 by The President and Fellows of Harvard College.

Sherwood Anderson, "Hands." From *Winesburg, Ohio,* by Sherwood Anderson. Copyright 1919 by B. W. Huebsch. Copyright renewed 1947 by Eleanor Copenhaver Anderson. Reprinted by permission of Viking Penguin Inc.

Martin Krovetz, "Going My Way." From *Newsweek,* September 22, 1975. Reprinted by permission of the author.

Loren Eiseley, "Sparrow Hawks." Copyright 1955 by Loren Eiseley. Reprinted from *The Immense Journey,* by Loren Eiseley, by permission of Random House, Inc.

Richard Rodriguez, "None of This Is Fair." From *Hunger of Memory* by Richard Rodriguez. Copyright 1981 by Richard Rodriguez. Reprinted by permission of David R. Godine, Boston.

Linda Bird Francke, "A Bedroom of One's Own." Copyright 1977 by Linda Bird Francke. Originally appeared in *The New York Times.* Reprinted by permission of the author.

Alastair Reid, "Curiosity." From *Weathering* (E. P. Dutton). 1959 by Alastair Reid. Originally in *The New Yorker.*

E. M. Forster, "My Wood." From *Abinger Harvest,* copyright 1936, 1964 by Edward Morgan Forster. Reprinted by permission of Harcourt Brace Jovanovich, Inc., and Edward Arnold (Publishers) Ltd.

Anne Morrow Lindbergh, "Channelled Whelk." From *Gift from the Sea,* by Anne Morrow Lindbergh. Copyright 1955 by Anne Morrow Lindbergh. Reprinted by permission of Pantheon Books, a Division of Random House, Inc.

Anne Morrow Lindbergh, From *War Within and Without: Diaries and Letters, 1939–1944,* copyright 1980 by Anne Morrow Lindbergh. Reprinted by permission of Harcourt Brace Jovanovich Inc.

James Baldwin, "If Black English Isn't a Language, Then Tell Me, What Is?" From *The New York Times,* July 29, 1979. Copyright 1979 by The New York Times Company. Reprinted by permission.

Lewis Thomas, "Death in the Open." From *The Lives of a Cell: Notes of a Biology Watcher,* by Lewis Thomas. Copyright 1973 by The Massachusetts Medical Society. Originally published in *The New England Journal of Medicine.* Reprinted by permission of Viking Penguin, Inc.

William Stafford, "Freedom." From *Stories That Could Be True: New and Collected Poems by William Stafford.* Copyright 1969 by William Stafford. Reprinted by permission of Harper & Row, Publishers, Inc.

Albert Camus, "The Guest." From *Exile and the Kingdom,* by Albert Camus, translated by Justin O'Brien. Copyright 1957 by Alfred A. Knopf, Inc. Reprinted by permission of the publisher.

INDEX OF AUTHORS

To the Student:

Part of our job as educational publishers is to try to improve the textbooks we publish. Thus, when revising a book, we take into account the experience of both instructors and students with the previous edition. At some time your instructor may be asked to comment extensively on *The Writer's I*, but right now we want to hear from you. After all, though your instructor assigned this book, you are the one who paid for it.

Please help us by completing this questionnaire and returning it to College English, Scott, Foresmann/Little, Brown, 34 Beacon Street, Boston, MA 02108.

School _____ Course Title _____

Instructor's name _____

Please rate the selections:	Liked best				Liked least	Didn't read
ONE: THE SELF						
Ved Mehta, "Sound Shadows of the New World"	5	4	3	2	1	____
Mary Ann Lynch, "December 22, 1972. New York City"	5	4	3	2	1	____
Toi Derricotte, "The Black Notebooks"	5	4	3	2	1	____
John Coleman, "Blue Collar Journal: A College President's Sabbatical"	5	4	3	2	1	____
Henry David Thoreau, "The Journals"	5	4	3	2	1	____
Wright Morris, *Will's Boy*	5	4	3	2	1	____
Zora Neale Hurston, "I Get Born"	5	4	3	2	1	____
Richard Rodriguez, *Hunger of Memory*	5	4	3	2	1	____
William Carlos Williams, "Danse Russe"	5	4	3	2	1	____
Pär Lagerkvist, "Father and I"	5	4	3	2	1	____
TWO: PEOPLE						
Sherwood Anderson, "Discovery of a Father"	5	4	3	2	1	____
Maya Angelou, "Sister Flowers"	5	4	3	2	1	____
John Gregory Dunne, "Quintana"	5	4	3	2	1	____
Alfred Kazin, "Cousin Sophie"	5	4	3	2	1	____
Joyce Maynard, "My Grandmother"	5	4	3	2	1	____
Yevgeny Yevtushenko, "People"	5	4	3	2	1	____
John Knowles, "Phineas"	5	4	3	2	1	____
THREE: PLACES						
Saul Bellow, "On a Kibbutz"	5	4	3	2	1	____
E. B. White, "Once More to the Lake"	5	4	3	2	1	____
Pete Hamill, "Home—378 Seventh Avenue"	5	4	3	2	1	____
Russell Baker, "Morrisonville"	5	4	3	2	1	____
Lillian Hellman, "In the Fig Tree"	5	4	3	2	1	____
Lawrence Ferlinghetti, "The pennycandystore beyond the El"	5	4	3	2	1	____
Bernard Malamud, "The Prison"	5	4	3	2	1	____
FOUR: EVENTS AND EXPERIENCES						
Richard Selzer, "An Absence of Windows"	5	4	3	2	1	____
Patrick Fenton, "A Style of My Own"	5	4	3	2	1	____
Hanna Wehle, "The Return"	5	4	3	2	1	____
Brent Staples, "A Brother's Murder"	5	4	3	2	1	____
Alice Walker, "Beauty; When the Other Dancer Is the Self"	5	4	3	2	1	____
Adrienne Rich, "Trying To Talk With a Man"	5	4	3	2	1	____
Kate Chopin, "The Story of an Hour"	5	4	3	2	1	____
FIVE: GOALS						
Gloria Steinem, "The Importance of Work"	5	4	3	2	1	____
Pete Hamill, "Winning Isn't Everything"	5	4	3	2	1	____
Robert Pirsig, "Gumption"	5	4	3	2	1	____
Jim Fusilli, "A Wall Street Rocker"	5	4	3	2	1	____
Steve Tesich, "An Amateur Marriage"	5	4	3	2	1	____

Gwendolyn Brooks, "Life For My Child Is Simple, and Is Good"	5	4	3	2	1	_____
Doris Lessing, "Notes for a Case History"	5	4	3	2	1	_____

SIX: EMOTIONS

George Orwell, "Revenge is Sour"	5	4	3	2	1	_____
Gloria Naylor, "What's in a Name?"	5	4	3	2	1	_____
Bertrand Russell, "Marriage"	5	4	3	2	1	_____
Maxine Hong Kingston, "The Misery of Silence"	5	4	3	2	1	_____
Anne Taylor Fleming, "The Fear of Being Alone"	5	4	3	2	1	_____
Emily Dickinson, "Wild Nights, Wild Nights"	5	4	3	2	1	_____
Sherwood Anderson, "Hands"	5	4	3	2	1	_____

SEVEN: CHOICES

Martin Krovetz, "Going My Way"	5	4	3	2	1	_____
Henry David Thoreau, "Simplicity"	5	4	3	2	1	_____
Loren Eiseley, "Sparrow Hawks"	5	4	3	2	1	_____
Richard Rodriguez, "None of This Is Fair"	5	4	3	2	1	_____
Linda Bird Francke, "A Bedroom of One's Own"	5	4	3	2	1	_____
Alastair Reid, "Curiosity"	5	4	3	2	1	_____
Mary Wilkins Freeman, "A Moral Exigency"	5	4	3	2	1	_____

EIGHT: PHILOSOPHIES

E. M. Forster, "My Wood"	5	4	3	2	1	_____
Ann Morrow Lindbergh, "Channelled Whelk"	5	4	3	2	1	_____
Ann Morrow Lindbergh, War Within and Without: Diaries and Letters (1939–44)	5	4	3	2	1	_____
Plato, "The Allegory of the Cave"	5	4	3	2	1	_____
James Baldwin, "If Black English Isn't a Language, Then Tell Me, What Is?"	5	4	3	2	1	_____
Lewis Thomas, "Death in the Open"	5	4	3	2	1	_____
William Stafford, "Freedom"	5	4	3	2	1	_____
Albert Camus, "The Guest"	5	4	3	2	1	_____

What did you think of the exercises following the readings?

_____

_____

Did you read the biographical material on the authors? _____

Did it help in your reading? _____

Please add any comments or suggestions on how we might improve this book. _____

_____

_____

_____

Your name _____ Date _____

Mailing address _____

May we quote you either in promotion for this book or in future publishing ventures?

Yes _____ No _____

Thank you.